A TEXT BOOK OF

DESCRIPTIVE STATISTICS, PROBABILITY AND PROBABILITY DISTRIBUTIONS – I

STATISTICS : PAPER – I

FOR

B.Sc. Part – I : Semester – I

As Per New Revised Syllabus (C.G.P.A. Pattern) of Solapur University, Solapur

Prof. P. G. DIXIT
M.Sc., M. Phil (Statistics)
Head, Department of Statistics,
Modern College,
Pune - 5

Prof. S. J. ALANDKAR
M.Sc., B.Ed., M.Phil
Diploma in Computer Science.
Head and Associate Professor,
Walchand College of Arts & Science,
Solapur

Prof. N. I. DHANSHETTI
M.Sc., M. Phil
C. B. Khedgis College,
Akkalkot,
Dist. Solapur

N3629

B.Sc. Part – I : Descriptive Statistics, Probability
and Probability Distributions - I (Stat.-I) (Solapur University)

First Edition	: July 2015	**ISBN 978-93-5164-738-6**
©	: Authors	

The text of this publication, or any part thereof, should not be reproduced or transmitted in any form or stored in any computer storage system or device for distribution including photocopy, recording, taping or information retrieval system or reproduced on any disc, tape, perforated media or other information storage device etc., without the written permission of Authors with whom the rights are reserved. Breach of this condition is liable for legal action.

Every effort has been made to avoid errors or omissions in this publication. In spite of this, errors may have crept in. Any mistake, error or discrepancy so noted and shall be brought to our notice shall be taken care of in the next edition. It is notified that neither the publisher nor the authors or seller shall be responsible for any damage or loss of action to any one, of any kind, in any manner, therefrom.

Published By :	**Printed By**
NIRALI PRAKASHAN Abhyudaya Pragati, 1312 Shivaji Nagar, Off J.M. Road, PUNE - 411005 Tel - (020) 25512336/37/39. Fax - 25511379 Email : niralipune@pragationline.com	Repro Knowledgecast Limited

DISTRIBUTION CENTERS

PUNE
Nirali Prakashan
119, Budhwar Peth, Jogeshwari Mandir Lane,
Pune - 411002, Maharashtra.
Tel : (020) 24452044, 66022708
Fax : (020) 2445 1538
Email : bookorder@pragationline.com

MUMBAI
Nirali Prakashan
385, S.V.P. Road, Rasdhara Co-op. Hsg.
Society, Girgaum,
Mumbai - 400004, Maharashtra
Tel : (022) 2385 6339 / 2386 9976,
Fax : (022) 2386 9976
Email : niralimumbai@pragationline.com

RETAIL SHOPS

PUNE
Pragati Book Centre
157, Budhwar Peth, Opp. Ratan Talkies,
Pune – 411002, Maharashtra
Tel : 2445 8887 / 6602 2707

Pragati Book Centre
676/B, Budhwar Peth,
Opp. Jogeshwari Mandir,
Pune – 411002, Maharashtra
Tel. : (020) 6601 7784, 2445 2254

PUNE
PBC Book Sellers and Stationers
152, Budhwar Peth,
Near Jogeshwari Mandir,
Pune – 411002, Maharashtra
Tel : (020) 6609 2463 / 2445 2254

PUNE
Pragati Book Centre
Amber Chamber, 28/A, Budhwar Peth,
Appa Balwant Chowk
Pune : 411002, Maharashtra
Tel. : (020) 20240335 / 66281669
Email : pbcpune@pragationline.com

Pragati Book Centre
917/22, Sai Complex,
F.C. Road, Shivaji Nagar,
Pune – 411004, Maharashtra
Tel. : (020) 2566 / 6602 2728

MUMBAI
Pragati Book Corner
Indira Niwas,
111-A Bhavani Shankar Road,
Dadar (W), **Mumbai** – 400028
Tel : (022) 2422 3525 / 6662 5254
Email : pbcmumbai@pragationline.com

DISTRIBUTION BRANCHES

NAGPUR
Pratibha Book Distributors
Above Maratha Mandir, Shop No. 3, First Floor, Rani Zanshi Square, Sitabuldi,
Nagpur 440012, Maharashtra, Tel : (0712) 254 7129
JALGAON
34, V. V. Golani Market, Navi Peth, Jalgaon 425001, Maharashtra,
Tel : (0257) 222 0395, Mob : 94234 91860
KOLHAPUR
New Mahadvar Road, Kedar Plaza, 1st Floor Opp. IDBI Bank
Kolhapur 416 012, Maharashtra. Mob : 9855046155

www.pragationline.com   info@pragationline.com

> *Statistical Thinking will one day be necessary for effective citizenship as the ability to read and write*
> — H.G. Wells

PREFACE

We feel indeed very happy to present this book of **'Statistics – Paper-I' 'Descriptive Statistics, Probability and Probability Distributions-I'** to the students of (C.G.P.A. Pattern) B.Sc. Part I. The book is written according to the revised syllabus of Solapur University, Solapur.

The main purpose of the book is to provide foundation as well as comprehensive background of 'Descriptive Measures', Probability and Probability Distributions to beginners in simple and interesting manner. In order to make the contents of the book easier to comprehend, we have included a requisite number of illustrations, remarks, figures, diagrams etc. to elucidate statistical concepts. Application of Statistics in real life situations is emphasized through illustrative examples. We have included the additional feature MS-EXCEL commands to obtain summary statistics. It will give an exposure to statistical computing package. Ample number of graded problems, theoretical as well as numerical are provided at the end of each chapter along with hints and answers. The numerical problems will also be useful for the F.Y.B.Sc. students' to prepare for Paper – III : Practicals.

We are thankful to Mr. D. K. Furia and the staff of Nirali Prakashan for bringing out this book Mrs. Anagha Medhekar and Mr. Santosh Bare deserve special thanks for the co-operation they have extended to us. Finally, our families deserve special thanks for their support, encouragement and tolerance.

We request our colleagues, teaching Statistics to offer their criticisms and suggestions, for further improvement of the book.

Pune

Authors

SYLLABUS

Section - I

Unit – 1 : (a) Introduction to Statistics (2)

1.1 Meaning of the world statistics.

1.2 Scope of statistics : In industry, Biological and Medical sciences, Economics, Social and Management sciences.

1.3 Statistical organizations in India : CSO, NSS, ISI (Indian Statistical Institute), IIPS (Indian Institute of Population Studies), Bureau of Economics and Statistics, Their aims and functions.

1.4 Indian statisticians and their contributions.

(b) Nature of Data : (7)

1.5 Meaning of primary and secondary data.

1.6 Qualitative data (attributes) : Nominal scale and Ordinal scale, Quantitative data (variable) : Interval scale and ratio scale, discrete and continuous variables, raw data.

1.7 Classification of data : Discrete and continuous frequency distribution, inclusive and exclusive methods of classification, cumulative frequency distribution, relative frequency.

1.8 Graphical representation of data : Histogram, Frequency polygon, Frequency curve and Ogive curves.

1.9 Illustrative Examples.

Unit – 2 : Measures of Central Tendency (10)

2.1 Concept of central tendency of statistical data, Statistical average, Requirements of good statistical average.

2.2 Arithmetic Mean (A.M.) : Definition, Effect of change of origin and scale, Deviation of observation from A.M., Mean of pooled data, Weighted A.M.

2.3 Geometric Mean (G.M.) : Definition.

2.4 Harmonic Mean (H.M.) : Definition.

2.5 Relation : A.M. ≥ G.M. ≥ H.M. (Proof for n = 2, positive observations).

G.M. = $\sqrt{\text{A.M.} \times \text{H.M.}}$ (Proof for n = 2, Positive observation)

2.6 Median : Definition, Derivation of formula for grouped frequency distribution.

2.7 Mode : Definition for ungrouped and grouped data derivation of formula.

2.8 Empirical relation between Mean, Median and Mode.

2.9 Partition values : Quartiles, Deciles and Percentiles.

2.10 Graphical method of determination of Median, Mode and Partition values.

2.11 Situations where one kind of average is preferable to others.

2.12 Examples to illustrate the concept.

Unit – 3 : Measures of Dispersion (8)

3.1 Concept of dispersion, Absolute and Relative measures of dispersion, Requirements of a good measure of dispersion.

3.2 Range : Definition, Coefficient of range.

3.3 Quartile deviation (Semi-interquartile range) : Definition, Coefficient of Q.D.

3.4 Mean derivation : Definition, Coefficient of M.D., Minimal property of M.D. (Statement only)

3.5 Mean square deviation, Definition, Minimal property of M.S.D.

3.6 Variance and Standard deviation : Definition, Effect of change of origin and scale, S.D. and variance (for proof take individual data of n observations $x_1, x_2, \ldots, x_n$ and $d_i = \dfrac{x_i - A}{h}$ S.D. of pooled data (without proof).

3.7 Coefficient of variation : Definition and use.

3.8 Comparison of absolute and relative measures of dispersion.

3.9 Examples to illustrate the concept.

Unit – 4 : Moments, Skewness and Kurtosis (8)

4.1 Moments : Raw moments (μ_r') and central moments (μ_r) for ungrouped and grouped data.

4.2 Effect of change of origin and scale on moments, Relation between central moments and raw moments (upto 4th order). Relation between row and factorial moments (upto 2nd order).

4.3 Sheppard's correction, Need of Sheppard's correction and its importance.

4.4 Skewness : Concept of skewness of a frequency distribution, Types of skewness and its interpretation.

4.5 Bowley's coefficient of skewness, Karl Pearson's coefficient of skewness, Measure of skewness based on moments.

4.6 Kurtosis : Concept of kurtosis of a frequency distribution, Types of kurtosis and its interpretations.

4.7 Measure of kurtosis based on moments.

4.8 Illustrative Examples.

Section - II

5. SAMPLE SPACE AND EVENTS (5)

5.1 Concept of experiments and random experiments.

5.2 Definitions : Sample space, discrete sample space (finite and countably infinite), event, elementary event, compound event.

5.3 Algebra of events (Union, intersection, complementation).

5.4 Definitions of mutuality exclusive events, exhaustive events, impossible events, certain events.

5.5 Power set IP (Ω) (sample space consisting at most 4 sample joints).

5.6 Symbolic representation of given events and description of events in symbolic form.

5.7 Illustrative examples.

6. PROBABILITY (12)

6.1 Equally like outcomes (events), apriori (classical), definition of probability of an event. Equiprobable sample space, simple examples of computation of probability of the events based on permutations and combinations.

6.2 Axiomatic definition of probability with reference to a finite and countably infinite sample space.

6.3 Proof of the results :
   (i) $P(\phi) = 0$.
   (ii) $P(A^c) = 1 - P(A)$
   (iii) $P(A \cup B) = P(A) + P(B) - P(A \cap B)$ (with proof), extension of this to $P(A \cup B \cup C)$.
   (iv) If $A \subset B$, $P(A) \leq P(B)$.
   (v) $0 \leq P(A \cap B) \leq P(A) \leq P(A \cup B) \leq P(A) + P(B)$.
   (vi) $P(A \cap B^c) = P(A) - P(A \cap B)$.

6.4 Illustrative examples based on the results in 6.3 above.

7. CONDITIONAL POROBABILITY AND INDEPENDENCE OF EVENTS (10)

7.1 Definition of conditional probability of an event.

7.2 Multiplication theorem for two events $P(A \cap B) = P(A) P(B|A)$

7.3 Partition of sample space.

7.4 Ideal of Posteriori probability, statement and proof of Bayes theorem, examples on Bayes theorem.

7.5 Concept of independence of two events.

7.6 Proof of the result that if A and B are independent then,
   (i) A and B^c, (ii) A^c and B, (iii) A^c and B^c are independent.

7.7 Pairwise and mutual independence for three events.

7.8 Elementary examples.

8. UNIVARIATE PROBABILITY DISTRIBUTION (DEFINED ON FINITE AND COUNTABLE INFINITE SAMPLE SPACE) (8)

8.1 Definition of discrete random variables.

8.2 Probability mass function (p.m.f.) and cumulative distribution function (c.d.f.), a discrete random variable, properties of c.d.f. (statements only).

8.3 Probability distribution function of a random variable.

8.4 Median and mode of a univariate discrete probability distribution.

8.5 Examples.

•••

CONTENTS

Section - I

1. Introduction to Statistics — 1.1 – 1.18
2. Nature of Data — 2.1 – 2.60
3. Measures of Central Tendency — 3.1 – 3.72
4. Measures of Dispersion — 4.1 – 4.44
5. Moments, Skewness and Kurtosis — 5.1 – 5.44

Section - II

6. Sample Space and Events — 6.1 – 6.24
7. Probability — 7.1 – 7.32
8. Conditional Probability and Independence of Events — 8.1 – 8.38
9. Univariate Probability Distributions — 9.1 – 9.28
10. Mathematical Expectations (Univariate) — 10.1 – 10.26

•••

SECTION - I

Chapter 1...
Introduction to Statistics

P. C. Mahalanobis (1893-1972) : The 1st Indian Statistician, Prof. Mahalanobis, is best remembered for the Mahalnobis Distance. He made pioneering studies in sampling theory and method. He founded Indian Statistical Institute at Kolkata in 1931. His contributions are design of large scale sample surveys, surveys for consumer expenditure, tea drinking habits, public opinion, crop acreage and plant disease, estimating crop yields. As a member of planning commission in the second five year plan, he employed a model for rapid industrialization of India. He established NSSO in 1950 and helped in setting-up the CSO. Starting formal teaching of statistics in Indian Universities is due to him. He was Fellow of Royal Society London, President of Indian Science Congress Association, Fellow of Royal Statistical Society UK, Fellow of American Statistical Association and PadmVibhushan. His birthday 29 June is celebrated as National Statistics Day.

P. C. Mahalanobis

Contents ...
1.1 Introduction
1.2 Definitions and Meaning of Statistics
1.3 Importance of Statistics
1.4 Scope of Statistics
1.5 Statistical Organisations in India
1.6 Statistical Organisation in the Maharashtra

Key Words :

Statistics, Definition of Statistics by Webster, Bowley, Yule and Kendall, Horace Secrist, Importance of Statistics, scope of statistics in various fields, CSO, NSSO, ISI, IIPS, Bureau of economics and statistics.

Objectives :

In this chapter what is statistics is explained. The importance and scope of statistics and statistical organisations are enumerated.

1.1 Introduction

It is believed that Statistics is in use from the time when man began to count and measure. In ancient days kings used to maintain records of land, agricultural yield, wealth, taxes, live stock, soldiers, weapons, deaths and births etc. There are references that Hebrews conducted population census. In ancient days Maurya kings, King Ashoka, Gupta kings had collected Statistics. Kautilya's Arthashastra mentions that the statistics of population, land etc. were collected from time to time. Emperor Akbar gave details of population, land, agriculture etc. in his publication Ain-i-Akbari.

It is considered that the word Statistics seems to be derived from the Italian word 'statista' or the Greek word 'statistika'. Both the words have the same meaning 'political states'.

The word statistics carries several meanings. Many times statistics is considered as statistical data, which contains numerical information of a characteristic under study.

For example : Statistics of a batsman, population statistics etc.

Statistics or statistical methods is treated as a branch of science which deals with (i) collection, (ii) presentation, (iii) analysis and (iv) interpretation of data.

Wherever data are generated, the use of statistics becomes inevitable. Statistics performs number of functions such as (i) presentation of facts and figures. This enables to get an overall idea about the phenomenon. (ii) forecasting, (iii) planning, (iv) controlling, (v) exploring etc.

Statistics plays a role in every walk of life right from simple situation such as finding average makes in examination to a very complex phenomenon such as rainfall prediction or measuring changes in prices.

Statistics helps in decision-making whenever phenomenon contains uncertainities. LIC, banks, defence department, government agencies, industries, business, trade etc. make use of statistics in planning, forecasting, controlling, decision-making. Index numbers are widely used in almost all fields such as economics, business, import, export etc. Now-a-days ISO 9000 makes use of statistical tools for standardising the quality of industrial production.

1.2 Definitions and Meaning of Statistics

Number of statisticians had made an attempt to define statistics. They used statistics for different purpose, with a different view-point. Accordingly they defined statistics emphasizing their view point. Some definitions are given below.

(a) Webster's Definition : Webster defines statistics as "the classified facts representing the conditions of people in the state, especially those facts which can be stated in a table or tables of numbers or in any tabular or classified arrangement."

The above definition gives importance to presentation of facts and figures. Remaining aspects of statistics are not considered in this definition.

(b) Bowley's Definition : Prof. A. W. Bowley gives some definitions :

'Statistics may be called as science of counting.'

'Statistics may rightly be called the science of averages'.

'Statistics is the science of the measurement of social organism regarded as a whole in all its manifestations'.

The area of operation of statistics is not limited to sociology. Apart from counting and measurement and finding averages, statistics performs many other functions. Bowley realised that the above definitions are not adequate and came to conclusion that 'statistics cannot be confined to any one science'. Boddington gave definition of statistics considering estimation aspect.

(c) Yule and Kendall's Definition : Yule and Kendall gave the following definition of statistics : 'By statistics we mean qualitative data affected to a marked extent by a multiplicity of causes'.

This definition ignores all other aspects of statistical analysis and gives stress on only one aspect of qualitative data.

(d) Horace Secrist's Definition : Secrist defines statistics as follows : 'By statistics we mean aggregates of facts affected to a marked extent by multiplicity of causes numerically expressed, enumerated or estimated according to resonable standards of accuracy, collected in a systematic manner for a predetermined purpose and placed in relation to each other.

The above definition takes into account almost all functions and aspects of statistics. It covers the fair important aspects viz. (i) collection, (ii) presentation, (iii) analysis and (iv) interpretation of data.

1.3 Importance of Statistics

We know that many phenomena in nature and activities, experiments are subject to measurements, moreover variation in different types of characteristics is inevitable. For example, income of a family, height of a person, sales of a company, electricity consumption of a city etc. This produces voluminous data. It becomes difficult to comprehend. This forces the use of statistical methods. Thus statistics is important from the following view points.

(i) Statistical methods enable to condense the data. It facilitates several functions apart from summerisation.

(ii) Statistical methods give tools of comparison.

(iii) Estimation, prediction is also possible using statistical tools.

(iv) We can get idea about the shape, spread, symmetry of the data.

(v) Inter-relation between two or more variables can be measured using statistical techniques.

(iv) Statistical methods help in planning, controlling, decision-making etc.

(vii) The use of statistical methods is important because considerable amount of time, money, manpower can be saved.

(viii) Uncertainities can be reduced to get reliable results.

(ix) Statistical methods give systematic methods of data collection and investigation.

Thus statistics reveals several aspects of phenomena.

H. G. Wells expresses the importance and need of statistics in the following words.

"Statistical thinking will one day be necessary for effective citizenship as the ability to read and write".

1.4 Scope of Statistics

The tools and techniques given by statistical methods are used in almost all fields at several phases. Because of diversified applications of statistics, an exhaustive list of fields is difficult to prepare. However, some of them are stated below. We find use of statistics indispensable in the agriculture, business, commerce, demography, economics, education, government agencies, industries, social sciences, biological sciences, medical sciences, management sciences etc. We discuss briefly the scope of statistics in some of the above stated fields.

(a) Statistics in industry : Industry makes use of statistics at several places such as administration, planning, production, growth and development. In many industries 'Statistical Quality Control' division is separately operating. Mainly, whether manufactured goods possess a desirable standard or not is examined using various control charts. These inspections are done at the time of production. On-line process capability study is conducted to set up the machines to give desired standards. Moreover purchased goods or semifinished goods are inspected using acceptance sampling plans of various types. Now-a-days, ISO 9000 makes use of Statistics to a large extent. Apart from this in some industries the technique known as designs of experiment is also used. Newly installed machinery is tested for its performance using statistical methods. Sampling is required to be used because of its several advantages. Multiple regression planes are used for forecasting, when several factors are interlinked. Efficiency measurement, index number of production, work sampling etc. are very much useful for administration and planning department.

(b) Statistics and Biological Sciences : Several experiments are being conducted in biological fields, which need the use of statistical methods. The use of statistics in this field is not new. Scientist Sir Francis Galton (1822 – 1911) used Statistics in studying heridity. He pioneered the use of statistical methods in biological sciences. The regression analysis was used by him in the field of genetics. Scientist Mendel performed number of experiments in the field of genetics. Statistical tests are applied now-a-days to test his theory. Optimum dose of fertiliser or adequate dose of amount of irrigation can be decided using statistical methods.

Demography uses, statistical methods for forecasting population, measuring death rates, birth rates, growth rates etc. Average longevity of human can be estimated using statistical tools. Infant mortality rates can also be measured using statistics. It serves as an indicator of health condition of a country. Population dynamics reveals several characteristics. Estimation of sex ratio is possible using statistical tools.

(c) Statistics and Agriculture : Analysis of agricultural experiments make heavy use of statistical method known as designs of experiment. Main advantage of this statistical technique is testing the interaction effects. For example, the interaction effect of fertilizer and irrigation. It saves amount of time due to statistical methods. Otherwise separate experiments are to be performed to verify the various factors, several times. These experiments help the scientists in developing various hybrid species having specific characteristics such as disease resistance, high yield, requirement of less irrigation facility etc. While planning the experiments, use of correlation is indispensable. Mainly correlation helps in selecting factors to be included in study. The correlated characteristics are to be simultaneously recorded. Regression lines and various methods of forecasting are immensely useful. Various methods of cultivation can be tested for better performance using statistical tools. Various methods of irrigation such as drip irrigation, pot irrigation, sprinkler etc. can be compared using statistical tests. The effect of alkalinity of water, hardness, impurities in the water on growth of plants which receive such a water; can be tested using statistical tests.

Estimation of number of trees in a jungle, forest density, number of animals in a jungle, fish in a lake etc. can be done using various statistical techniques.

(d) Statistics and Medical Sciences : In the field of medical sciences statistical methods are used to test various claims, such as (i) Does smoking increase the possibility of proneness of cancer ? (ii) Is there any correlation between age and blood pressure ? (iii) Is a particular vaccine useful in controlling a particular disease ? (iv) Whether growth of a baby is normal ? The conjectures made by experts can be supported by statistical data. Such conjectures can also be tested. Effectiveness of remedial medicines can be tested statistically. Thus statistics helps in every respect in this field.

(e) Statistics and Economics : In the field of economics, huge amount of data are needed to be processed and interpreted. Statistics is very much helpful in this field. In order to collect data, various statistical methods of investigations are used. Many a times questionnaires are drafted. A proper representative of a group is selected using sampling methods. Statistical methods are used in this activity to get reliable results. Estimation of national income, per capita income, poverty line, industrial production etc. is done using statistical techniques. Probability distribution of income can be useful in various economic activities. A tool known as index number developed in Statistics is used every now and then in economics. It performs number of functions. It measures average increase in prices, production, income, volume of import, export etc. Index numbers are called as economic barometers. Index numbers are used in determining real income, deflation, cost of living index numbers. To measure the changes in prices of shares in stock market index number provides the best tool. Several interlinked activities in economics can be studied. For example, (i) the relation between prices and supply (ii) the relation between demand and prices (iii) the relation between sales and profit.

Demand analysis, time series analysis techniques are mainly developed to study economics. They are the gifts given by statistics.

Richard Lipsey says "The role of statistical analysis is two fold. First, we wish to use observations from the real world to test our theories. Second, we wish to use such observations to give us measures of the quantitative relations between economic variables.

(f) Statistics and Social Sciences : Bowley says "Statistics is the science of measurement of social organism, regarded as a whole in all its manifestation". Research in social sciences need questionnaire. Further analysis is required to be done using statistical tools. In social sciences we need to test association between two variables such as (i) education and criminality (ii) education and marriage adjustment score (iii) sex and education (iv) richness and criminality etc.

(g) Statistics and Management Sciences : Most of the managerial functions make use of statistics. For efficient working various sections of management such as sales, production, marketing statistical method are used. Different statistical tools such as forecasting, tests of significance, index numbers, time series analysis, statistical quality control, estimation play vital role in management activities. Apart from this, various optimisation techniques known as linear programming, transportation techniques, job assignment problems, sequencing, CPM and PERT, replacement problems, inventory control are also useful.

Portfolio management makes use of regression analysis. The regression coefficient called beta index in portfolio is used in decision-making. Risk measurement is done using standard deviations, covariance. Various statistical techniques are used in decision making.

(h) Statistics and Insurance : Life table or mortality rates play keyrole in life insurance policies. In order to decide the premium, insurance company has to use mortality rates which are determined using statistical method. Mortality rates depend upon (i) age, (ii) sex, (iii) occupation, (iv) residential area, (v) heredity etc. Accordingly premium changes. As age advances beyond 20 years (approximately) death rate of human being increases slowly upto age 40. Beyond 40 it increases rapidly, the premium also increases similarly. The premium is decided on the basis averages. A simple principle given below is used by insurance companies.

Average premium = Average claims + Business charges

In case of general insurance also the chances of happening of events are determined using laws of probability.

Statistics is the only science which comes to help for prediction or forecasting in the presence of uncertainity. Thus, statistics has growing importance in this field.

(i) Statistics and Psychology : In the field of psychology human traits are interrelated. The powerful technique of measuring such dependence is correlation. The use of statistics in this field is to a great extent. Some complex phenomena may be a effect of several factors. The techniques of factor analysis, cluster analysis are very much useful to explain the phenomena. The causes behind the human work productivity can be studied by designing statistical experiments. Design of experiment is also a most useful technique. The research in this field makes heavy use of statistical methods. We can study relation between productivity and intelligence, productivity and emotional quotient etc. Multivariate analysis, correlation and regression are the most applicable tools of statistics which are used in the field of psychology.

(j) Statistics and Education : Statistical inference and statistical methods are useful to great extent in the field of research in education. Analysis of variance is also developed to test the most effective methods of teaching and communication. The relation between interrelated variables is studied using correlation and regression. Factor analysis and multivariate techniques are also used to great extent. Forecasting and predications are required every now and then.

In order to study equivalence between two examinations for example, SSC board score and CBSE broad score or score of arts and that of science students can be compared using percentile ranks.

Now-a-days in every competitive examination percentile rank is used to know the relative position of candidate in examination.

Sometimes examination results are in grades. How to combine the grades and how to find the average grade is a problem which is well answered using statistical methods.

(k) Statistics and Computer Science : Statistics and computer science both are together useful in providing solutions to the problems in various fields. Particularly, whenever data analysis techniques are employed to large data, use of computers become indispensable. Conjectures supported by statistical data have sound ground of approval. Now-a-days several statistical software packages like MINITAB, MATLAB, STATPACK, SAS, SPSS, SYSSTAT etc. are used for data analysis. Forecasting, prediction, estimation, curve fittings etc. are the commonly used statistical techniques. The use of software packages provides the unusual opportunities to get the data summarised in appropriate way. The suitability of modal used for analysis can be quickly determined by means of software package, otherwise it is a time consuming and tedious procedure. Although software packages are useful to great extent, it cannot replace totally the necessity of statistician. In order to interpret the output or to decide the suitability of statistical model for analysis, to design the quessionaire, to design the experiment etc. statisticians help is essential.

The other aspect of statistics and computer science may be discussed as follows. Computer is an assembly of several components. The life of each component is a variable having some probability distribution. The average life of each component as well the assembled product can be determined using statistical methods. Reliability of component and system may help the manufacturer to decide the guarantee period of computer as well to user to decide the policy of replacement of spare parts. In general to a computer consultant, theory of queues and optimisation techniques may be useful to plan out his work schedule.

1.5 Statistical Organisations in India

Statistical organisation in operation today is gradually developed over a considerable time period. Mughal emperors, Bristishers set some statistical system in India. After independence, according to Constitution of India, the Central Government modified the systems. The Central Statistical Organisation (CSO) associated with Cabinct Sccrctariat at the centre, looks after various activities such as collection and compilation of data. The concerned regular publications are taken care of by CSO. It is the main co-ordinating agency of various statistical organisations in centre as well as states of our country. We study some important statistical organisations in India.

(A) Central Statistics Office (C.S.O.) : Central Government has established central statistical office for co-ordination of statistical organisation within the states. This was set in May 1951. CSO works under the Cabinet Secretariat.

CSO was established with a view of (i) laying down the standards in the statistical fields (ii) co-ordination of statistical activities at the centre and in the states (iii) maintaining liaison in statistical matters with international agencies (iv) playing an advisory role in statistical matters. The National Income Unit was transferred from Ministry of Finance to the CSO in the year 1954. In 1957 industrial statistics was transferred to CSO.

In 1961 Department of statistics was set up in the Cabinet Secretariat and CSO became part of it. Hence the additional duties CSO had started performing are as follows : (i) preparation of national accounts, (ii) processing and publications of industrial statistics (iii) conduct of economic census and surveys, (iv) maintenance of consumer price index number, (v) organising various training programmes in official statistics, (vi) organising various conferences on a regular basis.

CSO functions through number of divisions such as Industrial statistics wing. Analytical Division, National Sample Survey Division, National Income Division, Population Division, Training Division, Price and Price Index No. Division.

Details are available on website www.mosphi.nic.in/cso.

CSO brings out number of publications, few important publications are listed below :

(i) Monthly Abstract Statistics.
(ii) Monthly Statistics of the Production of Selected Industries of India.
(iii) Statistical Pocket Book of the Indian Union.
(iv) Statistical Abstract of India.
(v) Annual Survey of Industries.

(B) National Sample Survey Office (N.S.S.O).

NSS was set-up in 1950 under the guidance of P. C. Mahalanobis and it was reorganised in 1970 under the name national sample survey office (NSSO). All aspects of survey work were considered together to form NSSO. It functions under the Department of Statistics. It is headed by a Chief Executive Officer. It functions through four divisions for conducting large scale sample surveys (i) Survey Design and Research (ii) Field Operations (iii) Data processing (iv) Co-ordination and Publication. It has about 170 offices throughout the country. The activities of NSSO are guided by Governing Council. Reconstitution of Governing Council took place in 1993.

The NSSO, field operation division (FOD) is situated at Akurdi, Pune 53.

The main functions of the Directorate of NSSO are as follows :

(a) Data collection for Estimation of National Income, for the activities of Planning Commission, for the activities of various Ministries. Collection of Socio-economic and demographic data.

(b) NSSO collects data regarding prices, wages, consumption, production, agriculture etc.

(c) NSSO conducts sample surveys in the registered industrial sectors.

(d) It provides guidance to the various states and does the job of supervision for conducting various surveys.

CSO helps NSSO in designs and tabulation, in fixing priorities and in co-ordination, whereas Indian Statistical Institute (ISI) helps in preparing designs, programming, processing of information, analysis, report writing etc. State Governments participate in the programmes of NSSO which are of common interest to both. NSSO gets assistance from its advisory committee, which consists of experts from the fields such as planning commission, ministries of food, agriculture, labour, employment.

NSSO Rounds of Surveys

NSSO conducted several surveys from time to time. First round of survey started in October 1950.

The brief table of latest round and future rounds is given below :

NSSO rounds for 2005-06 to 2014-15
(NSS 62nd to 72nd Rounds)

Round No.	Period of Survey	Subjects
62	July 2005 - June 2006	Unorganised Manufacturing Enterprises, Household Consumer Expenditure and Employment-Unemployment.
63	July 2006 - June 2007	Unorganised Service Sector Enterprises (excluding Trade) and Household Consumer Expenditure.
64	July 2007 - June 2008	Participation and Expenditure in Education, Employment-Unemployment, Migration and Household Consumer Expenditure.
65	July 2008-June 2009	Domestic Tourism, Housing Conditions, Urban Slums and Civic Amenities.
66	July 2009 - June 2010	Household Consumer Expenditure and Employment-Unemployment (quinquennial survey).
67	July 2010 - June 2011	Unincorporated Enterprises covering Manufacturing, Services and Trade.
68	July 2011 - June 2012	Employment and unemployment and household consumer expenditure.
69	July 2012 - Dec. 2012	Housing Condition, Disability and Slums.
70	Jan 2013 - Dec. 2013	Land and Livestock Holdings, Debt and Investment
71	Jan 2014 - June 2014	Social Consumption
72	July 2014 - June 2015	Consumer Expenditure and Employment-Unemployment (quinquennial survey).

In order to meet the various requirements, NSSO also conducts ad hoc surveys.

The details are available on website **www.mospi.gov.in**.

Reliability of Surveys : Every attempt is made to give correct and most reliable results. It is the primary concern of NSSO. The following are the main three steps taken in this regard.

(i) Internal checks : Expert statisticians directly collect the primary data and compare the results with those obtained by investigators.

(ii) External checks : The results of surveys are compared with those obtained by other entirely independent sources.

(iii) Comparison of estimates with the actual values.

(C) Indian Statistical Institute (ISI)

The Indian Statistical Institute at Calcutta was set up on 28th April 1932 by P. C. Mahalanobis. In the year 1959, the Indian Parliament passed an act and accordingly ISI is treated as an Institute of national importance. Moreover it is authourised to confer degrees and diplomas like any university.

The main functions of ISI are as follows :

(i) To carry out research qualifying high standards.

(ii) To provide training and to conduct statistical projects.

(iii) To provide technical and computational assistance to NSSO.

(iv) ISI runs B. Stat., M. Stat. courses with various specialisations such as statistical quality control (SQC), operations research, demography, probability, econometrics etc. Besides this Ph. D and research activities in various branches of Statistics and allied subjects are conducted by ISI. Apart from regular training and teaching there are some diploma courses conducted by ISI for external students.

At ISI the International Statistical Education centre functions with the collaboration of the International Statistical Institute, UNESCO and the Government of India and ISI. ISI has SQC division with 10 units located at key industrial centres. The division arranges training activities in SQC and Operations Research.

ISI is world renowned institute for its high standards research in Statistics and training.

The 'Sankhya' is regular publication of ISI as a research journal.

(D) International Institute for Population Sciences (IIPS) : The International Institute for Population Sciences (IIPS), formerly known as Demographic Training and Research Centre, was established at Mumbai in July 1956 to serve as the regional centre for training and research in Population Studies for the countries of Asia and Pacific region. It was renamed as International Institute for Population Studies in April 1971 and was redesignated to its present title in March 1984 of facilitate expansion of its academic activities. The institute was declared as a 'Deemed University' in August 1985 by the Ministry of Human Resource Development, Government of India, New Delhi. It is an autonomous institution under the administrative control of Department of Family Welfare, Ministry of Health and Family Welfare, Government of India. This is the only Institute of its kind in the world completely devoted to teaching and research in the population related areas.

Over the years, the institute has helped in building a nucleus of professional in the field of population in various countries in the ESCAP region. Many who are trained at the Institute, now occupy key positions in the field of population in reputed national and international organizations. During the past forty-five years, the institute has trained 1,956 students i.e. 1,321 from India and 635 from 39 different countries.

The Institute offers following regular teaching programmes :
1. Diploma in Population Studies (D.P.S.)
2. Master of Population Studies (M.P.S.)
   Master of Philosophy (M. Phil.) in Population Studies.
3. Master of Population Studies (M.P.S.)
   (Correspondence Course)
4. Doctor of Philosophy (Ph.D.) in Population Studies.
5. Diploma in Health Promotion Training and Research Centre (FWTRC), Mumbai, affiliated to IIPS.

Besides teaching and research activities, the Institute also provides consultancy to the governments and non-government organizations and other academic institutions. It also conducts short term training programmes on various issues related to population and other allied fields. The details are available on website www.iipsindia.org.

1.6 Statistical Organisation In The Maharashtra

Bureau of Economics and Statistics

The present statistical system in India does not specify the jurisdiction of centre and state clearly. Hence statistical units exist in Central Ministries as well as in State Government according to the subjects.

Statistical system in states varies from state to state. In Maharashtra State Statistical Bureau is functioning for various activities such as (i) Statistical co-ordination (ii) State Income (iii) Socio economic survey. Apart from this different departments have their own statistical units in respective fields.

The specific functions of Bureau of Economics and Statistics, Bombay are described below :
  (i) Co-ordinate statistics collected by various departments of State Government.

(ii) Provide guidance regarding statistics to various departments.

(iii) Collect statistical information, conduct statistical enquiries and statistical surveys.

(iv) Provide liaison between state and CSO.

(v) Conduct economic and statistical research.

(vi) Provide statistical assistance to state planning agencies.

(vii) Compile economic indicators and give State Income estimates.

(viii) Publish, Annual State Statistical Abstract and Quarterly District Statistical Abstracts, which include all the essential statistics of the state.

Statistical Systems in India

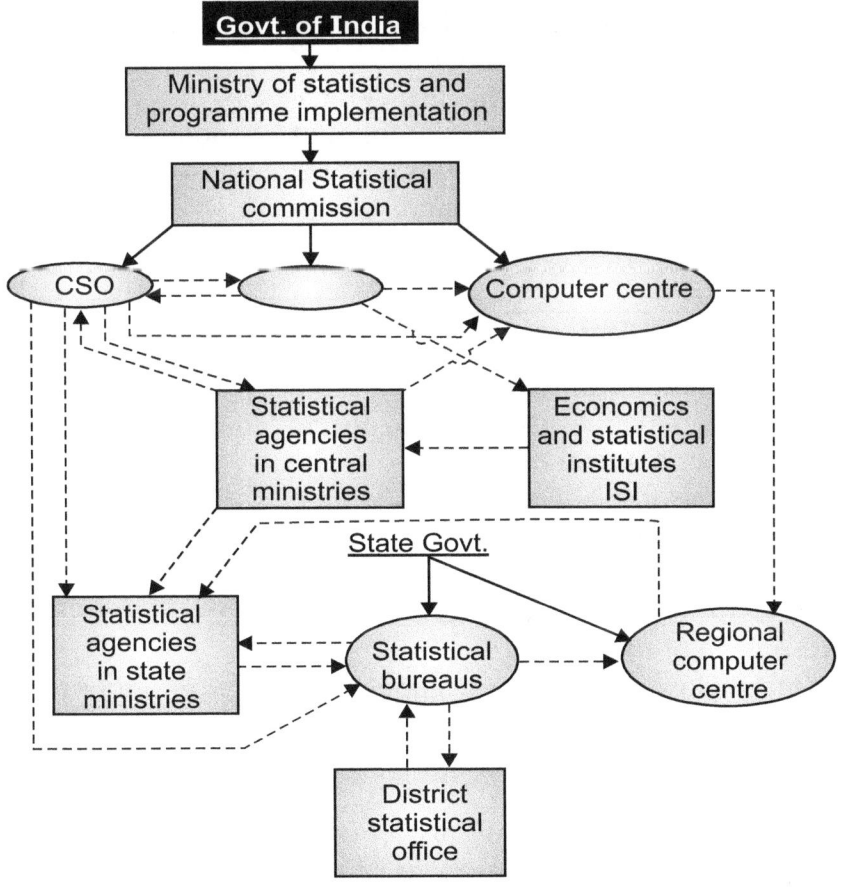

Fig. 1.1

EXERCISE 1 (A)

1. Give the definitions of statistics due to (i) Webster (ii) Bowley (iii) Yule and Kendall (iv) Horace Secrist.
2. Describe the importance of statistical methods.
3. Describe the utility and scope of Statistics with illustrations in the following fields.
   (i) Industry (ii) Biological sciences (iii) Medical sciences (iv) Economics (v) Social sciences (vi) Management sciences (vi) Agriculture, (vii) Insurance (ix) Information technology (x) Education (xi) Psychology.
4. Write a note on Statistical Organisations in India with special reference to (i) NSSO (ii) CSO and (iii) ISI (iv) IIPS.
5. Describe the functions of the following statistical organisation at the Central Government.
   (i) NSSO (ii) CSO (iii) ISI (iv) IIPS.
6. Describe the functions of 'Bureau of Economics and Statistics'.
7. Give an account of activities of CSO.
8. Write a note on NSSO rounds of survey.
9. Explain in brief how reliability of survey is maintained by NSSO.

Objective Type Questions

I. Multiple Choice Questions

- **Choose the correct alternative out of four alternatives given below for each questions.**

1. 'CSO' stands for
   (a) Central Standard Office
   (b) Control Statistical Office
   (c) Central Statistical Office
   (d) None of the above
2. Central Government has established CSO for co-ordination of statistical organisation with the states in
   (a) May, 1950 (b) May, 1951
   (c) May, 1952 (d) none of the above
3. National Sample Survey (NSS) was set-up in 1950 under the guidance of
   (a) C. R. Rao (b) P. V. Sukhatme
   (c) P. C. Mahalanobis (d) V. S. Huzurbazar

4. NSSO stands for
   (a) Natonal Service Scheme Office
   (b) National Scheme Service Office
   (c) National Statistical Service Office
   (d) National Sample Servey Office

5. The name of statistical institute which helps in preparing designs, programming, processing of information analysis, report writing and it is also centre of research and training etc. is
   (a) National Statistical Institute
   (b) National Sample Institute
   (c) Indian Statistical Institute
   (d) Indian Statistical Service

6. The name of Bureau exist in state govenment functioning for various activities such as (i) statistical co-ordination, (ii) state income, (iii) socio economic survey etc. is
   (a) Bureau of English and Statistics
   (b) Bureau of Economics and Statistics
   (c) Bureau of Economics and Socilology
   (d) None of the above

7. Statistical methods is treated as a branch of science which deals with
   (a) collection and presentation of data
   (b) analysis of data
   (c) interpretation of data
   (d) all the above

8. Statistics performs functions such as :
   (a) presentation of facts and figures
   (b) forecasting and planning
   (c) controlling and exploring
   (d) all the above

9. Statistics helps in almost all fields such as
   (a) decision-making, LIC, banks
   (b) government agencies and industries
   (c) business, trade, index numbers
   (d) all the above

10. Statistics as "the classified facts representing the conditions of people in the state, especially those facts which can be stated in a tables of numbers" was stated by :
    (a) Bowley's A. W. (b) Yule and Kendall's
    (c) Webster (d) Horace Secrist

11. Statistics may be called as : (i) science of ocunting or (ii) science of averages or (iii) science of the measurement of social organism regarded as a whole in all its manifestations was stated by :
    (a) Bowley's A. W. (b) Yule and Kendall's
    (c) Webster (d) Hoarce Secrist

12. Who stated that "by statistics we mean qualitative data affected to a marked extent by a multiplicity of causes"
    (a) Bowley's A. W. (b) Yule and Kendall's
    (c) Webster (d) Horace Secrist

13. The statement "by statistics we mean aggregates of facts affected to a marked extent by multiplicity of causes to reasonable standards of accuracy, collected in a symmatic manner for a predetermined purpose and placed in relation to each other :
    (a) Bowley's A. W. (b) Yule and Kendall's
    (c) Webster (d) Horace Secrist

Answers : Objective Type Questions

I. **Multiple Choice Questions :**
   (1) c (2) b (3) c (4) d (5) c
   (6) b (7) d (8) d (9) d (10) c
   (11) a (12) b (13) d

Chapter 2...
Nature of Data

Most statistical packages use Sturges' rule (or an extension of it) for selecting the number of classes when constructing a histogram. Sturges' rule is also widely recommended in introductory statistics textbooks. It is known that Sturges' rule leads to oversmoothed histograms, but Sturges' derivation of his rule has never been questioned.

Sturge

A rule for determining the desirable number of groups into which a distribution of observations should be classified; the number of groups or classes is $1 + 3.3 \log n$, where n is the number of observations.

Contents ...

2.1 Introduction
2.2 Types of Characteristics : Attributes and Variables
2.3 Collection and Organisation of Data
2.4 Classification
2.5 Frequency Distribution
2.6 Methods of Classification
2.7 Cumulative Frequencies
2.8 Relative Frequency
2.9 Guidelines for the Choices of Classes
2.10 Graphical Representation of Statistical Data
2.11 Stem and Leaf Chart
2.12 Advantages and Limitations of Graph
2.13 Process Control Tools
2.14 Diagrammatic Representation of Data
2.15 Tabular Representation

Key Words :

Data, Variable, Attributes, Nominal Scale, Ordinal Scale, Ratio Scale, Interval Scale, Circular Scale, Primary Data, Secondary Data, Cross-sectional Data, Time Series Data, Industrial Data, Failure Data Classification, Frequency, Inclusive and Exclusive Method of Classification, Class Limits, Class Boundaries, Class Mark, Open End Class, Relative Frequency, Cumulative Frequency, Histogram, Frequency Polygon, Frequency Curve, Ogive Curves, Stem and Leaf Chart, Check Sheet, Parato Diagram.

Objectives :

This chapter explains the first two aspects of statistics viz. collection and presentation of data. Classification is a tool of data condensation. It becomes easier to analyse the data after classification. Graphical representation has several advantages. Some process control tools which are used in industry are introduced here.

2.1 Introduction

While studying any phenomenon we come across two types of characteristics :
(i) constant and (ii) variable. The characteristic which does not change its value (or nature) is considered as **constant**. *For example* : Height of a person after 25 years of age, altitude of a certain place from sea level etc. On the other hand there are many characteristics which are qualitative or quantitative in nature and change their values (or nature). For *example* : Examination result of a candidate can be recorded as pass or fail which is a qualitative variable characteristics, whereas we can express a candidate's performance as percentage of marks which is a quantitative variable.

2.2 Types of Characteristics : Attributes and Variables

Statistics involves the study of variable characteristics. Hence, we include the related and necessary definitions.

Attribute : A qualitative characteristic like sex, nationality, religion, grade in examination, blood group, beauty, defectiveness of an article produced by a machine is called as *attribute*.

Steven S.S. introduced four types of scales of measurements viz. the nominal, ordinal, interval and ratio scales. Attributes are measured using nominal and ordinal scale.

Nominal Scale : Nominal scale consists of two or more named categories into which the objects are classified. *For example*, (a) classification of individuals using blood groups constitutes a nominal scale (b) Classification of students in various divisions of the same standard also represents nominal scale. (c) Classification of individuals using sex, caste, nationality etc. also use nominal scale. (d) House numbers, survey numbers, pincode numbers are also examples of nominal scale.

Remarks : (i) In nominal scale if numbers are used, then those are allotted in purely arbitrary manner. Those numbers are just for identification purpose used in place of labels. (ii) Those numbers are interchangeable.

Ordinal Scale : Ordinal scale of measurement gives numbers to groups of objects using some quantifiable characteristics. Therefore ordered arrangement of groups is possible in this type of scale. For example : (a) Groups of individuals according to income such as poor, middle class, rich. (b) Groups of students according to grades in examination, such as fail, second class, first class, first class with distinction (c) Groups using weight such as light, heavy (d) Groups using height such as short, medium, tall. Similarly groups of individuals as dull or intelligent; groups of objects as soft or hard etc. are all situations where ordinal scale can be used.

Remark : (i) In the ordinal scale, numbers given to groups as labels, serve the purpose of ranks. Hence those labels are not interchangeable.

(ii) In the ordinal scale, the groups are ordered according to some characteristic. Suppose three individuals A, B, C are given ranks 1, 2, 3 respectively according to their height. A is the shortest and C is the tallest. In this case heights of A, B, C may not be equispaced, however, they possess equispaced ranks.

(iii) Rank of individual B is 2, however, height of B is not double the height of A or height of C is not three times the height of A. Here we note that the heights of B, C are not exact integer multiples of height of A, however, they possess ranks 1, 2, 3 which are integer multiples of rank of A. Here we only mean that B is taller than A and C is taller than B.

Nominal and ordinal scales are used in the measurement of attributes.

Variable : A quantitative characteristic (which changes its value) like weight of person, examination marks, population of a country, profit of a salesman, is called as *variable*.

Note : Variables are measured using interval scale and ratio scale.

The drawback of ordinal scale that the units are not equispaced is overcome in interval scale.

Interval scale : Interval scale of measurement has equal units of measurement, however, the zero point is arbitrary.

The classic example of interval scale in our day-to-day life is the Centigrade or Fahrenheight scale of temperature measurement. In both the scales zero is arbitrary, it does not mean absence of heat. Moreover 60°C does not contain exactly double the heat that 30°C has. However, the difference in temperature between 10°C to 20°C is same as that between 50°C to 60°C (or that between similar pair).

Drawback : In interval scale 0 is arbitrary, it is chosen as per convenience, therefore we can add (or subtract) a constant in the readings on interval scale without affecting form of scale. However, we cannot multiply or divide the readings by constant.

Use : Inspite of the drawback in interval scale, it is used for convenience in behavioural sciences to study mental and social variables and traits.

All the drawbacks existing in the earlier three scales of measurement viz. nominal, ordinal, interval scales are overcome in ratio scale. It is the best scale of measurement. It is used in almost all places.

Ratio scale : Ratio scale of measurement has equal units of measurement and those are taken from a true zero.

All the measurements of type height (cm), weight (kg), time (hours) etc. are the examples of ratio scales. In this scale 60 kg weight is exactly double heavy as compared to 30 kg weight.

It can be clearly noticed that variables can be measured by numbers.

Further the variables can be divided into two categories : (i) discrete and (ii) continuous.

Definition : A variable taking only particular values is called as *discrete variable*.

For example : Number of students in a class, number of articles produced by a machine, population of a country, number of workers in a factory etc. are discrete variables. Most of the discrete variables have integral values.

Definition : A variable taking all possible values in a certain range is called as *continuous variable*.

For example : Weight of a person, length of a screw produced by a machine, temperature at a certain place, agricultural production, electricity consumption of a family, speed of a vehicle are the examples of continuous variable.

It is observed that many continuous variables such as marks, income, weight of a person etc. look like discrete variables after the measurement. This is mainly due to the limitations of the measuring instruments. Using better instruments one can have accurate measurement and overcome this difficulty.

The following diagram summarizes the various types of data :

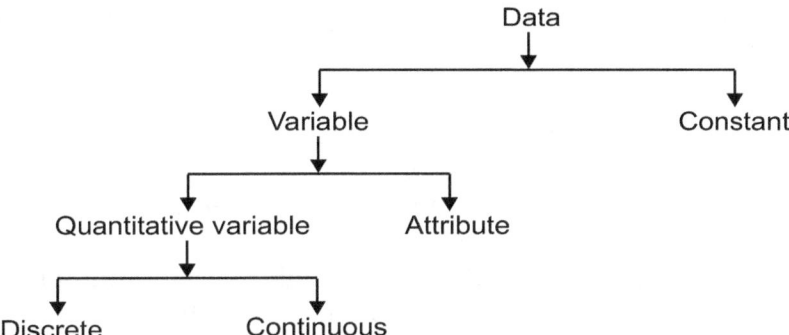

Directional Data and Circular Scale : Some variables are cyclic or rhythmic in nature according to time. *For example*, blood pressure, reproductive cycles, body temperature, mental alterness, sleep-wake cycles, hormonal pulsatility. Such variables are called as biological rhythms control characteristics. The corresponding data is considered as directional data or circular data. Moreover direction of wind, direction of earth's magnetic pole, direction of birds movement, direction of river flow are the examples of directional data. The variables measured in angles i.e. on circular scale rather than linear scale are called as directional data or circular data.

The statistical tools such mean variance used in usual manner do no remain meaningful and suitable. The statistical methods to be used in these instances are entirely different.

Directional data is also observed in circular movements of automobiles parts, oceanography, travel of ships etc.

The details are beyond the scope of book. The introduction of such non-trivial data and corresponding situation is the only purpose.

2.3 Collection and Organization of Data

Collection of data is a very important work and needs to be done carefully. One has to decide the objectives clearly before collecting the data. In order to determine dependable and reliable results, proper data should be collected in a proper way. The data according to the method of collection are of two types viz., (a) Primary data, (b) Secondary data.

Apart from the method of collection the type of data according its nature are also in existence. (viz. time series data, cross-sectional data).

(a) Primary Data :

Primary data means original data (i.e. facts and figures) obtained by an investigator himself. Primary data may be a result of a survey or enquiry conducted. This may be regarded as first-hand information. Population census results, is a classical example of primary data. Primary data are also called as *raw data*. No doubt, primary data are more reliable than any other type but are expensive and time consuming.

Primary data are collected by the following methods :

1. Direct personal investigation or interview.

In this method, the investigator meets concerned persons known as 'informants' and collects necessary information by the process of interview. Investigator should be thorough in handling problems of investigation. This will result into reliable data. Investigator has to go upto the source of original information. For example, if he wants to know the amount of production, in a particular industry, he should collect the figures by visiting the machine floor, rather than from office or bulletin. This is the best method of collecting primary data. However, the investigator has to take certain precautions.

2. Indirect oral investigation.
3. Investigation through questionnaire.

(b) Secondary Data :

Data taken from sources like office records, bulletins, reports etc. which are already collected by some other agency is called *'secondary data.'*

The data which are already collected may be tabulated, classified, ordered etc. Hence, it is called processed or finished data. Thus, secondary data can also be called *finished product*.

'Secondary data' is a relative term. For example, if 'A' collects original data, then it becomes primary data for him, whereas if the same data is used by B. Then it becomes secondary data for B. In this case, the only difference is that the user of secondary data may not have thorough understanding of the background as the user of primary data has.

Difference between primary and secondary data :

(a) The main difference lies in the method of collection.
(b) Primary data are original in nature. Hence those are more accurate than secondary data.

(c) Collection of primary data is expensive as well as time-consuming.

(d) Primary data can be elicited in accordance with the objectives of a study. Secondary data may fail in this regard.

The investigator has to decide whether primary data are to be collected or secondary data to be collected by considering advantages and disadvantages of each. Moreover he has to consider nature, scope of enquiry, funds and time available, accuracy etc. to decide which type of data are to be collected.

The following are the main sources of secondary data :

(a) Publications of the state and central Government and public sector organizations such as, Reserve Bank of India Bulletin, periodical reports of Central Statistical Organisation (CSO), National Sample Survey (NSS), demographical institutes, research institutes, observatories, meteorological institutes etc.

(b) Publications of international organizations such as UNO, WHO, UNESCO.

(c) Reports of municipal corporations, Zilla Parishad, and similar other organizations

(d) Reports of different commissions and organizations like chambers of commerce, stock exchanges, UGC etc.

(e) News papers, journals, periodicals such as Economic Times, Financial express, India Year Book, Manorama Year Book etc. provide required data.

(f) Publications of research institutes, universities also provide data.

To prepare an exhaustive list of all publications and sources is a difficult task. Apart from these sources, there are many other sources such as records of private concerns, unpublished reports prepared by consultants, research workers etc.

After deciding whether to collect primary or secondary data, the investigator has to fix up the method of collecting the data keeping in view the funds, time and other resources at his disposal. There are two ways of collecting data. (i) Sampling, (ii) Complete enumeration.

Thus the methods of data collection are (i) surveys, (ii) laboratory experiments, (iii) simulation.

Surveys : With the help of sample surveys or complete enumeration primary or secondary data can be collected.

Laboratory experiments : The observations generated in laboratory experiments will be a method of data collection.

Simulation : Some experiments cannot be conducted in laboratory for example, genetic experiments, experiments with hazardous material or radioactive material. In such cases, now-a-days the data are generated using simulation techniques with the help of computers. It has tremendous scope in industry, business etc. For example, howmany counters or salesmen are required in a departmental store can be simulated using queueing theory.

The Other Types of Data :

There is yet another angle of looking at data. Earlier we have considered the way of collection. However, the type of data exists due to the nature of data and some other characteristics. If we consider the data when it was collected. Thus, we introduce the time characteristics. It gives rise to the data specially termed as **time series data**. Sometimes at a fixed time moment we collect data, where time is considered but hold constant. Such data are referred to as **cross-sectional data**. The specific definitions are as follows :

Time series data : The data arranged in the chronological order (as per the order of occurrence) are called as time series data.

For example :

(1) Daily sales of a departmental store.

(2) Daily electricity consumption of a town.

(3) Prime of gold recorded daily.

Cross-sectional data : The values of variables observed at a particular time at several places or on several objects are called as cross-sectional data.

For example :

(1) Sales on a specific day of several departmental store is a cross-sectional data. However daily sales of a specific departmental store constitutes time series data.

(2) Electricity consumption on a specific day for several towns constitutes
cross-sectional data. However, daily electricity consumption of a specific town is a time series data.

The analysis of time series data is to be carried out in a different manner. Since time is also an important characteristic of data. Classification method cannot be used just because it losses time characteristics. Classification considers the smallness or largeness of numbers but do not consider the time of its occurrence. The details are beyond the scope of book.

Industrial Data : Industrial data consists of (i) dimensions of manufactured goods, (ii) number of items confirming specifications, (iii) number of imperfections per item. Thus, data may be by variables or attributes. The analysis of such data is done using statistical methods used in statistical quality control. The ultimate result that industry needs is the capability index or capability performance index. It is the indicator of quality of goods. The six sigma procedures of total quality management (TQM) need industrial data to be analysed. The seven process control tools required in ISO 9000 also require industrial data.

The upcoming branch in industrial atmosphere is the reliability engineering. It is based on the study of failure of system, machines and its components. Accordingly the life of system is determined. Warranty period is determined. It is based on failure time data.

We treat failure data a different type, since analysis of such data needs altogether different method.

Thus, failure data includes data of life of components. Number replacements in a specific period. Failure is determined for every component as well as for entire assembly of components. Further survival rate of reliability of components and that of system is also determined. Hazard rate, which is called as instantaneous failure rate also plays important role in the further analysis. It also requires theory of probability for further analysis.

Sometimes in failure data analysis we try to analyse various causes behind the failure. It is called as cause and effect analysis. The most frequent causes of failure are required to be considered on priority basis. It is done using Parato diagram a graphical tool in the analysis of failure data. The details are discussed in the later part of the discussion.

2.4 Classification

In order to study a characteristic or a group of characteristics of any type, the first phase is to collect the data. The unprocessed data are called as *raw* data. For the sake of further statistical analysis, the data items are arranged in increasing (or decreasing) order. However, if there is a huge amount of observations, merely ordered arrangement is not enough. It does not furnish much useful information nor does it reduce the bulk of data. Data in this form are difficult to comprehend, analyse and interpret.

For example : Income of 5000 individuals is given for analysis.

It becomes quite essential to condense the data in a suitable form. Classification can be used as a tool to condense the data.

The entire process of making homogeneous and non-overlaping groups of observations according to similarities is called as *classification*. The groups so formed are called as *class intervals* or *classes*.

The objectives of classification can be summarized as follows :

1. It condenses the data.
2. It omits unnecessary details.
3. It facilitates the comparison with other data.

For example : In case of classification of income of 5000 individuals, one can find the number of individuals below poverty line or income distribution of two countries can be compared.

4. It reveals prominent features of the data.

For example : We can find the income group in which majority of families lie.

5. It enables further analysis like computation of averages, dispersion etc.

2.5 Frequency Distribution

We proceed to study how the observations are classified and a frequency distribution is formed. First we consider the classification of discrete variable.

(A) Frequency distribution of discrete variable :

Procedure : 1. Find the smallest and the largest observation.

2. Prepare first column of all possible values of variables from the smallest to the largest.

3. Consider the observations one-by-one. Put a tally mark against the value to which it relates in second column.

4. Count the number of tally marks and place them in the third column in front of corresponding value.

Tally marks facilitate counting. Hence, they are popularly used.

Illustration 1 : In a manufacturing process of screws, packets of 10 screws are prepared. A lot of 50 packets was submitted for inspection. The following data give the number of defective screws observed in each packet.

3	1	0	1	5	0	1	0	0	1
1	0	0	1	0	1	2	1	1	0
0	0	2	0	0	1	0	1	1	1
2	1	3	0	1	0	4	1	5	3
0	2	1	2	1	0	3	0	4	2

Prepare a frequency distribution of the above data.

Solution : By inspection we can locate the largest value as 5 and the smallest as 0. We prepare first column with the entries 0 to 5. We consider the first observation, it is 3, so we put a vertical bar (I) called as tally mark or tally bar in the second column against the value 3. The next observation is 1, we put tally mark against 1. In this manner we classify all the observations. We put a tally mark adjacent to earlier tally mark if the observation is repeated next time. If there are four tally marks (IIII) and the observation occurs fifth time then a fifth tally is put across (/) the earlier bunch of four tallies. Finally the structure looks like (IIII). In this manner tally marks are arranged in a group of five. This facilitates counting of tallies. Finally the number of tallies are counted and placed in the third column. The procedure gives table 2.1

Table 2.1

Frequency distribution of number of defective screws in 50 packets

Number of Defectives	Tally Marks	Frequency
0	₩ ₩ ₩ III	18
1	₩ ₩ ₩ III	18
2	₩ I	6
3	IIII	4
4	II	2
5	II	2
	Total	50

Preparing frequency distribution using MS-Excel for discrete data : Consider example in illustration 1. Enter the data in column A as shown. Arrange all distinct numbers in the data in ascending order (column B). Use the command **= countif (range, criteria)** and holding shift and control keys, press enter. It counts the number of cells within a range that meets the given condition. The final output will be as follows.

	A	B	C	D
1	Data	No. of	Frequency	
2		Defectives		
3		3	0	=COUNTIF(A3 A52 B3)
4		1	1	18
5		0	2	6
6		1	3	4
7		5	4	2
8		0	5	2
9		1		50
10		0		
11		0		
12		1		
13		1		

Fig. 2.1

Frequency : The number of observations in a class is called as *frequency* or *class frequency*.

Frequency Distribution : A table containing class intervals along with frequencies is called as *frequency distribution.*

(B) Frequency distribution of continuous variable :

The procedure of classification of continuous variable differs slightly from that of a discrete variable.

Procedure :

1. Find the smallest and the largest observation. Calculate the difference between them. This difference is called as the *range*.

2. Decide the classes by dividing the range into several intervals. The number of classes be preferably between 7 to 20.

3. Prepare first column of table by entering the class intervals.

4. Classify the observations one-by-one in the appropriate class by putting tally marks in the second column against the corresponding class. Cross the observation from the original data to avoid double counting.

5. Count the tally marks and enter the number in the third column.

Illustration 2 : The following are the scores in intelligence test conducted for 80 candidates of a certain class.

```
112   77  115   91  137   88   89   71
100   93   64  116   95   95  106   92
 84   86   87  124   84  117   97   80
103  114   83   77   94  114   63   61
120  126   98   98  116  108   94  105
108   99   87   96   88   95   73   92
 91  129  108   81   82  102   86  111
119   90  109  101  107   75  123  104
106   84   75   99   72  128  114   93
 83   82  124  114  130   81  101   91
```

Prepare the frequency distribution of the data by taking suitable class intervals.

Solution : In the given problem we note that the highest and the lowest observations are respectively 137 and 61. Hence, the range is 137 − 61 = 76. In this case it is suitable to make 8 classes each of width 10. Since the lowest observation is 61, it is convenient to choose the first class as 60 to 69, the next a 70 to 79 and so on. The last class will be 130 to 139. According to the procedure described above, we classify the observations and prepare a table of three columns. First column includes classes, second includes tally marks and the third includes frequencies. The first observation is 112, it lies between 110-119, therefore, we put a tally mark to include the observation in this class. Likewise all the observations are classified and the process gives the following table 2.2.

Table 2.2 : Frequency distribution of scores of 80 candidates

Class Intervals	Tally Marks	Frequency
60 - 69	|||	3
70 - 79	⃒⃒⃒⃒ ||	7
80 - 89	⃒⃒⃒⃒ ⃒⃒⃒⃒ ⃒⃒⃒⃒		16
90 - 99	⃒⃒⃒⃒ ⃒⃒⃒⃒ ⃒⃒⃒⃒ ⃒⃒⃒⃒	20
100 - 109	⃒⃒⃒⃒ ⃒⃒⃒⃒ ||||	14
110 - 119	⃒⃒⃒⃒ ⃒⃒⃒⃒		11
120 - 129	⃒⃒⃒⃒ ||	7
130 - 139	||	2
	Total	80

Preparing frequency distribution using MS-EXCEL for continuous data : Consider example in illustration. Enter the data in column A as shown. Enter the upper limits of all classes in column B which are called as **bins**. Use the command **= frequency (data_array, bins_array)**. In this case, **= frequency (A4 : A83, B4 : B11)**. Press enter key by holding shift and control key. It gives frequencies against bins as follows

	A	B	C	D	E
1					
2	Data	Upper Class Limits	Frequency		
3	112	69	=FREQUENCY(A3:A82,B3:B10)		
4	100	79	7		
5	84	89	16		
6	103	99	20		
7	120	109	14		
8	108	119	11		
9	91	129	7		
10	119	139	2		
11	106	Total	80		
12	83				
13	77				
14	93				
15	86				
16	114				
17	126				
18	99				
19	129				

Fig. 2.2

2.6 Methods of Classification

There are two methods of classification : (i) inclusive method (ii) exclusive method. We bring out the difference between the two methods.

1. Inclusive Method : In this method the observation equal to upper limit is included in the same class. Therefore, the method is called as *inclusive method*. It can be observed that the upper limit of class is not the same as the lower limit of succeeding class. Therefore, a discontinuity is observed between the classes. e.g.

Table 2.3

Daily Sales in ₹
2000 - 2999
3000 - 3999
4000 - 4999

2. Exclusive Method : In this method the observation equal to upper limit does not belong to the same class. It is included in the next class. Therefore, the method is called as *exclusive method*. For example, the observation 4000 is included in 4000 - 5000. In other words, the observation equal to upper limit is excluded from the same class e.g.

Table 2.4

Daily Sales in ₹
2000 - 3000
3000 - 4000
4000 - 5000

In this case upper limit of one class is the lower limit of subsequent class. The classes are observed to be continuous without any gap in between them.

We explain below few more terms related to the frequency distribution.

Class - limits : The two numbers designating the class-interval are called as *class limits*. With reference to table 2.2, the first class interval is 60-90, in this case 60 and 69 are the class limits. The smallest possible observation that can be included in the class is *lower limit* and the largest possible observation that can be included in the class is the *upper limit*. In the above example 60 and 69 are lower and upper limits of the class interval 60-69.

Class boundaries : The class boundaries are the numbers upto which the actual magnitude of observation in the class can extend. The class boundaries are also called as actual limits or extended limits. For the sake of clarity let us consider the frequency distribution with classes 10-19, 20-29, ... etc. In this case an observation 19.2 will be rounded-off to 19 and placed in 10-19, whereas the observation 19.6 will be rounded-off to 20 and will be placed in 20-29. Therefore, the actual magnitude of the observation in the class 20-29 will be between 19.5 - 29.5. The table below will make out the difference between class limits and class boundaries.

Table 2.5

Class limits	Class boundaries
10 - 29	9.5 - 19.5
20 - 29	19.5 - 29.5
30 - 39	29.5 - 39.5

It can be clearly seen that in case of exclusive method of classification, class limits and class boundaries are same.

Using class-boundaries the classes are made continuous, however, original frequency associated do not alter.

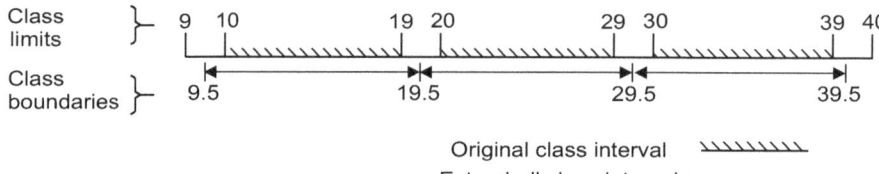

Original class interval
Extended class interval

Fig. 2.3

Class mark or Mid-values : It is the mid-point of class interval and the same can be obtained as follows :

$$\text{Mid-value} = \frac{\text{Upper limit} + \text{Lower limit}}{2}$$

$$= \frac{\text{Upper boundary} + \text{Lower boundary}}{2}$$

Class-width : It is the actual length of the class interval. We can find class width as follows.

Class width = Upper boundary − Lower boundary

$$= \begin{pmatrix} \text{Lower limit of the} \\ \text{succeeding class} \end{pmatrix} - \begin{pmatrix} \text{Lower limit of the} \\ \text{class under} \\ \text{consideration} \end{pmatrix}$$

$$= \begin{pmatrix} \text{Upper limit of the} \\ \text{class under} \\ \text{consideration} \end{pmatrix} - \begin{pmatrix} \text{Upper limit of the} \\ \text{preceding class} \end{pmatrix}$$

Open end class : A class in which one of the limits is not specified is called an open end class.

For example, in the following frequency distribution there are two open end classes.

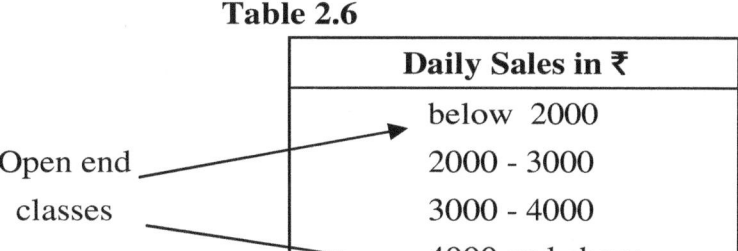

Table 2.6

The class 'below 2000' has no lower limit and the class 4000 and above has no upper limit. Therefore, these classes are open end classes. Whenever the extreme observations are widely spread, open end classes are used. In case of income distribution or the classification of sales of a company, open end classes may be required. Open end classes create some problems in further analysis, therefore, as far as possible the open end classes should be avoided.

2.7 Cumulative Frequencies

In many situations it is required to find the number of observations below or above a certain value. For *example*, in case of a frequency distribution of income, the number of persons below poverty line or in case of frequency distribution of examination marks, number of candidates above 60 etc. is required to be found. In this case cumulative frequencies are much useful. There are two types of cumulative frequencies : (i) less than type cumulative frequency (ii) more than type cumulative frequency.

Less than type cumulative frequency of a class is the number of observations less than or equal to the upper limit of the corresponding class. Similarly more than type cumulative frequency is the number of observations more than or equal to the lower limit of the corresponding class.

It is clear from the above explanation that the less than type cumulative frequencies can be obtained by computing cumulative sum of frequencies from the lowest class to highest class. We illustrate the procedure of computing the less than type and more than type cumulative frequencies.

Table 2.7

Marks	Frequency	Less than cumulative frequency	More than cumulative frequency
0 - 10	5	5	4 + 4 + 15 +12 + 5 = 40
10 - 20	12	5 + 12 = 17	4 + 4 + 15 + 12 = 35
20 - 30	15	5 + 12 + 15 = 32	4 + 4 + 15 = 23
30 - 40	4	5 + 12 + 15 + 4 = 36	4 + 4 = 8
40 - 50	4	5 + 12 + 15 + 4 + 4 = 40	4
Total	40		

It can be noted that the less than cumulative frequency is increasing in nature. Less than cumulative frequency of the lowest class is same as the usual frequency and the less than type cumulative frequency of highest class is the total number of observations. In case of more than cumulative frequencies exactly reverse pattern will be seen.

A table containing upper limits along with less than type cumulative frequency or lower limits along with more than type cumulative frequency is called as *cumulative frequency distribution*.

2.8 Relative Frequency

Two different frequency distributions may not have the same total frequency, hence for the purpose of comparison and interpretation, sometimes it is better to express the frequency of a class in terms of proportion (or percentage) of the total number of observations. The proportion of number of observations in a class is the *relative frequency*. Therefore,

$$\text{Relative frequency} = \frac{\text{Class frequency}}{\text{Total frequency}}$$

It can be noted that the relative frequency maintains the same pattern which is observed in class frequencies. The total of relative frequencies is 1.

Example :

Marks	0 - 10	10 - 20	20 - 30	30 - 40	40 - 50	50 - 60	Total
Frequency	5	25	27	32	6	5	100
Relative Frequency	0.05	0.25	0.27	0.32	0.06	0.05	1

2.9 Guidelines for the Choice of Classes

In further study we use frequency distribution instead of original data, hence classification of data is a sort of compromise, therefore, it becomes important to choose appropriate number of classes. The classes should be chosen, so that it will condense the data and it will also maintain the patterns in the original data.

1. The number of classes should not be too large, otherwise it will not serve the purpose of condensation.

2. The number of classes should not be too small. If the number of classes is too small, it will not reveal the pattern in the original data. Moreover, due to the small number of classes, each class will be too wide. For further computations it is assumed that the observations in a class are situated at the centre of the class. The assumption will not remain valid for wider classes.

The number of classes should be between 7 to 20. However, according to the needs and requirements of the situation appropriate number of classes is chosen.

If the number of observations is large, naturally the number of classes will be large.

Sturge's Rule : If N is the total number of observations to be classified, then according to Sturge's rule, the number of classes is approximately $1 + 3.322 \log N$.

By the other approach as a thumb rule, the number of classes is approximately $\sqrt{N}$.

3. As far as possible, classes should be of uniform width.
4. As far as possible open end classes should be avoided.
5. The class width should be preferably 5 or multiple of 5.
6. The lower limit of the starting class be preferably multiple of 5. For example : The classes may be of the type 0-9, 10-19 ... or 10-20, 20-30 ... etc.

2.10 Graphical Representation of Statistical Data

In the earlier discussion we have studied the methods of summarizing voluminous data. Those methods are adopted to serve the purpose of condensation, comparison and for revealing patterns. However, these methods have their own limitations, Especially when table is large in size, comparison becomes difficult. Perhaps a more effective way to serve the purpose of comparison and revealing the patterns, is graphical representation. Graphs are easy to understand and create an effect which lasts for a longer time. They use voluminous, uninteresting, dry data and present the facts in an attractive and impressive manner. They facilitate comparison and hence, conclusions can be drawn quickly, which is not possible with the help of a table or frequency distribution to the same extent. Moreover, patterns present in the data are more clearly exhibited by graphs. Due to such several advantages, graphs are believed to be powerful tools to convey information to a layman. Therefore, graphs are found to be of immense use in several fields to emphasize the facts. LIC, banks, government agencies, industries use graphs to show their growth, development, extension activities etc.

Here we discuss various graphs associated with frequency distribution. Generally graphs are used to represent mathematical relationship between two variables.

(i) Histogram (April 2011) : It is one of the popularly used graphs for the representation of frequency distribution. It is a series of adjacent rectangles erected on X-axis with class interval as base, hence width of rectangle is equal to class width. Area of rectangle is taken as proportional to class frequency. In case of inclusive method of classification, extended class interval is used as base, where extended class interval is an interval designated by class boundaries.

Since the base of rectangle is classwidth, there is slight difference in the procedure of construction of histogram when the classes are of equal width and when those are of unequal width.

Case (i) Classes of equal width : In this case height of rectangle is proportional to frequency.

Case (ii) Classes of unequal width : In this case height of rectangle is proportional to frequency density where,

$$\text{Frequency density} = \frac{\text{Class frequency}}{\text{Class width}}$$

Note : 1. A serious drawback of histogram is that, it cannot be drawn for a frequency distribution with open end class.

2. In case of discrete variable, histogram need not contain adjacent rectangles, those may be separated like bar diagram.

3. Histograms are useful to find mode, which is discussed in the 5th chapter.

4. Histogram remains same if class width is changed.

Illustration 3 : Draw a histogram to represent the following frequency distribution :

Size of farm in hectares	1 - 20	21 - 40	41 - 60	61 - 80	81 - 100	101 - 120
No. of farms	12	38	16	5	3	1

Solution :

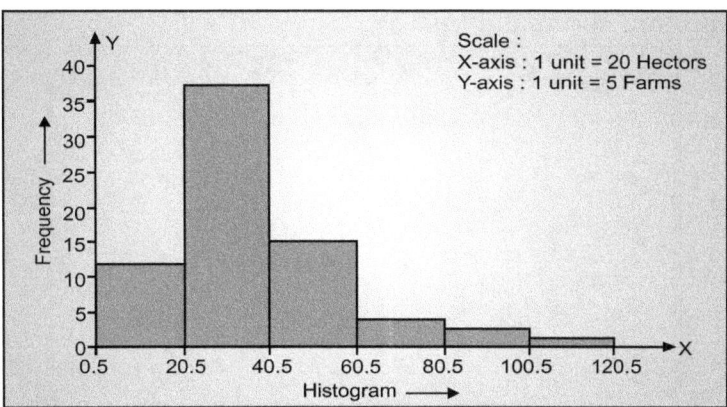

Fig. 2.4

Histogram using MS-Excel : To draw histogram follow steps given below. Take mid values on X-axis and frequency on Y-axis. Enter mid values in column A and corresponding frequencies in column B on worksheet. Select the frequencies by clicking the mouse then go to insert command on main menu. Select

Insert – – > chart.

Then following windows will appear on the screen one-by-one.

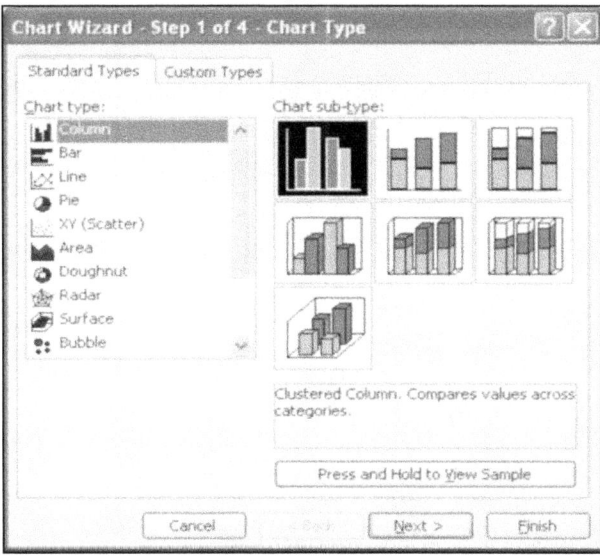

Fig. 2.5 (a)

Select chart type **(column)** and click **next**.
It is at bottom command line.

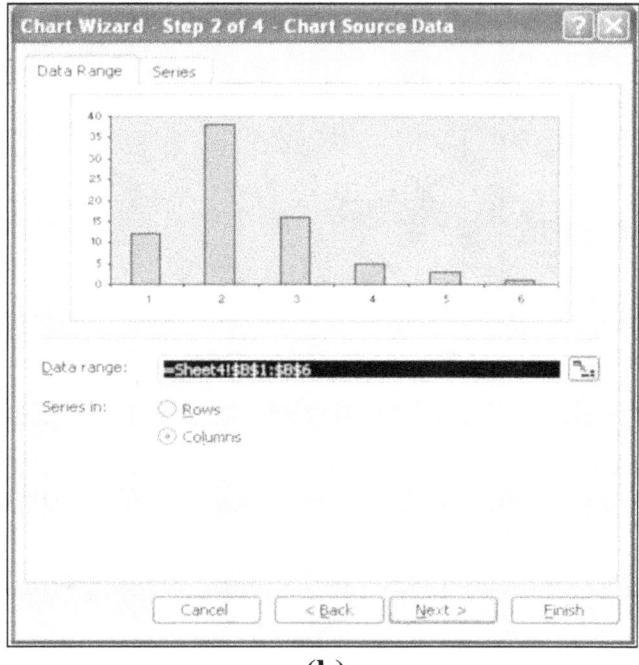

(b)

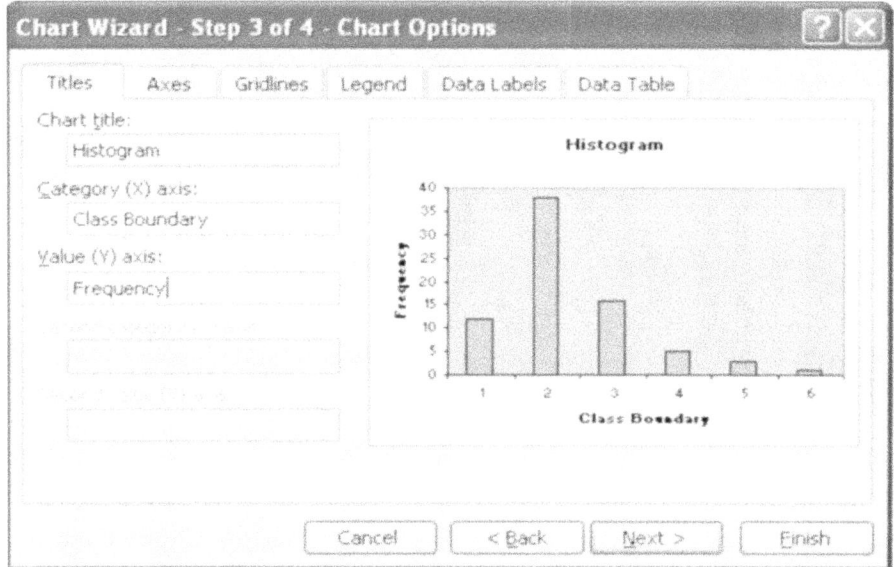

(c)

Fig. 2.5

In the data range, select frequencies and click Next.

Give chart title and x, y axis, click Finish, Right click on one of the bar as shown in Fig. 2.6 (a), select sub-menu Format Data Series to get Fig. 2.6 (b) then select Gap width 0 as shown in Fig. 2.6 (b). Click OK to get histogram as shown in Fig. 2.6 (c).

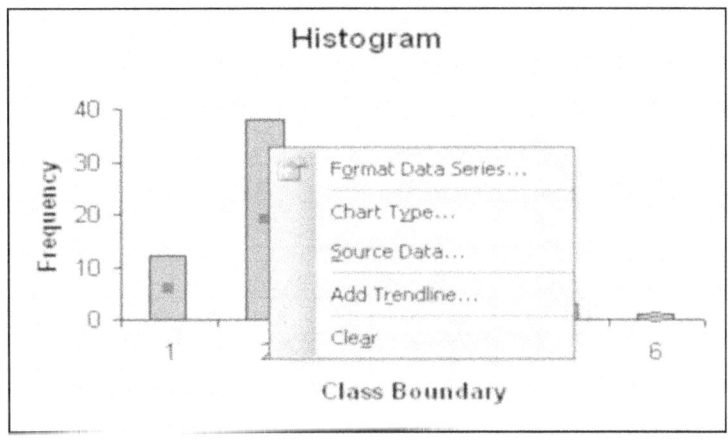

(a)

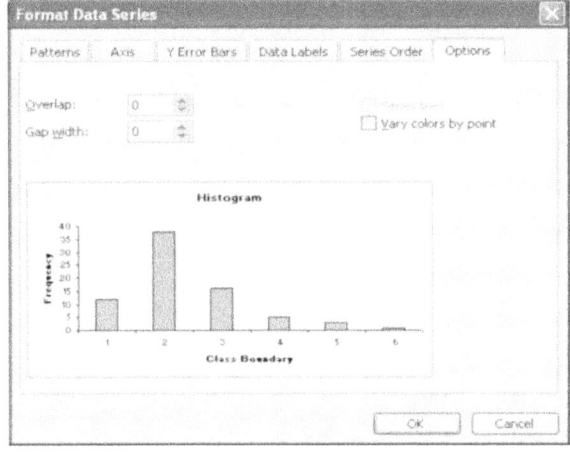

(b)

Fig. 2.6

After going through all steps of chart wizard, following histogram will appear on the screen.

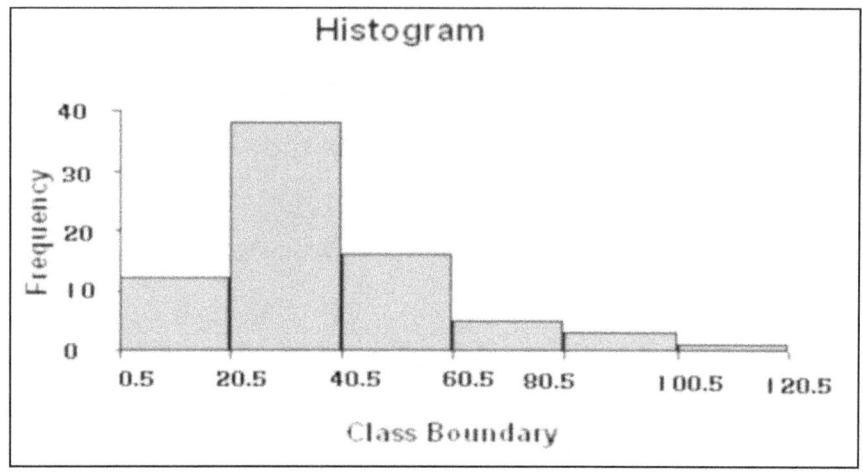

Fig. 2.7

Illustration 4 : Represent the following data by histogram.

Age-group (in years)	0 - 5	5 - 20	20 - 30	30 - 40	40 - 60	60 - 100
Population :	500	2100	2200	2000	1600	400

Solution : Since classes are of unequal width, we need to compute frequency density.

Age-group	0 - 5	5 - 20	20 - 30	30 - 40	40 - 60	60 - 100
Frequency density	$\frac{500}{5} = 100$	$\frac{2100}{15}$ $= 140$	$\frac{2200}{10}$ $= 220$	$\frac{2000}{10}$ $= 200$	$\frac{1600}{20}$ $= 80$	$\frac{400}{40}$ $= 10$

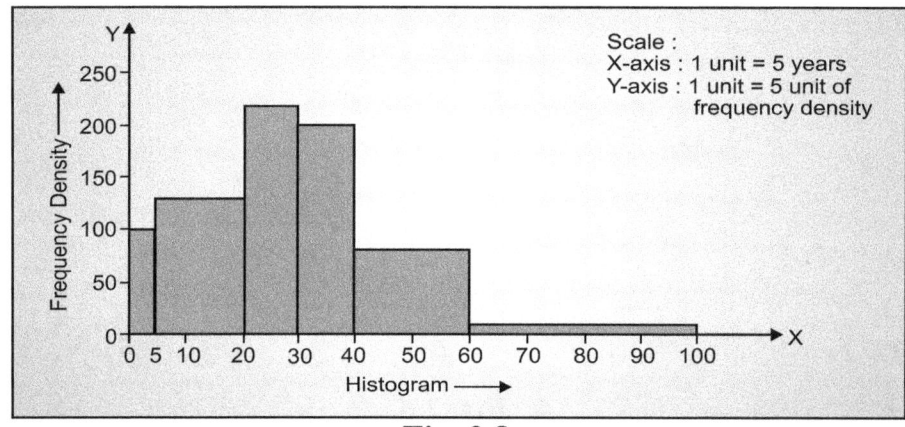

Fig. 2.8

Illustrative Examples

Example 2.1 : Draw histogram for the following frequency distribution.

Monthly income	Frequency	Mid values
1000 – 3000	6	2000
3000 – 5000	16	4000
5000 – 7000	24	6000
7000 – 9000	30	8000
9000 – 11000	10	10000
11000 – 13000	4	12000

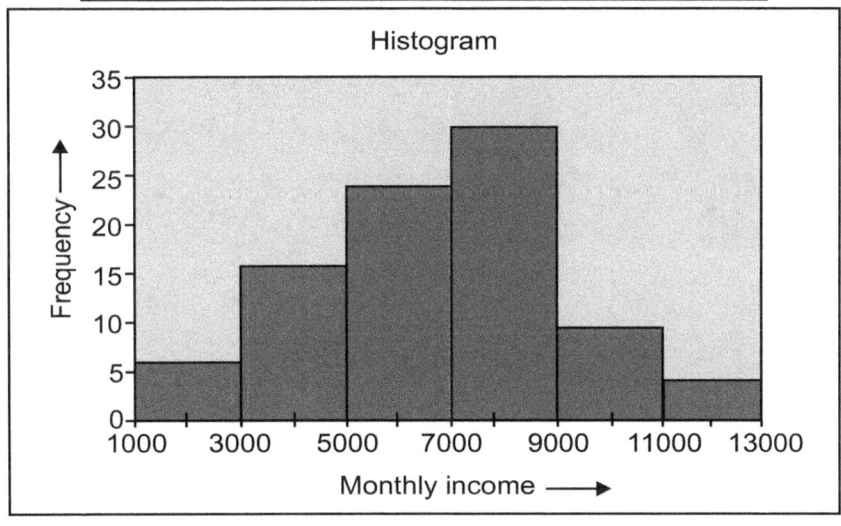

Fig. 2.9

To draw frequency polygon and ogive curve, select chart type option LINE.

Histogram and ISO 9000 : Now-a-days manufacturing units and industries have to maintain quality of their product as per norms laid down by Indian Standards (IS) or International Standards Organisation (ISO). To achieve quality standards several statistical tools are used. Such tools are known as Quality Control (QC) or Process Control (PC) tools. Histogram is an important tool. It has three fold purpose (i) It displays the pattern of variation, (ii) It gives idea about process behaviour, (iii) It helps to decide where to focus the efforts for improvement. Some interpretations based on histogram are illustrated below :

Symmetric distribution.

Non-symmetric distribution

Bimodal (having two centres) distribution. It is a mixture of two distributions.

Lower extreme values are not recorded separately.

Left end is not tapered.

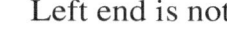

Upper extreme values are not recorded separately.

Right end is not tapered.

Narrow spread distribution.

Widely spread distribution.

(ii) Frequency Polygon : Generally a graph is expected to be in the form of a smooth curve. Histogram does not fulfill this requirement. Therefore, another way of presentation of frequency distribution is frequency polygon or frequency curve. This type of graph enables us to understand the pattern in the data more clearly. Mid-values are taken on X-axis and frequencies on Y-axis to draw the graph. Successive points are joined by the line segments. Further, to complete polygon we obtain closed figure by taking two more classes, one preceding to first class and the other succeeding to last class. Frequency of these classes is taken to be zero. Mid-points of these classes are used to get closed figure. The figure so obtained is called as frequency polygon.

Note : **(1)** We can draw frequency polygon using histogram. In this case we join the mid-points of upper sides of all the rectangles by line segments. Further to get closed figure we join the mid-values of preceding class and succeeding class to the frequency distribution.

(2) Histogram gives rough idea about the nature of frequency distribution. The border of histogram represents the frequency distribution. The boarder is zigzag, so we need to make it more smooth. Using frequency polygon and frequency curve it is possible to do so. The following figures will demonstrate how to make the border smooth by reducing the class width.

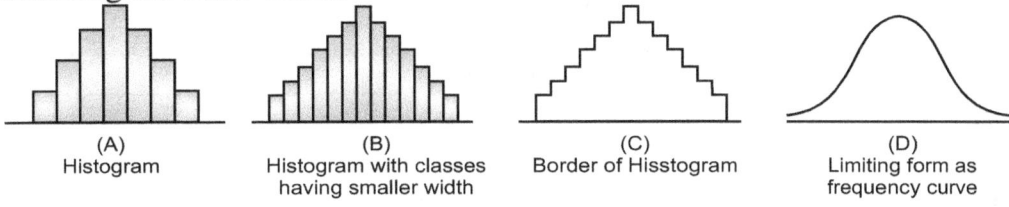

(A) Histogram (B) Histogram with classes having smaller width (C) Border of Hisstogram (D) Limiting form as frequency curve

Fig. 2.10

(iii) **Frequency Curve :** There is little difference in frequency polygon and frequency curve. If the points (or vertices of frequency polygon) are joined by a smooth curves instead of straight lines we get a closed figure called as *frequency curve*. While drawing frequency curve we should take care that the area under the curve is same as that of frequency polygon.

It can also be noticed that, we can draw frequency curve using histogram by the similar procedure which is used in case of frequency polygon.

Illustration 5 : Draw a frequency polygon and a frequency curve for the following data :

Monthly house rent	100 - 300	300 - 500	500 - 700	700 - 900	900 - 1100	1100 - 1300
No. of families	6	16	24	20	10	4

Solution : Mid-values of classes are taken on X-axis and frequency is taken on Y-axis. First point we need to plot is (200, 6), second point will be (400, 16) and so on. The last point will be (1200, 4). To get a closed figure we take two more points (0, 0) and (1400, 0). Joining these points by line segments (or smooth curve) we get frequency polygon (or frequency curve).

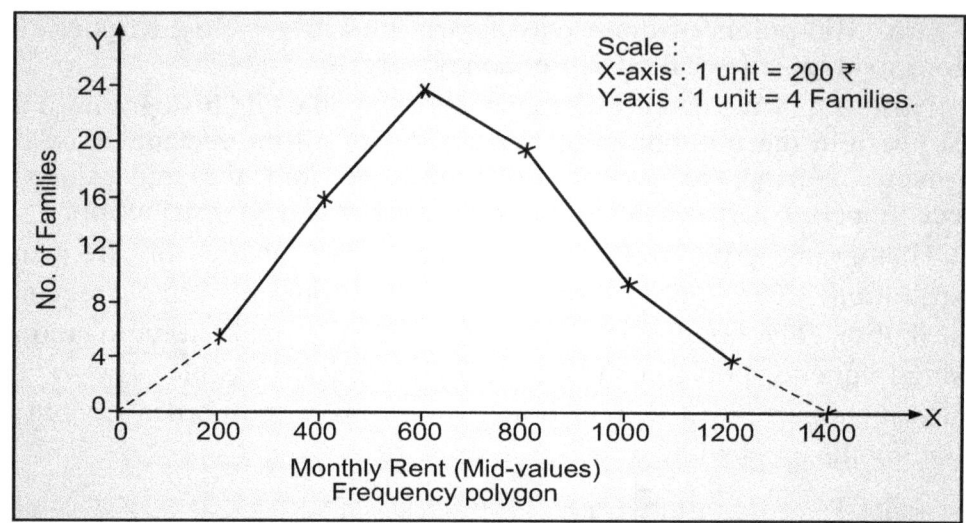

Fig. 2.11

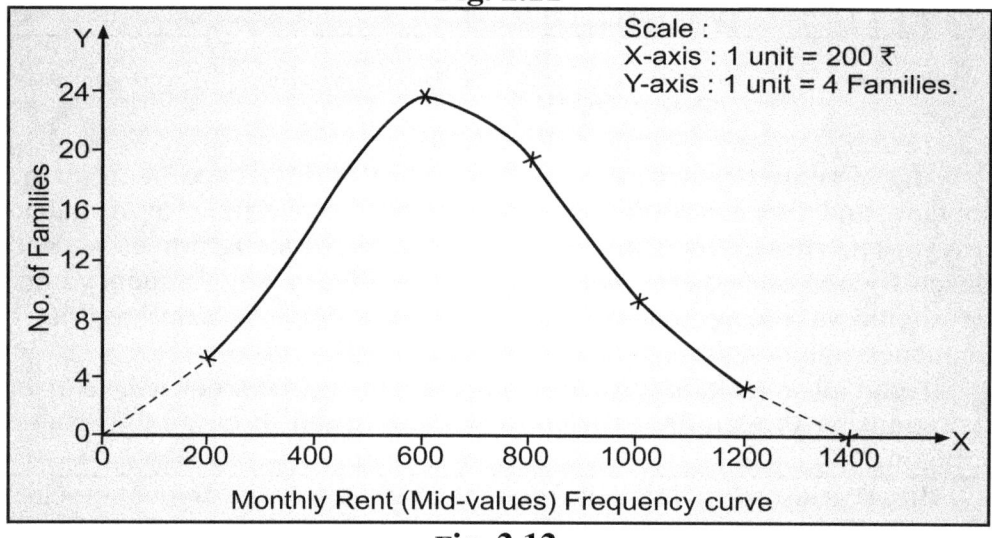

Fig. 2.12

(iv) Cumulative Frequency Curve or Ogive : Cumulative frequency distribution is represented by cumulative frequency curve (or ogive). There are two types of cumulative frequencies, hence, there are two types of cumulative frequency curves. For less than type cumulative curve upper boundaries of classes are taken on X-axis and less than cumulative frequencies on Y-axis. A preceding class before first class is also taken into consideration for drawing this curve. Cumulative frequency of this class is taken to be zero. Similarly, to draw more than type cumulative frequency curve lower boundaries are taken on X-axis and more than cumulative frequencies on Y-axis. In this case a succeeding class to the last class is taken with cumulative frequency zero. Those points are joined by smooth curve to get the cumulative frequency curve.

This type of curve is useful in finding median which is discussed in 5th chapter.

Illustration 6 : Draw less than cumulative frequency curve and more than cumulative frequency curve for the following frequency distribution :

Marks	0 - 10	10 - 20	20 - 30	30 - 40	40 - 50
No. of students	5	12	43	32	8

Solution : To draw less than type cumulative frequency curve we find out the required cumulative frequencies. In this problem class limits and class boundaries are same.

Upper boundaries	0	10	20	30	40	50
Cumulative frequencies	0	5	17	60	92	100

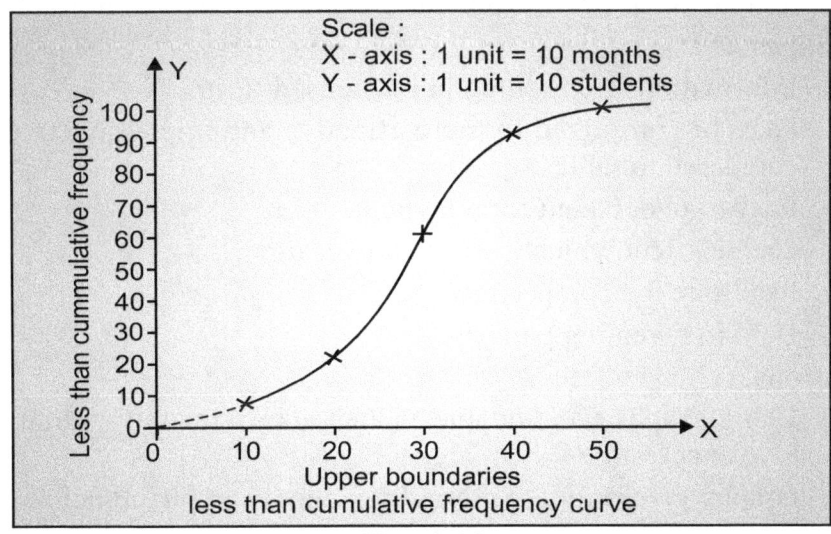

Fig. 2.13

In order to draw more than cumulative frequency curve we obtain more than cumulative frequencies.

Lower boundaries	0	10	20	30	40	50
Cumulative frequencies	100	95	83	40	8	0

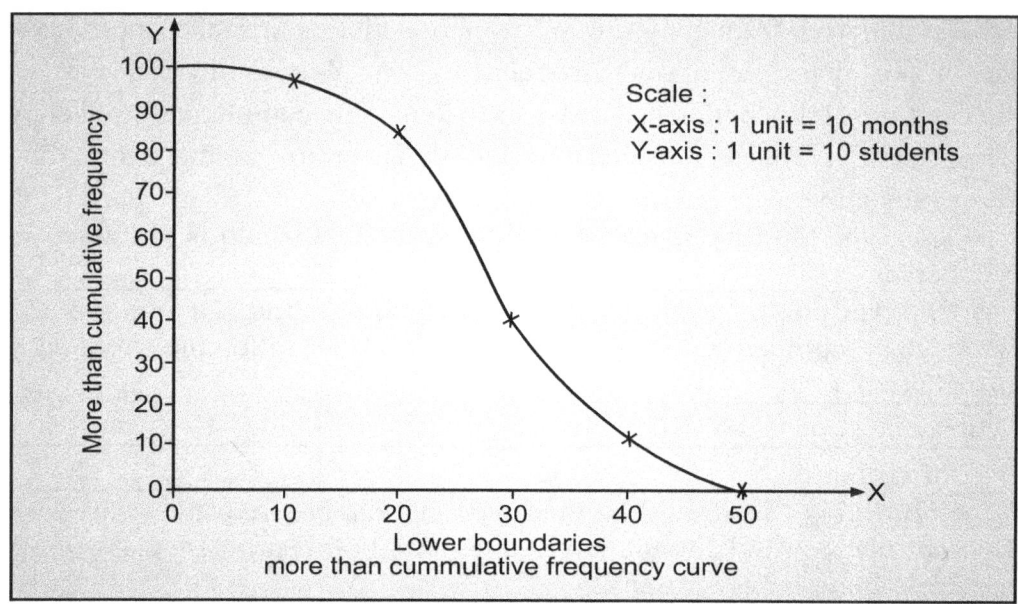

Fig. 2.14

2.11 Advantages and Limitations of Graphs

We summarize below, the advantages and limitations of graphs.

Advantages :
1. Information is presented in condensed form.
2. Facts are presented in more effective and impressive manner as compared to tables.
3. Easy to understand for a layman.
4. Create effect which lasts for longer time.
5. Facilitate the comparison.
6. Help in revealing patterns.

Limitations :
1. Using graphs we find the values approximately, while, tables give exact values.
2. Graphs give only a general idea about the phenomenon, which is not sufficient for further statistical analysis.

2.12 Diagrammatic Representation of Data

Types of diagrams : Several types of diagrams are used in practice to represent the information in a statistical table, some of then viz. simple bar diagram, subdivided bar diagram, pie diagram are discussed below.

(i) Simple bar diagram : In order to represent data related to a single variable, a simple bar diagram or a bar diagram is used.

For example : Yearly sales, monthly production, yearly population, countrywise population, yearly inputs etc. In this type of diagram, year, month, country etc. are taken on X-axis and corresponding values of the variable are taken to Y-axis. In this case, rectangles of equal width and height proportional to the value of the variable are erected on the horizontal axis.

Illustration 12 : Represent the following data using simple bar diagram.

Year	1981	1982	1983	1984	1985
Production in million tonnes	45	40	50	52	47

Solution : Scale : Y-axis : 1 unit = 10 million tonnes

X-axis : 1 unit = 1 year

Fig. 2.15 (a) : Simple bar diagram

Simple bar diagram using MS-EXCEL

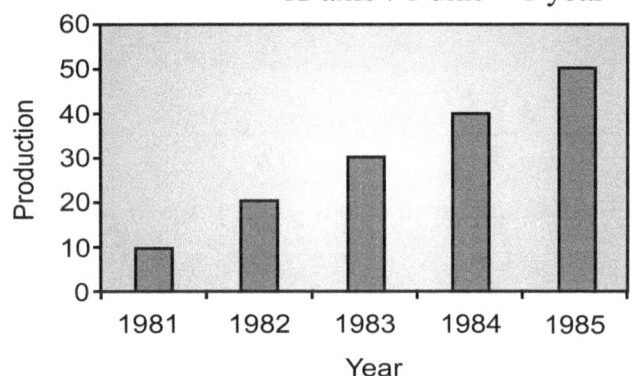

Fig. 2.15 (b)

Click on INSERT, CHART and follow the same path explained for plotting Histogram (Fig. 2.16). Select CHART TYPE column and first chart in CHART SUBTYPE.

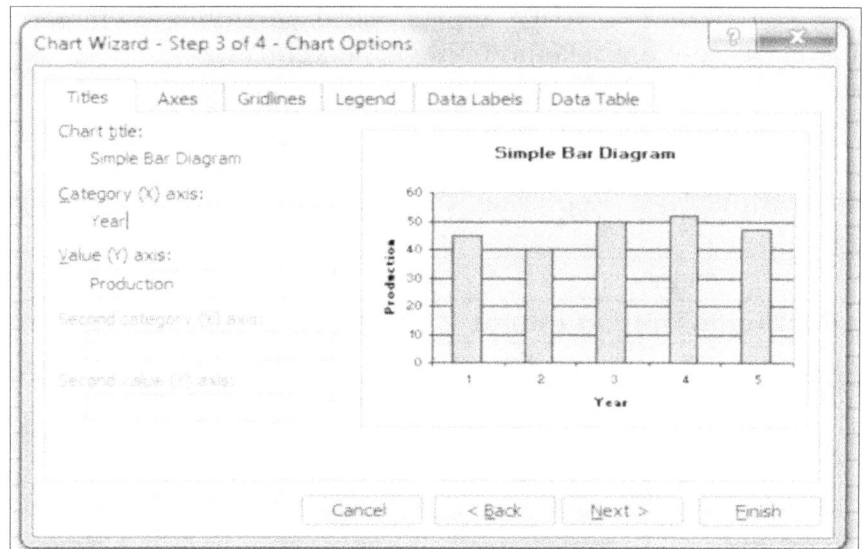

Fig. 2.16

Click on **FINISH** and simple bar diagram will appear on screen.

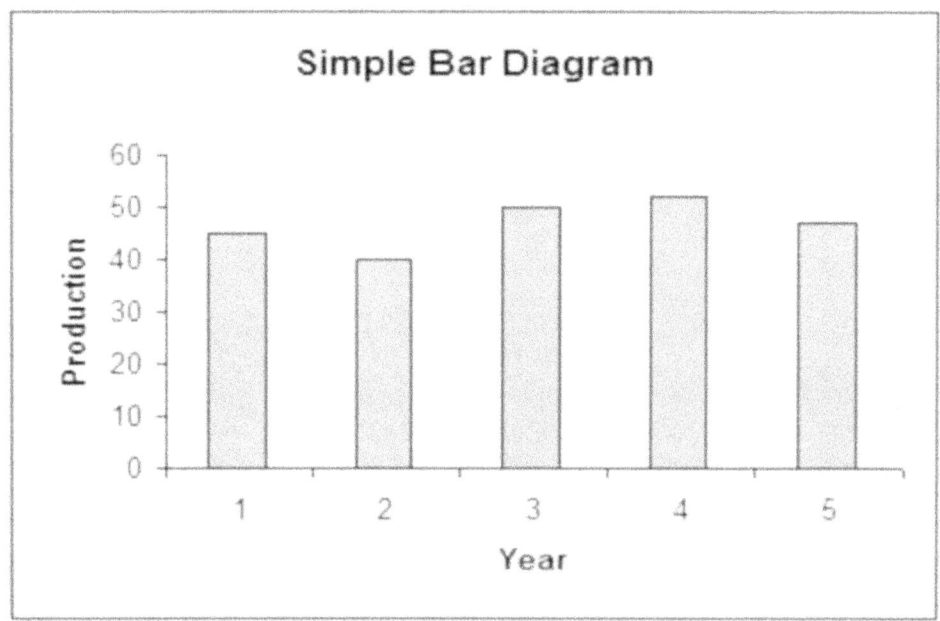

Fig. 2.17

Illustration 13 : Use a bar diagram to represent following data :

Year	1983	1984	1985	1986	1987
Profits of a company (In lakhs ₹)	2.5	2.0	− 1.0	2.8	3.0

Solution : Scale : X-axis : 1 unit = 1 year
Y-axis : 2 unit = 1 lakh ₹

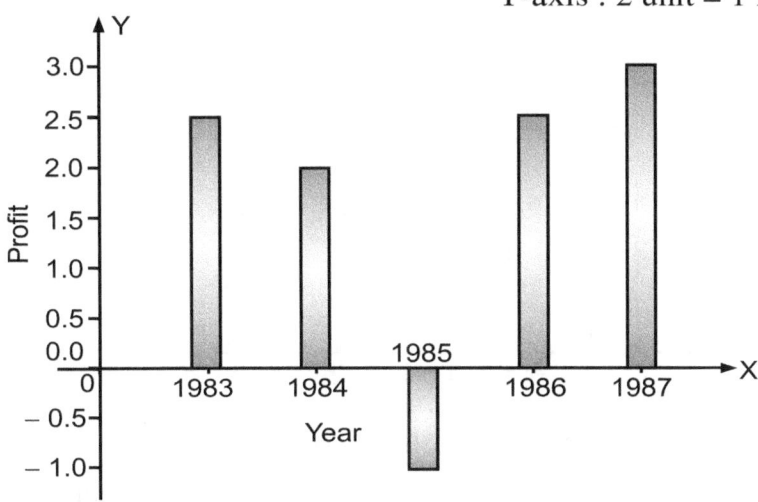

Fig. 2.18 : Bar diagram

Note :
1. Sometimes horizontal bars are used instead of vertical bars.
2. When two or more variables are involved, multiple bar diagram can be used.

(ii) Sub-divided bar diagram : When a single variable involves two or more components, subdivided bar diagram is used. A bar representing the total value is divided into several parts. Those parts represent the different components. The parts are chosen in such a way that the height is proportional to the respective component. These parts are displayed in different colours or shades.

Illustration 14 : The given table shows a faculty-wise strength for 4 years.

Represent the data by subdivided bar diagram.

Year	No. of students			
	Arts	Science	Commerce	Total
1982 – 83	800	800	1400	3000
1983 – 84	750	1000	1750	3500
1984 – 85	700	1100	1800	3600
1985 – 86	900	1200	1900	4000

Solution :

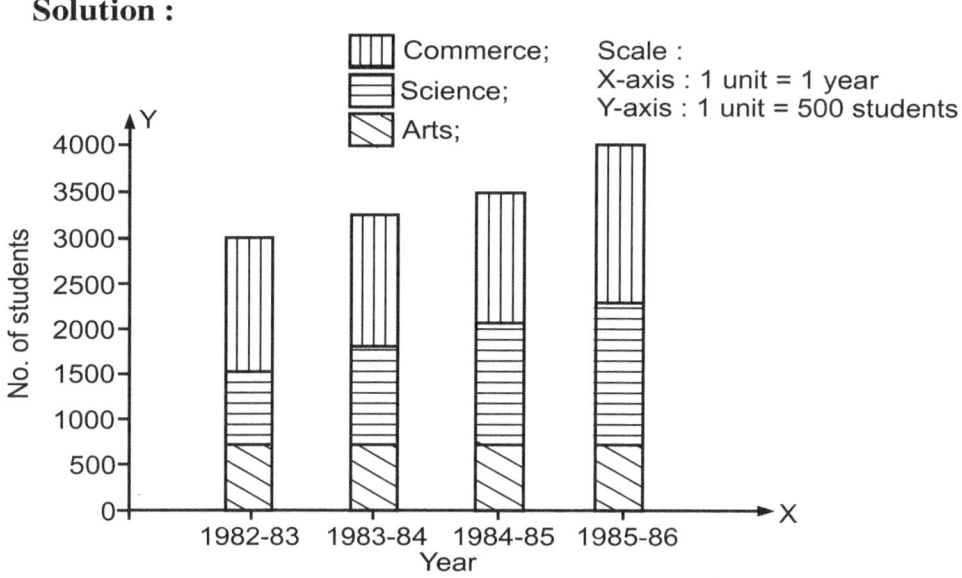

Fig. 2.19 : Sub-divided bar diagram

Illustration 15 : Present the following data using a suitable diagram.

Class	F.Y.	S.Y.	T.Y.
Pass	300	325	210
Fail	100	125	90
Total	400	450	300

Solution : In this case subdivided bar diagram is suitable because along with total components are also known.

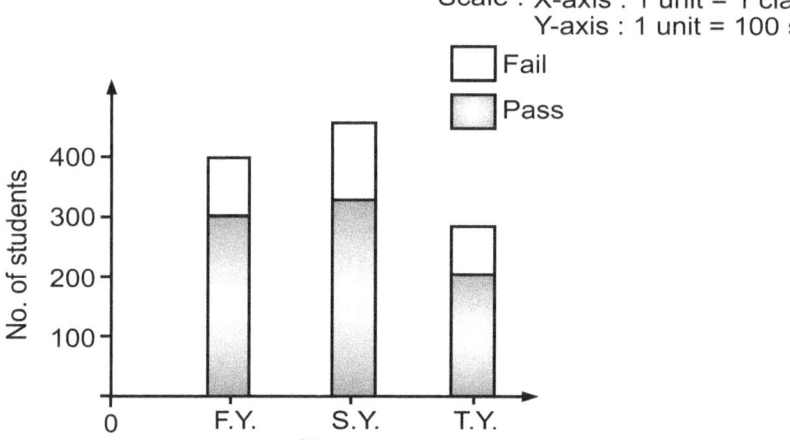

Fig. 2.20 : Sub-divided bar diagram

Sub-divided Bar Diagram using MS-EXCEL

	A	B	C	D
1	Class	F.Y.	S.Y.	T.Y
2	Pass	300	325	210
3	Fail	100	125	90
4	Total	400	450	300

Fig. 2.21

Click on INSERT, CHART and follow the same path explained for plotting Histogram (Fig. 2.21 (a)). Select chart type column and second chart in chart subtype.

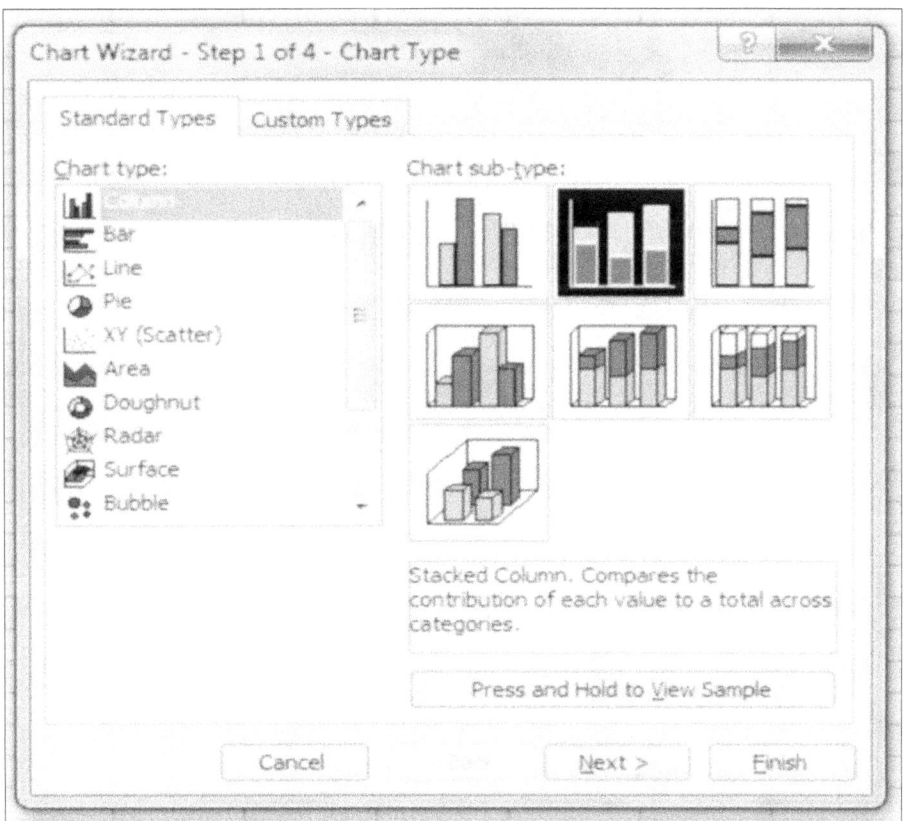

Fig. 2.21 (a)

Click on NEXT and enter the data range.

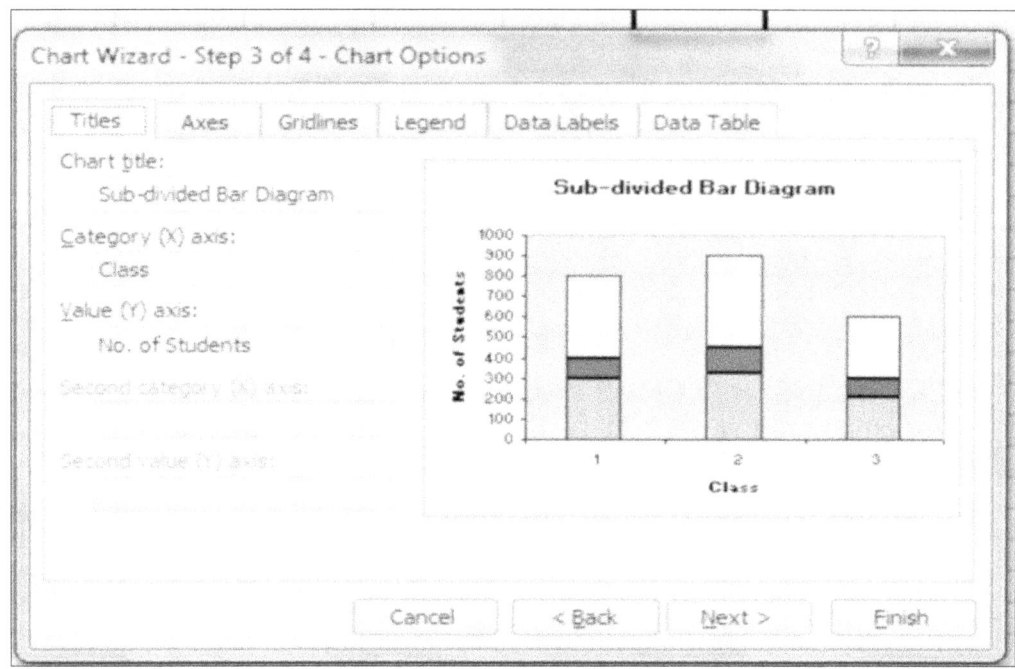

Fig. 2.22

Click on Finish and sub-divided bar diagram will appear on screen.

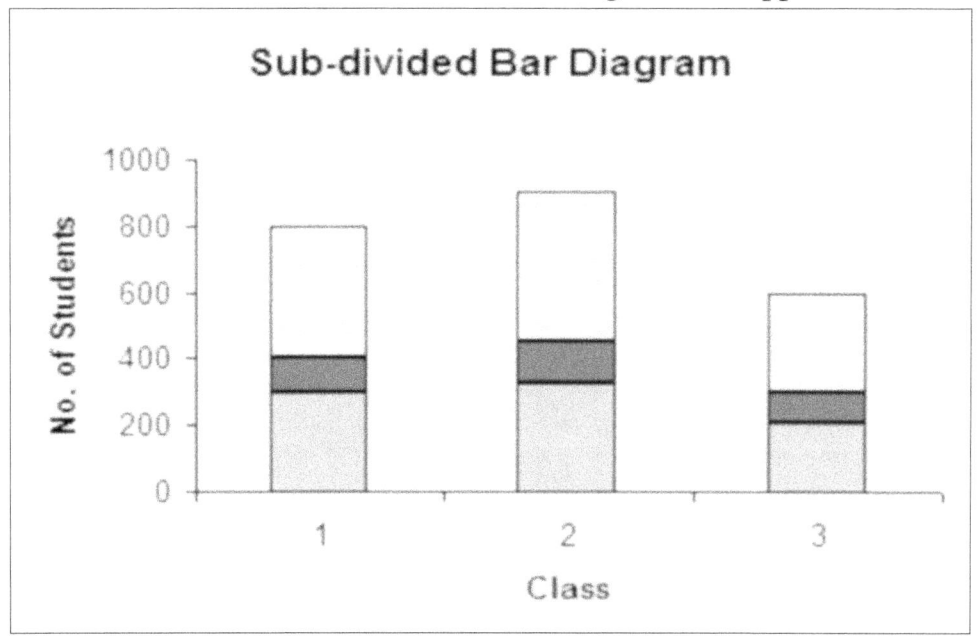

Fig. 2.23

EXERCISE 2 (A)

1. Explain the terms : Variable, attribute.
2. Distinguish between variable and attribute.
3. Explain the terms : nominal scale, ordinal scale, ratio scale, interval scale.
4. Give examples of directional data.
5. Distinguish between primary data and secondary data.
6. Explain the terms : time series data, cross-sectional data, failure data.
7. Explain the need of classification.
8. Explain the different methods of classification briefly.
9. Explain the following terms with illustrations :
   (i) attribute (ii) discrete variable (iii) continuous variable.
10. Explain the following terms :
    (i) class limits (ii) class boundaries (iii) class width (iv) class frequency (v) less than type cumulative frequency (vi) more than type cumulative frequency (vii) relative frequency (vii) open end class.
11. Explain the general guidelines or principles of choosing the classes.
12. (a) What do you mean by classification ?
    (b) Write a note on various scales of measurement.
    (c) Describe the four different scales of measurement.
13. Discuss the importance of classification in statistical analysis.
14. Distinguish between 'inclusive method of classification' and 'exclusive method of classification'.
15. Explain how to classify qualitative data.
16. State the advantages and limitations of graphical representation of data.
17. What are uses of histogram, stem and leaf plot and ogives ?
18. Discuss the importance of graphs in presentation of statistical data.
19. State the advantages of (i) stem and leaf plot (ii) check sheet (iii) Parato diagram.

Diagrams :

20. State the advantages and limitations diagrammatic representation of data.

21. Explain the construction of the following diagrams. Also give rough sketch of each of the following :
    (i) bar diagram, (ii) multiple bar diagram, (iii) percentage bar diagram, (iv) pie diagram, (v) subdivided bar diagram.
22. Explain the construction of the following graphs along with the rough sketches : (i) histogram, (ii) frequency polygon, (iii) frequency curve, (iv) ogives.
23. What are uses of histogram and ogives ?
24. Discuss the importance of graphs in presentation of statistical data.

EXERCISE 2 (B)

1. A teacher gave a dictation of 10 words for a spelling test, for a class of 50 students of Vth standard. Number of mistakes observed among each of the 50 students are given below :

5	1	0	1	3	6	2	0	2	4
1	5	1	2	1	3	4	4	0	2
0	1	1	0	2	1	5	0	2	3
3	5	0	3	5	0	1	4	3	8
2	4	7	6	1	4	3	1	2	2

   Construct a frequency distribution of number of mistakes.

2. The data given below relates to the number of T.V. sets sold by a dealer on 25 working days of a certain month. Prepare a frequency distribution of number of T.V. sets sold.
   1, 4, 2, 1, 1, 2, 2, 1, 2, 1, 0, 1, 1, 3, 0, 1, 5, 4, 1, 2, 3, 1, 1, 4, 1

3. Heights in cm of 50 students in a class are given below :

168.9	163.1	161.5	168.0	167.1	157.5	163.9	168.9
166.7	160.8	161.3	161.5	162.0	166.3	162.6	168.0
170.1	165.8	165.2	164.5	171.3	158.0	158.7	159.6
167.4	162.1	166.7	169.0	167.0	160.3	167.7	157.7
164.9	168.3	164.0	157.6	172.5	171.1	168.2	172.6
169.3	159.2	171.7	163.7	162.3	171.9	169.7	167.7
170.2	169.0						

   Classify the above data by using exclusive method of classification. Take the first class interval as 157 - 160.

4. Daily wages received by 50 workers in factory are as follows :

   68 44 55 56 52 72 54 75 60 48
   60 42 60 50 56 65 45 65 55 55
   55 50 60 44 45 58 58 59 48 66
   50 50 70 70 64 53 65 55 65 60
   40 55 70 63 70 45 75 46 76 80

   Classify the data taking classes as 40-44, 45-49, 50-54, ... Also obtain a more than cumulative frequency distribution.

5. Prepare a frequency distribution for each of the following :

   (a)

Mid-value	47.5	52.5	57.5	62.5
Frequency	4	9	17	10

   (b)

Class mark	4	8	12	16	20
Frequency	24	45	20	10	1

6. Prepare the frequency distribution for the following :

Marks below	Number of students
10	1
20	8
30	35
40	46
50	50

7. Prepare the frequency distribution for the following :

Income more than ₹	No. of persons
500	100
1000	96
1500	92
2000	59
2500	28
3000	2

8. Following is a frequency distribution of heights in cm.

Classes	150-154	155-159	160-164	165-169	170-174
Frequency	2	17	29	21	1

   (a) Obtain class boundaries of each of the classes.

   (b) Determine the class width.

9. Among a group of students, 10% scored marks below 20, 20% scored marks between 20 and 40, 35% scrod marks between 40 and 60, 20% scored marks between 60 and 80, and the remaining 30 students scored marks between 80 and 100.

   (a) Using the information prepare a frequency distribution of marks of students.

   (b) If minimum 40 marks are required for passing, how many students have passed the examination?

   (c) If maximum 60 marks are required for getting first class, how many students secured first class?

10. Draw the histogram, frequency polygon and ogive curves for the following frequency distribution :

Weight in lb	80-89	90-99	100-109	110-119	120-129	130-139	140-149
Frequency	8	16	20	26	50	13	5

11. Draw a histogram for the following income distribution :

Monthly income	1000-2000	2000-2500	2500-3500	3500-5000
Frequency	120	125	180	150

12. Draw less than cumulative frequency curve for frequency distribution of intelligence quotient given below. Also obtain number of candidates having intelligence quotient between 105 and 125.

I.Q.	60-69	70-79	80-89	90-99	100-109	110-119	120-129
Frequency	21	37	51	49	21	13	4

13. Draw a frequency curve, frequency polygon and histogram for the following data.

Mid-values	25	35	45	55	65
Frequencies	5	12	33	13	7

14. Draw less than cumulative frequency curve and more than cumulative frequency curve for the following frequency distribution of marks in Statistics :

Marks	0-20	20-40	40-60	60-80	80-100
No. of students :	2	18	42	28	5

EXERCISE 2 (C)

15. A cube with all sides painted is subdivided into smaller cubes, all of the same size. If each side of the smaller cube is 1/4 times that of the original cube we get various types of cubes some with none of the side painted, some with only one side painted etc. Prepare frequency distribution of number of sides painted.

16. A certain diet was introduced to a group of 20 individuals. Weights before starting the new diet and after using the new diet for the period of two months were recorded. The results were as follows :

Individual	1	2	3	4	5	6	7	8	9	10
Weight in kg (before)	53	54	52	54	56	52	55	57	57	53
Weight in kg (after)	56	53	57	55	56	51	60	56	59	55
Individual	11	12	13	14	15	16	17	18	19	20
Weight in kg (before)	54	52	55	57	53	59	51	53	54	51
Weight in kg (after)	56	56	57	54	54	60	52	52	59	51

(i) Prepare frequency distribution for both the sets of observations (before the change of diet and after the change of diet). Draw their frequency polygons. Prepare their relative frequency distributions. Take classes as 51-52, 53-54 ......

(ii) Determine the increase in weight for every individual and classify the same using classes as −3 to −1, 0 to 2, ...

17. In order to construct a dam on a certain river a survey was conducted. In all 200 locations in the river-blade were studied. Water flow at those locations were classified as follows :

River flow (thousands of gallons per minute)	No. of locations
1000 - 1050	7
1050 - 1100	15
1100 - 1150	26
1150 - 1200	39
1200 - 1250	48
1250 - 1300	34
1300 - 1350	22
1350 - 1400	9
Total	200

Using less than cumulative frequency curve find,
(i) The number of locations having flow less than or equal to 1325 thousand gallons per minute.
(ii) The number of locations having flow between 1120 gallons per minute and 1370 gallons per minute.

ANSWERS 2 (D)

Diagrams :

18. Represent the following data by a suitable diagram.

Country	India	Shri Lanka	U. S. A.	U. K.	Mexico
Population growth rate	2.5 %	1.8 %	2.0 %	1.8 %	3.2 %

19. Using a suitable diagram represent the following data :

Year	Birth rate (per thousand)	Death rate (per thousand)
1921 - 30	46.4	36.3
1931 - 40	45.2	31.2
1941 - 50	39.9	27.4
1951 - 60	41.7	22.8
1961 - 70	41.1	18.9
1971 - 80	37.0	14.0
1981 - 90	32.5	11.4
1991 - 00	26.0	9.0

20. Draw a pie diagram and percentage bar diagram to represent the following data :

Components	Cost of construction of a house
Labour	25 %
Bricks	15 %
Cement	20 %
Steel	15 %
Timber	10 %
Supervision	15 %

21. Draw a suitable diagram to represent the following data :

Year	Exports (crores ₹)	Imports (crores ₹)
1983 - 84	430	260
1984 - 85	350	300
1985 - 86	360	290
1986 - 87	400	300

Nature of Data

22. Draw a bar diagram and pie diagram to represent following data :

Gas	Oxygen	Nitrogen	Carbon dioxide	Others
Percentage in atmosphere	21	78	0.03	0.97

23. Draw a pie diagram and subdivided bar diagram to represent the following data :

Country	Percentage of population in the world in 1980 - 81
India	15.53
China	21.72
Russia	6.05
U.S.A.	5.04
Others	23.69

24. Draw a bar diagram to represent the following data related to the capacity of production of electricity (in crores kilowatt).

Year	Total
1975 - 76	7920
1976 - 77	8850
1977 - 78	9130
1978 - 79	9790
1979 - 80	10560

25. Present the following information using suitable diagram :

Mode of transport	Bus	Train	Aeroplane	Private vehicle	Own vehicle	Total
No. of passengers	1250	2250	100	600	500	5000

26. Draw a suitable diagram and represent the following data of ABC steel company.

Year	1994 – 95	1995 – 96	1996 – 97	1997 – 98	1998 – 99
Iron production	2100	2140	2200	2300	2500
Saleable steel production	1800	1830	1850	1900	1900

27. Draw a suitable diagram to represent the following data of a company.

Year	1994 – 95	1995 – 96	1996 – 97	1997 – 98	1998 – 99
Gross assets (in crores)	1900	2000	2200	3000	4000
Net assets (in crores)	900	1000	1050	2000	3000

28. The data given below relates to export performance in crores of ₹ of a company.

Year	Total
1995 – 96	93
1996 – 97	145
1997 – 98	210
1998 – 99	450

Draw a suitable diagram to represent the above data.

29. Represent the following data by a suitable diagram

Date (July 1999)	1	2	5	6	7	8	9
Stock Exhange Index	4140	4140	4194	4306	4322	4321	4326

30. Following data are regarding cashewnut export by Indian market, represent the same by a suitable diagram.

Year	92-93	93-94	94-95	95-96	96-97	97-98	98-99
Export (tons)	0.58	0.74	0.80	0.71	0.70	0.77	0.75
Revenue (crores ₹)	749	1048	1253	1241	1288	1396	1610

31. Marks scored by Sunil in the annual examination are given below :

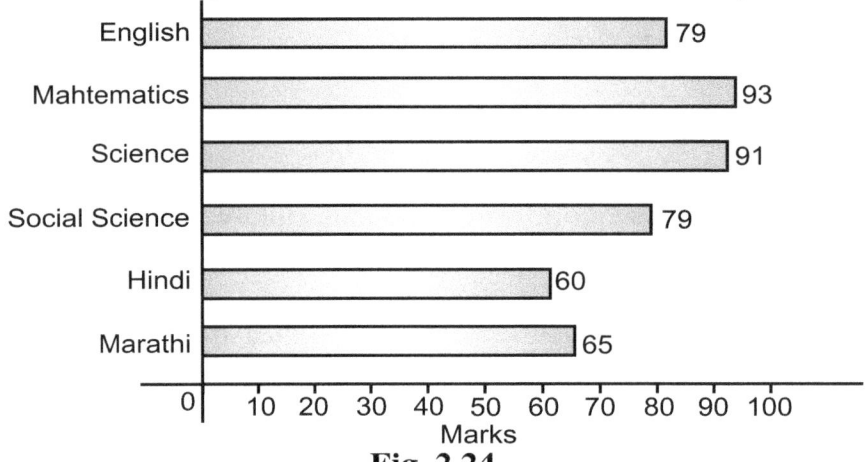

Fig. 2.24

(a) Which is the type of diagram ?
(b) State the subject in which he has scored maximum marks.
(c) State the subject in which he has scored least marks.

ANSWERS 2 (B)

1.

No. of mistakes :	0	1	2	3	4	5	6	7	8
No. of students :	8	11	9	7	6	5	2	1	1

2.

No. of T.V. Sets sold :	0	1	2	3	4	5
No. of days :	2	12	5	2	3	1

3.

Class	157 - 160	160 - 163	163 - 166	166 - 169	169 - 172	172 - 175
Frequency	7	9	8	14	10	2

4.

Class	Frequency	Class	Frequency
40 - 44	4	65 - 69	6
45 - 49	6	70 - 74	5
50 - 54	7	75 - 79	3
55 - 59	11	80 - 84	1
60 - 64	7		

5. (a)

Class	Frequency
45 - 50	4
50 - 55	9
55 - 60	17
60 - 65	10

(b)

Class	Frequency
2 - 6	24
6 - 10	45
10 - 14	20
14 - 18	10
18 - 22	1

6.

Class	0 - 10	10 - 20	20 - 30	30 - 40	40 - 50
Frequency	1	7	27	11	4

7.

Class	Frequency
500 - 1000	4
1000 - 1500	4
1500 - 2000	33
2000 - 2500	31
2500 - 3000	26
above 300	2

8. (a)

Class limits	Class boundaries
150 - 154	149.5 - 154.5
155 - 159	154.5 - 159.5
160 - 164	159.5 - 164.5
165 - 169	164.5 - 169.5
170 - 174	169.5 - 174.5

(b) Width of each class is 5

9. (a)

Class	0 - 20	20 - 40	40 - 60	60 - 80	80 - 100
Frequency	20	40	70	40	30

(b) 140

(c) 70

ANSWERS 2 (C)

15.

No. of sides painted :	0	1	2	3	4	5	6
No. of cubes :	8	24	24	8	0	0	0

16.

(i)

Class	Usual frequency distribution		Relative frequency distribution	
	Before	After	Before	After
51 - 52	5	4	0.25	0.20
53 - 54	8	3	0.40	0.15
55 - 56	3	7	0.15	0.35
57 - 58	3	2	0.15	0.10
59 - 60	1	4	0.15	0.20

(ii)

Class :	− 3 to − 1	0 to 2	3 to 5
Frequencies :	5	10	5

17. (i) 180 (ii) 163.

ANSWERS 2 (D)

18. Bar diagram
19. Multiple bar diagram or several bar diagrams
21. Multiple Bar diagram or several bar diagrams
26. Multiple bar diagram or several bar diagrams
27. Multiple bar diagram or several bar diagrams
28. Bar diagram
29. Bar diagram
30. Multiple bar diagram or several bar diagrams

Objective Type Questions

(A) Multiple Choice Questions

- **Choose the correct alternative out of four alternatives given below for each questions.**

1. Which limits are excluded in case of exclusive type of class intervals ?
   - (a) lower limits
   - (b) upper limits
   - (c) either (a) and (b)
   - (d) both (a) and (b)

2. If 19, 28, 37, 46, 55, 64 are mid-points of class intervals then the first class of the distribution is :
   - (a) 13.5 – 23.5
   - (b) 18.5 – 28.5
   - (c) 14 – 24
   - (d) 12.5 – 25.5

3. The mid-point of the class intervals 34.5 to 44.5 is
   - (a) 01.5
   - (b) 39
   - (c) 39.5
   - (d) 40.5

4. A grouped frequency distribution in which one of the limits of class interval is not specified is called
   - (a) discrete frequency distribution
   - (b) exclusive class distribution
   - (c) inclusive class distribution
   - (d) open end distribution

5. In the following table the first and last classes are of :

Daily sales in ₹
below 2000
2000 – 3000
3000 – 4000
4000 and above

   - (a) exclusive type
   - (b) inclusive type
   - (c) both (a) and (b)
   - (d) open end type

6. In constructing frequency distribution for a sample, the number of classes depend on
   - (a) the number of data points
   - (b) the range of the data collected
   - (c) the size of the population
   - (d) (a) and (b) but not (c)

7. Which of the following statements is true ?
   (a) the size of sample can never be as large as the size of the population from which it is taken.
   (b) classes describe only one characteristic of the data being organized.
   (c) as a rule statisticians generally use between 6 and 15 classes.
   (d) all of these
8. A relative frequency distribution represents frequencies in terms of
   (a) proportions   (b) whole numbers
   (c) percentages   (d) both (a) and (c)
9. In frequency distributions are all inclusive ?
   (a) no data point falls in to more than one class
   (b) there are always more classes than data points
   (c) all data fit into only one class of another
   (d) all of these
10. In the following table

Name of the state	Sugarcane produced (in million tone)
U.P.	48
Bihar	18
Tamil Nadu	8
Maharashtra	4
Other	2

the given data are classified on the basis of
   (a) industrial   (b) time series
   (c) chronological   (d) geographical
11. In the following table

Year	Profit (in 1000)
1992	120
1993	121
1994	180
1995	136

the given data are classified on the basis of
   (a) geographical   (b) chronological
   (c) census   (d) none of the above

12. The number of children in each family is an example of
    (a) time series   (b) an individual series
    (c) a discrete series   (d) a continuous series
13. The number of observations (frequency) corresponding to a variable is always
    (a) a fractions   (b) may be negative
    (c) an integer   (d) (a) and (c) but not (b)
14. The following frequency distribution :

No. of T.V. sets sold	No. of days
0	2
1	12
2	5
3	2
4	3
5	1

is classified as :
(a) discrete frequency distribution
(b) continuous frequency distribution
(c) cumulative frequency distribution
(d) none of the above distribution

15. The distribution

Marks below	10	20	30	40	50
No. of students	2	7	35	46	50

is of :
(a) cumulative frequency distribution
(b) inclusive class type
(c) exclusive class type
(d) none of the above

16. The type of following frequency distribution is :

Marks	0-20	20-40	40-60	60-100
No. of students	2	18	42	5

(a) individual observation series
(b) discrete frequency distribution series
(c) grouped frequency distribution series
(d) cumulative frequency distribution

17. The following frequency distribution :

Income more than ₹	No. of persons
500	100
1000	96
1500	92
2000	59
2500	28
3000	2

is known as :
(a) discrete frequency distribution
(b) continuous frequency distribution
(c) cumulative distribution in less than type
(d) cumulative distribution in greater than type

18. The following frequency distribution

Classes	0-20	0-40	0-60
Frequency	14	38	50

is known as
(a) discrete frequency distribution
(b) continuous frequency distribution
(c) cumulative distribution is less than type
(d) cumulative distribution is greater than type

19. In the following distribution, which one of the following is given in second columns ?

Age in years	No. of persons
below 10	15
below 20	32
below 30	51
below 40	78
below 50	97
below 60	110

(a) frequency
(b) cumulative frequency gerater than type
(c) cumulatve frequency less than type
(d) mid-points

20. The class intervals of the grouped data :

5-9	10-14	15-19	20-24

is of the type :
(a) inclusive class   (b) discrete class
(c) exclusive class   (c) none of the above

21. The width of class intervals given in Q. No. 21 is :
    (a) 5 (b) 4
    (c) 7 (d) 2

22. The following data gives :

Mid-values	25	35	45
Frequencies	5	12	7

    The first class for the above frequency distribution is :
    (a) 10-40 (b) 17.5–32.5
    (c) 15-35 (d) 20-30

23. While we are going to construct a frequency distribution table, one may not have :
    (a) mutually exclusive classes
    (b) exhaustive classes (c) both (a) and (b)
    (d) none of the above

24. Which of the following statements about histogram rectangles is correct ?
    (a) The heights of rectangles are proportional to class frequencies.
    (b) There are generally five rectangles in every histogram
    (c) The height of rectangle is proportional to cumulative frequency
    (d) all of these

25. In order to draw histogram the data presented is of the type :
    (a) individual observations
    (b) discrete frequency distribution
    (c) continuous frequency distribution
    (d) all the above

26. In order to draw histogram for frequency distribution with classes of unequal width, we have to consider
    (a) height of rectangles proportional to class inrervals
    (b) height of rectangles proportional to class frequency
    (c) height of rectangles proportional to frequency density
    (d) all the above

27. Which of the following statements is true for less than cumulative frequency curve ?
    (a) the curve is non-decreasing in nature
    (b) the curve is strictly decreasing in nature
    (c) the curve is non-increasing in nature
    (d) the curve is strictly increasing.

28. In order to construct histogram for equal class interval, what is taken on the X axis and Y axis respectively ?
    (a) lower limit and less than cumulative frequency
    (b) upper limit and less than cumulative frequency
    (c) class interval and frequency
    (d) mid-points and frequency
29. In order to construct a frequency polygon for equal class interval along X axis and Y axis respectively is :
    (a) lower limit and less than cumulative frequency
    (b) upper limit and less than cumulative frequency
    (c) class interval and frequency
    (d) mid points and frequency
30. If the points (or vertices of frequency polygon) are joined by a smooth curves instead of straight lines we get a closed figure called as :
    (a) frequency distribution
    (b) trend
    (c) cumulative distribution curve
    (d) frequency curve
31. If we plot values of upper boundaries on X-axis and points of less than type cumniative frequency on Y-axis and points are joined by a smooth curve we get figure called as :
    (a) frequency distribution
    (b) less than type ogive
    (c) greater than type ogive
    (d) none of the above
32. Which one of the following is true for histogram ?
    (a) It can not be drawn for a frequency distribution with open end class
    (b) It is used to locate value of mode
    (c) It remains same if class width is changed
    (d) all of the above
33. The base of histogram is
    (a) class limits
    (b) class intervals
    (c) class boundries
    (d) extended class intervals.
34. From Histogram we can prepare :
    (a) frequency distribution   (b) frequency polygon
    (c) frequency curve   (d) all the above

35. With the help of histogram. one can determine :
    (a) median   (d) deciles
    (c) percentiles   (d) mode
36. With the help of ogive curve, one can not determine
    (a) median   (b) deciles
    (c) percentiles   (d) mode
37. Parato diagram is used to find the
    (a) average number of defectives
    (b) major causes behind the imperfections
    (c) spread of the data
    (d) symmetry of data
38. Check sheet is a ....
    (a) list of checks and counter checks
    (b) systematic record of inspections
    (c) frequency distribution of qualitative variables
    (d) table containing cause of failure alongwith the number of defectives.
39. Primary data means :
    (a) original data
    (b) it may be result of survey
    (c) it may be result of equiry
    (d) all the above
40. Primary data are collected by method of :
    (a) direct personal investigation
    (b) indirect oral investigation
    (c) investigation through questionnaire
    (d) all the above
41. Secondary data is
    (a) already collected by some other agency
    (b) a processed data
    (c) a finished data
    (d) all the above
42. Which one of the following is false ? Secondary data have sources like :
    (a) office records   (b) bulletins
    (c) reports   (d) direct interview

43. The term primary data refers precisely to the statistical information
    (a) obtained directly by an investigator from an inquiry, from data banks, interviews surveys and journals
    (b) collected by government or semi-government agencies for the creation of data bank
    (c) collected directly by an investigator from periodicals or journals
    (d) collected by an investigator from sampling units
44. For obtaining secondary data, a researcher may rely on :
    (a) direct personal interviews
    (b) indirect personal interviews through a team of investigators appointed for an inquiry
    (c) direct personal scrutiny of periodicals
    (d) questionnaires filled by a group of enumerators appointed for the project
45. Data taken from the "Reserve Bank of India Bulletin" will be considered as
    (a) primary data   (b) secondary data
    (c) primary and secondary data
    (d) neither (a) nor (b)
46. Statistical data are :
    (a) in exact numbers   (b) in fractions
    (c) in rounded numbers   (d) in any of these forms
47. Statistical data may release to
    (a) only discrete variate   (b) only continuous variate
    (c) none of these   (d) any of these
48. Which one of the following scales is the crudest scale is the measurement of data ?
    (a) nominal scale   (b) ordinal scale
    (c) internal scale   (d) ratio scale
49. Which one of the following scale is the best scale in measurement of data ?
    (a) nominal scale   (b) ordinal scale
    (c) interval scale   (d) ratio scale
50. In which one of the following scales, data can be measured by using non-numeric notations or non-comparable symbols ?
    (a) nominal scale   (b) ordinal scale
    (c) interval scale   (d) ratio scale

51. The registration of two wheelers of four wheelers by allocating the series A, B, MH, GA or the sex-wise condification of 'males' or 'females' by M and F, are examples on :
    (a) nominal scale   (b) ordinal scale
    (c) interval scale   (d) ratio scale

52. In which one of the following scales, measurements can be made with the help of symbols/notations, where in there is a provision of carrying out comparisons between and within data items belonging to a group ?
    (a) nominal scale   (b) ordinal scale
    (c) interval scale   (d) ratio scale

53. Which scale uses the concept of absolute zero ?
    (a) nominal scale   (b) ordinal scale
    (c) interval scale   (d) ratio scale

54. The measurements on height and weight are made on :
    (a) nominal scale   (b) ordinal scale
    (c) interval scale   (d) ratio scale

55. Suppose A, B and C scores on an IQ test 120, 100 and 140 respectively. Let the test be based on an interval scale of measurement. Which one of the following statement is true ?
    (a) A exceeds B in intelligence, by the same degree, as B exceeds C.
    (b) B exceeds A in intelligence, by the same degree, as A exceeds C
    (c) C exceeds A in intelligence, by the same degree, as A exceeds B
    (d) none of the above

56. Which one of the following is not an example of Nominal scale ?
    (a) Classification of individuals using blood groups.
    (b) Classification of students in various divisions of the same standard.
    (c) Classification of individuals using sex, caste, nationality.
    (d) Classification of students according to grades.

57. Which one of the following is an example of ordinal scale ?
    (a) Groups of student using weight such as light and heavy.
    (b) Groups of student using height such as short, medium, tall.
    (c) Groups of individual according to income such as poor, middle class, rich.
    (d) all of the above.
58. Which one of the following is not an example of ratio scale ?
    (a) Farenheight scale of temperature measurement
    (b) Scale of type height (cm)
    (c) Scale of type weight (kg)
    (d) Scale of type time (cm)
59. Attributes are measured using
    (a) normal scale only   (b) ordinal scale only
    (c) both (a) and (b)   (d) neither (a) nor (b)
60. Variables are measured using
    (a) nominal scale   (b) ordinal scale
    (c) interval scale and ratio scale
    (d) both (a) and (b)
61. Discrete variable is :
    (a) a variable taking all possible values in a certain range
    (b) a variable taking all values between 0 and ∞
    (c) a variable taking only particular values
    (d) all of the above
62. Which one of the following is not an example of continuous variable ?
    (a) number of articles produced by a machine
    (b) length of screw produced by a machine
    (c) speed of a vehicle
    (d) temperature at accretion place
63. The variate is discrete variate if it relates to
    (a) measurements   (b) counting
    (c) temperature   (d) heights

II. Fill in the suitable word(s) or pharse(s) in the blanks :

1. A original data which may be result of survey or result of enquiry conducted is called ....
2. Zero is a point on a ..... scale, means, the absence of the property.
3. The data may be already collected by some other agency or processed data is called as ....

4. The data taken from sources like office records, bulletins, reports etc. are of the type ....
5. The statistical information collected by an investigator from sampling units termed as .... data.
6. Data taken from the demographical institutes will be termed as ......
7. The crudest scale in the measurement of data is .... scale.
8. The best scale in measurement of data is .... scale.
9. .... scale is used for measurement of non-numeric notations or non-comparable symbols.
10. .... scale uses the concept of absolute zero.
11. .... scale is used for measurements on weight and height.
12. Classification of students in various divisions of the same standard is done by .... scale.
13. The groups of individuals according to income such as poor, middle class, rich class measured by .... scale.
14. The centigrade or Farenheight scale of temperature measurement is an example of .... scale.
15. The qualitative characteristics can be measured by ..... and..... scale.
16. The quantitative characteristics can be measured by .... and .... scale.
17. A variable which can takes only particular values is called as .... variable.

III. State Whether the following statements are True or False

1. The classification of data invariably depends on the scale of measurement.
2. The frequency distribution has the advantage of representing data in compressed form.
3. Discrete data can be expressed only in whole numbers.
4. A univariate frequency distribution organizes data into groups of values describing one or more characteristics of the data.
5. The class widths of frequency distribution are of equal size.
6. A more than ogive is S-shaped.
7. The vertical scale of an ogive for a relative frequency distribution marks the fraction of the total number of observations that corresponds to resepctive class.

8. A histogram is a series of rectangles, with width proprotional to class frequencies.
9. A 'less than' ogive is S-shaped ingenral.
10. Histogram cannot be drawn for a frequency distribution with open end class.
11. While drawing frequency curve it is not necessary to take care that the area under the curve is same as that of frequency polygon.
12. After plotting mid-points on X-axis and frequencies on Y-axis for frequency polygon it is not necessary to join the mid values of preceding class and succeeding class with zero frequency.
13. In case the data items are three digit, stem will be two digit and leaf will be signle digit at unit place.
14. If the observations are of the type 102.3, 102.8, 103.5 then integers such as 102, 103 can be taken as stem and fractional part as leaf.
15. Stem and leaf is another way of representing data, gives bar like structure infront of stem and no loss of data due to condensation.
16. The facts and figures obtained by an investigator himself is called as primary data.
17. Population census result is a classical example of secondary data.
18. Primary data are more reliable but are expensive and time consuming.
19. The collection of data of production amount, in a particular industry is an example of primary data.
20. Primary data are more accurate than secondary data.
21. The data obtained from reports of municipal corporations and zilla parishad is an example of secondary data.
22. Examination result of a candidate can be recorded as pass or fail which is an example of quantitative variable.
23. We can express candidate's performance as percentage of marks which is an example of quantitative variable.
24. In an ordinal scale of measurement' 'distance' is an important factor in the measurements.
25. The zero point on an interval scale signifies absence of the property.
26. The zero point on a ratio scale signifies absence of the property.

Answers : Objective Type Questions

I. Multiple Choice Questions :

(1) b   (2) a   (3) c   (4) d
(5) d   (6) d   (7) c   (8) a
(9) a   (10) d   (11) b   (12) c
(13) c   (14) a   (15) a   (16) c
(17) d   (18) b   (19) a   (20) a
(21) a   (22) d   (23) d   (24) a
(25) c   (26) c   (27) d   (28) c
(29) d   (30) d   (31) d   (32) d
(33) d   (34) d   (35) d   (36) d
(37) b   (38) b
(39) d   (40) d   (41) d   (42) d
(43) d   (44) c   (45) b   (48) d
(47) d   (48) a   (49) d   (50) a
(51) a   (52) b   (53) d   (54) d
(56) d   (57) d   (58) a   (59) c
(60) c   (61) c   (62) c   (63) b

II. Fill in the blanks :

(1) Primary data   (2) ratio
(3) secondary data   (4) secondary data
(5) primary data   (6) secondary data
(7) nominal
(8) ratio   (9) nominal
(10) ratio   (11) ratio
(12) nominal   (13) ordinal
(14) interval   (15) nominal, ordinal
(16) interval ratio   (17) discrete

III True or False :

1. True   2. True   3. False   4. False
5. False   6. True   7. True   8. False
9. True   10. True   11. True   12. True
13. True   14. True   15. True

(16) True   (17) False (18) True   (19) True
(20) True   (21) True   (22) False (23) True
(24) False (25) False (26) True

Chapter 3...
Measures of Central Tendency

Vasant Shankar Huzurbazar (September 15, 1919 – November 15, 1991) was an Indian statistician from Kolhapur. Huzurbazar was the founder head of the department of statistics, University of Pune from 1953 to 1976. From 1979 to 1991, he served as professor at University of Denver, Colorado until his death. He served as visiting professor for two years to the Iowa State University in 1962. In 1974, Huzurbazar was awarded the Padma Bhushan from Government of India for his contributions to the field of statistics.

Vasant Shankar Huzurbazar

Contents ...

- 3.1 Introduction
- 3.2 Objectives or Requisites of Average
- 3.3 Types of Averages or Measures of Central Tendency
- 3.4 Arithmetic Mean
- 3.5 Trimmed Mean
- 3.6 Properties of Arithmetic Mean
- 3.7 Merits and Demerits of A.M.
- 3.8 Median
- 3.9 Mode
- 3.10 Geometric Mean
- 3.11 Harmonic Mean
- 3.12 Weighted Means
- 3.13 Partition Values
- 3.14 Box and Whisker Plot
- 3.15 Choice of an Average

Key Words :

Central tendency, Average, Arithmetic mean, Outliers, Trimmed mean, Median, Mode, Geometric mean, Harmonic mean, Weighted means, Partition values, Quartiles, Deciles, percentiles, Box plot.

Objectives :

Averages are tools of summersing data, finding representative. It facilitates the comparison. Different averages suitable to different situations are to used. The first and second aspects of data analysis are collection of data, presentation of data respectively. The third aspect is analysis and fourth is interpretation. Averages are useful in both analysis and interpretation. Box plot technique gives us quick overall view. Percentile rank is another important indicator or tool of comparison.

3.1 Introduction

We have studied in the previous chapters various methods of summarizing data and its graphical representation. However it becomes essential to condense the data into a single value for comparison purpose. This value is treated as a representative of data. There are various methods of selecting a single central value, we will discuss those in detail in this chapter.

Central Tendency : By means of classification and frequency curve we get an idea about the shape of frequency distribution. In most of the frequency distributions we observe that, all the class-frequencies are not same. Initially frequency is small in magnitude, later on it increases, it reaches to maximum in the middle part of the data and then falls down. In other words the frequency curve is bell-shaped. Here we note a property that, the observations are not uniformly spread. However, most of the observations get clustered in the central part of the data. This property of observations is described as **central tendency.**

Naturally we select a representative observation from the central part. This is referred to as an **average** or **measure of central tendency**.

It is desired that all the important properties of the observations in the data should be represented in the average. The word average is very commonly used in day-to-day life.

For example : Average marks, average profit, average run-rate of a team in one day. A single value is suitable for comparison. Therefore, average is essential quantity. Average is a value around which most of the observations are clustered, hence this single value itself gives clear idea regarding phenomenon under study.

There are several types of averages used in practice according to the type of data and purpose.

3.2 Objectives and Requisites of Average

Objectives of average :
1. To obtain a single representative quantity for the entire data.
2. To facilitate comparison.

There are several averages in use, hence it is necessary to discuss the requisites of good or ideal average.

Requisites of good average :
1. It should be simple to understand and easy to calculate.
2. It should be rigidly defined.
3. It should be based on all observations in the data.
4. It should be capable of further mathematical treatment.
5. It should be least affected by extreme observations.
6. It should possess sampling stability.

3.3 Types of Averages or Measures of Central Tendency

There are various types of averages used in practice. Those are listed below :
1. Arithmetic mean (simple and weighted)
2. Median
3. Mode.

Moreover there two more averages obtained after transforming data. These are (i) Geometric Mean, (ii) Harmonic Mean.

Among the above stated averages arithmetic mean, geometric mean and harmonic mean, three are called as mathematical averages and the median and mode are called as positional averages.

According to the nature of data, type of average is decided. Different averages possess different advantages and disadvantages. The details are discussed later.

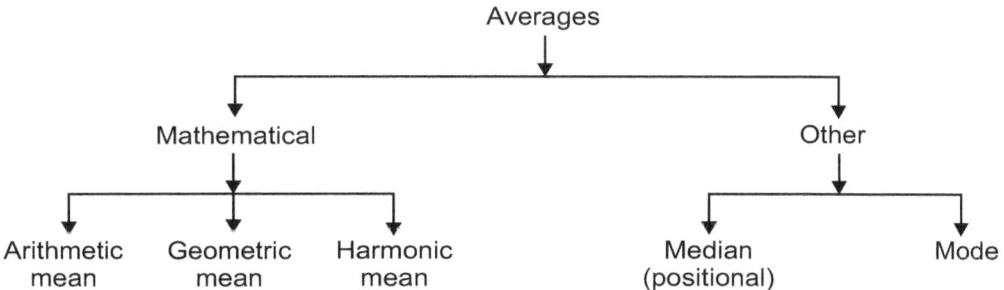

3.4 Arithmetic Mean

This is very commonly used and widely applicable average.

Definition : Arithmetic mean (A.M.) or mean is a sum of observations divided by number of observations i.e.

$$\text{A.M.} = \frac{\text{Sum of the observations}}{\text{Number of observations}}$$

According to the different types of data calculation of A.M. differs slightly. We consider these cases as given below :

Case (i) Individual observations or ungrouped data :

Suppose $x_1, x_2, \ldots, x_n$ is a set of n observations. By definition, arithmetic mean will be

$$\text{A.M.} = \frac{x_1 + x_2 + \ldots + x_n}{N} \quad \ldots (1)$$

Numerator of right side of (1) can be symbolically written as $\sum_{i=1}^{n} x_i$

i.e. $x_1 + x_2 + \ldots + x_n$ (See Appendix - I)

Symbol $\sum$ (sigma) represents the sum. Further it is a customary to denote A.M. by $\bar{x}$.

Hence, $$\text{A.M.} = \bar{x} = \frac{\sum_{i=1}^{n} x_i}{n}$$

For simplicity $\sum_{i=1}^{n} x_i$ will be written as $\sum x$.

Case (ii) Discrete frequency distribution :

Suppose $x_1, x_2, \ldots, x_n$ are values with $f_1, f_2, \ldots, f_n$ as the corresponding frequencies. Clearly to find the sum of observations we need to add observation x_1, f_1 times, observation x_2, f_2 times and so on. Hence sum of observations will be $f_1 x_1 + f_2 x_2 + \ldots + f_n x_n$ and total number of observations will be $f_1 + f_2 + \ldots + f_n$. Hence,

$$\bar{x} = \frac{f_1 x_1 + f_2 x_2 + \ldots + f_n x_n}{f_1 + f_2 + \ldots + f_n} \quad \text{(using } \sum \text{ notation we get)}$$

$$\bar{x} = \frac{\sum_{i=1}^{n} f_i x_i}{\sum_{i=1}^{n} f_i}$$

Case (iii) Continuous frequency distribution :

In this case, frequency is associated to the entire class and not to any specific single value. This creates difficulty in choosing $x_1, x_2, ..., x_n$.

For calculation purpose we make a reasonable assumption that the frequency is associated with mid-point of class or equivalently we say the frequency is distributed over the respective class uniformly. Thus, taking $x_1, x_2, ..., x_n$ as the mid-values of class intervals we calculate mean by the same formula discussed in case (ii), i.e.

$$\bar{x} = \frac{\sum f_i x_i}{\sum f_i} = \frac{\sum f_i x_i}{N}$$

Example 3.1 : Calculate the arithmetic mean of marks scored by a student in 7 subjects given below :

61, 68, 69, 70, 63, 60, 78

Solution :

$$\bar{x} = \frac{61 + 68 + 69 + 63 + 70 + 60 + 78}{7} = \frac{469}{7} = 67$$

Note : Arithmetic mean possesses central position on linear scale,

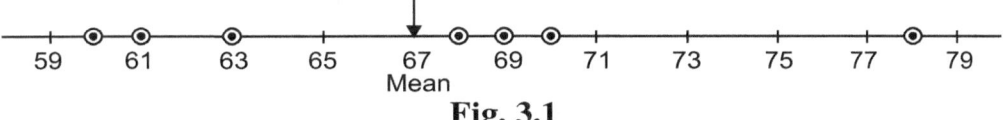

Fig. 3.1

It can be noticed in the above illustration that the observations are nearer to 60, so for convenience we assume the mean to be 60 and obtain the sum of excess of marks. It will be $1 + 8 + 9 + 3 + 10 + 0 + 18 = 49$. We find the average of excess and add in the assumed mean. Thus mean will be $60 + 49/7 = 67$.

The above discussion leads to a short-cut method of finding arithmetic mean. We will discuss it later.

To find out mean of given data using MS-Excel :

Use command = **average(range)**. It will return arithmetic mean of given data.

	A	B
1		
2		
3	Data	
4	61	
5	68	
6	69	
7	63	
8	70	
9	60	
10	78	
11		
12	= AVERAGE(A4:A10)	
13	MEAN = 67	
14		

Fig. 3.2

3.5 Trimmed Mean

Outliers : Some observations in data set · fall outside the usual pattern of the data. Such poits are called as outliers (which lie outside the pattern).

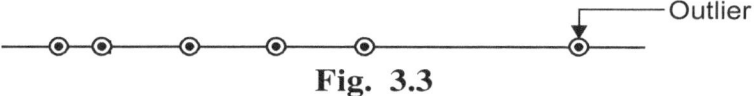

Fig. 3.3

Some observations at the extreme are considered to be outliers. The computation of arithmetic in the presence of outliers may give faulty results. The interpretation based on such summary will not be that much reliable. For example, the examination score, data will have minimum and maximum score far off from the remaining observations.

To overcome this difficulty it is suggested to ignore or to trimm-off the outliers. The trimming factor α % means ignore topmost α% and lowest α% observations (i.e. $\alpha n/100$ observations).

Trimmed mean : Arithmetic mean obtained by ignoring lowest α% as well as highest α% observation is called as α% trimmed mean.

Note :

(1) In general, may be taken as 5% to 10% or even 20% also there is no hard and fast rule.

(2) We need to arrange the observations in increasing or in decreasing order of magnitude before computing trimmed mean.

(3) Many statistical softwares determine trimmed mean.

(4) If α% is not integer it may be rounded-off.

(For example : 10% of 45 comes to 4.5, so we ignore 5 highest and 5 lowest observations).

Illustration 1 : Weights of 20 students in kg are given below :

50, 28, 32, 30, 42, 26, 40, 31, 38, 51, 48, 33, 45, 36, 40, 29, 43, 48, 52, 60.

Obtain :

(i) 5% trimmed arithmetic mean.

(ii) 10% trimmed arithmetic mean.

(iii) arithmetic mean.

Solution : Step 1 : We arrange the observations in increasing order of magnitude.

26, 28, 29, 30, 31, 32, 33, 36, 38, 40, 40, 42, 43, 45, 48, 48, 50, 51, 52, 60.

(i) The number of observations : n = 20 trimming factor is 5%, thus 5% of 20 is $20 \times \frac{5}{100}$ = 1. We have to ignore one highest (60) and one lowest observations (26) to find 5% trimmed mean. Thus, the mean of middle 18th observation is the required mean.

$$\frac{28 + 29 + 30 + \ldots + 50 + 51 + 52}{18} = \frac{716}{18} = 39.7778.$$

(ii) 10% of 20 is $20 \times \frac{10}{100}$ = 2. We need to ignore the 2 highest observations (52, 60) and the two lowest observations (26, 28). The mean of middle 16 observations is the required mean

$$\frac{29 + 30 + 31 + \ldots + 50 + 51}{16} = \frac{636}{16} = 39.75.$$

(3) Usual arithmetic mean is = $\frac{26 + 28 + 29 + \ldots + 51 + 52 + 60}{20}$

= $\frac{802}{20}$ = 40.1%.

MS-EXCEL Command :

Note : To obtain trimmed mean using MSEXCEL command.

The command is of the nature TRIMMEAN (data range, $2\alpha\%$).

If α is 5% then 2α we need type as 0.2. It is exhibited in the following MS-EXCEL sheet.

	A	B	C	D
1	50	AVERAGE MEAN	40.1	
2	28			
3	32	TRIMMED MEAN (5 %)	39.77778	
4	30			
5	42	TRIMMED MEAN (10 %)	39.75	
6	26			
7	40			
8	31			
9	38			
10	51			
11	48			
12	33			
13	45			
14	36			
15	45			
16	36			
17	40			
18	29			
19	43			
20	48			
21	52			
22	60			

Fig. 3.4

3.6 Properties of Arithmetic Mean

(1) The algebraic sum of deviations of observations from their arithmetic mean is zero. (i.e. $\sum (x_i - \bar{x}) = 0$)

Proof : Note that $x_1 - \bar{x}, x_2 - \bar{x}, ..., x_n - \bar{x}$ are deviations.

$$\text{Algebraic sum of deviations} = \sum(x_i - \bar{x}) = \sum x_i - n\bar{x}$$
$$= n\bar{x} - n\bar{x} = 0$$
$$\left(\because \text{from property (1)} \sum x_i = n\bar{x}\right)$$

(2) The sum of squares of the deviations taken from arithmetic mean is minimum. i.e. $\sum(x_i - \bar{x})^2 \leq \sum(x_i - a)^2$.

Proof : Suppose 'a' is any arbitrary constant. Then $x_i - \bar{x}$ is deviation of x_i from $\bar{x}$ and $x_i - a$ is deviation of x_i from a.

Let us evaluate $\sum(x_i - a)^2 = \sum(x_i - \bar{x} + \bar{x} - a)^2$

$$= \sum\{(x_i - \bar{x}) + (\bar{x} - a)\}^2$$

$$= \sum(x_i - \bar{x})^2 + 2\sum(\bar{x} - a)(x_i - \bar{x}) + \sum(\bar{x} - a)^2$$

$$= \sum(x_i - \bar{x})^2 + 2(\bar{x} - a)\sum(x_i - \bar{x}) + n(\bar{x} - a)^2$$

$$= \sum(x_i - \bar{x})^2 + n(\bar{x} - a)^2$$

$$(\because \text{ From property (2), } \sum(x_i - \bar{x}) = 0$$

$$= \sum(x_i - \bar{x})^2 + \text{Non-negative quantity}$$

Therefore, $\sum(x_i - a)^2 \geq \sum(x_i - \bar{x})^2$

Alternative Method

Using calculus method we find minima of the quantity $\sum(x_i - a)^2$.

Let $\phi = \sum(x_i - a)^2$. Therefore, $\frac{\partial \phi}{\partial a} = 0$ gives $\frac{\partial}{\partial a} \sum_{i=1}^{n}(x_i - a)^2 = 0$

$$\therefore \quad \sum_{i=1}^{n} \frac{\partial}{\partial a}(x_i - a)^2 = 0$$

$$\therefore \quad \sum_{i=1}^{n} 2(x_i - a) \times (-1) = 0$$

$$\therefore \quad \sum_{i=1}^{n}(x_i - a) = 0$$

$$\therefore \quad \sum_{i=1}^{n} x_i - \sum_{i=1}^{n} a = 0$$

$$\therefore \quad n\bar{x} - na = 0$$

$$\therefore \quad a = \bar{x}$$

Further $\dfrac{\partial^2 \phi}{\partial a^2} = \dfrac{\partial}{\partial a} \sum_{i=1}^{n} -2(x_i - a) = \sum_{i=1}^{n} 2 = 2n$

Therefore $\dfrac{\partial \phi}{\partial a} = 0$ at $a = \bar{x}$ and $\dfrac{\partial^2 \phi}{\partial a^2} = 2n > 0$ at $a = \bar{x}$. Hence, ϕ is minimum at $a = \bar{x}$. Therefore $\sum(x_i - \bar{x})^2 \leq \sum(x_i - a)^2$.

Effect of change of origin and scale

If we add (or subtract) a constant from each observation, then we say that the origin is changed. Similarly if each observation is multiplied (or divided) by some constant then we say that the scale is changed. Here we study the effect of change of origin and scale.

(3) If $u_i = \dfrac{x_i - a}{h}$ then $\bar{u} = \dfrac{\bar{x} - a}{h}$; a and h being constants.

Proof : $\bar{u} = \dfrac{\sum u_i}{n} = \dfrac{1}{n} \sum \left(\dfrac{x_i - a}{h} \right) = \dfrac{1}{nh} [\sum x_i - na]$

$= \dfrac{1}{h} \left[\dfrac{\sum x_i}{n} - a \right] = \dfrac{\bar{x} - a}{h}$

Similarly we get, if $y_i = cx_i + d$ then $\bar{y} = c\bar{x} + d$.

Remark : (a) This property simplifies the computations of arithmetic mean [See examples 3.2 and 3.2].

(b) If we take $h = 1$, $c = 1$ then we get $u_i = x_i - a$, $y_i = x_i + d$. Hence $\bar{u} = \bar{x} - a$ and $\bar{y} = \bar{x} + d$. In this case we have changed only the origin and scale is not changed.

(c) If we take $a = 0$, $d = 0$, then we get $u_i = \dfrac{x_i}{h}$ and $y_i = cx_i$. Hence $\bar{u} = \bar{x}/h$, $\bar{y} = c\bar{x}$. This amounts to change of scale only and no change of origin.

Mean of Combined Groups :

Many times it is required to compute mean of two groups combined together. If means and sizes of groups are known, we can determine the combined A.M. mean i.e. A.M. of combined group. Units of measurement in both the groups should be same.

(4) Let $\bar{x}_1$ be the arithmetic mean of first group of size n_1. Similarly $\bar{x}_2$ be arithmetic mean of second group of size n_2, then the combined mean $\bar{x}_c$ is given by $\dfrac{n_1\bar{x}_1 + n_2\bar{x}_2}{n_1 + n_2}$.

Proof : Note that $\bar{x}_1 = \dfrac{(\text{Sum of observations in first group})}{n_1}$

Hence, $n_1 \bar{x}_1$ = sum of observations in first group.

Similarly $n_2 \bar{x}_2$ = sum of observations is second group. Thus, the combined mean $\bar{x}_c$ is

$$\bar{x}_c = \frac{\begin{pmatrix}\text{Sum of the observations in} \\ \text{first group}\end{pmatrix} + \begin{pmatrix}\text{Sum of the observations} \\ \text{in second group}\end{pmatrix}}{(\text{Size of first group}) + (\text{Size of second group})}$$

$$\bar{x}_c = \frac{n_1\bar{x}_1 + n_2\bar{x}_2}{n_1 + n_2}$$

Remark : The above result can be generalised to k (k ≥ 2) groups as follows :

Let there be k groups with size of ith group as n_i and the arithmetic mean as $\bar{x}_i$ (i = 1, 2, 3, ... k). Then $\bar{x}_c$, the arithmetic mean of all the k groups combined together is given by

$$\bar{x}_c = \frac{n_1\bar{x}_1 + n_2\bar{x}_2 + ... + n_k\bar{x}_k}{n_1 + n_2 + ... + n_k} = \frac{\sum n_i \bar{x}_i}{\sum n_i}$$

(5) $\min \{x_1, x_2, ..., x_n\} \leq \bar{x} \leq \max \{x_1, x_2, ..., x_n\}$.

Proof : Let $\min \{x_1, x_2, ..., x_n\} = a$, $\max \{x_1, x_2, ..., x_n\} = b$

∴ $\quad \sum a \leq \sum x_i \leq \sum b$

∴ $\quad na \leq \sum x_i \leq nb$

∴ $\quad a \leq \dfrac{\sum x_i}{n} \leq b$

∴ $\quad a \leq \bar{x} \leq b.$ ... (1)

This gives bounds for arithmetic mean. If $\bar{x}$ does not lie within minimum and maximum of the observations then it is indication of error in computations.

Note that, equalities in (1) will be satisfied if all the observations are same.

ILLUSTRATIVE EXAMPLES

Example 3.2 : Calculate arithmetic mean for the following frequency distribution :

Observations (x)	103	110	112	118	95
Frequency (f)	4	6	10	12	3

Solution : We solve the problem by both the methods.

x_i	f_i	$f_i x_i$
103	4	$103 \times 4 = 412$
110	6	$110 \times 6 = 660$
112	10	$112 \times 10 = 1120$
118	12	$118 \times 12 = 1416$
95	3	$95 \times 3 = 285$
Total	N = 35	$\sum f_i x_i = 3893$

$$\therefore \quad \bar{x} = \frac{\sum f_i x_i}{\sum f_i} = \frac{3893}{35} = 111.2286$$

Example 3.3 : The following is a distribution of weekly salaries of the employees of a firm.

Salary in ₹	No. of employees
0 – 500	2
500 – 1000	8
1000 – 1500	12
1500 – 2000	23
2000 – 2500	25
2500 – 3000	20
3000 – 3500	9
3500 – 4000	1

Compute arithmetic mean of salaries.

Solution : For computations of arithmetic mean of continuous variables, we compute mid-point of each class interval. In most of the problems of this type, we get mid-points equispaced (if the classes are of uniform width). We choose 'a' as far as possible closer to $\bar{x}$. Thus any mid-point in the central part can be taken as 'a'. We define $u_i = (x_i - a)/h$, where, h is the width of class interval (or any suitable number). It can be easily seen that computation of $\bar{u}$ is simpler than that of $\bar{x}$.

Class	Mid-values x_i	$u_i = \dfrac{x_i - 1750}{500}$	f_i	$f_i u_i$
0 – 500	250	– 3	2	– 6
500 – 1000	750	– 2	8	– 16
1000 – 1500	1250	– 1	12	– 12
1500 – 2000	1750	0	23	0
2000 – 2500	2250	1	25	25
2500 – 3000	2750	2	20	40
3000 – 3500	3250	3	9	27
3500 – 4000	3750	4	1	4
Total	–	–	100	62

Here, $u_i = \dfrac{x_i - 1750}{500}$, therefore $\bar{u} = \dfrac{\bar{x} - 1750}{500}$

Hence, $\bar{x} = 500\bar{u} + 1750$, $\bar{u} = \dfrac{\Sigma f_i u_i}{\Sigma f_i} = \dfrac{62}{100} = 0.62$

∴ $\bar{x} = 500 \times 0.62 + 1750 = 310 + 1750 = 2060$ ₹

Example 3.4 : A variable takes values $a, a + d, a + 2d, \ldots, a + (n - 1)d$. Find its arithmetic mean.

Solution : Here $x_1 = a$, $x_2 = a + d$, $\ldots$, $x_i = a + (i - 1)d$.

∴ $\bar{x} = \dfrac{\Sigma x_i}{n} = \begin{pmatrix} \text{Sum of n terms in Arithmetic} \\ \text{progression with first term a and} \\ \text{common difference d} \end{pmatrix} \div n$

$= \dfrac{S_n}{n} = \dfrac{na + \dfrac{n(n-1)}{2}d}{n} = a + \dfrac{(n-1)d}{2}$

Alternative method : Let $u_i = (x_i - a)/d$.

Thus, $u_1 = 0, \; u_2 = 1, \; u_3 = 2, \ldots, u_n = n - 1$

$$\therefore \quad \bar{u} = \frac{\sum u_i}{n} = \frac{0 + 1 + 2 + \ldots + (n-1)}{n} = \frac{n(n-1)/2}{n}$$

$$= \frac{n-1}{2}$$

Since, $u_i = \dfrac{x_i - a}{d}, \quad \bar{u} = \dfrac{\bar{x} - a}{d}$

Hence, $\bar{x} = a + \bar{u}\, d = a + \left(\dfrac{n-1}{2}\right) d$

Note : We state a general rule for the arithmetic mean of terms in arithmetic progression.

$$\text{A.M. of A.P.} = \frac{\text{First term + Last term}}{2}$$

It can be proved easily.

Example 3.5 : A variable takes values $1, 2, \ldots, n$ with frequencies $1, 2, 3, \ldots, n$ respectively. Find its arithmetic mean.

Solution :

x_i	1	2	3	………	n	**Total**
f_i	2	2	3	………	n	$n(n+1)/2$
$f_i x_i$	1^2	2^2	3^2	………	n^2	$n(n+1)(2n+1)/6$

$$\bar{x} = \frac{\sum f_i x_i}{\sum f_i} = \frac{n(n+1)(2n+1)}{6} \div \frac{n(n+1)}{2} = \frac{2n+1}{3}$$

Example 3.6 : Arithmetic mean of weight of 100 boys is 50 kg and the arithmetic mean of 50 girls is 45 kg. Calculate the arithmetic mean of combined group of boys and girls.

Solution : Let $\bar{x}_1$ and n_1 be the mean and size of group of boys and $\bar{x}_2$ and n_2 be the mean and size of group of girls. So $n_1 = 100$, $\bar{x}_1 = 50$, $n_2 = 50$, $\bar{x}_2 = 45$. Hence, combined mean is

$$\bar{x}_c = \frac{n_1 \bar{x}_1 + n_2 \bar{x}_2}{n_1 + n_2} = \frac{(100 \times 50) + (50 \times 45)}{100 + 50} = \frac{7250}{150} = 48.3333$$

Example 3.7 : The mean weekly salary paid to 300 employees of a firm is ₹ 1,470. There are 200 male employees and the remaining are females. If mean salary of males is ₹ 1,505, obtain the mean salary of females.

Solution : Suppose $\bar{x}_1$ and n_1 are mean and group size of males. $\bar{x}_2$ and n_2 are mean and size of group of females, $\bar{x}_c$ mean of all the employees considered together.

Now, $$\bar{x}_c = \frac{n_1\bar{x}_1 + n_2\bar{x}_2}{n_1 + n_2}$$

$\therefore \quad 1470 = \frac{(200 \times 1505) + (100 \times \bar{x}_2)}{200 + 100}$

$\therefore \quad 1470 = \frac{301000 + 100x_2}{300}$

$\therefore \quad 441000 = 301000 + 100\bar{x}_2$

$\therefore \quad 4410 = 3010 + \bar{x}_2$

$\therefore \quad \bar{x}_2 = 1,400$ ₹

Example 3.8 : From the following data find the missing frequencies, it is given that mean is 15.3818 and total frequency is 55.

Class	9 - 11	11 - 13	13 - 15	15 - 17	17 - 19	19 - 21
Frequency	3	7	–	20	–	5

Solution : Let the missing frequencies be a and b.

Class	Mid-value x_i	Frequency f_i	$f_i x_i$
9 - 11	10	3	30
11 - 13	12	7	84
13 - 15	14	a	14a
15 - 17	16	20	320
17 - 19	18	b	18b
19 - 21	20	5	100
	Total	35 + a + b = N = 55	534 + 14a + 18b = $\Sigma f_i x_i$

We get two equations from the given information

i.e. $\quad 35 + a + b = 55 \therefore a + b = 20 \quad \ldots (1)$

$$\bar{x} = \frac{\Sigma fx}{N} \text{ gives } 15.3818$$

$$= \frac{534 + 14a + 18b}{55}$$

$\therefore \quad 845.999 = 534 + 14a + 18b$

$\therefore \quad 14a + 18b = 311.999 \quad \ldots (2)$

Solving (1) and (2) we get, $a = 12.0002$, $b = 7.9998$.

After rounding-off the values, $a = 12$ and $b = 8$

Thus, frequency of the class 13 – 15 is 12 and that of 17 – 19 is 8.

Example 3.9 : Find the arithmetic mean given that $\Sigma(x - 10) = 230$ and n = 50

Solution : Let $\quad u = x - 10$, hence $\Sigma u = 230$

$\therefore \quad \bar{x} = 10 + \bar{u} = 10 + \dfrac{230}{50} = 14.6$

Example 3.10 : Arithmetic mean of 50 items is 104. While checking, it was noticed that observation 98 was misread as 89. Find the correct value of mean.

Solution : Incorrect mean $= 104 = \dfrac{\text{Incorrect sum}}{n}$

$\therefore \quad$ Incorrect sum $= 104 \times 50 = 5200$

Correct sum $=$ Incorrect sum + Correct observation – Incorrect observation.

$= 5200 + 98 - 89 = 5209$

$\therefore \quad$ Correct mean $= \dfrac{\text{Correct sum}}{n} = \dfrac{5209}{50} = 104.18$

3.7 Merits and Demerits of A.M.

A.M. possesses most of the requisites of a good average. Hence it is widely used. We state below its merits and demerits :

Merits :

1. It is easy to calculate and simple to follow.
2. It is based on all observations.
3. It is rigidly defined.
4. It possesses sampling stability.

5. It is capable of further mathematical treatment. Given the means and sizes of two or more groups, we can find mean of combined group.

Demerits :
1. It is applicable only for quantitative data.
2. It is unduly affected by extreme observations. (Hence, trimmed mean is used in some cases).
3. It cannot be computed for frequency distribution with open end class. (For an open end class we cannot find mid point).
4. It cannot be determined graphically.
5. Sometimes arithmetic mean may not be an actual observation in a data. For example average number of T.V. sets daily sold in a particular month is 5.25. On any day actually 5. 25 T.V. sets cannot be sold.

3.8 Median

We have seen that arithmetic mean cannot be calculated for qualitative observations like debating skill, honesty, blindness. Moreover, if a frequency distribution includes open end class, mean does not exist and it is unduly affected by extreme observations. In order to overcome these drawbacks, other measures of central tendency such as median or mode are used.

Illustration 2 : The A.M. of 38, 43, 41, 39, 52, 48, 60, 167 is 61. This cannot be said to be a representative value, because among these 8 observations 7 are smaller than A.M. Thus in case extreme items are widely separated from most of the observations, A.M. does not remain suitable, median is suitable.

Definition : Median is the value of middle most observation in the data when the observations are arranged in increasing (or decreasing) order of their values.

Thus, median is the central observation. It divides the data into two equal parts. There are equal number of observations above as well as below the median. It is also called as positional average. It is also trimmed mean obtained by ignoring $(n - 1)/2$ topmost and $(n - 1)/2$ lowest observations.

(i) Computation of Median – Ungrouped data : It may be noticed that in case of individual observations or ungrouped data, computation of median does not require any formula. It can be determined by inspection.

Suppose n is the number of observations in the data. If n is odd then there is only one middle most observation which is $\left(\frac{n+1}{2}\right)^{th}$ observation. On the other hand, if n is even then there are two middle most observations namely the $(n/2)^{th}$ and $(n/2 + 1)^{th}$. In this case we take median to be mean of these two middle most observations. We follow the procedure described below for calculating median.

Step 1 : Arrange the observations in increasing (or decreasing) order.

Step 2 : Compute the median by the following criteria :

Median = The value of $(n + 1)/2^{th}$ observation if n is odd

$$\text{Median} = \frac{\left(\begin{array}{c}\text{The value of } n/2^{th} \\ \text{observation}\end{array}\right) + \left(\begin{array}{c}\text{The value of } (n/2 + 1)^{th} \\ \text{observation}\end{array}\right)}{2}$$ if n is even.

ILLUSTRATIVE EXAMPLES

Example 3.11 : Following are the temperatures recorded in a certain city, observed in a certain week.

$$35, \ 38, \ 40, \ 39, \ 35, \ 36, \ 37$$

Obtain the median temperature.

Solution : The ordered arrangement of 7 observations is

$$35, \ 35, \ 36, \ \boxed{37}, \ 38, \ 39, \ 40$$

Since n = 7 is odd we get

Median = The value of $(n + 1)/2^{th}$ observation

= The value of 4th observation = 37.

Median using MS-EXCEL :

Enter the data at A_1 to A_7 and use command = MEDIAN $(A_1 : A_7)$.

```
       A     B        C
   1  35
   2  38
   3  40   = MEDIAN(A1:A7)
   4  39   MEDIAN = 37
   5  35
   6  36
   7  37
```

Fig. 3.5

Example 3.12 : The following are the sales in ₹ for 6 days in a certain week.

3020, 4120, 3600, 3250, 3830, 4000

Obtain the median sale.

Solution : The ordered arrangement of 6 observations is

3020, 3250, $\boxed{3600, 3830}$, 4000, 4120

Since n = 6 is even we get two middle observations. Hence,

$$\text{Median} = \frac{\left(\text{The value of } n/2^{\text{th}} \text{ observation}\right) + \left(\text{The value of } (n/2 + 1)^{\text{th}} \text{ observation}\right)}{2}$$

$$\text{Median} = \frac{\left(\text{The value of 3}^{\text{rd}} \text{ observation}\right) + \left(\text{The value of 4}^{\text{th}} \text{ observation}\right)}{2}$$

$$= \frac{3600 + 3830}{2} = 3715 \text{ ₹}$$

(ii) Computation of Median–Continuous frequency distribution : Suppose N is the total frequency. Since the variable under consideration is continuous, we can estimate the value of $N/2^{\text{th}}$ observation. Hence, regardless of N, whether it is even or odd in continuous frequency distribution, we take median to be the value of $N/2^{\text{th}}$ observation.

Computational procedure :

Step 1 : Obtain the class boundaries.

Step 2 : Obtain less than cumulative frequencies.

Step 3 : Locate the median class. Median class is the class in which median i.e. $N/2^{\text{th}}$ observation falls. In other words, it is in a class where less than cumulative frequency is equal to or exceeds N/2 for the first time.

Step 4 : Apply the formula and find the median.

$$\text{Median} = l + \frac{N/2 - c.f.}{f} \times h$$

where, l = Lower boundary of the median class
N = Total frequency
c.f. = Less than cumulative frequency of the class just preceding the median class.
f = Frequency of median class
h = Class width

Example 3.13 : Calculate median for the following frequency distribution :

Marks	below 20	21 – 40	41 – 60	61 – 80	81 – 100
No. of students	1	9	32	16	7

Solution :

Class boundaries	Frequency	Less than cumulative frequency
0 – 20.5	1	1 < N/2
20.5 – 40.5	9	c.f. = 10 < N/2
40.5 – 60.5 Median class	f = 32	42 > N/2
60.5 – 80.5	16	58
80.5 – 100	7	65 = N

Median = The value of N/2 i.e. 32.5^{th} observation.

Median class : 40.5 – 60.5, because N/2 exceeds less than cumulative frequency for the first time in this class.

Therefore, l = 40.5, N/2 = 32.5, c.f. = 10, f = 32, h = 20.

Hence, $\text{Median} = l + \dfrac{N/2 - c.f.}{f} \times h$

$= 40.5 + \dfrac{32.5 - 10}{32} \times 20 = 54.5625$

Median - by Graphical Method :

Median can be obtained graphically by means of ogive curve. Plot less than cumulative frequency curve taking upper boundaries on x-axis, and less than cumulative frequency on y-axis. Draw a line parallel to x-axis passing through point N/2 on y-axis. From the point of intersection of the line and ogive curve, draw a perpendicular to x-axis. The value at the foot of perpendicular is the median.

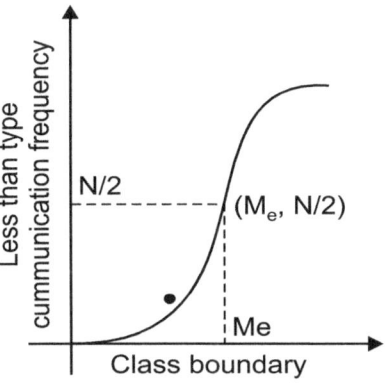

Fig. 3.6

Merits and Demerits of Median :

Merits :
1. It is easy to understand and easy to calculate.
2. It is not affected due to extreme observations.
3. It can be computed for a distribution with open end classes.
4. It can be determined graphically.
5. It is applicable to qualitative data also. In this case observations are arranged in order according to the quality and the middle most observation is obtained. The quality of this item is taken to be average quality or median quality.

Demerits :
1. It is not based on all the observations, hence it is not proper representative.
2. It is not capable of further mathematical treatment.
3. It is not as rigidly defined as the arithmetic mean.

3.9 Mode

It is yet another measure of central tendency developed to overcome the drawbacks of arithmetic mean. Apart from this, in some situations mode is the proper average.

Definition : The observation with maximum frequency or the most repeated observation is called as mode.

It is clear from earlier discussion that the general nature of frequency curve is bell shaped in majority of situations. Thus initially frequency is small, it increases and reaches the maximum and then it declines. The value on x-axis at which the maxima or the peak of the frequency curve appears is a mode.

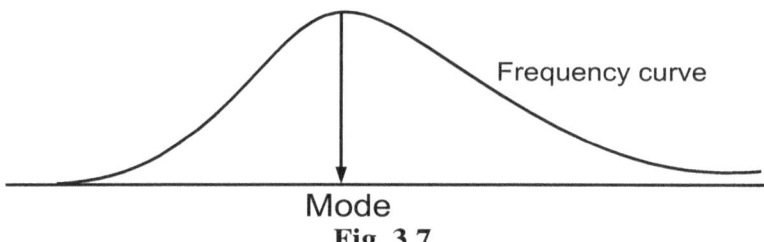

Fig. 3.7

In case of election results, a political party with largest votes (i.e. maximum frequency) is considered as representative. Thus, it is mode or modal opinion. In this situation, mode is the appropriate average. Similarly, to estimate the crop yield, too good quality or too poor quality crop is not considered. A quality of crop most commonly found is taken into account, which is nothing but mode. In titration experiment, out of three readings a repeated reading is taken to be final reading. It is mode and not the arithmetic mean. Thus in number of situations mode is appropriate.

(i) Computation of mode–Individual observations and Discrete frequency distribution : In this case we can find the observation with the largest frequency just by inspection. If the largest frequency occurs twice (or more), then we say there are two (or many) modes.

Example 3.14 : Find the mode of the following frequency distribution :

x	10	11	12	13	14	15
f	2	5	10	21	12	13

Solution : Since maximum frequency is associated with observation 13, the mode is 13.

Example 3.15 : Determine mode of the data given below :

35, 38, 40, 39, 35, 36, 37 (i) using formula (ii) using MS-EXCEL.

Solution : (i) It can be clearly seen that observation 35 has maximum frequency hence it is mode.

(ii) If the data items are entered in spreadsheet in column A at A_1 to A_7. The MS-EXCEL command = **MODE (A_1 : A_7)** gives mode. It is displayed in following Fig. 3.8.

	A	B	C
1	35		
2	38		
3	40	= MODE(A1:A7)	
4	39	MODE = 35	
5	35		
6	36		
7	37		

Fig. 3.8

Mode (For continuous frequency distribution) :

Mode lies in the class with maximum frequency. The position of mode depends upon premodal and postmodal frequency. Clearly if premodal and post modal frequencies are equal mode occupies the centre B of modal class (AC) as shown in following figure.

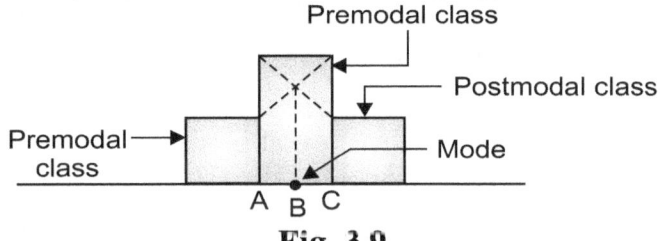

Fig. 3.9

However, if premodal frequency is larger than postmodal frequency, mode shifts earlier to the centre proportionality i.e. B shifts towards A, on the other hand if postmodal frequency is larger than premodal frequency then mode shifts towards C. It is like tug-off war between premodal and postmodal class frequencies. In the derivation we need to find exactly by how much quantity mode shifts from the centre.

Suppose, f_m = frequency of modal class i.e. maximum frequency

f_1 = premodal class frequency
f_2 = postmodal class-frequency

The shift in the mode from centre is in the proportion $(f_m - f_1)$ to $(f_m - f_2)$. In other words the mode (point B) divides the line AB internally in the ratio $(f_m - f_1) : (f_m - f_2)$.

$$\therefore \quad \frac{AB}{BC} = \frac{f_m - f_1}{f_m - f_2}$$

Using the above equation one can find AB and hence the value mode.

(ii) Computation of mode – Continuous frequency distribution :

Step 1 : Obtain the class – boundaries.

Step 2 : Locate the modal class. Modal class is class in which mode lies or a class with the largest frequency.

Step 3 : Apply the formula and find the mode.

$$\text{Mode} = l + \frac{f_m - f_1}{2f_m - f_1 - f_2} \times h$$

where,
- l = Lower boundary of modal class
- f_m = Frequency of modal class
- f_1 = Frequency of premodal class
- f_2 = Frequency of postmodal class
- h = Width of modal class

Example 3.16 : Calculate modal income from the following income distribution :

Daily income (₹)	30 and below	31-60	61-90	91-120	121-150	above 150
No. of Persons	22	198	110	95	42	33

Solution :

Class boundaries	Frequency
below 30.5	f_1 = 22
30.5 – 60.5	f_m = 198 Modal class
60.5 – 90.5	f_2 = 110
90.5 – 120.5	95
120.5 – 150.5	42
above 150.5	33

Modal class is 31–60.

Here we get $l = 30.5$, $f_m = 198$, $f_1 = 22$, $f_2 = 110$, $h = 30$

$$\text{Mode} = l + \frac{f_m - f_1}{2f_m - f_1 - f_2} \times h$$

$$= 30.5 + \frac{198 - 22}{2 \times 198 - 22 - 110} \times 30 = 50.5$$

Note :
1. If the maximum frequency is repeated, to find the mode uniquely, a method of grouping is adopted and a modal class is determined. The method of grouping is beyond the scope of book.
2. Mode cannot be determined if modal class is at the extreme. (i.e. the maximum frequency occurs at the beginning or at the end of the frequency distribution.)
3. Modal, pre-modal and post-modal classes should be of the same width.

(iii) Computation of mode – by Empirical relation : Arithmetic mean, mode and median are averages, hence we expect that those should be identical in value. However, this is true only in ideal situation. It is true whenever the frequency curve is perfectly symmetric and bell-shaped. For a moderately asymmetric unimodal frequency distribution the following empirical relationship holds approximately.

Mean – Mode ≃ 3 (Mean – Median) ... (1)

In some situations mode is ill-defined (see notes 1, 2 stated above). To overcome this difficulty in computing mode, the empirical relation (1) is used. If any two averages included in (1) are known, the remaining third can be computed. Therefore, if mean and median are known, then mode can be determined.

The empirical relation cannot be theoretically proved. Karl Pearson has stated it on the basis of vast experience. This relationship is observed to be valid for number of data sets after actual computations.

(iv) Computation of mode – by graphical method : Mode can be obtained graphically with the help of histogram. Mode is the x-co-ordinate of point P or the value at foot of perpendicular from P to x-axis, shown in Fig. 3.10.

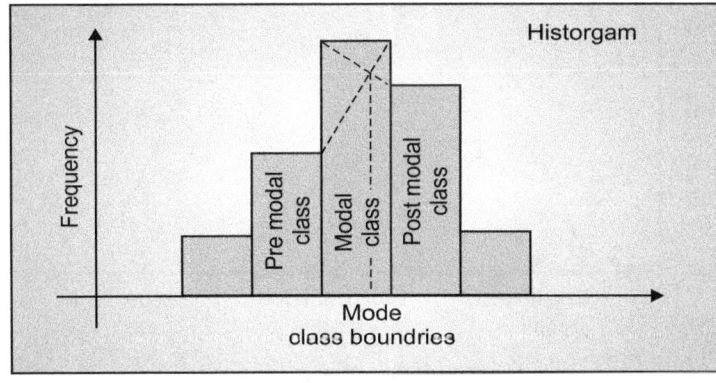

Fig. 3.10

Merits and Demerits of mode :

Merits :

1. It is simple to understand and easy to compute.
2. It is applicable for qualitative and quantitative data.
3. It is not affected by extreme observations.
4. It can be computed for distribution with open end classes.
5. It can be determined graphically.

Demerits :

1. It is not based on all the observations.
2. It is not capable of further mathematical treatment.
3. It is not rigidly defined.
4. It is indeterminate if the modal class is at the extreme of the distribution.

Note : It is possible to have two modes, such frequency distribution is called as bimodal frequency distribution. Sometimes bimodal frequency distribution is an indication of mixture of two frequency distributions.

For example, operator or machine is changed in manufacturing process. In medical sciences, two types of anaemia viz. microcytic and macrocytic are found in same population which give bimodal frequency curve.

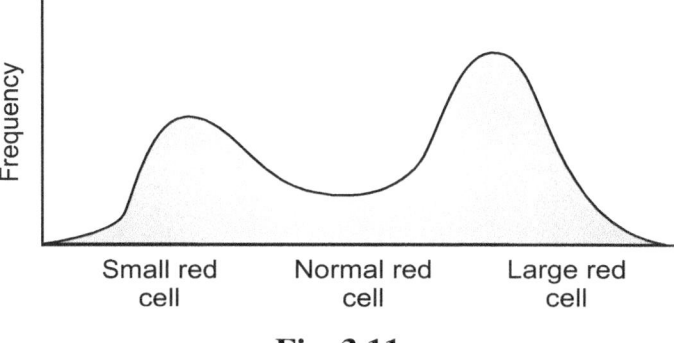

Fig. 3.11

Example 3.17 : Calculate arithmetic mean and mode for the following data :

Daily salary (₹)	Number of workers
Below 400	0
Below 600	4
Below 800	14
Below 1000	33
Below 1200	45
Below 1400	49
Below 1600	50

Solution : We need to prepare frequency distribution from the given cumulative frequency distribution.

Class	Frequency	Mid-values x	$u = \dfrac{x - 900}{200}$	fu
400 - 600	4 − 0 = 4	500	− 2	− 8
600 - 800	14 − 4 = 10	700	− 1	− 10
800 - 1000	33 − 14 = 19	900	0	0
1000 - 1200	45 − 33 = 12	1100	1	12
1200 - 1400	49 − 45 = 4	1300	2	8
1400 - 1600	50 − 49 = 1	1500	3	3
Total	50	−	−	5

$$\text{Mean} = a + \frac{\Sigma fu}{N} \times h, \text{ where } a = 900, \Sigma fu = 5,$$

$$N = 50, h = 200 = 900 + \frac{5}{50} \times 200 = 920 \text{ ₹}$$

Modal class : 800 − 1000

$$\text{Mode} = l + \frac{f_m - f_1}{2 f_m - f_1 - f_2} \times h$$

Here $l = 800$, $f_m = 19$, $f_1 = 10$, $f_2 = 12$, $h = 200$

$$\therefore \text{ Mode} = 900 + \frac{19 - 10}{38 - 10 - 12} \times 200 = 1012.5$$

3.10 Geometric Mean (G.M.)

The following example illustrates the need of an average other than arithmetic mean.

Illustration 3 : Suppose the price of an article is increased by 100% in 1992. It is reduced by 50% in the next year. Find the average change in the price.

Solution :

Year	Change in price
1992	100
1993	− 50

Arithmetic mean of change in price $= \dfrac{100 + (-50)}{2} = 25$

Thus average change (increase) in price is 25%.

However we notice that the average change is zero. Suppose price in 1991 is ₹ a, then in 1992 it will become ₹ 2a, due to 100% increase. Further due to 50% decrease, in the price, in 1993 it will be ₹ a. Thus in the span of those two years original price is retained. Thus average change is likely to be zero.

This situation demands average other than arithmetic mean. We compute average change in price as follows :

Here we need to determine the relative change in price. We call it as growth ratio (y). It is computed as follows :

$$\text{Growth ratio (y)} = \dfrac{\text{Current year price}}{\text{Previous year price}}$$

Therefore y indicates per unit change in price. In 1992 price is increased by 100% which means it is doubled, hence the corresponding y = 2. In 1993 the price is decreased by 50%, it means that the price is reduced to 1/2. Therefore the corresponding y = 1/2. Suppose price in 1991 is ₹ a

Year	Percent change	Current year price	$y = \dfrac{\text{Current year price}}{\text{Previous year price}}$
1991	-	a	-
1992	100	2a	2a ÷ a = 2
1993	− 50	a	a ÷ 2a = 1/2

$$\text{Average of y} = \sqrt{2 \times \dfrac{1}{2}} = 1$$

Average change in x = (Average of y − 1) × 100
= (1 − 1) × 100 = 0

The average of y determined in (1) is called a geometric mean. Therefore in this situation geometric mean gives the correct value.

Definition : Geometric mean (G.M.) of n observations is defined as n^{th} root of their product.

If $x_1, x_2, ..., x_n$ are the observations then geometric mean G of these observations is given by

$$G = (x_1 \times x_2 \times x_3 \times x_4 ... \times x_n)^{1/n} \quad ...(2)$$

The product $x_1 \cdot x_2 \cdot x_3 ... x_n$ can be symbolically written as $\prod_{i=1}^{n} x_i$.

(Π read as pi, represents product).

Therefore, $G = (\Pi x_i)^{1/n}$

Sometimes Πx_i is too large, hence it is difficult to compute. Therefore we use logarithms and simplify it.

Clearly, $\log G = \frac{1}{n} \log(\Pi x_i)$

$$\log G = \frac{1}{n} \sum \log x_i$$

∴ $G = \text{Antilog} \left(\frac{1}{n} \sum \log x_i \right)$

If $\{(x_i, f_i), i = 1, 2, ... k\}$ is a frequency distribution, then geometric mean is

$$G = \left(x_1^{f_1} \cdot x_2^{f_2} ... x_k^{f_k} \right)^{1/N} \quad \text{where, } N = \sum f_i$$

Using Π notation we get $G = \left(\prod_i x_i^{f_i} \right)^{1/N}$

The simplification using logarithm is as follows :

$$G = \text{Antilog} \left[\frac{1}{N} \sum_{i=1}^{k} f_i \log x_i \right]$$

Example 3.18 : Find the geometric mean of 2, 8, 20, 62, 54.

Solution : G.M. $= (2 \cdot 8 \cdot 20 \cdot 62 \cdot 54)^{1/5}$
$= (1071360)^{1/5} = 16.0689$

Alternative Method : Using logarithms computations will be as follows :

x_i	2	8	20	62	54
$\log x_i$	0.3010	0.9031	1.3010	1.7924	1.7324

$$G = \text{Antilog}\left(\frac{1}{n}\sum \log x_i\right) = \text{Antilog}\left(\frac{6.0299}{5}\right) = 16.068$$

Geometric mean by using MS-EXCEL :

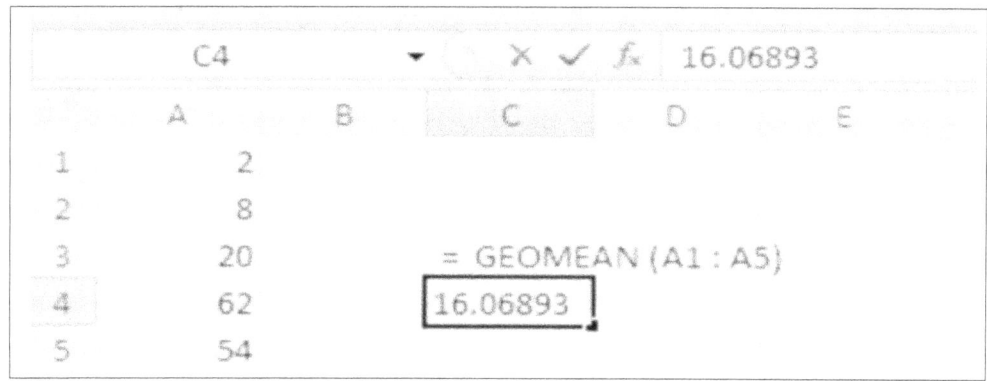

Fig. 3.12

Example 3.19 : A xyz co-operative bank gave interest at the rate of 10% p.c.p.a. on a fixed deposit for the first year. In the second year and third year the rate of interest was 12% and 15% respectively. If the amount is compounded yearly, find the average rate of interest.

Solution : In this case geometric mean is appropriate. Let x = rate of interest. y = current year amount ÷ previous year amount = $\frac{x}{100} + 1$.

y is the relative change in amount. In other words y indicates per unit change in amount due to interest.

x	10	12	15
y	1.10	1.12	1.15

$$\begin{aligned}\text{Average rate of interest} &= (\text{G.M. of } y - 1) \times 100\% \\ &= [(1.1 \times 1.12 \times 1.15)^{1/3} - 1] \times 100\% \\ &= (1.1231 - 1) \times 100 = 12.31\%\end{aligned}$$

Therefore average rate of interest is 12.31%.

Example 3.20 : A variable takes values a, ar, ar^2, ... , ar^{n-1}. Find its geometric mean.

Solution : By definition

$$G = (a \cdot ar \cdot ar^2 \cdots ar^{n-1})^{1/n}$$
$$= (a^n r^{1+2+3+\cdots+(n-1)})^{1/n}$$
$$= (a^n r^{n(n-1)/2})^{1/n} = a r^{(n-1)/2}$$

Note : G.M. of all the terms in geometric progression is same as that of the first term and the last term.

In the above example,

G.M. of $\{a, ar, ..., ar^{n-1}\}$ = G.M. of $\{a, ar^{n-1}\}$

$$= \sqrt{a \cdot ar^{n-1}} = ar^{(n-1)/2}$$

Example 3.21 : A population of a certain city is given below. Obtain the average rate of increase in population between the period 1991 - 1994.

Year	1991	1992	1993	1994
Population (in lakhs)	15.22	15.61	15.97	16.45

Solution : Let x = population, $y = \dfrac{\text{Current year population}}{\text{Previous year population}}$, y is relative change or per unit change in population.

Year	x	y	Percent increase
1992	15.61	15.61 ÷ 15.22 = 1.0256	2.56
1993	15.97	15.97 ÷ 15.61 = 1.0231	2.31
1994	16.45	16.45 ÷ 15.97 = 1.0300	3.00

Average percent increase in x = (G.M. of y − 1) × 100
= $[(1.0256 \times 1.0231 \times 1.03)^{1/3} - 1] \times 100$
= $(1.0808^{1/3} - 1)\,100 = (1.0262 - 1) \times 100 = 2.62\%$

Therefore average increase in population is 2.62% per year.

Uses of G.M. : Arithmetic mean is an important and widely used average, whereas geometric mean is not much in use. However, in certain situations geometric mean is more appropriate. The following are situations where G.M. is preferred.
1. Average change in percent.
2. Average of bank interest rates.
3. Average of depreciation in the cost of a certain machine.
4. Average of population growth.
5. Average rate of returns on share.

In general, G.M. is appropriate if the values are ratios or percentages. Similarly if the values are approximately in geometric progression then also G.M. is proper average to find rate of growth.

Due to some mathematical properties of G.M., it is popularly used in the construction of index numbers.

Merits of G.M.
1. It is based on all the observations.
2. It is rigidly defined.
3. It is capable for further mathematical treatment, such as combined G.M. of two sets.
4. It is not unduly affected by extreme observations.

Demerits of G.M.
1. The serious drawback of G.M. is, it is zero if any of the observations is zero.
2. It is not simple to understand and calculate.
3. It may be imaginary if some observations are negative. Therefore it is calculated only for the data containing positive values.
4. It is not applicable to qualitative data.
5. It cannot be determined graphically.
6. It cannot be computed if frequency distribution includes open end class.
7. It may not be an actual observation in the data.

Result 1 : If $x_1, x_2, ..., x_n$ and $y_1, y_2, ..., y_n$ are the two sets of observations then

$$\text{G.M.}\left(\frac{x}{y}\right) = \frac{\text{G.M. }(x)}{\text{G.M. }(y)}$$

Proof :
$$\text{G.M.}\left(\frac{x}{y}\right) = \left(\frac{x_1}{y_1} \cdot \frac{x_2}{y_2} \cdot ... \cdot \frac{x_n}{y_n}\right)^{1/n}$$

$$= \frac{(x_1 \cdot x_1 \cdot ... x_n)^{1/n}}{(y_1 \cdot y_2 \cdot y_n)^{1/n}} = \frac{\text{G.M. }(x)}{\text{G.M. }(y)}$$

Remark : It is a noteworthy property. In case of arithmetic mean,

$$\text{A.M.}\left(\frac{x}{y}\right) \neq \frac{\text{A.M. }(x)}{\text{A.M. }(y)}$$

Moreover, except geometric mean no other average satisfies the above property.

3.11 Harmonic Mean (H.M.)

The following example, illustrates the need of an average other than A.M. and G.M.

Illustration 4 : Suppose a train while leaving the terminus travels first kilometer distance at a speed of 10 km. per hour. For the next kilometer, the speed is 15 km. per hour. Compute average of the speed in these two kilometers journey.

Solution : Average speed $= \dfrac{\text{Total distance travelled}}{\text{Total time required}}$

Clearly, the total distance travelled is 2 km. Time required to travel first km. distance will be $\dfrac{1}{10}$ hours. Similarly the time required to travel the next kilometer distance will be $\dfrac{1}{15}$ hours. Therefore the total time required is $\dfrac{1}{10} + \dfrac{1}{15}$. Thus average speed $= \dfrac{2}{\dfrac{1}{10} + \dfrac{1}{15}} = 12$. This is neither A.M. nor G.M.. This type of average is called as harmonic mean. Here average speed is 12 km. per hour whereas A.M. is $\dfrac{10 + 15}{2} = 12.5$ km. per hour.

Definition : A harmonic mean (H.M.) is defined as reciprocal of arithmetic mean of reciprocals of observations.

If $x_1, x_2, ..., x_n$ are the observations then harmonic mean H is given by

$$H = \text{Reciprocal of (A.M. of reciprocals)}$$

$$H = \dfrac{1}{\left(\dfrac{1}{x_1} + \dfrac{1}{x_2} + ... + \dfrac{1}{x_n}\right) \div n}$$

$$H = \dfrac{n}{\dfrac{1}{x_1} + \dfrac{1}{x_2} + ... \dfrac{1}{x_n}} = \dfrac{n}{\sum \dfrac{1}{x_i}}$$

If $\{(x_i, f_i), i = 1, 2, ... k\}$ is a frequency distribution then

$$H = \dfrac{N}{\dfrac{f_1}{x_1} + \dfrac{f_2}{x_2} + ... + \dfrac{f_k}{x_k}} = \dfrac{N}{\sum(f_i/x_i)} \qquad \text{where, } N = \sum f_i$$

Example 3.22 : Suppose price of tea of first grade is 10 grams per rupee, whereas that of second grade is 12.5 grams per rupee. If equal quantity of both types of tea are mixed together, determine the price of mixture in gm. per Re.

Solution : Suppose x gm. of tea of each type is purchased. Therefore total tea purchased is 2x gm.

Cost of first grade x gm. tea is $\frac{x}{10}$ ₹

Similarly cost of second grade x gm tea is $\frac{x}{12.5}$ ₹

$\therefore$ Average price (gm per Re) $= \dfrac{\text{Total quantity purchased}}{\text{Total cost}}$

$$= \dfrac{2x}{\dfrac{x}{10} + \dfrac{x}{12.5}} = \dfrac{2}{\dfrac{1}{10} + \dfrac{1}{12.5}}$$

$$= 11.11 \text{ gm per Re.}$$

H.M. using MS-EXCEL :

Illustration 5 : Compute H.M. of 73, 84, 47, 91, 56. Also verify the result using MS-EXCEL command.

Solution : H.M. $= \dfrac{n}{\sum (1/x_i)} = \dfrac{5}{\dfrac{1}{73} + \dfrac{1}{84} + \dfrac{1}{47} + \dfrac{1}{91} + \dfrac{1}{56}} = 66.0274$

To compute H.M. using MS-EXCEL; enter data at A_1 to A_5.

Use Command **= HARMEAN ($A_1 : A_5$)** to get the H.M.

	A	B	C	D	E
1	73				
2	84				
3	47		= HARMEAN (A1 : A5)		
4	91		66.0274		
5	56				

Fig. 3.13

Merits of H.M.:
1. It is based on all observations.
2. It is rigidly defined.
3. It is capable of further mathematical treatment.

Demerits of H.M.:
1. If any of the observation is zero, H.M. cannot be defined.
2. It is not simple to compute and easy to understand as compared to A.M.
3. It is not applicable to qualitative data.
4. It cannot be computed for frequency distribution with open end class.
5. It cannot be computed graphically.
6. It may not be an actual observation in the data.
7. Since H.M. is calculated to find average of rates etc. it is meaningful to compute for positive observations.

Uses of H.M.

Harmonic mean is appropriate to compute average speed, average rates etc. (where the rates are specified in units per Re.)

ORDERING OF A.M., G.M., H.M.

We observe the following type of ordered arrangement of A.M., H.M., G.M. for any data.

A.M. ≥ G.M. ≥ H.M.

Result 2 : If a and b are two positive observations then their A.M. ≥ G.M. ≥ H.M..

Proof : Note that A.M. = $\frac{a+b}{2}$, G.M. = $\sqrt{ab}$ and H.M. = $\frac{2}{\frac{1}{a}+\frac{1}{b}}$

= $\frac{2ab}{a+b}$

It is enough to prove that $\frac{a+b}{2} \geq \sqrt{ab} \geq \frac{2ab}{a+b}$

To prove that $\frac{a+b}{2} \geq \sqrt{ab}$

We need to prove $a + b \geq 2\sqrt{ab}$

$(a+b)^2 \geq 4ab$

$a^2 + b^2 + 2ab \geq 4ab$

$$a^2 + b^2 - 2ab \geq 0$$
$$(a-b)^2 \geq 0$$

which is always true, hence A.M. $\geq$ G.M.

Similarly to prove that G.M. $\geq$ H.M., we need to prove $\sqrt{ab} \geq \dfrac{2ab}{a+b}$

$$a + b \geq 2\sqrt{ab}$$
$$(a+b)^2 \geq 4ab$$
$$a^2 + b^2 + 2ab \geq 4ab$$
$$a^2 + b^2 - 2ab \geq 0$$
$$(a-b)^2 \geq 0$$

which is always true. Hence G.M. $\geq$ H.M.

Therefore A.M. $\geq$ G.M. $\geq$ H.M.

Result 3 : If a, b, c are three positive observations then the corresponding A.M. $\geq$ G.M. $\geq$ H.M. (equality holds when all observations are equal)

Proof : Note that A.M. $= \dfrac{a+b+c}{3} = \bar{x}$, G.M. $= (abc)^{1/3}$

$$\text{H.M.} = \dfrac{3}{\dfrac{1}{a} + \dfrac{1}{b} + \dfrac{1}{c}}$$

To prove that A.M. $\geq$ G.M. $\geq$ H.M., it is sufficient to prove

$$\dfrac{a+b+c}{3} \geq (abc)^{1/3} \geq \dfrac{3}{\dfrac{1}{a} + \dfrac{1}{b} + \dfrac{1}{c}}$$

Suppose the fourth observation is d = A.M.

Part I : Therefore,

$$\dfrac{a+b+c+d}{4} = \dfrac{\left(\dfrac{a+b}{2}\right) + \left(\dfrac{c+d}{2}\right)}{2} \quad \text{Let } x = (a+b)/2$$

$$= \dfrac{x+y}{2} \quad\quad y = (c+d)/2$$

$$\geq \sqrt{xy} \quad \text{(Result 1 gives A.M.} \geq \text{G.M.)}$$

$$= \sqrt{\dfrac{a+b}{2} \times \dfrac{c+d}{2}}$$

$$= \sqrt{\sqrt{ab}\sqrt{cd}}$$

$$\geq (abcd)^{1/4} \quad\quad\quad\quad\quad\quad\quad\quad \ldots (1)$$

Since $\frac{a+b+c}{3} = \bar{x}$ we get $a + b + c = 3\bar{x}$ and $(abc)^{1/3} = G$, hence $abc = G^3$. Therefore inequality (1) becomes

$$\frac{3\bar{x} + \bar{x}}{4} \geq \left(G^3 \bar{x}\right)^{1/4}$$

$\therefore \qquad \bar{x} \geq \left(G^3 \bar{x}\right)^{1/4}$

$\therefore \qquad (\bar{x})^4 \geq G^3 \bar{x}$

$\therefore \qquad (\bar{x})^3 \geq G^3$

$\therefore \qquad \bar{x} \geq G$

Therefore A.M. $\geq$ G.M.

Part II : To prove G.M. $\geq$ H.M., we use the above result.
Note that A.M. $\geq$ G.M. for any data

$\therefore$ A.M. of $\left(\frac{1}{a}, \frac{1}{b}, \frac{1}{c}\right) \geq$ G.M. of $\left(\frac{1}{a}, \frac{1}{b}, \frac{1}{c}\right)$

$$\frac{1/a + 1/b + 1/c}{3} \geq \left(\frac{1}{a} \cdot \frac{1}{b} \cdot \frac{1}{c}\right)^{1/3}$$

Taking reciprocals we get

$$\frac{3}{1/a + 1/b + 1/c} \leq (abc)^{1/3}$$

H.M. $\leq$ G.M.

Therefore A.M. $\geq$ H.M. $\geq$ G.M. Clearly when $a = b = c$, A.M. = H.M. = G.M.

Note :
1. The above result can be generalised and proved for any number of observations.
2. For frequency distribution also the above result holds good.
3. A.M. $\geq$ H.M. can be proved using Cauchy – Schwartz's inequality; as follows :

If $a_1, a_2, ..., a_n$ and $b_1, b_2, ..., b_n$ are real numbers then Cauchy – Schwartz's inequality states that

$$(\Sigma a_i b_i)^2 \leq \left(\Sigma a_i^2\right) \times \left(\Sigma b_i^2\right)$$

Using the above inequality for $a_i = \sqrt{x_i}$ and $b_i = \frac{1}{\sqrt{x_i}}$ we get,

$$\left(\Sigma \frac{1}{\sqrt{x_i}} \times \sqrt{x_i}\right)^2 \leq (\Sigma x_i) \times \left(\Sigma \frac{1}{x_i}\right)$$

$$n^2 \leq (\Sigma x_i) \times \left(\Sigma \frac{1}{x_i}\right)$$

$$\frac{n}{\Sigma \frac{1}{x_i}} \leq \frac{\Sigma x_i}{n}$$

$$\text{H.M.} \leq \text{A.M.}$$

Result : If a, b are two observations then the corresponding A.M., G.M., H.M. satisfy the relation (a > 0, b > 0).

$$\text{G.M.} = \sqrt{\text{A.M.} \times \text{H.M.}}$$

In other words G.M. of a and b is G.M. of their A.M. and H.M.,

Proof : $\text{A. M.} = \frac{a+b}{2}$, $\text{G. M.} = \sqrt{ab}$, $\text{H. M.} = \frac{1}{1/a + 1/b}$

$$\begin{aligned}
\text{A.M.} \times \text{H.M.} &= \frac{a+b}{2} \times \frac{2}{1/a + 1/b} \\
&= \frac{a+b}{2} \times \frac{2ab}{a+b} = ab \\
&= (\text{G.M.})^2
\end{aligned}$$

$\therefore \qquad \text{G.M.} = \sqrt{\text{A.M.} \times \text{H.M.}}$

3.12 Weighted Means

There are two isotopes of chlorine atom. One is with atomic weight 35 and the other is with atomic weight 37. Average atomic weight of chlorine used in practice is 35.5. Surely it is not the usual arithmetic mean of the weights of these two types of atoms. How the average atomic weight 35.5 is determined, may be question of interest. The occurrence of these two types of atoms in the atmosphere is in the ratio 3 : 1. Treating these numbers as frequencies, the arithmetic mean will be as follows :

$$\text{Average atomic weight} = \frac{(35 \times 3) + (37 \times 1)}{3 + 1} = \frac{142}{4} = 35.5$$

The multipliers 3 and 1 to 35 and 37 respectively are called as weights.

The corresponding average is called weighted average.

In the above example we see that the two numbers are not equally important. Therefore usual arithmetic mean (called simple arithmetic mean) is not suitable average. In this situation we need to modify the formula of arithmetic mean suitable to the purpose.

Weight : A device of giving due or proper importance to the observation is called as **weight.**

Weight is a positive number. It is used in place of frequency while computing means. Frequency is not fractional, however, weight can be fractional. Sometimes weights are expressed in terms of percentages, then the total of weights is 100%. We define below weighted averages.

Suppose $x_1, x_2, \ldots, x_n$ are observations with weights $w_1, w_2, \ldots, w_n$ respectively. The weighted arithmetic mean is given by

$$\bar{x}_w = \frac{\sum_{i=1}^{n} w_i x_i}{\sum_{i=1}^{n} w_i} \qquad \ldots (1)$$

The weighted geometric mean is given by

$$G_w = \left(\prod_{i=1}^{n} x_i^{w_i} \right)^{\frac{1}{\sum_{i=1}^{n} w_i}} = \text{Antilog} \left(\frac{\sum_{i=1}^{n} w_i \log x_i}{\sum_{i=1}^{n} w_i} \right) \qquad \ldots (2)$$

The weighted harmonic mean is given by

$$H_w = \frac{\sum_{i=1}^{n} n_i}{\sum_{i=1}^{n} \left(\frac{w_i}{x_i} \right)} \qquad \ldots (3)$$

Remark : If all the weights are same, then the formulae given by (1), (2), and (3) reduce to simple averages or unweighted averages.

Note that the combined arithmetic mean formula for k groups given their sizes and arithmetic means is an example of weighted arithmetic mean.

$$\bar{x}_c = \frac{\sum_{i=1}^{k} n_i \bar{x}_i}{\sum_{i=1}^{k} n_i}$$

Here the weights are the group sizes.

Uses of Weighted Means :

1. In the construction of index numbers weighted means are preferred to simple means.
2. In the computation of death rates, birth rates etc. weighted means are found to be suitable.
3. For obtaining combined means of two or more groups, given the means and sizes of individual groups, weighted means are used.
4. Whenever we need to compute mean of ratios, percentages, rates etc. weighted averages are preferred.

Example 3.23 : The prices of tea of grade I and grade II are ₹ 200 per kg. and ₹ 160 per kg respectively.

If these two grades of tea are mixed together in the ratio 3 : 2, find the average price of mixture.

Solution : Let x be price of tea and w be proportion in the mixture.

x_i	w_i	$x_i w_i$
200	3	600
160	2	320
Total	5	920

$$\bar{x}_w = \frac{\sum w_i x_i}{\sum w_i} = \frac{920}{5} = 184$$

Thus the average price of mixture is ₹ 184 per kg.

Example 3.24 : Suppose $A(x_1, y_1)$ and $B(x_2, y_2)$ are the points on straight line, $C(x, y)$ divides the line segment in the ratio m : n. Show that the co-ordinates of C given by section formula are the weighted averages of co-ordinates of A and B with weights $\frac{1}{m}$ and $\frac{1}{n}$ respectively.

Solution :

$$\begin{array}{ccc} \overset{m}{\longmapsto} & \overset{n}{\longmapsto} & \\ A(x_1, y_1) & C(x, y) & B(x_2, y_2) \end{array}$$

Weighted average of x_1, x_2 with weights $\frac{1}{m}, \frac{1}{n}$ will be

$$x = \frac{\frac{1}{m}x_1 + \frac{1}{n}x_2}{\frac{1}{m} + \frac{1}{n}} = \frac{nx_1 + mx_2}{n + m}$$

Similarly, $\quad y = \frac{ny_1 + my_2}{n + m}$

Thus co-ordinates given by section formula for weighted averages of corresponding co-ordinates.

Example 3.25 : The following table gives the number of employees and their weekly salary in two factories of a particular city.

Factory A		Factory B	
Salary in ₹	No. of employees	Salary in ₹	No. of employees
5500	4	5250	1
2000	20	2125	8
1725	22	1750	10
1675	80	1725	30
1650	30	1700	20
1575	300	1575	100

Compare salaries of two factories by means of

(i) Simple arithmetic mean and

(ii) Weighted arithmetic mean, taking number of employees as weights.

Solution : Let x : salary of employee in factory A, y : salary of employee in factory B and w : number of employees.

	x_i	w_i	$x_i w_i$		y_i	w_i	$y_i w_i$
	5500	4	22000		5250	1	5250
	2000	20	40000		2125	8	17000
	1725	22	37950		1750	10	17500
	1675	80	134000		1725	30	51750
	1650	30	49500		1700	20	34000
	1575	300	472500		1575	100	157500
Total	14125	456	755950	Total	14125	169	283000

Simple arithmetic mean

$$\bar{x} = \frac{\sum x_i}{n} = \frac{14125}{6} = 2354.17 \text{ ₹}$$

$$\bar{y} = \frac{\sum y_i}{n} = \frac{14125}{6} = 2354.17 \text{ ₹}$$

Weighted arithmetic mean

$$\bar{x}_w = \frac{\sum x_i w_i}{\sum w_i} = \frac{755950}{456} = 1657.79 \text{ ₹}$$

$$\bar{y}_w = \frac{\sum y_i w_i}{\sum w_i} = \frac{283000}{169} = 1674.56 \text{ ₹}$$

Comment : Since $\bar{x} = \bar{y}$, we say that on the basis of simple A.M., both companies pay same average salary. However, $\bar{x}_w < \bar{y}_w$, hence we say that on the basis of weighted A.M., company B pays more average salary than that of company A. Weighted A.M. is appropriate in this situation.

3.13 Partition Values

Quartiles, Deciles and Percentiles : Earlier we have seen that median divides the total number of observations into two equal parts. Similarly in order to make four equal parts we use quartiles, for making 10 equals parts we use deciles and for making 100 equal parts we use percentiles, when the observations are ordered.

Definitions : The observations Q_1, Q_2, Q_3 which divide the total number of observations into 4 equal parts are called *quartiles.*

The observations D_1, D_2, ..., D_9 which divide the total number of observations into 10 equals parts are called *deciles.*

The observations P_1, P_2, ..., P_{99} which divide the total number of observations into 100 equal parts are called *percentiles.*

Median, quartiles, deciles and percentiles are called **partition values** in common. The procedure of obtaining median is used to compute other partition values with appropriate changes. To obtain the partition values of series of individual observations, many calculations or formulae are not required. However, to compute partition values of a continuous frequency distribution, corresponding formula of median can be suitably modified. In this case, first of all less than cumulative frequency is determined. Using these cumulative frequencies a class in which partition value lies is decided and then using the formula, partition value is determined.

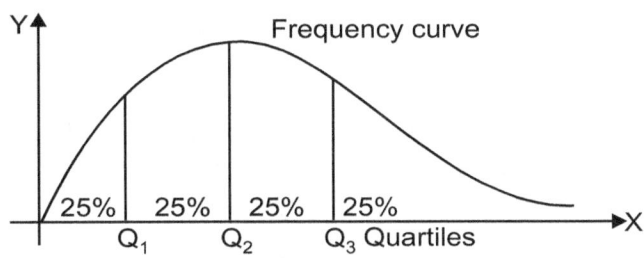

Fig. 3.14

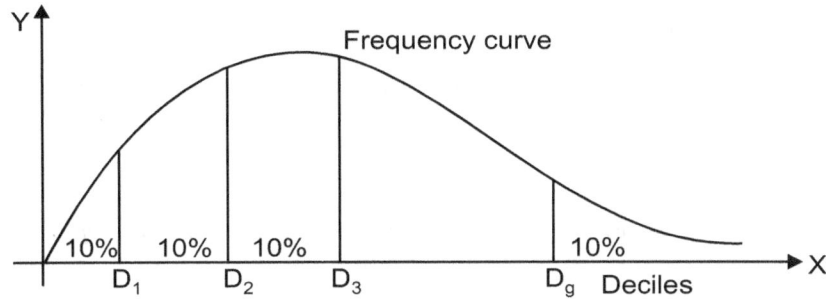

Fig. 3.15

$$\text{First quartile } (Q_1) = l + \left(\frac{\frac{N}{4} - \text{C.F.}}{f} \right) \times h$$

$$\text{Third quartile } (Q_3) = l + \left(\frac{\frac{3N}{4} - \text{C.F.}}{f} \right) \times h$$

$$k^{th} \text{ Decile } (D_k) = l + \left(\frac{\frac{kN}{10} - \text{C.F.}}{f} \right) \times h$$

where, $k = 1, 2, \ldots, 9$

$$k^{th} \text{ Percentile } (P_k) = l + \left(\frac{\frac{kN}{100} - \text{C.F.}}{f} \right) \times h$$

where, $k = 1, 2, \ldots, 99$

Note :
1. Median $= Q_2 = D_5 = P_{50}$
2. $D_1 = P_{10}, D_2 = P_{20}, \ldots, D_9 = P_{90}$
3. $Q_1 = P_{25}, Q_3 = P_{75}$.

4. Partition values are not equispaced. However, area under the curve between any two successive partition values of the same type is same. Therefore area between any two successive quartiles in 25% of the total area under the frequency curve, whereas that of between any two consecutive deciles is 10% between any two consecutive percentiles is 1% of the total area under the frequency curve.

5. Partition values can be obtained graphically using less than cumulative frequency curve.

6. Minimum $< Q_1 < Q_2 < Q_3 <$ Maximum.

Example 3.26 : Compute the quartiles for the following series of observations.

26, 30, 35, 5, 6, 7, 9, 20, 40, 45, 11, 18, 15, 49, 60.

Solution : To find the quartiles first we arrange the observations in increasing (or decreasing) order of their magnitudes. Ordered arrangement will be

5, 6, 7, $\boxed{9}$, 11, 15, 18, $\boxed{20}$, 26, 30, 35, $\boxed{40}$, 45, 49, 60.

First quartile or lower quartile Q_1

$$= \left(\frac{(n+1)}{4}\right)^{th} \text{observation}$$

$$= \left(\frac{15+1}{4} = 4\right)^{th} \text{observation} = 9$$

Second quartile or median Q_2

$$= \left(\frac{n+1}{2}\right)^{th} \text{observation}$$

$$= \left(\frac{15+1}{2} = 8\right)^{th} \text{observation} = 20$$

Third quartile or upper quartile Q_3

$$= \left(\frac{3(n+1)}{4}\right)^{th} \text{observation}$$

$$= \left(\frac{3(15+1)}{4} = 12\right)^{th} \text{observation} = 40.$$

Example 3.27 : Obtain the first quartile, 6th decile and 43rd percentile from the following frequency distribution using formula and also graphically.

Monthly Salary (₹)	1400-1600	1600-1800	1800-2000	2000-2200	2200-2400	2400-2600
Frequency	12	30	55	40	35	28

Solution : Here the classes are continuous, hence they can be used as they are :

Class	Frequency	Less than type cumulative frequency
1400 – 1600	12	12
1600 – 1800	30	42
1800 – 2000	55	97
2000 – 2200	40	137
2200 – 2400	35	172
2400 – 2600	28	200 = N

$Q_1 = \left(\frac{N}{4}\right)^{th}$ observation $= \left(\frac{200}{4} = 50\right)^{th}$ observation.

First quartile $(Q_1) = l + \left(\dfrac{\frac{N}{4} - C.F.}{f}\right) \times h$

Since we have to consider 50th observation, and 42 < 50 < 97, we have to consider the class of less than cumulative frequency in which partition value lies. Therefore,
1800 – 2000 is the first quartile class.

∴ Q_1 lies in (1800 – 2000) class

∴ $Q_1 = 1800 + \dfrac{50 - 42}{55} \times 200$

$= 1800 + 29.0909 = 1829.0909$

Similarly, 6th decile $D_6 = \left(\dfrac{6N}{10}\right)^{th}$ observation

D_6 lies in the (2000 – 2200) class

$$\therefore \quad D_6 = l + \left(\frac{\frac{6N}{10} - \text{C.F.}}{f}\right) \times h$$

$$= 2000 + \left(\frac{120 - 97}{40}\right) \times 200$$

$$= 2000 + \frac{23}{40} \times 200$$

$$= 2000 + 115 = 2115 \ ₹$$

Similarly, 43rd percentile $(P_{43}) = \left(\frac{43N}{100}\right)^{th}$ observation = 86th observation. 86th observation lies in (1800 – 2000) class.

$$\therefore \quad P_{43} = l + \left(\frac{\frac{43N}{100} - \text{C.F.}}{f}\right) \times h$$

$$= 1800 + \frac{86 - 42}{55} \times 200$$

$$= 1800 + \frac{44}{55} \times 200$$

$$= 1800 + 160 = 1960 \ ₹$$

To obtain Q_1, D_6, P_{43} graphically we use less than type cumulative frequency curve.

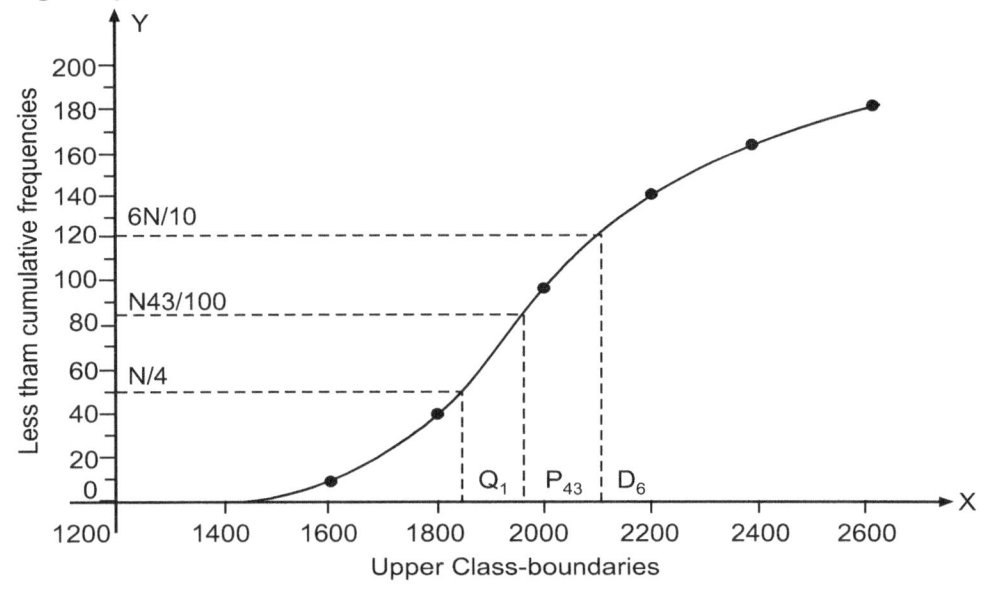

Fig. 3.16

Example 3.28 : Heights in cm of 30 students are given below. Determine the quartiles.

171	145	153	162	145	172	159	168
148	171	158	151	154	159	152	163
154	165	152	161	154	164	153	156
162	151	152	146	147	161		

Solution : The ordered arrangement is,

145, 145, 146, 147, 148, 151, 151, 152, 152, 152, 153, 153, 154, 154, 154, 156, 158, 159, 159, 161, 161, 162, 162, 163, 164, 165, 168, 171, 171, 172.

The first quartile Q_1 = The values of $\left(\frac{n+1}{4}\right)^{th}$ observation (n = 30)

= The value of $7\frac{3}{4}^{th}$ observation

= The value of 7th observation $+\frac{3}{4}$ (8th observation $- 7^{th}$ observation)

$= 151 + \frac{3}{4} (152 - 151)$

$= 151 + 0.75 = 151.75$ cm

Second quartile or median Q_2

$- \left(\frac{(n+1)}{4}\right)^{th}$ observation

$= \left(\frac{30+1}{4} = \frac{31}{4}\right)^{th}$ observation $= \left(15\frac{1}{2}\right)^{th}$ observation

= (15th observation + 16th observation)/2

or 15th observation $+ \frac{1}{2}$ (16th observation $- 15^{th}$ observation)

$= \frac{154 + 156}{2} = 155$ cm

Or median $= 154 + \frac{1}{2} (156 - 154) = 155$ cm)

Third quartile = The value of $\left(\frac{3(n+1)}{4} = \frac{3 \times 31}{4} = 23\frac{1}{4}\right)^{th}$ in the ordered arrangement.

= The value of 23rd observtion

$+ \frac{1}{4}$ (24th observation $- 23^{rd}$ observation)

$= 162 + \frac{1}{4} (163 - 162) = 162.25$ cm

3.14 Box and Whisker Plot

There is one more way of graphical representation of data known as box and whisker plot.

To draw box plot we find the three quartiles and the extreme observations. We illustrate the procedure by the following example.

Illustration 6 : Construct box plot to represent the data given below

26, 30, 35, 5, 6, 7, 9, 20, 40, 45, 11, 18, 15, 49, 60.

Solution : Clearly the ordered arrangement is

5, 6, 7, $\boxed{9}$, 11, 15, 18, $\boxed{20}$, 26, 30, 35, $\boxed{40}$, 45, 49, 60.

Note that the minimum is 5, maximum is 60 and the three quartiles are respectively
9, 20, 40. We take observations from minimum to maximum on line and put the rectangular box to include the first quartile and the third quartile. Thus the length of box is $Q_3 - Q_1$. In this case it is $40 - 9 = 31$. We divide the box in two boxes by putting horizontal line at median.

The box pot is drawn below.

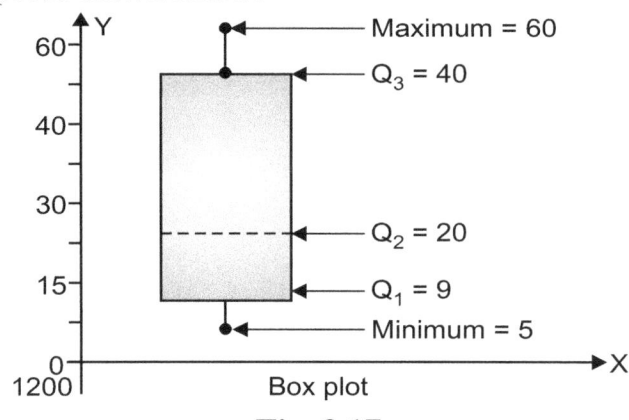

Fig. 3.17

Note : The box plot may be horizonal also.

Uses of box plot :
1. It gives the idea about the spread of data.
2. The box represents the interquartile range $Q_3 - Q_1$ of the data. In other words it gives the range in which middle 50% observations lie.

3. It gives the idea about the symmetry of the data around the median.
4. Median divides the data in two equal parts, box plot gives idea about how the observations are clustered or spread in each part of data.
5. The box plot facilitates the comparison of the aspects (i) central tendency, (ii) spread, (iii) symmetry.

3.15 Choice of an Average

Proper choice of an average is essential otherwise results based on it will not be reliable. The choice depends upon the type of data and purpose of collection of data or survey. We have already discussed the various situations suitable for each average. Once again we summarize the same in short.

In majority of situations A.M. is preferred, G.M. is used to compute average of changes, growth rates, interest rates etc. whereas H.M. is used to compute average speeds, rates specified in terms of units per Re. etc.

In case of quantitative data and frequency distributions having open end class, means cannot be computed, median or mode are suitable.

Sometimes single average is not sufficient as descriptive measure of data, we use two or more averages.

Limitations of Averages :
1. Mean, mode, median are proper representatives for bell-shaped frequency distributions.
2. Averages cannot give the idea about the internal variation among the items.
3. Averages cannot give the idea about the nature of data.

Illustration 7 : The following data gives dividend paid by two companies.

Year	1985	1986	1987	1988	1989
Company A	40%	30%	20%	15%	15%
Company B	10%	20%	20%	35%	35%

A.M. of dividends paid by companies A and B are same and the common value is 24%. However, company B is prospering and A is declining. This nature of data cannot be focused by averages.

Case Study :

Shriram Oxygen Ltd. is a company in a manufacturing of industrial oxygen based in a industrial area of Washi, Navi Mumbai. There are in all about 1000 employees in this company. They are of various grades. For example, there is a managing director, about 10 directors, 30 senior general managers, about 200 managers, 150 officers and rest are workers of different grades. Company's monthly salary budget is about ₹ 30 lac.

Management of this company is of the opinion to increase the productivity by not increasing the man power but through increasing the salary of existing employees.

Existing salary of managing director is approximately ₹ 1 lacs per month, directors get around ₹ 75,000/- per month, general manager gets around ₹ 50,000. Whereas workers salary varies from ₹ 20,000 to ₹ 50,000 as per their grades.

Company has a revised budget of ₹ 40 lacs per month. Company would like to know about what is the average salary per month. Whether to find mean would be appropriate or should median be used. What would be average revised salary per month ?

Points to Remember

1. Arithmetic mean $(\bar{X}) = \dfrac{\Sigma x}{n}$ for ungrouped data

   $= \dfrac{\Sigma fx}{\Sigma f}$ for frequency distribution.

2. Median $= l + \left(\dfrac{\frac{N}{2} - Cf}{f}\right) \times h$.

3. Mode $= l + \left(\dfrac{f_m - f_1}{2f_m - f_1 - f_2}\right) \times h$

4. If $y = ax + b$ then $\bar{y} = a\bar{x} + b$, $y = \dfrac{x - c}{d}$ then $\bar{y} = \dfrac{\bar{x} - c}{d}$

5. Combined arithmetic mean $= \dfrac{n_1 \bar{x} + n_2 \bar{y}}{n_1 + n_2}$

6. Median can be obtained graphically using ogive curves.
7. Mode can be obtained graphically using histogram.
8. Arithmetic mean is the best average.
9. Arithmetic mean cannot be determined by graph.

EXERCISE 3 (A)

A. Theory Questions :

1. What do you mean by central tendency ? Explain the purpose of measures of central tendency. Describe the various measures of central tendency.
2. State requisites of a good measure of central tendency.
3. Define arithmetic mean, median, mode and state the formula for each, in case of individual observations and frequency distributions.
4. Explain the concept of $\alpha\%$ trimmed mean. State its necessity.
5. Discuss merits and demerits of arithmetic mean, median, mode, geometric mean and harmonic mean.
6. Explain graphical method of determination of median, mode and partition values.
7. Define geometric mean and harmonic mean and state the formula for each, in case of individual observations and frequency distributions.
8. Define quartiles, deciles, and percentiles.
9. Describe what is box plot. State its uses.
10. Define weighted means. How weighted means are superior to simple means ?
11. State and prove the properties of A.M.
12. Let $x_1, x_2, ..., x_n$ be the set of observations, show that
    $\min \{x_1, x_2, ..., x_n\} \leq$ A.M. $\leq \max \{x_1, x_2, ..., x_n\}$.
    When will either of the equalities be satisfied ?
13. Show that the algebraic sum of deviations of all observations from A.M. is equal to zero.
14. Show that the sum of squares of deviations of all observations taken from arithmetic mean is minimum.
15. Derive formula for combined A.M. of k groups given their sizes and arithmetic means.
16. Give two situations where the following measures of central tendency are proper : (a) A.M. (b) G.M. (c) H.M. (d) median (e) mode (f) weighted means.
17. If a, b, c are three positive observations then show that
    (i) $\dfrac{a+b}{2} \geq \sqrt{ab} \geq \dfrac{2ab}{a+b}$
    (ii) $\dfrac{a+b+c}{3} \geq (abc)^{1/3} \geq \dfrac{3}{1/a + 1/b + 1/c}$.

18. Discuss the effect of change of origin and scale an arithmetic mean.
19. Find the formula for combined geometrical mean of two groups with size n_1, n_2 and geometric means G_1, G_2.

B. Problems :

1. A variable takes values 1, 4, 9, ..., n^2. Find its A.M.
2. A variable takes values 1, 4, 9, ..., n^2 with frequencies 1, 2, 3, ..., n respectively. Find its A.M.
3. A variable takes values 7, 10, 13, ... (50 terms), find its A.M. and median.
4. A variable takes values a, ar, ar^2, ..., ar^{n-1}, find its A.M. and G.M.
5. For 20 observations on Y, $\sum y^2 = 500$. Show that the mean of the data cannot exceed 5.
6. Suppose $\{(x_i, f_i) \ i = 1, 2, ..., k\}$ is frequency distribution. Show that A.M. does not change if each frequency is doubled.
7. Find A.M. of the following frequency distribution.

x	1	2	3	4
f	a	2a	3a	4a

'a' being positive integer.

8. If $y = 3x + 2$, then show that $\bar{y} = 3\bar{x} + 2$.
9. A variable x takes values 0, 1, 2, ..., n with frequencies n_{C_0}, n_{C_1}, n_{C_2}, ..., n_{C_n}. Find the A.M. of x.
10. Arithmetic mean of the following frequency distribution is 5, find the value of x.

Variable	2	4	6	8
Frequency	x – 1	x + 1	x + 1	2x – 5

11. Suppose a, b, c are three positive numbers such that
    a : b : : (a + b) : (b + c). Show that b is G.M. of a and c.

C. Numerical Problems :

1. Find the geometric mean of 5, 10, 17, 0, 256.
2. Monthly consumption of electricity in units of a certain family in a year is given below. Find arithmetic Mean and Mode for the given data :
   210, 207, 315, 250, 240, 232, 216, 208, 209, 215, 300, 290.

3. Find the arithmetic mean, median and mode of the following observations :
   61, 62, 63, 62, 63, 62, 64, 64, 60, 65. Also find 10% trimmed mean.

4. Calculate arithmetic mean and median weight of the group of students with weights (in kg) given below :
   51, 52, 53, 51, 53, 54, 54, 50, 55, 53. Also find 20% trimmed mean.

5. Represent the following data using box plot technique
   15, 11, 11, 28, 22, 14, 13, 18, 30, 12, 25
   Also obtain 10% trimmed mean.

6. Draw the box plot for the following data
   30, 26, 24, 23, 20, 13, 13, 9, 9, 6, 6, 5, 5, 4, 3, 3, 3, 3, 2, 2, 2, 1, 1.
   Also obtain 20% trimmed mean.

7. Find the mean, mode and median of the following data.

X	5	6	7	8	9	10	11	12
Frequency	8	10	9	6	5	4	4	1

8. Find the mean, median and mode of the following frequency distribution.

Marks	0 - 20	20 - 40	40 - 60	60 - 80	80 - 100
No. of frequency	5	12	32	40	11

Obtain mode and median by graph.

9. Find arithmetic mean, mode and median of following frequency distribution.

Marks	0 - 20	20 - 40	40 - 60	60 - 80	80 - 100
No. of students	4	8	9	20	9

Draw appropriate graphs and find median, mode.

10. Compute mode and median of the following frequency distribution.

Weight in kg.	Below 40	40 - 50	50 - 60	60 - 70	Above 70
No. of students	3	5	12	20	10

11. The monthly profit in rupees of 100 shops is distributed as follows :

Profit (in ₹) per shop	Below 100	100 - 200	200 - 300	300 - 400	400 - 500	Above 500
No. of shops	12	18	27	20	17	6

(i) Calculate the median and mode for above data. (ii) Find median, mode graphically.

12. For the following frequency distribution find the median, seventh decile and eighty-fifth percentile.

Class	0-100	100-200	200-300	300-400	400-500	500-600	600-700
Frequency	9	15	18	21	18	14	5

13. Following is a frequency distribution of marks scored by 250 students.

Marks	0-10	10-20	20-30	30-40	40-50	50-60	60-70	70-80	80-90	90-100
No. of students	5	12	16	26	70	85	16	8	8	4

(i) Find the marks within which middle 60% students lie. (ii) Find median, third quartile, sixty fifth percentile. (iii) Draw the box plot.

14. Calculate median and mode wage from the following data : (i) by using the formula (ii) by graphical method. Also find 3rd decile and 85th percentile.

Wages in ₹	No. of workers
above 130	520
above 140	470
above 150	399
above 160	210
above 170	105
above 180	45
above 190	7

15. Find the quartiles and mode of the following data by computational method and graphical method :

No. of days absent	No. of students
less than 5	29
less than 10	224
less than 15	465
less than 20	582
less than 25	634
less than 30	644
less than 35	650
less than 40	653
less than 45	655

16. Obtain the mean, median and mode from following data. Also find the quartiles, 9th decile 37th percentile.

Monthly Rent (in ₹)	No. of families
221 - 240	6
241 - 260	9
261 - 280	11
281 - 300	14
301 - 320	20
321 - 340	15
341 - 360	10
361 - 380	8
381 - 400	7

17. A study of a certain operation shows the following distribution for 180 workers. Calculate the (i) median, (ii) 6th decile, (iii) 73rd percentile.

Class interval (in seconds)	10 - 30	30 - 50	50 - 70	70 - 90	90 - 110
Frequency	10	40	80	35	15

Also find median, 6th decile and 73rd percentile graphically.

D. Missing Values :

18. If mean of the following frequency distribution is 15.82 find the missing value of *.

X	10	12	13	17	*	25	18	30
Frequency	25	17	13	15	14	8	6	2

19. Find the missing frequency of the following frequency distribution if the arithmetic mean is 26.90.

Class	10 - 15	15 - 20	20 - 25	25 - 30	30 - 35	35 - 40	40 - 45
Frequency	5	6	8	*	7	5	4

20. You are given the following complete frequency distribution. It is known that the total frequency is 100 and the median is 44. Find the missing frequencies. Also compute the mean after finding missing frequencies.

Class	Frequency	Class	Frequency
10-20	5	50-60	–
20-30	12	60-70	10
30-40	–	70-80	4
40-50	20		

21. Mean daily salary of 50 employees in a firm is ₹ 188.40. Frequency distribution of salaries of these employees in which some frequencies are missing is given below :

Salary	140-160	160-180	180-200	200-220	220-240
Frequency	6	–	17	–	5

Find the missing frequencies.

22. The daily expenditure of 100 families is given below :

Expenditure	20-29	30-39	40-49	50-59	60-69
No. of families	14	–	27	–	15

If the mode of the distribution is 43.5, find the missing frequencies.

23. Arithmetic mean of marks of 30 candidates was 40. Later on it was found that a score of 47 was misread as 74. Find the correct arithmetic mean.

24. The arithmetic mean of weight of 98 students as calculated from a frequency distribution is 50 kg. It was later found that the frequency of the class 30 – 40 was wrongly taken as 8 instead of 10. Calculate the correct arithmetic mean.

E. Combined Mean :

25. A salesman has given a target to complete average daily sales of ₹ 5000. In a particular week average of first 6 days is ₹ 4990. What should be his sales on seventh day in order to make up the target ?

26. Find the combined mean of the following data :

   Group I $\bar{x}_1 = 2100$ $n_1 = 100$

   Group II $\bar{x}_2 = 1500$ $n_2 = 200$

27. Average monthly sale of certain departmental store for first 11 months was ₹ 56000. Due to repairs and renewal of shop in the last month the sales dropped down to ₹ 8000. Find the average monthly sales in the year.

28. Find the combined arithmetic mean and salary given that :

Group	Male	Female
No. of employees	100	50
Arithmetic mean of salary	6000 ₹	5100 ₹

29. Given   **Group 1**   **Group 2**

    $n_1 = 100$ $n_2 = 100$

    $\sum x = 600$ $\sum y = 800$

    Find $\bar{x}$, $\bar{y}$ and combined mean of the two groups.

30. Obtain the combined mean profit per salesman from the following data

	Mean profit per salesman	No. of salesman
Shop 1	2000	5
Shop 2	3000	12
Shop 3	5000	3

31. The weekly salary paid to all employees in a certain company was ₹ 600. The arithmetic mean of weekly salary paid to the male and female employees were ₹ 620 and ₹ 520 respectively. Obtain the percentage of male and female employees in the company.

32. The mean monthly salary of 77 workers in a certain factory is ₹ 1560. The mean salary of 32 of them is ₹ 1500 and that of the next 25 of the remaining is ₹ 1640. What is the mean salary of remaining 20 workers ?

F. Geometric Mean, Harmonic Mean, Weighted Means :

33. Compute weighted A.M. and weighted G.M. of index numbers from the following table :

Group	A	B	C	D	E
Index number	300	200	250	150	250
Weight	62	4	6	12	16

34. A train travels the first half distance of its journey with a speed of 25 km. per hour; the next one-fourth distance at a speed of 60 km. per hour, the remaining one-fourth distance at a speed of 40 km. per hour. Find the average speed of the train during the journey.

35. Suppose the typist X types 8 pages per hour, whereas typists Y and Z can type 10 pages and 15 pages per hour respectively. What is the mean time required to type per page ?

36. Scores of students alongwith weights are given below :

Test	Written	Viva-voce	Group discussion
Scores out of 100	75	60	65
Weights	2	1	2

Find the weighted arithmetic mean of scores.

37. Sales of a company increased by 5% in the first year, 7% in the second year and 10% in the third year. Find average increase in percentage of sales using appropriate average.

38. A cost of machine is depreciated by 15%, 20%, and 30% in the first year, second year and third year respectively. Find the average percentage of depreciation using appropriate average.

39. Find the weighted arithmetic mean of first n natural numbers with the same numbers as weights.

40. A cyclist pedals from his house to his college at a speed of 10 km/h and back from college to his house at 15 km/h. Find the average speed of his journey.

41. The arithmetic mean and geometric mean of two items as 5 and 2.5 respectively. Find the harmonic mean.

42. The values 3, 5 and 7 are assigned weights $(K-4)$, $(K-2)$ and $(K+1)$ respectively. If we weighted arithmetic mean is 6 and K.

G. Miscellaneous Problems and Objective Problems :

43. For a moderately asymmetrical frequency distribution, the values of arithmetic mean and median are 144 and 156 respectively. Estimate the modal value.

44. Arithmetic mean of five items is 20, if the smallest item is 10 and the largest item is greater than the smallest by 14. Find the arithmetic mean of three items ignoring the largest and the smallest.

45. Five lots of items were inspected. The results are as follows :

Lot No.	1	2	3	4	5
No. of items	100	200	100	300	150
Proportion of defectives	0.05	0.04	0.02	0.01	0.04

Using suitable average, find average of proportion of defectives.

46. Obtain the average bonus per employee for the following frequency distribution.

Salary Group (₹)	1000-2000	2000-4000	4000-6000	above 6000
Bonus (₹)	300	400	450	500
Frequency	5	12	5	3

47. In a batch of 15 students 5 students failed in a test. The marks of 10 students who passed were 9, 6, 7, 8, 8, 9, 6, 5, 4, 7. What is the median of marks of all the 15 students ?

48. In a batch of 10 students, 3 failed in certain examination. The marks obtained by 7 successful candidates were 77, 87, 40, 52, 82, 70, 50. Find median of marks obtained by all 10 students.

49. The mean of 5 numbers is 27. If one of them is excluded then their mean will be 25. What is the excluded number ?

50. If $n = 10$ and $\dfrac{\Sigma(x-5)}{5} = 18$, find the mean.

51. A set of 10 values has arithmetic mean 20. Find the arithmetic mean if, (i) each value is doubled and then increased by 2, (ii) each value is increased by 5 and then doubled, (iii) each value is decreased by 5.

52. In a set of 50 items arranged in ascending order of magnitude the values of 24th, 25th and 26th items are 40, 42 and 45 respectively. Find the median. Also find the median if the number of observations was 51.

53. Arithmetic mean of a group is 20. If each observation is increased by 5, find the mean of new observations.

54. State the imperical relation between mean, mode and median.

55. If $n = 10$, $\Sigma(x-6) = 30$, find $\bar{x}$.

56. State the mode of following frequency distribution (with calculations) :

Class	0-10	10-20	20-30	30-40	40-50
Frequency	7	10	22	10	8

57. If each frequency is doubled, then what will happen to the arithmetic mean.

58. If frequency distribution has open end class, which average will be possible to compute.

59. Individual observations are not known but the total of 10 observations is known. Suggest the average which can be computed.
60. Suggest the average which you can compute if all the observations except the largest and smallest are known.

ANSWERS 3 (A)

B.
1. $(n+1)(2n+1)/6$,
2. $n(n+1)/2$,
3. A.M. = Median = 80.5
4. A.M. $= \dfrac{a(r^n - 1)}{n(r-1)}$,   G.M. $= a\, r^{(n-1)/2}$,
5. 3
6. $\dfrac{n}{2}$
7. 4

C.
1. 0
2. $\bar{X} = 241$, Median = 224
3. $\bar{X} = 62.6$, median = 62.5, mode = 28.59, trimmed mean = 62.625
4. $\bar{X} = 52.6$, median = 53, trimmed mean = 52.6667
5. $Q_1 = 12$, $Q_2 = 15$, $Q_3 = 25$, trimmed mean = 17.56
6. $Q_1 = 3$, $Q_2 = 5$, $Q_3 = 13$, trimmed mean = 6.3077
7. Mean = 7.4894, Mode = 6, median = 7.
8. Mean = 58, Median = 60.2857, Mode = 64.32
9. Mean = 58.8, Median = 64, Mode = 65,
10. Mean = 60.8, Mode = 64.44, Median = 62.5,
11. 256.25
12. Median = 338.0952, $D_7 = 438.8888$, $P_{85} = 566.6667$.
13. (i) $D_2 = 36.5385$, $D_8 = 58.3529$, (ii) Median = 49.4286
    $Q_3 = 56.8824$, $P_{65} = 53.9412$.
14. Median = 157.3545, Mode = 155.8416, $D_3 = 151.8519$, $P_{85} = 174.5$

15. Median = 12.1473, Mode = 11.35, Q_1 = 8.4551, Q_3 = 16.1218
16. Mean = Median = 310.5, Mode = 311.409, Q_1 = 278.6818, Q_3 = 340.5, P_{37} = 296.2143, D_9 = 373.
17. Median = 60,
18. 24
19. 15
20. Missing frequencies 25, 24, Mean = 44.2
21. 12, 20
22. 23, 21
23. 39.5
24. 49.7
25. ₹ 5600
26. 1700
27. 52,000
28. ₹ 5700
29. $\bar{X}$ = 6, $\bar{Y}$ = 8, Combined mean = 7.
30. 3050
31. Male 80%, Female 20%
32. 1556
33. AM = 267, G.M. = 260.9
34. 32.8767 kmph
35. 5.8333 minutes
36. 68
37. 7.3137%
38. 21.9207%
39. $(2n + 1)/3$
40. 12 kmph
41. 1.25
42. 5
43. 180
44. 22
45. 0.02824
46. 402
47. 6
48. 51

49. 35
50. 14
51. (i) 42, (ii) 50, (iii) 15, (iv) 23
52. 43.5, 45
53. 25   55. 9
56. 25   57. Will not change
58. Mode, Median   59. Mean
60. Median

Objective Types Questions

I. Multiple Choice Questions

- **Choose the correct alternative :**

1. Which one of the following is not a measure of central tendency ?
   - (a) mean deviation
   - (b) mean
   - (c) median
   - (d) mode

2. When calculating the average rate of profit made by a company, the correct mean to use is the :
   - (a) arithmetic mean
   - (b) weighted mean
   - (c) geometric mean
   - (d) either (a) or (c)

3. What is the major assumption we make while computing a mean from grouped data ?
   - (a) all values are discrete
   - (b) every value in a class is equal to the midpoint
   - (c) no value occurs more than once
   - (d) each class contains exactly the same number of values

4. Which of the following is the first step in calculating the median of a data set ?
   - (a) average the middle two values of the data set
   - (b) array the data in order
   - (c) determine the relative weights of the data values in terms of importance
   - (d) not necessary to arrange

5. Which of the following is NOT correct ?

(a) extreme values affect the median less strongly than they do affect the mean.
(b) a median can be calculated for qualitative descriptions.
(c) the median can be calculated for every set of data, even for all sets containing open ended classes.
(d) the median is adaptable for further mathematical manipulations.

6. Which one of the following is true for $\bar{x} = a + \dfrac{\Sigma(x-a)}{n}$ when 'a' is
   (a) positive or negative
   (b) less than mean
   (c) greater than mean
   (d) any number

7. The formula for geometric mean G is :
   (a) $\dfrac{1}{n} \Sigma \log x_i$
   (b) $\log\left[\dfrac{1}{n} \Sigma x_i\right]$
   (c) $\text{antilog}\left[\dfrac{1}{n} \Sigma \log x_i\right]$
   (d) $\text{antilog}\left[\dfrac{1}{n} \log \Sigma x_i\right]$

8. If $x_1, x_2, \ldots x_n$ is a set of n observations, then harmonic mean of X is the reciprocal of :
   (a) the given observations and their arithmetic mean
   (b) the arithmetic mean of the given observations
   (c) the arithmetic mean of the reciprocals of the given observations
   (d) reciprocal of mean

9. For n-observations, the harmonic mean is given by :
   (a) $\dfrac{\Sigma 1/x}{n}$
   (b) $\dfrac{n}{\Sigma 1/x}$
   (c) $\dfrac{1/\Sigma x}{n}$
   (d) $\dfrac{\Sigma 1/x}{1/n}$

10. With usual notation the formula of median for grouped data is :
    (a) $l_1 + \dfrac{N/c.f}{f} \times h$
    (b) $l_2 + \dfrac{[N/c.f-1]}{f} \times h$
    (c) $l_1 + \dfrac{[N/2 - c.f]}{f} \times h$
    (d) none of the above

11. Median for arranged data is :
    (a) mean of first and last value
    (b) most frequent value
    (c) least frequent value
    (d) middle most value

12. Which one of the following is false ?

(a) Q_2 = Median
(b) Q_2 = 50th percentile
(c) Q_2 = 25th percentile
(d) Q_2 = 5th decile

13. Which of the following measures of central tendency are not affected by the extreme values ?
    (a) Geometric mean and harmonic mean
    (b) Arithmetic mean and median
    (c) Median and mode
    (d) Arithmetic mean and mode

14. If $x_1, x_2, \ldots x_n$ are n observations with mean $\bar{x}$ then $\sum (x_i - \bar{x})$ is :
    (a) necessarily zero
    (b) necessarily non-negative
    (c) may be non-negative
    (d) may be zero

15. The arithmetic mean of first n natural numbers is :
    (a) n (n + 1) /2
    (b) $(n^2 + 1)/2$
    (c) $n(n^2 + 1)/2$
    (d) $(n^2 + n)/2n$

16. The value of 20th percentile is equal to :
    (a) second quartile
    (b) median
    (c) second decile
    (d) fourth decile

17. The value of lower quartile is equal to :
    (a) P_{25}
    (b) D_3
    (c) median
    (d) Q_3

18. The value of P_{50} :
    (a) can not be equal to mode
    (b) can not be equal to Q_1
    (c) is equal to fifth decile
    (d) is equal to Q_3

19. Mode is :
    (a) middle most value
    (b) the minimum value
    (c) most frequent value
    (d) the maximum value

20. Which one of the following is least affected by extreme values ?

(a) arithmetic mean (b) geometric mean
(c) harmonic mean (d) median

21. Median can be
    (a) calculated when measurements are on the nominal scale
    (b) affected by number and values of the observations
    (c) affected by extreme values
    (d) calculated for open end classes

22. Which one of the following cannot be found when terminal classes are open end ?
    (a) mode (b) median
    (c) arithmetic mean (d) any one of the above

23. Which one of the following is true ? When a single extreme observation in the given data is missing, one can use :
    (a) mode and arithmetic mean
    (b) median and arithmetic mean
    (c) median
    (d) any measure

24. Which measure of central tendency can be located by a mere inspection for series of individual observations ?
    (a) mode and arithmetic mean
    (b) median and arithmetic mean
    (c) median and mode
    (d) mode only

25. Mode for data with frequencies vary haphazardly
    (a) can be located by a formula
    (b) can be found by grouping class interval
    (c) can be found by graphical method
    (d) cannot be found

26. Mean > Median > Mode valid for
    (a) symmetrical distribution
    (b) moderate negatively skewed distribution
    (c) moderate positively skewed distribution
    (d) both (a) and (b)

27. Given mean ($\bar{x}$), median (Me), the Mode (Mo) can be found by formula
   ($\bar{x}$ − Mo) = 3 ($\bar{x}$ − Me)
   (a) in symmetrical distribution
   (b) in widely skewed distribution
   (c) in moderately skewed distribution
   (d) in all cases

28. Which one of the relation is true ?
   (a) Mean = $\frac{1}{2}$ (Median − Mode)
   (b) Mean − 3(Mean − Median) = 2 Mode
   (c) Median = Mode + 2/3 (Mode − $\bar{x}$)
   (d) Mode = 2 Me − 3 $\bar{x}$

29. Usually one can find arithimetic mean median and mode, when data are collected repectively on the scale :
   (a) nominal, ratio or interval
   (b) interval, ordinal or nominal
   (c) ratio, nominal or interval
   (d) nominal, ratio or ordinal

30. Which one of the following is true for first n natural numbers ?
   (a) $\frac{1}{n} \sum \frac{1}{x} \neq \frac{n}{\sum x}$
   (b) $\frac{1}{n} \sum \frac{1}{x} \neq \frac{n}{\sum x}$
   (c) $\frac{1}{n} \sum \frac{1}{x} = \frac{n}{\sum n}$
   (d) $\frac{1}{n} \sum \frac{1}{x} < \frac{n}{\sum x}$

31. If $\bar{X}s$ = simple arithmetic mean and $\bar{X}w$ = weighted mean of n observations then which one of the following statement about the weighted arithmetic mean is false ?
   (a) $\bar{X}s = \bar{X}w$ if weight are the same
   (b) $\bar{X}w$ is used to calculate standardised birth rate
   (c) $\bar{X}w$ is used to compute index numbers
   (d) $\bar{X}s < \bar{X}w$ if smaller weights are assigned to the greater values and greater weights are assigned to the smaller values

32. Which one of the following statement is false ?
   (a) Average changes if scale is changed.
   (b) Average changes if origin is changed.

(c) In a negatively skewed distribution, the value of mode is greater than the arithmetic mean

(d) geometric mean is the square root of the product of all the observations

33. Which one of the following statement is false for harmonic mean ?

    (a) It is quite useful for the analysis of data pertaining to rates etc.
    (b) It is not computed when even a single observation in a given data is zero.
    (c) In a negatively skewed distribution, the value of mode is greater than the arithmetic mean
    (d) It gives small items more importance

34. If 10 is subtracted from each observation then mean of the set of n observations is :

    (a) not affected　　　　　　　(b) zero
    (c) increased by 10　　　　　(d) decreased by 10

35. If we add 15 in each observation of a set, then arithmetic mean is :

    (a) 15 times the original data
    (b) not affected
    (c) increased by 15
    (d) decreased by 15

36. The geometric mean of three numbers 7, 21 and 63 is equal to :

    (a) 30.3　　　　　　　　　　(b) $\sqrt{91}$
    (c) $\sqrt{9251}$　　　　　　　(d) 21

37. If X_1 and X_2 are two observations then geometric mean is calculated only if :

    (a) X_1 and X_2 are equal to zero
    (b) X_1 and X_2 are negative
    (c) X_1 and X_2 are positive
    (d) X_1 is negative and X_2 is positive

38. If each of the observation in a series is divided by 5 then the mean of new data set is

    (a) unchanged　　　　　　　(b) half of the old mean
    (c) decreased by 5
    (d) the old mean is five times the new mean

39. If each value in a data set of observations is multiplied by 20, the median of the new series will be :
    (a) increased by 20
    (b) 1/20th of the old median
    (c) twenty times the old mean
    (d) unchanged

II. State Whether the following statement are True or False

1. Measures of central tendency in a data set refer to the value around which the observations are scattered.
2. If we arrange the observations in a data set from highest to lowest, the data point lying in the middle is the median of the data set.
3. With ungrouped data, the mode is most frequently used as the measure of central tendency.
4. The value most often repeated in a data set is called the arithmetic mean.
5. When working with grouped data, we may compute an approximate mean by assuming that each value in a given class is equal to its mid-point.
6. Extreme values in a data set have a strong effect on the median.
7. The aritthmetic mean of a variable with values which are all equal, is same as their common value.
8. The sum of the deviations of given values of a variable from its measure of central tendency is necessarily zero.
9. Unlike geometric mean, harmonic mean can not be computed when one or more observations in data are zero.
10. If a non-negative variable changes over time exponentially, then the appropriate average is harmonic mean.
11. Mode is the only measure of central tendency that can be obtained without calculation.
12. If we arrange 50 observations in ascending order than the median will be the value of the 25th observation in the series.
13. We can compute a mean for any data set.
14. The geometric mean of the ratio of x and y is the ratio of their geometric means.
15. The value of every observation in the data set is taken into account when we calculate its median.

16. A mean calculated from grouped data always gives a good estimate of the true value, although it is seldom exact.
17. The geometric mean of a group of numbers is less than the arithmetic mean in all cases, except in the special case in which numbers are all the same.
18. Mean, median and mode never be same.
19. Simple arithmetic mean is less than the weighted arithmetic mean, if greater weights are attached to the smaller values and smaller weights are attached to the greater values.
20. In order to compute median if class intervals are unequal, the frequencies are ought to be adjusted to make the class intervals equal before proceeding with standard formulae.
21. The harmonic mean of n observations is the reciprocal of the arithmetic mean of the reciprocals of the numbers.
22. Harmonic mean becomes zero when one of the item is zero.
23. The arithmetic mean is an average which is such that if each value of the variable is replaced by it, the total remains the same.
24. Sachin travels by car for 4 days. He drove 10 hours each day. He drove first day at the rate of 45 km per hour, second day at the rate of 40 km per hour, third day at the rate of 38 km per hour, and fourth day at the rate of 37 km per hour then average speed of Sachin is 40 km per hour.
25. The mean will be the same whether the values of the variate are expressed in inches or in cms.
26. Mean cannot be worked out if the class intervals are unequal.
27. Harmonic mean for 2, 7, 0, 12, 15 is positive.
28. Mode cannot be calculated if the distribution does not have frequency.
29. Sachin travels 8 km at 4 km per hour, 6 km at 3 km per hour and 4 km at 2 km per hour, the average rate per hour at which sachin travelled is 6.
30. The $\sum (x_i - \bar{x})^2 \leq \sum (\bar{x} - a)^2$ always holds.
31. Arithmetic mean is dependent on change of origin and change of scale.

32. Sometimes arithmetic mean may be determined graphically.
33. Geometric mean is prefered for the situations like a average population growth, average rate of returns on share, average bank interest rates etc.
34. The serious drawback of geometric mean is, it is not equal to zero, if any of the observation is zero.
35. Geometric mean not applicable to qualitative type data.
36. Geometric mean cannot be computed if frequency distribution includes open end class and also cannot be determined graphically.
37. Since G.M. $\left[\dfrac{x}{y}\right] = \dfrac{G.M.(x)}{G.M.(y)}$ then A.M. $\left[\dfrac{x}{y}\right] = \dfrac{A.M.(x)}{A.M.(y)}$
38. Harmonic mean can not be computed if frequency distribution includes open end class and also can not be determined graphically.
39. Arithmetic mean, geometric mean and also harmonic mean may not be an actual observation in the data.
40. G.M. of x and y is G.M. of their A.M. and H.M.
41. Median can be computed for qualitative data.
42. Median is not capable of further mathematical treatment.
43. If the maximum frequency is repeated, to find the mode uniquely a method of grouping is adopted and a modal class is determined.
44. Mode can be determined if modal class is at the extreme.
45. Modal, premodal and postmodal classes should be of the same width.
46. Mode is applicable for qualitative and quantitative data.
47. Wherever we need to compute mean of ratios, percentage rates etc. weighted averages are preferred.
48. In the construction of Index numbers, death rates birth rates weighted means are found to be suitable.
49. Average cannot give the idea about the nature of data.
50. If n = 10 and $\dfrac{\Sigma(x-5)}{5} = 18$ then value of mean will be 12.

Answers : Objective Type Questions

I. Multiple Choice Questions :

(1) a   (2) a   (3) a   (4) d   (5) d
(6) a   (7) b   (8) c   (9) b   (10) c
(11) a   (12) d   (13) a   (14) a   (15) a
(16) b   (17) a   (18) c   (19) d   (20) c
(21) d   (22) d   (23) b   (24) d   (25) d
(26) d   (27) d   (28) d   (29) d   (30) a
(31) d   (32) a   (33) c   (34) c   (35) b
(36) b   (37) a   (38) c   (39) c

II. True or False :

1. False : clustered
2. True
3. False
4. False
5. True
6. False
7. True
8. False : it is true when the measures is arithmetic mean
9. False : both can not be computed
10. False : geometric mean
11. False : in some cases median also
12. False
13. False
14. True
15. False
16. True
17. True
18. False : maybe
19. False : true if greater weights are attached to greater values
20. False : frequency need not be adjusted
21. True
22. False : infinity
23. True
24. True
25. True
26. False
27. False
28. False
29. False : 3
30. True
31. True
32. False : never

33.	True	34.	False : zero	35.	True
36.	True	37.	False	38.	True
39.	True	40.	True	41.	True
42.	True	43.	True	44.	False : never
45.	True	46.	True	47.	True
48.	True	49.	True	50.	False : 14

Chapter 4...
Measures of Dispersion

Prof. Ranald A. Fisher (1890-1962) : Born in London, Prof. Fisher was a genius who single handedly created the foundations for modern statistics. By collecting data over many years at Rothamsted Experimental Station, near London, he published a series of reports titled 'Studies in Crop variation'. This led to the theory of Design of Experiments. He pioneered the basic principles of DOE and the technique of Analysis of Variance. He developed distribution theory of small and large samples. His book 'Statistical Methods for Research Workers' went through many editions and translations. It is the standard reference book for scientists in many disciplines.

Prof. Ranald A. Fisher

Prof. Fisher developed the method of maximum likelihood, concepts of sufficiency, Fisher information, ancillary statistic, Fisher's discriminant analysis. These contributions made him a major figure in 20th century statistics and he is rightly called as 'The father of Modern Statistics'. He was also a well known geneticist.

Contents ...

4.1   Introduction

4.2   Measures of Dispersion

4.3   Range and Coefficient of Range

4.4   Quartile Deviation or Semi-interquartile Range

4.5   Mean Deviation and Coefficient of Mean Deviation

4.6   Mean Square Deviation

4.7   Variance, Standard Deviation, Coefficient of Variation

Key Words :

Deviation, Dispersion, Range, Mean Deviation, Standard Deviation (SD), Variance, Coefficient of Variance (C.V.).

Objectives :

The reliability of average is more if dispersion is less. Measures of dispersion is a tool which summerizes the internal variation or variation within the observations. The techniques of measurement of variation are discussed in this chapter. Statistics is in existence because of variation. Statisticians has to talk in terms of S.D. There are some situations in life sciences, genetics, biodiversity etc. where larger the S.D. or C.V. better is situation.

4.1 Introduction

We have seen that average condenses information into a single value. However, average alone is not sufficient to describe the distribution completely. There may be two distributions with same means but distributions may not be identical.

Illustration 1 : Marks of students A, B, C in 5 subjects are as follows :

Student	Marks					A.M.
A	51	52	50	48	49	50
B	30	35	50	65	70	50
C	0	15	45	95	95	50

Notice that the average marks of all students are the same but they differ in variation. Clearly we can see that A is more consistent than B and B is more consistent than C.

For further study and analysis it becomes essential to measure the extent of variation. Observations are scattered or dispersed from central value. This variation is called as *dispersion.* Thus, next important aspect of comparison or study of frequency distribution is dispersion. Moreover, it plays very important role in further analysis.

Average remains good representative if dispersion is less (i.e. if the observations are close to it). Thus, dispersion decides the reliability of average.

4.2 Measures of Dispersion

In this chapter we study the following measures of dispersion : (i) range, (ii) quartile deviation, (iii) mean deviation, (iv) standard deviation. These measures have the same units as that of the observation.

For example, ₹, cm., hours etc.

Measure of Comparison of Dispersion :

It can be very well seen that these measures possess units and hence create difficulty in comparison of dispersion for two or more frequency distributions.

For example : For a group of persons, variation in height and variation in weight are to be compared. Height may be in cm and weight may be in kg. Therefore, comparison is not possible until a unitless quantity is available. Therefore, with respect to every such a measure of dispersion, measure of dispersion for comparison is defined. Such measure can be obtained by dividing the measure by corresponding average. Such a measure is called as coefficient of the respective measure of dispersion.

4.3 Range and Coefficient of Range

Range is a crude measure of dispersion. However, it is the simplest measure and suitable if the extent of variation is small.

Definition : If L is the largest observation and S is the smallest observation then range is the difference between L and S. Thus,

$$\text{Range} = L - S$$

and the corresponding relative measure is

$$\text{Coefficient of range} = \frac{L - S}{L + S}$$

In case of frequency distribution mid-values of first and last class intervals are taken to be the largest and the smallest observations respectively.

Note : Requisites of good measures of dispersion are same as those of average.

Merits of Range : There is only one merit viz. it is simple to understand and easy to calculate.

Demerits of Range : It is not based on all observations. It does not give proper idea regarding variation between the extreme observations. *For example :* Range of 0, 3, 5, 200 is same as that of 0, 50, 100, 150, 200. However, variation patterns are different.

Applications of Range : Range is suitable measure of dispersion in case of small group with less variation. (i) It is widely used in the branch of statistics known as Statistical Quality Control. (ii) The changes in prices of shares, the lowest and highest values are recorded. (iii) Temperature at certain place is recorded using maximum and minimum value. (iv) Range is used in medical science to check whether blood pressure HB count etc. is normal.

4.4 Quartile Deviation or Semi-interquartile Range

The range uses only two extreme items. Hence, any change in the inbetween observations is not going to affect the range. This is a main drawback of range. Moreover in many situations extreme items are widely separated from remaining items.

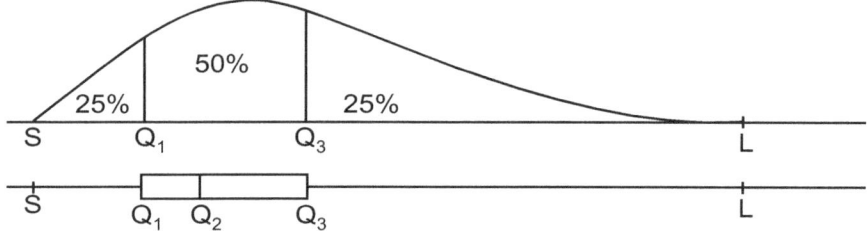

Fig. 4.1

In this situation range will overestimate the dispersion. Thus, range fails to give true picture of dispersion. In order to overcome these drawbacks range of middle 50% items is computed.

Clearly the middle 50% items lie inbetween the two quartiles Q_1 and Q_3. The measure of dispersion based on these quartiles is given below :

Quartile Deviation (Q.D.) or Semi-Interquartile Range $= \dfrac{Q_3 - Q_1}{2}$.

And the corresponding relative measure is

Coefficient of Quartile Deviation $= \dfrac{Q_3 - Q_1}{Q_3 + Q_1}$

Illustrative Examples

Example 4.1 : Compute (i) range and coefficient of range (ii) quartile deviation and coefficient of quartile deviation for the following data :

100, 24, 14, 105, 21, 35, 106, 16, 100, 72, 68, 103, 61, 90, 20.

Solution : (i) Here, Smallest observation (S) = 14

Largest observation (L) = 106

$$\text{Range} = L - S = 106 - 14 = 92$$

$$\text{Coefficient of range} = \frac{L - S}{L + S} = \frac{92}{106 + 14} = \frac{92}{120}$$

$$= 0.7667$$

(ii) To find quartile deviation, we arrange the observations in ascending order as follows :

14, 16, 20, $\boxed{21}$, 24, 35, 61, 68, 72, 90, 100, $\boxed{100}$, 103, 105, 106

Q_1 = The value of $\left(\dfrac{n+1}{4} = \dfrac{15+1}{4} = 4\right)^{th}$ item in the ordered arrangement

= 21

Q_3 = The value of $\left(\dfrac{3(n+1)}{4} = \dfrac{3 \times 16}{4} = 12\right)^{th}$ item in the ordered arrangement

= 100

∴ Q.D. = $\dfrac{Q_3 - Q_1}{2} = \dfrac{100 - 21}{2} = 39.5$

Coefficient of Q.D. = $\dfrac{Q_3 - Q_1}{Q_3 + Q_1} = 0.6529$

Example 4.2 : Compute Q.D. and Coefficient of Q.D. for the following frequency distribution.

Daily Wages (in ₹)	below 35	35–40	40–45	45–50	50–55	55–60	60–65	above 65
No. of workers	12	18	22	26	36	23	19	8

Solution :

Class	Frequency	Less than type cumulative frequency	
below 35	12	12	
35–40	18	30	
40–45	22	52............	... → Q_1 class
45–50	26	78	
50–55	36	114	
55–60	23	137............	... → Q_3 class
60–65	19	156	
above 65	8	164 = N	

Q_1 = The value of $\left(\dfrac{N}{4} = \dfrac{164}{4} = 41\right)^{st}$ observation

Therefore, (40 – 45) is Q_1 class

∴ $Q_1 = l + \dfrac{N/4 - C.F.}{f} \times h = 40 + \dfrac{41 - 30}{22} \times 5 = 42.5$

Q_3 = The value of $\left(\dfrac{3N}{4} = \dfrac{3 \times 164}{4} = 123\right)^{rd}$ observation

Therefore, Q_3 lies in (55 – 60)

∴ $Q_3 = l + \dfrac{3N/4 - C.F.}{f} \times h = 55 + \dfrac{123 - 114}{23} \times 5 = 56.9565$

∴ Q.D. $= \dfrac{Q_3 - Q_1}{2} = \dfrac{56.9565 - 42.5}{2} = 7.2283$

Coefficient of Q.D. $= \dfrac{Q_3 - Q_1}{Q_3 + Q_1} = \dfrac{55.9565 - 42.5}{55.9565 + 42.5} = 0.1454$

Remark : One of the requisites of a good measure is that, it should be based on all the observations. However, Q.D. depends upon only two partition values. Therefore, it is not affected by any changes except the upper and lower quartile.

4.5 Mean Deviation and Coefficient of Mean Deviation

A prime requirement of a good statistical measure is that it should be based on all the observations. It is not satisfied by both the range and quartile deviation. Here we discuss the measure of dispersion which take into account all the observations. Naturally, the use of deviations taken from a certain point of reference is appropriate. Preferably we take deviations from arithmetic mean (A.M.). We require to combine all these deviations into a single value. One of the appropriate techniques is to take arithmetic mean. However, the sum of deviations taken from A.M. is zero. Therefore, A.M. of deviations fails to serve the purpose. A.M. behaves like a centre of gravity, it balances both positive and negative deviations giving total zero. Hence, it is required to get rid of the algebraic signs of deviations. This can be done in two ways (a) taking absolute deviations (b) taking squares of the deviations.

Definition : The arithmetic mean of absolute deviations from any average (mean or median or mode) is called as mean deviation about the respective average.

(i) Mean deviation (M.D.) about mean :

$$= \frac{\sum_{i=1}^{n} |d_i|}{n} \quad \text{for individual observations, where } |d_i| = |x_i - \bar{x}|$$

$$= \frac{\sum_{i=1}^{n} f_i |d_i|}{N} \quad \text{for frequency distribution where } N = \sum f_i$$

Relative measure of dispersion is

Coefficient of M.D. about mean $= \dfrac{\text{M.D. about mean}}{\text{Mean}}$

(ii) M.D. about mean :

$$= \frac{\sum_{i=1}^{n} |d_i|}{n} \quad \text{for individual observations where } |d_i| = |x_i - \text{median}|$$

$$= \frac{\sum_{i=1}^{n} f_i |d_i|}{N} \quad \text{for frequency distribution}$$

Relative measure of dispersion is

Coefficient of M.D. about median $= \dfrac{\text{M.D. about median}}{\text{Median}}$

(iii) M.D. about mode :

$$= \frac{\sum_{i=1}^{n} |d_i|}{n} \quad \text{for individual observations where } |d_i| = |x_i - \text{mode}|$$

$$= \frac{\sum_{i=1}^{n} f_i |d_i|}{N} \quad \text{for frequency distribution}$$

Relative measure of dispersion is

Coefficient of M.D. about mode $= \dfrac{\text{M.D. about mode}}{\text{Mode}}$

Computational Procedure :

Step 1 : Obtain the required average (mean or mode or median).

Step 2 : Obtain the absolute deviation $|d_i| = |x_i - \text{average}|$ for each observation.

Step 3 : Find the sum of $|d|$ as $\sum |d_i|$ for individual observation and $\sum f_i |d_i|$ for frequency distribution.

Step 4 : Compute M.D. as

$\dfrac{\sum |d_i|}{n}$ for individual observations and

$\dfrac{\sum f_i |d_i|}{N}$ for frequency distribution.

Step 5 : Obtain coefficient of M.D. (if required) by formula $\dfrac{\text{M.D.}}{\text{Average}}$.

Example 4.3 : Compute (i) M.D. about mean and coefficient of M.D. about mean (ii) M.D. about median and coefficient of M.D. about median for the prices per 10 kg of sugar for 7 days in a certain week. 80, 82, 79, 78, 85, 80, 83.

Solution :

(i) Arithmetic mean $= \dfrac{\sum x}{n} = \dfrac{567}{7} = 81$

x_i	80	82	79	78	85	80	83	Total
$|d_i| = |x_i - 81|$	1	1	2	3	4	1	2	14

M.D. about mean $= \dfrac{\sum |d|}{n} = \dfrac{14}{7} = 2$ ₹

Coefficient of M.D. about mean $= \dfrac{\text{M.D.}}{\text{Mean}} = \dfrac{2}{81} = 0.0247$.

(ii) To find the median we use the ordered arrangement :

78, 79, 80, $\boxed{80}$, 82, 83, 85

Median $= \left(\dfrac{n+1}{2}\right)^{\text{th}}$ i.e. 4th observation = 80.

x_i	80	82	79	78	85	80	83	Total
$|d_i| = |x_i - 80|$	0	2	1	2	5	0	3	13

M.D. about median $= \dfrac{\sum |d|}{n} = \dfrac{13}{7} = 1.8571$ ₹

Coefficient of M.D. about median $= \dfrac{\text{M.D.}}{\text{Median}} = \dfrac{1.8571}{80} = 0.0232$

Example 4.4 : Obtain M.D. about (i) mean (ii) median and the absolute measure of dispersion in each case for the following frequency distribution.

Class	2–4	4–6	6–8	8–10
Frequency	3	4	2	1

Solution : First we find mean and median which we need for further calculations.

Class	Mid-values x_i	f_i	$f_i x_i$	Cumulative frequency
2–4	3	3	9	3
4–6	5	4	20	7
6–8	7	2	14	9
8–10	9	1	9	10
Total	–	10	52	–

$$\text{Mean} = \frac{\Sigma fx}{N} = 5.2$$

Median = The size of $(N/2)^{th}$ i.e. 5th observation.

Median class : 4 – 6

$$\text{Median} = l + \frac{N/2 - c.f.}{f} \times h \qquad (l = 4, N/2 = 5, c.f. = 3, h = 2)$$

∴ Median = 5

x_i	f_i	$\|x_i - \bar{x}\|$	$f_i \|x_i - \bar{x}\|$	$\|x_i - Me\|$ = $\|x - 5\|$	$f_i \|x_i - Me\|$
3	3	2.2	6.6	2	6
5	4	0.2	0.4	0	0
7	2	1.8	3.6	2	4
9	1	3.8	3.8	4	4
Total	10	–	14.8	–	14

$$\text{M.D. about mean} = \frac{\Sigma f_i |x_i - \bar{x}|}{N} = \frac{14.8}{10} = 1.48$$

$$\text{Coefficient of M.D. about mean} = \frac{\text{M.D.}}{\text{Mean}} = \frac{1.48}{5.2} = 0.2846$$

$$\text{M.D. about median} = \frac{\sum f_i |x_i - Me|}{N} = \frac{14}{10} = 1.4$$

$$\text{Coefficient of M.D. about median} = \frac{1.4}{5} = 0.28$$

Minimality property of M.D. : Among all mean deviations, mean deviation about median is minimum.

Therefore, in order to avoid the effect of choice of average, mean deviation about median is preferred.

Merits of M.D. :
1. It is simple to understand and easy to calculate.
2. It is rigidly defined.
3. It is based on all observations.

Demerits of M.D. :
1. It is not applicable for qualitative data.
2. Since algebraic signs of deviations are ignored, it is not applicable for further mathematical treatment.
3. It cannot be computed for the frequency distribution with open end class.

A serious drawback mentioned in demerits of M.D. (2) can be overcome by taking squares of the deviations. Based on the squares of deviations a measure of dispersion is defined and it is discussed below :

4.6 Mean Square Deviation

Supposed $d = x - a$ is a deviation taken from an arbitrary reference point 'a'. To get rid of algebraic sign of d, we either use |d| of d^2. The measure of dispersion based on |d| viz. mean deviation, we have already studied. Using d^2 we can develop a measure of dispersion, which is better than mean deviation. The arithmetic mean of d^2 is used as a measure of deviation. It is known as *mean square deviation* (M.S.D.).

Clearly,

$$\text{M.S.D.} = \sum_{i=1}^{n} (x_i - a)^2 / n \quad \text{for individual observations}$$

$$= \left.\sum_{i=1}^{n} f_i (x_i - a)^2 \middle/ \sum_{i=1}^{k} f_i \right. \quad \text{for frequency distribution}$$

However, M.S.D. is affected by choice of a. Thus, it creates difficulty in measuring the dispersion properly. We try to find a measure which will overcome this difficulty.

We have studied properties of arithmetic mean. One of the properties states that, the sum of squares of deviations taken from arithmetic mean is the minimum. Using this fact we get the minimal property of M.S.D. It will enable us to develop a measure of dispersion.

Minimality property of M.S.D. : Mean square deviation is the least if the deviations are taken from arithmetic mean.

Since, sum of squares of deviations taken from arithmetic mean is the minimum we get,

$$\sum (x_i - a)^2 \geq \sum (x_i - \bar{x})^2$$

∴ $\quad \sum (x_i - a)^2/n \geq \sum (x_i - \bar{x})^2/n$

∴ $\quad$ M.S.D. about a $\geq$ M.S.D. about $\bar{x}$.

4.7 Variance, Standard Deviation and Coefficient of Variation

The lower bound of M.S.D. is taken as a measure of dispersion. It is called as *variance*.

Definition : The arithmetic mean of squares of deviations taken from arithmetic mean is called as **variance.**

Clearly, Variance $= \sum_{i=1}^{n} (x_i - \bar{x})^2/n \quad$ for individual observations

$$= \sum_{i=1}^{k} f_i (x_i - \bar{x})^2 \Big/ \sum_{i=1}^{k} f_i$$

for frequency distribution

Note : Symbolically we write variance of x as Var (x). The term Variance is suggested by R. A. Fisher.

Remark : The units of original items and that of the variance are not same.

For example, if items are measured in cm., then the variance will be expressed in (cm)². Therefore we take positive square root of variance. It is called as standard deviation or least root mean square deviation.

Definition : The positive square root of mean of squares of the deviations taken from arithmetic mean is called as **Standard Deviation** (S.D.).

It is denoted by σ (read as sigma, a lower case Greek letter).

Therefore, $\sigma = \sqrt{\dfrac{\sum_{i=1}^{n}(x_i - \bar{x})^2}{n}}$ for individual observations

$= \sqrt{\dfrac{\sum_{i=1}^{k} f_i(x_i - \bar{x})^2}{\sum_{i=1}^{k} f_i}}$ for frequency distribution

For computational purpose the above formulae can be simplified as follows :

Case (i) : Individual observations

$$\sigma^2 = \dfrac{1}{n}\sum_{i=1}^{n}(x_i - \bar{x})^2 = \dfrac{1}{n}\sum_{i=1}^{n}\left(x_i^2 - 2\bar{x}x_i + (\bar{x})^2\right)$$

$$= \dfrac{1}{n}\left[\sum_{i=1}^{n} x_i^2 - 2\bar{x}\sum_{i=1}^{n} x_i + \sum_{i=1}^{n}(\bar{x})^2\right]$$

$$= \dfrac{1}{n}\left[\sum x_i^2 - 2n(\bar{x})^2 + n(\bar{x})^2\right] \qquad (\because \sum x_i = n\bar{x})$$

$$= \dfrac{1}{n}\sum x_i^2 - (\bar{x})^2$$

$$\therefore \quad \sigma = \sqrt{\dfrac{\sum x_i^2}{n} - (\bar{x})^2}$$

Case (ii) : Frequency distribution

$$\sigma^2 = \sum_{i=1}^{k} f_i(x_i - \bar{x})^2 \bigg/ \sum_{i=1}^{k} f_i$$

$$= \dfrac{1}{N}\sum_{i=1}^{k} f_i\left(x_i^2 - 2\bar{x}x_i + (\bar{x})^2\right) \qquad \left(\text{Let } N = \sum_{i=1}^{n} f_i\right)$$

$$= \dfrac{1}{N}\left[\sum_{i=1}^{k} f_i x_i^2 - 2\bar{x}\sum_{i=1}^{k} f_i x_i + \sum_{i=1}^{k} f_i(\bar{x})^2\right]$$

$$= \dfrac{\sum f_i x_i^2}{N} - 2\bar{x}\dfrac{\sum f_i x_i}{N} + (\bar{x})^2 \qquad \left(\because \dfrac{\sum f_i x_i}{\sum f_i} = \bar{x}\right)$$

$$= \frac{\sum f_i x_i^2}{N} - 2(\bar{x})^2 + (\bar{x})^2$$

$$= \frac{\sum f_i x_i^2}{N} - (\bar{x})^2$$

$$\therefore \quad \sigma = \sqrt{\frac{\sum f_i x_i^2}{N} - (\bar{x})^2}$$

Standard deviation is a measure of dispersion which satisfies most of the requisites of a good measure. It is free from the drawbacks present in the other measures of dispersion.

Coefficient of Variation : Prof. Karl Pearson suggested the relative measure of standard deviation. It is called as coefficient of variation (C.V.)

It is given by C.V. = $\frac{S.D}{|A.M.|} \times 100 = \frac{\sigma}{|\bar{x}|} \times 100\%$ ... (1)

Coefficient of variation is always expressed in percentage.

Remarks (1) R.H.S. of (1) includes the multiplier 100, because $\frac{\sigma}{|\bar{x}|}$ is too small in many cases. Thus, for convenience it is multiplied by 100.

2. Frequently we need to compare dispersions of two or more groups. If the values in data set are large in magnitude, naturally variation among them will be proportionately larger.

For example, S.D. of weights of a group of elephants will be larger than that of a group of human beings. Suppose S.D. of weights of a group of elephants is 15 kg and that of human beings is also 15 kg. In this case we cannot say, both the groups have identical variation. This is because average weight of a group of elephants is larger than that of the average weight of a group of persons. Therefore for comparing variations between two different data sets, a measure based on the ratio of σ and $\bar{x}$ would be appropriate. This is achieved in coefficient of variation. It measures variation in all data sets using a common yard stick; moreover it is free from units.

3. According to Prof. Karl Pearson C.V. is the percentage variation in mean whereas S.D. gives the total variation in the mean.

C.V. and Least Count :

Using proper measuring instrument is also a way to check whether C.V. is maintained properly. If appropriate instrument is not used, C.V. will be inflated. As a thumb rule in industry.

Least count $\approx \frac{1}{10}$ specified range.

For example, if the inner diameter of cylinder is required to be between 0.95 cm and 1.05 cm the least count of the gauge should be $\frac{1}{10}$ th of the specified range which is $\frac{1}{10}(1.05 - 0.95) = 0.01$ cm $= 0.1$ mm.

Properties of Variance and S.D. :

1. Mean square deviation $\geq$ Variance.
2. **Effect of change of origin (P.U. April 2010) :** Variance (S.D.) is invariant to the change of origin. In other words, if a constant is added to (or subtracted from) each item, the variance (S.D.) remains same.

Proof : Case (i) Individual observations : Suppose $x_1, x_2, \ldots, x_n$ is set of observations. Let $y_i = x_i - a$ where 'a' is constant. We have to show that var (y) = var (x). or $\sigma_y = \sigma_x$.

Since $y = x - a$, we get $\bar{y} = \bar{x} - a$.

By definition
$$\text{Var}(y) = \frac{1}{n} \sum_{i=1}^{n} (y_i - \bar{y})^2$$
$$= \frac{1}{n} \sum_{i=1}^{n} \left[(x_i - a) - (\bar{x} - a)\right]^2$$
$$= \frac{1}{n} \sum_{i=1}^{n} \left(x_i - \bar{x}\right)^2 = \text{var}(x)$$

Case (ii) Frequency distribution : Suppose $\{(x_i, f_i), i = 1, 2, \ldots, k\}$ is a frequency distribution. Let $y = x - a$, hence $\bar{y} = \bar{x} - a$.

By definition,
$$\text{Var}(y) = \frac{1}{N} \sum_{i=1}^{k} f_i \left(y_i - \bar{y}\right)^2 \quad \text{where, } N = \sum_{i=1}^{k} f_i$$
$$= \frac{1}{N} \sum_{i=1}^{k} f_i \left[(x_i - a) - (\bar{x} - a)\right]^2$$
$$= \frac{1}{N} \sum_{i=1}^{k} f_i \left(x_i - \bar{x}\right)^2 = \text{Var}(x)$$

3. Effect of change of origin and scale :

If $u = (x - a)/h$, a and h being constants, then $\text{var}(u) = \frac{1}{h^2} \text{var}(x)$ or $\sigma_u = \sigma_x/h$.

Proof : Since $u = \frac{x-a}{h}$, $\bar{u} = \frac{\bar{x}-a}{h}$

For $\{(x_i, f_i), i = 1, 2, \ldots, k\}$ frequency distribution

$$\text{Var}(u) = \frac{1}{N} \sum_{i=1}^{k} f_i (u_i - \bar{u})^2 \quad \text{where, } N = \sum_{i=1}^{k} f_i$$

$$= \frac{1}{N} \sum_{i=1}^{k} f_i \left[\frac{x_i - a}{h} - \frac{\bar{x} - a}{h}\right]^2$$

$$= \frac{1}{h^2 N} \cdot \sum_{i=1}^{k} f_i (x_i - \bar{x})^2 = \frac{1}{h^2} \text{Var}(x)$$

$$\therefore \quad \sigma_u = \frac{1}{h} \sigma_x$$

Note :
(a) The properties (2) and (3) simplify the computations of variance and S.D. to a large extent.
(b) If we define $y = ax + b$ then $\text{Var}(y) = a^2 \text{Var}(x)$ or $\sigma_y = a\sigma_x$.
(c) In property (3) if we take $h = 1$, then we get $u = x - a$. This amounts to change of origin and not the change of scale.
(d) In property (3) if we take $a = 0$, then we get $u = x/h$. It is equivalent to change of scale only.

4. Combined Variance and S.D. :

Suppose there are two groups. First is of size n_1 with arithmetic mean $\bar{x}$ and variance σ_1^2. Second group is of size n_2 with arithmetic mean $\bar{y}$ and variance σ_2^2. Then the variance of combined group of size $n_1 + n_2$ is given by

$$\sigma_c^2 = \frac{n_1 (\sigma_1^2 + d_1^2) + n_2 (\sigma_2^2 + d_2^2)}{n_1 + n_2}$$

where, $d_1 = \bar{x} - \bar{x}_c$, $d_2 = \bar{y} - \bar{x}_c$, and $\bar{x}_c$ is combined arithmetic mean.

Derivation : Let n_1 be the size of first group, $\bar{x}$ and σ_1^2 be the arithmetic mean and variance of the first group. Let n_2 be the size of second group, $\bar{y}$ and σ_2^2 be the arithmetic mean and variance of the second group. Suppose $x_1, x_2, \ldots, x_n$ are the observations in the first group.

Note that
$$\sigma_1^2 = \sum_1^{n_1} (x_i - \bar{x})^2 / n_1$$

$\therefore$
$$n_1 \sigma_1^2 = \sum_1^{n_1} (x_i - \bar{x})^2 \qquad \ldots (1)$$

Suppose $y_1, y_2, \therefore, y_{n_2}$ are the observations in the second group.

$\therefore$
$$n_2 \sigma_2^2 = \sum_1^{n_2} (y_i - \bar{y})^2 \qquad \ldots (2)$$

The combined mean $= \bar{x}_c = \dfrac{n_1 \bar{x} + n_2 \bar{y}}{n_1 + n_2}$ and the combined variance

$$\sigma_c^2 = \dfrac{\sum_1^{n_1} (x_i - \bar{x}_c)^2 + \sum_1^{n_2} (y_i - \bar{y}_c)^2}{n_1 + n_2} \qquad \ldots (3)$$

We simplify (3) as follows :

$$\sum_1^{n_1} (x_i - \bar{x}_c)^2 = \sum_1^{n_1} (x_i - \bar{x} + \bar{x} - \bar{x}_c)^2$$

$$= \sum_1^{n_1} [(x_i - \bar{x})^2 + (\bar{x} - \bar{x}_c)^2 + 2 (\bar{x} - \bar{x}_c)(x_i - \bar{x})]$$

$$= \sum_1^{n_1} (x_i - \bar{x})^2 + \sum_1^{n_1} (\bar{x} - \bar{x}_c)^2 + 2 (\bar{x} - \bar{x}_c) \sum_1^{n_1} (x_i - \bar{x})$$

$$= n_1 \sigma_1^2 + n_1 (\bar{x} - \bar{x}_c)^2 + 0 \qquad \text{from (1)}$$

$$= n_1 \sigma_1^2 + n_1 d_1^2 \quad (\text{where } d_1 = \bar{x} - \bar{x}_c) \qquad \ldots (4)$$

Similarly,

$$\sum_1^{n_2} (y_i - \bar{x}_c)^2 = n_2 \sigma_2^2 + n_2 d_2^2 \quad (\text{where } d_2 = \bar{y} - \bar{x}_c) \qquad \ldots (5)$$

From (4) and (5) we can write (3) as

$$\sigma_c^2 = \frac{n_1 \sigma_1^2 + n_1 d_1^2 + n_2 \sigma_2^2 + n_1 d_2^2}{n_1 + n_2}$$

$$\sigma_c^2 = \frac{n_1 (\sigma_1^2 + d_1^2) + n_2 (\sigma_2^2 + d_2^2)}{n_1 + n_2}$$

Generalisation : Let there be k groups ($k \geq 2$) with size of ith group as n_i, arithmetic mean $\bar{x}_i$ and variance σ_i^2, $i = 1, 2, 3, \ldots, k$. The combined variance of k groups is given by

$$\sigma_c^2 = \frac{\sum_{i=1}^{k} n_i (\sigma_i^2 + d_i^2)}{\sum_{i=1}^{k} n_i}$$

where, $d_i = \bar{x}_i - \bar{x}_c$, and $\bar{x}_c$ = combined arithmetic mean.

5. S.D. ≥ M.D. about arithmetic mean :

Proof : Suppose $x_1, x_2, \ldots, x_n$ are the observations with mean $\bar{x}$. Let $d_i = x_i - \bar{x}$ then S.D. $= \sqrt{\sum d_i^2 / n}$ and M.D. about mean $= \frac{\sum |d_i|}{n}$.

Let $y_i = |d_i|$

Note that $(y_i - \bar{y})^2 \geq 0$ being a square.

$\therefore \quad \sum_{i=1}^{n} (y_i - \bar{y})^2 \geq 0$

$\therefore \quad \sum y_i^2 - 2\bar{y} \sum y_i + \sum (\bar{y})^2 \geq 0$

Dividing by n we get,

$\therefore \quad \frac{\sum y_i^2}{n} - 2(\bar{y})^2 + (\bar{y})^2 \geq 0$

$\therefore \quad \frac{\sum y_i^2}{n} \geq (\bar{y})^2$

$\therefore \quad \sqrt{\frac{\sum y_i^2}{n}} \geq \bar{y}$

$\therefore \quad \sqrt{\frac{\sum |d_i|^2}{n}} \geq \frac{\sum |d_i|}{n}$

$$\therefore \qquad \sqrt{\frac{\sum(x_i - \bar{x})^2}{n}} \geq \text{M.D.} \qquad (\because d_i^2 = |d_i|^2)$$

$\therefore$ S.D. $\geq$ M.D. about arithmetic mean.

Illustrative Examples

Example 4.5 : Compute S.D. and C.V. for the following data :
36, 15, 25, 10, 14

Solution : We use computational formula

$$\sigma = \sqrt{\frac{\sum x_i^2}{n} - \bar{x}^2}$$

						Total
x_i	36	15	25	10	14	100
x_i^2	1296	225	625	100	196	2442

$$\therefore \quad \bar{x} = \frac{\sum x_i}{n} = \frac{100}{5} = 20$$

$$\therefore \quad \sigma = \sqrt{\frac{\sum x_i^2}{n} - (\bar{x})^2} = \sqrt{\frac{2442}{5} - 20^2} = \sqrt{88.4} = 9.4021$$

$$\text{C.V.} = \frac{\sigma}{|\bar{x}|} \times 100 = \frac{9.4021}{20} \times 100 = 45.2105\%$$

Compute S.D. and C.V. for above data using MS-Excel.

Solution : Using the command **=stdevp (range)** in this case type = stdevp (A5 : A9), we get S.D.

$$\text{C.V.} = (\text{S.D./Mean}) \: 100\%$$

	A	B	C	D
1				
2		Find S.D. and C.V. of given data		
3				
4	Data			
5	36			
6	15			
7	25	Mean =		20
8	10	S.D. =	=STDEVP(A5 A9)	9.40212742
9	14	C.V. =		47.0106371
10				

Fig. 4.2

This is not possible for frequency distribution, therefore we use worksheet.

Example 4.6 : Compute S.D. of first n natural numbers.

Solution : We have to find S.D. of 1, 2, 3, ... , n.

x_i	1	2	......	r	......	n	Total: $n(n+1)/2$
x_i^2	1^2	2^2	......	r^2	......	n^2	$n(n+1)(2n+1)/6$

$$\bar{x} = \frac{\sum x_i}{n} = \frac{n(n+1)/2}{n} = \frac{n+1}{2}$$

$$\sigma = \sqrt{\frac{\sum x_i^2}{n} - (\bar{x})^2} = \sqrt{\frac{n(n+1)(2n+1)}{n \times 6} - \frac{(n+1)^2}{4}}$$

$$= \sqrt{\frac{2(n+1)(2n+1) - 3(n+1)^2}{12}}$$

$$= \sqrt{\frac{(n+1)}{12}[4n + 4 - 3n - 3]}$$

$$= \sqrt{\frac{n^2 - 1}{12}}$$

Example 4.7 : Compute S.D. and C.V. of marks scored by 10 candidates given below :

54, 61, 64, 69, 58, 56, 49, 57, 55, 50.

Solution : Let $a = 57$, $u = x - 57$

x_i	54	61	64	69	58	56	49	57	55	50	Total
u_i	-3	4	7	12	1	-1	-8	0	-2	-7	3
u_i^2	9	16	49	144	1	1	64	0	4	49	337

$$\sigma = \sqrt{\frac{\sum u_i^2}{n} - \left(\frac{\sum u}{n}\right)^2} = \sqrt{\frac{337}{10} - \left(\frac{3}{10}\right)^2}$$

$$= \sqrt{33.61} = 5.7974$$

To compute C.V. we require $\bar{x}$. Note that $u = x - 57$.

$$\therefore \quad \bar{x} = \bar{u} + 57 = \frac{\sum u}{n} + 57 = \frac{3}{10} + 57 = 57.3$$

$$\text{C.V.} = \frac{\sigma}{|\bar{x}|} \times 100 = \frac{5.7974}{57.3} \times 100 = 10.1176\%$$

Example 4.8 : Calculate the standard deviation and coefficient of variation for the frequency distribution of marks of 100 candidates given below :

Marks	0–20	20–40	40–60	60–80	80–100
Frequency	5	12	32	40	11

Solution : Let $u = \dfrac{x - 50}{20}$

Class	Mid-values x_i	Frequency f_i	$u_i = \dfrac{x_i - 50}{20}$	$f_i \times u_i$	$f_i u_i^2$
00–20	10	5	– 2	– 10	– 10 × – 2 = 20
20–40	30	12	– 1	– 12	– 12 × – 1 = 12
40–60	50	32	0	0	0
60–80	70	40	1	40	40 × 1 = 40
80–100	90	11	2	22	22 × 2 = 44
Total	–	100	–	40	116

Here, $u = \dfrac{x - 50}{20}$, therefore $x = 50 + 20u$

$$\therefore \bar{x} = 50 + 20 \bar{u} = 50 + 20 \dfrac{\Sigma f_i u_i}{\Sigma f_i} = 50 + 20 \times \dfrac{40}{100} = 58$$

$$\text{Var}(x) = 20^2 \text{ Var}(u) = 400 \left[\dfrac{\Sigma f_i u_i^2}{\Sigma f_i} - (\bar{u})^2 \right]$$

$$= 400 \left[\dfrac{116}{100} - \left(\dfrac{40}{100}\right)^2 \right] = 400$$

$\therefore$ S.D. of $x = \sqrt{\text{var}(x)} = \sqrt{400} = 20$

$\therefore$ C.V. of $x = \dfrac{\text{S.D.}}{\text{A.M.}} \times 100 = \dfrac{20}{58} \times 100$

$= 34.4828\%$

Merits of S.D. :
1. It is based on all observations.
2. It is rigidly defined.
3. It is capable of further mathematical treatment.

4. It does not ignore algebraic signs of deviations.
5. It is not much affected by sampling fluctuations.

Demerits of S.D. :
1. It is difficult to understand and to calculate.
2. It cannot be computed for a distribution with open-end class.
3. It is unduly affected due to extreme deviations.
4. It cannot be calculated for qualitative data.

Use of variance and S.D. :

Practically, in almost all advanced statistical methods such as sampling, statistical quality control, statistical inference deal with variance.

As far as variance is concerned, smaller variance is better in many situations. However, there are some situations in genetical sciences where larger variance is better.

Variance and standard deviation are used in number of situations. Some of them are discussed below :

(a) Precision of an instrument is inversely proportional to variance. Therefore precision = k/variance.
(b) In portfolio analysis, risk is described in terms of variance of prices of shares.
(c) For the comparison of performance of two or more instruments, machines, coefficient of variation is used.
(d) The spread of variable is approximately taken as $(\bar{x} - 3\sigma, \bar{x} + 3\sigma)$.

Thus, standard deviation helps in estimating lower limit and upper limit of the items.

We state below the notes, which will be useful in solving numerical problems.

Note :
1. If all the observations are equal, S.D. is zero (why ?)
2. If data contains only one observation, S.D. is zero (why ?)

Illustrative Examples

Example 4.9 : A group of 50 items have mean and S.D. 61 and 8 respectively. Another group of 100 observations has mean and S.D. 70 and 9 respectively. Find mean and S.D. of combined group.

Solution : We are given that : $n_1 = 50$, $\bar{x}_1 = 61$, $\sigma_1 = 8$, $n_2 = 100$, $\bar{x}_2 = 70$ and $\sigma_2 = 9$. Therefore combined mean is

$$\bar{x}_c = \frac{n_1\bar{x}_1 + n_2\bar{x}_2}{n_1 + n_2} = \frac{(50 \times 61) + (100 \times 70)}{50 + 100} = 67$$

∴ $d_1 = \bar{x}_1 - \bar{x}_c = 61 - 67 = -6$ and $d_2 = \bar{x}_2 - \bar{x}_c = 70 - 67 = 3$.

∴ Combined S.D. is

$$\sigma_c = \sqrt{\frac{n_1(\sigma_1^2 + d_1^2) + n_2(\sigma_2^2 + d_2^2)}{n_1 + n_2}}$$

$$\sigma_c = \sqrt{\frac{50(64 + 36) + 100(81 + 9)}{150}} = 9.6609$$

Example 4.10 : The mean weight of 150 students is 60 kg. The mean weight of boys is 70 kg, with S.D. of 10 kg. For girls the mean weight is 55 kg with S.D. of 15 kg. Find the number of boys and combined S.D.

Solution : Let there are n_1 boys with mean $\bar{x}_1$ and S.D. σ_1. Similarly, there are n_2 girls with mean $\bar{x}_2$ and S.D. σ_2. Hence, we get $n_1 + n_2 = 150$, $\bar{x}_c = 60$, $\bar{x}_1 = 70$, $\bar{x}_2 = 55$, $\sigma_1 = 10$, $\sigma_2 = 15$.

$$\bar{x}_c = \frac{n_1\bar{x}_1 + n_2\bar{x}_2}{n_1 + n_2}$$

∴ $$60 = \frac{70n_1 + 55n_2}{n_1 + n_2}$$

$$60n_1 + 60n_2 = 70n_1 + 55n_2$$

$$n_2 = 2n_1 \qquad \ldots (1)$$

$$n_1 + n_2 = 150$$

∴ $$n_1 + 2n_1 = 150 \qquad \ldots \text{from (1)}$$

$$n_1 = 50$$

∴ Number of boys = 50.

We get $d_1 = \bar{x}_1 - \bar{x}_c = 70 - 60 = 10$ and $d_2 = \bar{x}_2 - \bar{x}_c = 55 - 60 = -5$

∴ Combined S.D. $= \sigma = \sqrt{\frac{n_1(\sigma_1^2 + d_1^2) + n_2(\sigma_2^2 + d_2^2)}{n_1 + n_2}}$

$$\therefore \quad \sigma = \sqrt{\frac{50(100+100)+100(225+25)}{150}} = 15.2753 \text{ kg.}$$

Example 4.11 : The mean and S.D. of 10 observations were 9.5 and 2.5 respectively. If one more observation with value 15 is included in group, obtain the mean and S.D. of these 11 observations.

Solution : Let there be two groups, first group of original 10 observations and second group of new single observation. Hence,

$$n_1 = 10, \quad n_2 = 1$$

$$\bar{x}_1 = 9.5, \quad \bar{x}_2 = 15 \text{ (why ?)}$$

$$\sigma_1 = 2.5, \quad \sigma_2 = 0 \text{ (why ?)}$$

$$\text{Combined mean} = \bar{x}_c = \frac{n_1\bar{x}_1 + n_2\bar{x}_2}{n_1 + n_2}$$

$$= \frac{10 \times 9.5 + 15}{11} = 10$$

$$\therefore \quad d_1 = \bar{x}_1 - \bar{x}_c = -0.5 \text{ and } d_2 = \bar{x}_2 - \bar{x}_c = 5$$

$$\therefore \quad \sigma_c = \sqrt{\frac{10(6.25+0.25)+(25+0)}{11}} = 2.8604$$

Example 4.12 : The number of runs scored by cricketers A and B in 10 test matches are shown below :

A	5	20	90	76	102	90	6	108	20	16
B	40	35	60	62	58	76	42	30	30	20

Find (i) which cricketer is better in average ? (ii) which cricketer is more consistent ?

Solution : Mean of A $= \frac{\Sigma x}{n} = \frac{533}{10} = 53.3$

$$\text{S.D. of A} = \sqrt{\frac{\Sigma x^2}{n} - \left(\frac{\Sigma x}{n}\right)^2}$$

$$= \sqrt{\frac{45161}{10} - (53.3)^2} = 40.9293$$

$\therefore \quad$ C.V. of A $= 76.79\%$

Mean of B $= \frac{\Sigma y}{n} = \frac{453}{10} = 45.3$

$$\text{S.D. of B} = \sqrt{\frac{\Sigma y^2}{n} - \left(\frac{\Sigma y}{n}\right)^2}$$

$$= \sqrt{\frac{23373}{10} - (45.3)^2}$$

$$= 16.8882$$

$$\therefore \quad \text{C.V. of B} = 37.28\%$$

(i) A gives better average runs (mean A > mean B).

(ii) B is more consistent (C.V. of B < C.V. of A)

Example 4.13 : Arithmetic mean and S.D. of 12 items are 22 and 3 respectively. Later on it was observed that the item 32 was wrongly taken as 23. Compute correct mean, S.D. and C.V.

Solution :

$$\text{Incorrect sum } (\Sigma x) = n \times \text{Incorrect mean} = 12 \times 22 = 264.$$

$$\text{Correct } \Sigma x = \text{Incorrect } \Sigma x + \text{Correct item} - \text{Incorrect item}$$

$$\Sigma x = 264 - 23 + 32 = 273$$

$$\text{Correct mean} = \frac{273}{12} = 22.75$$

$$\sigma^2 = \frac{\Sigma x^2}{n} - (\bar{x})^2$$

$$\therefore \quad n\left[\sigma^2 + (\bar{x})^2\right] = \Sigma x^2$$

$$\therefore \quad \text{Incorrect } \Sigma x^2 = n\left[\sigma^2 + (\bar{x})^2\right] \text{ with } \sigma \text{ and } \bar{x} \text{ incorrect}$$

$$= 12 (9 + 484) = 5916$$

$$\text{Correct } \Sigma x^2 = \text{Incorrect } \Sigma x^2 + (\text{Correct item})^2 - (\text{Incorrect item})^2$$

$$= 5916 + 32^2 - 23^2 = 6411$$

$$\text{Correct } \sigma = \sqrt{\frac{\Sigma x^2}{n} - \left(\frac{\Sigma x}{n}\right)^2}$$

with correct Σx^2 and Σx

$$= \sqrt{\frac{6411}{12} - (22.75)^2}$$

$$= \sqrt{16.6875} = 4.0850$$

Correct C.V. $= \dfrac{\sigma}{|\bar{x}|} \times 100 = 17.9562\%$

Example 4.14 : For a set of 90 items the mean and S.D. are 59 and 9 respectively. For 40 items selected from those 90 items the mean and S.D. are 54 and 6 respectively. Find the mean and S.D. of the remaining items.

Solution :

Group 1	Group 2	Combined Group
$n_1 = 40$	$n_2 = 50$	$n = 90$
$\bar{x}_1 = 54$	$\bar{x}_2 = ?$	$\bar{x}_c = 59$
$\sigma_1 = 6$	$\sigma_2 = ?$	$\sigma_c = 9$

To find $\bar{x}_2$ we use $\bar{x}_c$.

$$\bar{x}_c = \dfrac{n_1 \bar{x}_1 + n_2 \bar{x}_2}{n_1 + n_2} \text{ gives } 59 = \dfrac{40 \times 54 + 50 \bar{x}_2}{90}$$

∴ $\bar{x}_2 = 63$

∴ $d_1 = \bar{x}_1 - \bar{x}_c = -5, \; d_2 = \bar{x}_2 - \bar{x}_c = 4$

∴ $\sigma_c^2 = \dfrac{n_1 (\sigma_1^2 + d_1^2) + n_2 (\sigma_2^2 + d_2^2)}{n_1 + n_2}$

$81 = \dfrac{40(36 + 25) + 50(\sigma_2^2 + 16)}{90}$

∴ $\sigma_2 = 9$.

Example 4.15 : Given that :
$n = 10, \; \Sigma(x - 20) = 8, \; \Sigma(x - 20)^2 = 762$. Find mean and S.D.

Solution : Let $u = x - 20$, Hence $\bar{x} = 20 + \dfrac{\Sigma u}{n} = 20.8$

$$\text{S.D.} = \sqrt{\dfrac{\Sigma u^2}{n} - \left(\dfrac{\Sigma u}{n}\right)^2} = \sqrt{\dfrac{762}{10} - \left(\dfrac{8}{10}\right)^2} = 8.6925$$

Example 4.16 : A variable takes values
$a - kd, \; a - (k-1)d, \; \ldots, \; a - d, \; a, \; a + d, \; \ldots, \; a + kd$.
Find its M.D. about arithmetic mean and S.D.

Solution : First of all we find A.M.

$$\bar{x} = \frac{(a - kd) + (a - (k-1)d) + \ldots + (a - d) + a + (a + d) + \ldots + (a + kd)}{2k + 1}$$

$$= \frac{(2k+1)a}{2k + 1}$$

We need to compute $(x_i - \bar{x})$. It is useful for M.D. as well as S.D.

Therefore, $\sqrt{\sum(x_i - \bar{x})^2/n}$ is a convenient formula for computations.

x_i	$|d_i| = |x_i - \bar{x}| = |x_i - a|$	d_i^2
a − kd	kd	k^2d^2
a − (k − 1) d	(k − 1) d	$(k-1)^2 d^2$
⋮	⋮	⋮
⋮	⋮	⋮
a − d	d	d^2
a	0	0
a + d	d	d^2
⋮	⋮	⋮
⋮	⋮	⋮
a + (k − 1) d	(k − 1) d	$(k-1)^2 d^2$
a + kd	kd	k^2d^2

$$\text{M.D. about } \bar{x} = \frac{\sum |d_i|}{n} = \frac{2(d + 2d + \ldots + kd)}{2k + 1}$$

$$= \frac{k(k+1)d}{2k + 1}$$

$$\text{S.D.} = \sqrt{\frac{\sum d_i^2}{n}} = \sqrt{\frac{2d^2(1^2 + 2^2 + \ldots + k^2)}{2k + 1}}$$

$$= \sqrt{\frac{2d^2 k(k+1)(2k+1)}{6(2k+1)}}$$

$$= d\sqrt{\frac{k(k+1)}{3}}$$

Example 4.17 : Suppose $x_1, x_2, \ldots, x_n$ are the observations.

$$\sigma^2 = \frac{1}{2n^2} \sum_{i=1}^{n} \sum_{j=1}^{n} (x_i - x_j)^2,$$

Solution : Suppose $\bar{x}$ is the A.M. Let us evaluate

$$\frac{1}{2n^2} \sum_i \sum_j (x_i - x_j)^2 = \frac{1}{2n^2} \sum_i \sum_j (x_i - \bar{x} - x_j + \bar{x})^2$$

$$= \frac{1}{2n^2} \sum_i \sum_j \left[(x_i - \bar{x}) - (x_j - \bar{x}) \right]^2$$

$$= \frac{1}{2n^2} \left[\sum_i \sum_j (x_i - \bar{x})^2 + \sum_i \sum_j (x_j - \bar{x})^2 - 2 \sum_i \sum_j (x_i - \bar{x})(x_j - \bar{x}) \right]$$

$$= \frac{1}{2n^2} \left[\left\{ n \sum_i (x_i - \bar{x})^2 + n \sum_j (x_j - \bar{x})^2 - 2 \sum_i \left[(x_i - \bar{x}) \sum_j (x_j - \bar{x}) \right] \right\} \right]$$

$$= \frac{\sum (x_i - \bar{x})^2}{2n} + \frac{\sum (x_j - \bar{x})^2}{2n} - \frac{2 \sum (x_i - \bar{x}) \times 0}{2n} = \frac{\sigma^2}{2} + \frac{\sigma^2}{2} - 0 = \sigma^2$$

Case Study :

Parag Infotech Pvt. Ltd. is a company to provide a software solutions. Directors of the company have taken a decision to double the capital and expand it in a big way. In view of this company decides to recruit at least 50 computer engineers. Company invited applications from fresh computer engineering graduates having at least 70% marks at their final examination. Company also expected furnish details of marks obtained from their SSC examination onwards.

Company received 200 applications. Most of the applications have secured marks between 70% to 73% in their final examination. Due to short of time to recruit, company is not interested to conduct personal interview of all the applicants but to select 70 of the best applicants for personal interview of the final selection. Company feels that 2% to 3% variation in final examination marks may be due to chance and has no effect in the performance.

Statisticians have advised to company to use the concept of measures of dispersion. Discuss the use of range and standard deviation in this regard to take the proper decision.

Points to Remember

1. Range = Largest observations − Smallest observation.
   Coefficient of range
   $$= \frac{\text{Largest observation} - \text{Smallest observation}}{\text{Largest observation} + \text{Smallest observation}}$$

2. Standard deviation (S.D.) $= \sigma = \sqrt{\dfrac{\sum x^2}{n} - \bar{x}^2}$ for discrete series

   $$= \sqrt{\frac{\sum fx^2}{\sum f} - \bar{x}^2}$$
   for frequency distribution

3. Coefficient of variation (C.V.) $= \dfrac{\sigma}{\bar{X}} \times 100\%$.

4. C.V. is used for the comparison of variation.

5. Quartile deviation $= \dfrac{Q_3 - Q_1}{2}$.

6. Coefficient of quartile deviation $= \dfrac{Q_3 - Q_1}{Q_3 + Q_1}$.

7. M.D. about m $= \dfrac{\sum f_i |x_i - m|}{\sum f_i}$ m is mean or median or mode.

8. Coefficient of mean deviation about m is $= \dfrac{\text{M.D. about m}}{m}$.

EXERCISE 4 (A)

A. Theory Questions :

1. What is dispersion ? What purpose does it serve in the study of distribution ?
2. What type of measures will you use for comparison of dispersion in different distributions ? Mention any two of such measures.
3. Explain relative measure of dispersion and state its utility.
4. Define : Range, Quartile deviation, Mean deviation and standard deviation. State the formula for each in case of ungrouped data and frequency distribution.
5. Compare critically the measures of dispersion (i) range and Q.D. (ii) M.D. and S.D.

6. State the merits and demerits of each of the following measures of dispersion :
   (i) range (ii) M.D. (iii) S.D.
7. Explain why S.D. is the best measure of dispersion.
8. What is utility of C.V. ?
9. Show that S.D. ≥ M.D. about arithmetic mean.
10. Show that mean squared deviation is greater than or equal to variance.
11. State and prove minimal property of mean squared deviation.
12. Discuss the effect of change of origin on variance and S.D.
13. Discuss the effect of change of scale on variance and S.D.
14. Suggest a suitable measure of dispersion if (i) the frequency distribution includes open end class (ii) the data are qualitative.
15. Show that all the measures of dispersion are invariant to the change of origin.
16. Define deviation about $\bar{x}$ and explain how it can be used to measure dispersion.
17. Given the size, A.M. and S.D. of each of k (k ≥ 2) groups, state the formula for combined S.D.
18. Two groups of n_1 and n_2 observations have the arithmetic means $\bar{x}_1$ and $\bar{x}_2$, the standard deviations σ_1 and σ_2 respectively. State the formula for combined S.D. Also discuss the cases for combined S.D. (i) $\bar{x}_1 = \bar{x}_2$ (ii) $n_1 = n_2$ (iii) $n_1 = n_2$ and $\bar{x}_1 = \bar{x}_2$ (iv) $n_1 = n_2$, $\bar{x}_1 = \bar{x}_2$ and $\sigma_1 = \sigma_2$.
19. Suppose $x_1, x_2, \ldots, x_n$ are n values of a variable x with A.M. $\bar{x}$. Can we measure dispersion of x using $\sum (x_i - \bar{x})$? If not, give reason and suggest how the deviations $(x_i - \bar{x})$; i = 1, 2, ... n, can be used to measure dispersion.
20. Compare mean deviation and standard deviation as measures of dispersion.
21. Suggest a measure of dispersion which can be obtained graphically. Also explain the procedure for obtaining the same.

B. Problems :

1. If $Y = 2X + 3$ then show that $\sigma_y^2 = 9\sigma_x^2$.
2. If $Y = aX + b$ then show that $\bar{Y} = a\bar{X} + b$ and $\sigma_y^2 = a^2 \sigma_x^2$.
3. Show that S.D. of $\{x_1, x_2\} = \dfrac{|x_1 - x_2|}{2}$.
4. Show that S.D. of $\{x_1, x_2, \ldots, x_n\}$ = S.D. of $\{-x_1, -x_2, \ldots, -x_n\}$.
5. Show that (i) $\sum x_i^2 \geq n\bar{X}^2$, (ii) $\sum x_i^2 \geq \dfrac{(\sum x_i)^2}{n}$.
6. Find the variance of $1, 2, \ldots, n$.
7. A variable takes values $a, a + d, a + 2d, \ldots, a + (n - 1) d$; find its variance.
8. A variable takes values $1, 2, \ldots, n$ with frequencies $1, 2, \ldots, n$ respectively. Find the standard deviation.
9. A variable takes values $0, 1, \ldots, n$ with frequencies $^nC_0, {}^nC_1, \ldots, {}^nC_n$ respectively. Find the variance.
10. Find the standard deviation of the following frequency distribution :

X	1	2	3	4	5
Frequency	a	2a	3a	4a	5a

C. Numerical Problems : Discrete Series :

1. Compute the (i) standard deviation (ii) mean deviation about mean (iii) coefficient of mean deviation about mean for the following data :
   15, 18, 22, 25, 10.
2. Calculate the (i) coefficient of variation (ii) mean deviation about the median for the following series :
   12, 18, 15, 20, 16.
3. Find the standard deviation of the following observations :
   2, 3, 5, 2, 7, 5, 7, 6, 11, 12.
4. Find the (i) standard deviation (ii) coefficient of variation (iii) mean deviation about median (iv) coefficient of mean deviation about median for the following data :
   6, 4, 5, 3, 12, 10.

5. Which of the following two series A and B is more stable? Why?

A	4	4	2	3	6	8	2	0	1	−1
B	8	7	5	5	6	7	4	3	4	1

6. Using coefficient of variation find which of the following batsman is more consistent in scoring:

Score of A	42	115	6	73	7	19	119	36	84	29
Score of B	47	12	76	42	4	51	37	48	13	0

7. Compare the variation between the weight and the height of a group of 10 persons using coefficient of variation.

Sr. No.	1	2	3	4	5	6	7	8	9	10
Weight (kg)	70	65	65	64	69	63	65	70	71	62
Height (cm)	170	140	151	145	165	167	156	160	153	168

D. Numerical Problems : Frequency Distribution :

8. Calculate the standard deviation and coefficient of variation for the following frequency distribution:

X	2	4	6	8	10
Frequency	2	4	14	8	2

Also find the quartile deviation, coefficient of quartile deviation.

9. A survey conducted to determine distance travelled (in kms) per litre of petrol by newly introduced motorcycle gives the following distribution:

Distance (km)	40-45	45-50	50-55	55-60	60-65
No. of Motorcycles	10	17	23	40	10

Find the (i) standard deviation, (ii) quartile deviation and coefficient of quartile deviation, (iii) mean deviation about median and coefficient of mean deviation.

10. Find the variance for the following frequency distribution and the mean deviation about the mode.

Class	5-15	15-25	25-35	35-45	45-55
Frequency	05	15	22	18	10

11. Compute the standard deviation for the following data. Also find mean deviation about median and its relative measure.

Marks	0-9	10-19	20-29	30-39	40-49
No. of Students	3	7	25	10	5

12. Calculate the coefficient of variation (C.V.) for the following data :

Class	1-10	11-20	21-30	31-40	41-50	51-60
Frequency	5	9	15	21	6	4

13. Find the standard deviation and the coefficient of variation from the following data :

Marks	0 - 10	10 - 20	20 - 30	30 - 40	40 - 50
Frequency	10	16	30	32	12

14. Find the quartile deviation and coefficient of quartile deviation of distribution of daily wages.

Daily wages	Below 20	21 - 40	41 - 60	61 - 80	Above 80
Frequency	5	32	45	17	1

15. Two automatic tea filling machines A and B tested for the performance. Machines are supposed to fill 500 gm. tea in each packet. A random sample of 100 filled packets on each machine showed the following distribution.

Weight in gm.	Frequency A	Frequency B
485–490	12	10
490–495	18	15
495–500	20	24
500–505	22	20
505–510	24	18
510–515	4	13

Which machine is more consistent ? Why ?

16. The following data pertain to two workers doing the same job in a factory :

	Worker A	Worker B
Mean time of completing the job (minutes)	40	42
Standard deviation (minutes)	8	6

Who is more consistent worker ? Why ?

E. Combined Standard Deviation :

17. Two samples of sizes 40 and 50 have the same mean and standard deviations 20 and 10 respectively. Find the variance of the combined group.

18. The mean weight of 150 students is 60 kg. The mean weight of boys is 70 kg, with standard deviation of 10 kg. For girls the mean weight is 55 kg with standard deviation of 15 kg. Find the number of boys and combined standard deviation.

19. Out of 400 observations, 100 observations have one each and the test of the observations are zero. Find the mean and standard deviation of 400 observations together.

20. For a set of 90 observations the mean and standard deviations are 59 and 9 respectively. For 40 observations selected from these observations, mean and standard deviations are 54 and 6 respectively. Find the mean and standard deviation of the remaining observations.

21. The arithmetic mean and the standard deviation of the values of 100 items in a group are 80 and 5 respectively. In a second group of 25 items, each item has a value equal to 60. Find the combined standard deviation of two groups taken together.

22. Suppose X denotes the time required to complete a job by workers A and Y denotes the time required to complete a job by workers B. Ten jobs were assigned to both workers A and B. Information regarding completion times is as follows :
$\Sigma x_i = 300$, $\Sigma y_i = 250$, $\Sigma x_i^3 = 9360$, $\Sigma y_i^2 = 7850$.
   (i) Which worker appears to be faster in completing the jobs ?
   (ii) Which worker is more consistent ?

23. Find combined standard deviation from the following data :

Workers	Number	Average Salary	Standard Deviation
Male	80	1520	06
Female	20	1420	05

24. Two workers on the same job show the following results over long period of time :

	Worker 'A'	Worker 'B'
Mean time of completing the job (in minutes)	30	24
Standard Deviation	6	4
Number of jobs	10	10

(i) Which worker appears to be more consistent in the time he requires to complete the job ? Why ?
(ii) Which worker is faster in completing the job ? Why ?
(iii) Find the combined mean and standard deviation of the two workers together.

25. Information about the daily salaries of employees in firms A and B is stated below :

Firm	No. of employees	Mean Salary	S.D. of Salary
A	60	₹ 400	₹ 10
B	40	₹ 500	₹ 11

(i) Which firm gives more amount as salary ?
(ii) Which firm has smaller variation in salary ?
(iii) Find the combined mean and S.D. of two firms.

26. Information regarding daily salaries of two companies A and B is given below :

	Company A	Company B
No. of workers	600	400
Mean salary	₹ 180	₹ 200
S.D. of salary	₹ 9	₹ 10

(i) Which company pays larger salary ? Why ?
(ii) Which company has less variation in salaries ? Why ?
(iii) Find combined mean and S.D. of two firms A and B.

27. Find the combined S.D. from the following data :

	Group A	Group B	Group C
Size	100	150	250
Arithmetic mean	50	55	60
S.D.	10	11	12

F. Corrected Standard Deviation :

28. A sample of 10 numbers gave a mean of 13 and a variance of 4. Later it was discovered that the number 12 included in the sample should have been 21. Find the corrected mean and variance.

29. The mean and standard deviation of 100 observations are 40 and 5.1 respectively. During cross-checking, it was found that an observation 40 was misread as 50. Compute correct values of mean and standard deviation.

30. The mean and standard deviation of 20 observations are 10 and 2 respectively. Later on it was noticed that item 8 was incorrect. Calculate arithmetic mean and standard deviation if (i) the wrong item is omitted. (ii) the wrong item is replaced by 12.

G. Miscellaneous Problems :

31. Find the missing observations, if the arithmetic mean and standard deviation of the following series are 10 and 4 respectively.
    14, ?, 11, 10, 13, 16, ?, 9, 12, 2.

32. In a group of 10 children, the heaviest boy weighs 10 kg. more than the average weight of other children. Show that the standard deviation of the group cannot be less than 3 kg.

33. The range, arithmetic mean and standard deviation of a group of 10 items is 20, 62, 10 respectively. If each observation is increased by 5, what will be the range and the coefficient of variation ?

34. If $n = 10$, $\sum (x - 120) = 20$, $\sum (x - 120)^2 = 200$. Find the mean and the standard deviation.

35. If $n = 100$, $\sum x = -20$, $\sum x^2 = 220$, find standard deviation and coefficient of variation.

36. Find the standard deviation of set A, Set B, Set C and Set D and comment on findings.

Set A :	1	2	3	4	5
Set B :	11	12	13	14	15
Set C :	10	20	30	40	50
Set D :	4	4	4	4	4

37. The range, arithmetic mean and standard deviation of 10 items are 12, 50, 6 respectively. If each observation is increased by 10, what will be the range, arithmetic mean and standard deviation ?

ANSWERS

B.
6. $(n^2 - 1)/2$
7. $n(n-2)d^2/12$
8. $\sqrt{(n^2 + n - 1)/18}$
9. $n/4$
10. 55.6

C.
1. S.D. = 5.2536, M.D. = 44, Coefficient of M.D. = 0.2444.
2. C.V. = 16.75%, M.D. = 2.2
3. 3.2558
4. $\sigma = 3.1842$, C.V. = 46.5975%, M.D. = 2.5, Coefficient of M.D. = 0.4167
5. Series B more stable, C.V. (A) = 89.1898% C.V. (B) = 40%
6. B is more consistent C.V. (A) = 75.54 %, C.V. (B) = 70.82 %
7. C.V. (weight) = 4.67 % < C.V. (height) = 6.18 %

D.
8. $\sigma = 1.9137$, C.V. = 43.73%, Q.D. = 1, Coefficient of Q.D. = 1/7
9. $\sigma = 5.7383$, Q.D. = 4.3566 Coefficient of Q.D. = 0.08103
   M.D. = 4.85 Coefficient of M.D. = 0.0882
10. $\sigma^2 = 129.4082$, M.D. = 9.2727
11. $\sigma = 9.8$, M.D. = 7 Coefficient of M.D. = 0.2745
12. C.V. = 42.9986
13. $\sigma = 11.4891$, C.V. = 42.5522
14. Q.D. = 12.1944, Coefficient of Q.D. = 0.1349
15. C.V. (A) = 1.4294 % C.V. (B) = 1.5084 %, Machine A is more consistent.
16. B, since C.V. (A) = 20% > C.V. (B) = 14.2857%

E.
17. $\bar{X}_C = 20$, $\sigma_c^2 = 10$
18. Number of boys = 50, $\sigma_c = 15.2753$
19. Mean = $\frac{1}{4}$, Variance = $\frac{5}{8}$
20. Mean = 63, S.D. = 9
21. $\bar{X}_C = 76$, $\sigma_c = \sqrt{84}$
22. (i) B (ii) A since C.V. (A) = 20% < C.V. (B) = 50.5964%
23. 40.42029

24. (i) C.V. (A) = 20% > C.V. (B) = 16.6667%,
    B is more consistent
    (ii) B (iii) Combined mean = 27, Combined S.D. = 5.9161
25. (i) B (ii) C.V. (A) = 2.5% > C.V. (B) = 2.2%,
    B has smaller variation
    (iii) Combined mean = 440, Combined S.D. = 50.0839
26. (i) B (ii) Both have same C.V. = 5%,
    both are equal in variation
    (iii) Combined mean = 188, Combined S.D. = 14.2969%
27. 11.9812

F. 28. Mean = 13.9, Variance = 9.49
29. Mean = 39.9, S.D. = 5
30. (i) Mean = 10.1053, S.D. = 1.9922 (ii) Mean = 10.2, S.D. = 1.99.

G. 31. 8, 5
33. 20, 14.9254
34. Mean = 122, S.D. = 2
35. S.D. = 1.4697, C.V. = 734.8469%
36. $\sigma_A = \sigma_B = \sqrt{2}$, $\sigma_C = 10\sqrt{2}$, $\sigma_D = 0$.
37. Range = 12, $\bar{X} = 60$, $\sigma = 6$.

Objective Type Questions

(A) Multiple Choice Questions

- **Choose the correct alternative :**

1. Which one of the following measure is the crudest measure of dispersion ?
   (a) range
   (b) quartile deviation
   (c) mean deviation
   (d) standard deviation

2. In the following, which is not a measures of dispersion ?
   (a) central deviation from mean
   (b) mean deviation
   (c) quartile deviation
   (d) standard deviation

3. The wide application of 'range' is in the field of :
   (a) statistical quality control
   (b) economics
   (c) psychometries
   (d) none of the above
4. In the case when first and last class intervals are openend type, one can find :
   (a) range
   (b) mean deviation
   (c) standard deviation
   (d) quartile deviation
5. The mean deviation can be obtained about :
   (a) arithmetic mean
   (b) mode
   (c) median
   (d) all the above
6. Let $x_1, x_2, ..., x_n$ a set of n observations, then the formula of standard deviation is :
   (a) $\sqrt{\dfrac{\sum(x_i - \bar{x})^2}{n}}$
   (b) $\dfrac{\sum(x_i - \bar{x}^2)}{N}$
   (c) $\dfrac{\sqrt{\sum(x_i - \bar{x})^2}}{n}$
   (d) $\dfrac{\sum(x^2 - \bar{x}^2)}{n}$
7. Let $x_1, x_2 .... x_n$ is a set of n observations, the formula of mean deviation from mean is :
   (a) $\sqrt{\dfrac{\sum|x_i - \bar{x}|^2}{\sqrt{n}}}$
   (b) $\dfrac{\sum|x_i - \bar{x}|}{n}$
   (c) $\dfrac{\sum|x_i - \bar{x}|^2}{n}$
   (d) $\dfrac{\sum|x_i - \bar{x}|}{\sqrt{n}}$
8. Let $x_1, x_2, ..., x_n$ be a set of an observations, L = Largest and S = Smallest value in the data then the formula of range is :
   (a) R = S – L
   (b) R = $x_n - x_1$
   (c) R = L – S
   (d) R = |S – L|
9. Mean deviation is the least when meansured from :
   (a) mean
   (b) median
   (c) mode
   (d) zero

10. The formula of quartile deviation or semi inter-quartile range is :
    (a) $Q_3 - Q_1$
    (b) $(Q_3 - Q_1)/(Q_3 + Q_1)$
    (c) $(Q_3 - Q_1)/2$
    (d) $(Q_1 - Q_3)/2$

11. With usual notations formula for coefficient of range of the set of observations $x_1, x_2, ..., x_n$ is :
    (a) $(L - S)/(L + S)$
    (b) $(L - S)/L$
    (c) $(L + S)/(L - S)$
    (d) L/S

12. Formula for coefficient of quartile deviation is equal to :
    (a) $(Q_3 - Q_1)/(Q_1 - Q_3)$
    (b) $(Q_3 + Q_1)/(Q_1 - Q_3)$
    (c) $(Q_3 + Q_1)/(Q_3 - Q_1)$
    (d) $(Q_3 - Q_1)/(Q_3 + Q_1)$

13. In standard deviation, the deviations of the items x_i are always taken from :
    (a) mean
    (b) median
    (c) mode
    (d) zero

14. If the coefficient of range of series A is less than that of the series B, then standard deviation of A is :
    (a) series A is more consistent
    (b) series B is more consistent
    (c) both series are equally consistent
    (d) none of the above

15. The concept of standard deviation was introduced by :
    (a) Karl Pearson
    (b) R. A. Fisher
    (c) Gauss
    (d) W. S. Gossett

16. Which one of the following relation between standard deviation (S.D.) and variance (Var (X)) of a variable X is true ?
    (a) S.D. = Var (X)
    (b) $(S.D.)^2$ = Var (X)
    (c) S.D. = $[Var (X)]^2$
    (d) None of the above

17. Mean square deviation is minimum when deviations are taken from :
    (a) mean
    (b) mode
    (c) median
    (d) zero

18. Let $\{(x_i, f_i), i = 1, 2, ... n\}$ be a discrete frequency distribution having an average A and $\sum f_i = N$, then the mean deviation is :
    (a) $\frac{1}{N} \sum f_i (x_i - A)^2$
    (b) $\frac{1}{N} \sum f_i (x_i - A)$
    (c) $\frac{1}{N} \sum f_i |x_i - A|$
    (d) $\frac{1}{N} \sum |f_i x_i - A|$

19. The value of standard deviation of a set of values will be :
    (a) zero if all observations are equal
    (b) always positive
    (c) positive although the values are negative
    (d) all the above

20. If mean deviation = M.D. and standard deviation = S.D. of n values $x_1, x_2 .... x_n$ then :
    (a) M.D. = S.D.
    (b) M.D. > S.D.
    (c) M.D. < S.D.
    (d) any one of the above

21. The quartile deviation (Q.D.), mean deviation (M.D.) and the standard deviation (S.D.) respectively normally related by the expression :
    (a) M.D. ≤ Q.D. ≤ S.D.
    (b) S.D. ≤ Q.D. ≤ M.D.
    (c) M.D. ≤ S.D. ≤ Q.D.
    (d) Q.D. ≤ M.D. ≤ S.D.

22. Which one of the following measures of dispersion ignores the signs of deviations from a central value ?
    (a) quartile deviation
    (b) standard deviation
    (c) range
    (d) mean deviation

23. The formula for quartile deviation or semi inter-quartile range is given by :
    (a) Q.D. = $(Q_3 - Q_1)/4$
    (b) Q.D. = $(Q_3 - Q_1)/2$
    (c) Q.D. = $(Q_3 - Q_1) \times 2$
    (d) Q.D. = $(Q_3 + Q_1)/2$

24. If a constant value 10 is subtracted from each observation of a set, the variance is :
    (a) increased by 100
    (b) decreased by 10
    (c) decreased by 100
    (d) not changed

25. If each observation of a set is divided by 15 the S.D. of the coded set is :
    (a) 15 times of S.D. of original set of observations
    (b) unaltered
    (c) $\frac{1}{225}$ th of S.D. of original set of observations
    (d) $\frac{1}{15}$ th of S.D. of original set of observations

26. Let $\{(x_i, f_i), i = 1, 2, \ldots n\}$ be a discrete frequency distribution and $\bar{x}$ be the arithmetic mean Let $\sum f_i = N$, then the standard deviation is :
   (a) $\sqrt{\sum(f_i x_i^2 - \bar{x}^2)/N}$
   (b) $\sqrt{(f_i x_i - \bar{x})^2/N}$
   (c) $\sqrt{\sum(x_i - \bar{x})/N}$
   (d) $\sqrt{\sum f_i (x_i - \bar{x})^2/N}$

27. There are two series with n_1 and n_2 values, having arithmetic means $\bar{x}_1$, $\bar{x}_2$ and standard deviations σ_1, σ_2 respectively, then for $d_1 = \bar{x}_1 - \bar{x}$ and $d_2 = \bar{x}_2 - \bar{x}$ where $\bar{x}$ = combined or pooled mean. The variance of the combined series is :
   (a) $[n_1 \sigma_1^2 + n_2 d_1^2 + n_2 \sigma_2^2 + n_1 d_2^2] / (n_1 n_2)$
   (b) $[n_1 \sigma_1^2 + n_2 d_1^2 + n_2 \sigma_2^2 + n_1 d_2^2] / (n_1 + n_2)$
   (c) $[n_1 \sigma_1^2 + n_1 d_1^2 + n_2 \sigma_2^2 + n_2 d_2^2] / (n_1 n_2)$
   (d) $[n_1 \sigma_1^2 + n_1 d_1^2 + n_2 \sigma_2^2 + n_2 d_2^2] / (n_1 + n_2)$

28. Which one of the following measures satisfies all the characteristics of an ideal measure ?
   (a) the range
   (b) the mean deviation
   (c) the quartile deviation
   (d) the standard deviation

29. If the smallest value in a set is 7 and its range is 85. The largest value of the set is :
   (a) 85.7
   (b) 12.14
   (c) 78
   (d) 92

30. If the largest value in a set is 89 and its range is 82. The smallest value of the set is :
   (a) 7
   (b) 9
   (c) 86
   (d) 6

31. Which one of the following is called as the best measures of dispersion ?
   (a) range
   (b) mean deviation
   (c) coefficient of variation
   (d) standard deviation

32. If mean $\bar{x}$, median Me, mode Mo and standard deviation σ are given then coefficient of variation is :
   (a) $\sigma/\bar{x} \times 100$
   (b) $\bar{x}/\sigma \times 100$
   (c) $\sigma/Me \times 100$
   (d) $\sigma/Mo \times 100$

33. If $N = 10$, $\sum X = 120$, $\sum X^2 = 1530$ then value of coefficient of variation (C.V.) is equal to :
   (a) 12%
   (b) 30%
   (c) 25%
   (d) 40%

34. The value of range and Q.D. for the following data :
   125, 70, 156, 100, 190 175, 250 is respectively :
   (a) 160, 54
   (b) 160, 45
   (c) 180, 45
   (d) 180, 54

35. Following data shows the performance of two batsman A and B :

	Batsman A	Batsman B
No. of innings	60	40
Mean runs	30	25
S.D. of runs	6	4

   The combined average runs of two batsmen are :
   (a) 8
   (b) 28
   (c) 20
   (d) 22

36. For the problem given is Q. No. 35 which batsman is more consistent in score ?
   (a) batsman A
   (b) batsman B
   (c) both A and B
   (d) any one of the above

37. For the problem given in Q. No. 35 the combined variance is equal to :
   (a) 40.4
   (b) 20
   (c) 16
   (d) 6.25

38. A measure of dispersion which is independent of units is :
   (a) range
   (b) mean deviaiton
   (c) coefficient of variation
   (d) standard deviation

39. In order to compare the variability of different groups, the best measure of dispersion is :
   (a) range
   (b) mean deviation
   (c) coefficient of variation
   (d) standard deviation

40. A set of values with mean 20 and its coefficient of variation is 15 percent the variance of the series is :
    (a) 30 (b) 3
    (c) 9 (d) 300
41. If mean and standard deviation of a set of values are 33 and 2, respectively. If a constant value 7 is added to each value, the coefficient of variation of the new coded set of values is :
    (a) 330 percent (b) 5 percent
    (c) 40 percent (d) 35 percent
42. The mean and variance of a distribution are 80 and 6.25 respectively, the coefficient of variation is :
    (a) 2.5 percent (b) 12.5 percent
    (c) 3.125 percent (d) 7.8 percent
43. If each value of set of observations is multiplied by 15, the coefficient of variation will be increased by :
    (a) zero percent (b) five percent
    (c) ten percent (d) fifteen percent
44. If each value of set of observations is divided by 10, its coefficients of variation is decreased by :
    (a) zero percent (b) five percent
    (c) ten percent (d) fifteen percent

II. State whether the following statements are True or False :

1. The dispersion of a data set gives insight into the reliability of the measure of central tendency.
2. The stadard deviation is equal to the positive square root of the variance.
3. The difference between the highest and lowest observations in a data set is called the inter-quartile range.
4. The inter-quartile range is based on only two values taken from the data set.
5. The standard deviation is measured in the same units as the observations in the data set.
6. The variance, like the standard deviation takes into account every observation in the data set.
7. It is possible to measure the range of an open ended distribution.
8. The measure of dispersion ensures credibility to the measure of central tendency.

9. The mean deviation is minimum when computed from the median.
10. Let $x_1, x_2, \ldots, x_n$ be a set of values of X then the least root mean square deviation of X about $\bar{x}$ is known as standard deviation.
11. The standard deviation of a variable whose values are all equal, must be zero and converse is also true.
12. The standard deviation is less affected by extreme values than the mean deviation.
13. Consistent player has more variability in test score.
14. If standard derivation of two groups are known then value of combined standard derivation lies between two group standard derivation.
15. Range is not based on all observations and it does not give proper idea regarding variation between the extreme observations.
16. The range is widely used in the Statistical Quality Control.
17. The range of middle 50% items is computed with the help of quartile deviation.
18. Variance is invariant to the change of origin.

Answers : Objective Type Questions

I. Multiple Choice Questions :

(1) a (2) a (3) a (4) d (5) d
(6) a (7) b (8) c (9) b (10) c
(11) a (12) d (13) a (14) a (15) a
(16) b (17) a (18) c (19) d (20) c
(21) d (22) d (23) b (24) d (25) d
(26) d (27) d (28) d (29) d (30) a
(31) d (32) a (33) c (34) c (35) b
(36) b (37) a (38) c (39) c (40) c
(41) b (42) c (43) a (44) a

II. True or False :

(1) True (2) True (3) False (4) True
(5) True (6) True (7) False (8) True
(9) True (10) False : It is positive square root.
(11) True (12) False : Mean deviation is less affected.
(13) False : Less variability.
(14) False (15) True
(16) True (17) True (18) True.

Chapter 5...
Moments, Skewness and Kurtosis

C. R. Rao

Dr. C. R. Rao (1920) : Born in Karnataka, Prof. C. R. Rao is the most celebrated Indian American Statistician. He is a professor emeritus at Penn State University and Research professor at the University of Buffalo, USA. In 1946, he completed his Ph.D. at Cambridge University under the guidance of Prof. R. A. Fisher. His contributions are Cramer-Rao inequality, Rao-Blackwell theorem, Fisher-Rao theorem, Rao distance and orthogonal arrays. He is honored with over 36 doctoral degrees by different universities of 19 countries. He is included in to the Hall of Fame of India's National Institution for Quality and Reliability.

Prof. Rao was awarded the US National of Science in 2002. American Statistical Association has described him as 'a living legend' for his far reaching work in statistics applied to economics, genetics, anthropology, geology, national planning and medicinal problem.

Contents ...

Moments

5.1 Introduction
5.2 Raw Moments
5.3 Central Moments
5.4 Relation between Raw and Central Moments
5.5 Moments about 'a'
5.6 Sheppard's Correction

Skewness and Kurtosis

5.7 Introduction
5.8 Symmetry
5.9 Skewness
5.10 Karl Pearson's Coefficient of Skewness
5.11 Bowley's Coefficient of Skewness
5.12 Pearsonian Coefficient of Skewness (β_1)
5.13 Kurtosis
5.14 Measures of Kurtosis (β_2)

Key Words :
Moments, raw moments, central moments, moments about value a, Sheppard's correction.
Symmetry, Skewness, Positive Skewness, Negative Skewness, Moments, Quartiles, Kurtosis, Leptokurtic, Mesokurtic, Platykurtic.

Objectives :
Moments give tools for comparison of data sets. Using moments we can study the four aspects of comparison viz. average, dispersion, symmetry and kurtosis.

To measure departure from symmetry. To compare data sets of asymmetric nature. To find the relative height of symmetric frequency distributions. There are four aspects of comparison of data sets viz. average, dispersion, symmetry and kurtosis. The last two aspects are studied in this chapter.

Moments

5.1 Introduction

There are several aspects of studying frequency distribution. In earlier chapters we have studied two of them viz. average and dispersion. In order to study few more aspects such as symmetry, shape of frequency distribution (or frequency curve) moments are useful. For quantitative data, we have used $\bar{x} = \sum x_i/n$ and $\sigma^2 = \sum(x_i - \bar{x})^2/n$ as the best measures of average and dispersion respectively. Here we study a more general type of descriptive measure such as $\sum(x_i - a)^r/n$. It is called as moment. Particularly for $a = 0$, $r = 1$, we get arithmetic mean and for $a = \bar{x}$ and $r = 2$, we get variance.

Moments : The quantity $\sum(x_i - a)^r/n$ is called as r^{th} moment (or moment of order r) about 'a'.

According to the choice of 'a', we make three categories of moments, viz. raw materials, central moments, moments about a.

5.2 Raw Moments

Raw moment of order r (or r^{th} raw moment) is denoted by μ_r and given by the following formula.

$$\mu_r' = \frac{\sum_{i=1}^{n} x_i^r}{n} \quad \text{for individual observations}$$

$$= \frac{\sum_{i=1}^{k} f_i x_i^r}{\sum_{i=1}^{k} f_i} \quad \text{for frequency distribution}$$

The first four moments are of prime importance for defining various descriptive measures of data. Therefore, for r = 1, 2, 3, 4 we get the first four raw moments μ_1', μ_2', μ_3', μ_4' respectively. We state the corresponding formulae in the following table.

Moments	Formula For	
	Individual observations	Frequency distribution
μ_1'	$\sum x_i / n = \bar{x}$	$\sum f_i x_i / N = \bar{x}$
μ_2'	$\sum x_i^2 / n$	$\sum f_i x_i^2 / N$
μ_3'	$\sum x_i^3 / n$	$\sum f_i x_i^3 / N$
μ_4'	$\sum x_i^4 / n$	$\sum f_i x_i^4 / N$ where $N = \sum f_i$

Note : (i) μ_1' = Arithmetic mean

(ii) The raw moments are also called as the moments about origin.

5.3 Central Moments

Central moment of order r (or r^{th} order moment) μ_r is given by the following formula.

$$\mu_r = \sum (x_i - \bar{x})^r / n, \text{ for individual observations}$$

$$= \sum f_i (x_i - \bar{x})^r / \sum f_i, \text{ for frequency distribution.}$$

Substituting r = 1, 2, 3, 4 in the above formula we get first four central moments, μ_1, μ_2, μ_3 and μ_4 respectively.

Moments	Formula For	
	Individual observations	Frequency distribution
μ_1	$\sum(x_i - \bar{x})/n = 0$	$\sum f_i (x_i - \bar{x})^2/N = 0$
μ_2	$\sum(x_i - \bar{x})^2/n = \sigma^2$	$\sum f_i (x_i - \bar{x})^2/N = \sigma^2$
μ_3	$\sum(x_i - \bar{x})^3/n$	$\sum f_i (x_i - \bar{x})^3/N$
μ_4	$\sum(x_i - \bar{x})^4/n$	$\sum f_i (x_i - \bar{x})^4/N$ where $N = \sum f_i$

Mainly we need central moments. However, these are difficult to compute as compared to raw moments. Therefore, we require to find relation between raw moments.

5.4 Relation between Raw and Central Moments

$$\mu_1 = \frac{\sum f_i (x_i - \bar{x})}{N} = \frac{\sum f_i x_i}{N} - \frac{\sum f_i \bar{x}}{N} = \bar{x} - \frac{N\bar{x}}{N} = 0$$

$$\mu_2 = \sum f_i (x_i - \bar{x})^2 / \sum f_i \quad (\text{Let } \sum f_i = N)$$

$$= \frac{1}{N} \sum f_i (x_i - \bar{x})^2$$

$$= \frac{1}{N} \sum f_i \left(x_i^2 - 2\bar{x} x_i + (\bar{x})^2 \right)$$

$$= \frac{\sum f_i x_i^2}{N} - 2\bar{x} \frac{\sum f_i x_i}{N} + \frac{\sum f_i (\bar{x})^2}{N}$$

$$= \frac{\sum f_i x_i^2}{N} - 2(\bar{x})^2 + (\bar{x})^2$$

$$= \frac{\sum f_i x_i^2}{\sum f_i} - (\bar{x})^2 = \mu_2' - \left(\mu_1'\right)^2 \qquad \ldots (1)$$

$$\mu_3 = \frac{\sum f_i (x_i - \bar{x})^3}{\sum f_i}$$

$$= \frac{1}{N} \left[\sum f_i \left(x_i^3 - 3x_i^2 \bar{x} + 3x_i (\bar{x})^2 - (\bar{x})^3 \right) \right]$$

$$= \frac{\sum f_i x_i^3}{N} - 3\bar{x} \frac{\sum f_i x_i^2}{N} + 3(\bar{x})^2 \frac{\sum f_i x_i}{N} - \frac{\sum f_i (\bar{x})^3}{N}$$

$$= \frac{\sum f_i x_i^3}{N} - 3\bar{x} \frac{\sum f_i x_i^2}{N} + 3(\bar{x})^3 - (\bar{x})^3$$

$$= \mu_3' - 3\mu_2' \mu_1' + 3\mu_1'^3 - \mu_1'^3$$

$$= \mu_3' - 3\mu_2' \mu_1' + 2\mu_1'^3 \qquad \ldots (2)$$

$$\mu_4 = \frac{\sum f_i (x_i - \bar{x})^4}{\sum f_i}$$

$$= \frac{1}{N} \left[\sum f_i \left(x_i^4 - 4x_i^3 \bar{x} + 6x_i^2 (\bar{x})^2 - 4x_i (\bar{x})^3 + (\bar{x})^4 \right) \right]$$

$$= \frac{\sum f_i x_i^4}{N} - 4\bar{x} \frac{\sum f_i x_i^3}{N} + 6(\bar{x})^2 \frac{\sum f_i x_i^2}{N} - 4(\bar{x})^3 \frac{\sum f_i x_i}{N} + \frac{\sum f_i (\bar{x})^4}{N}$$

$$= \mu_4' - 4\mu_3' \mu_1' + 6\mu_2' (\mu_1')^2 - 4(\mu_1')^4 + (\mu_1')^4$$

$$= \mu_4' - 4\mu_3' \mu_1' + 6\mu_2' (\mu_1')^2 - 3(\mu_1')^4 \quad \ldots (3)$$

In general μ_r can be expressed in terms of raw moments as follows :

$$\mu_r = \frac{\Sigma f_i (x_i - \bar{x})^r}{N}$$

$$= \frac{1}{N}\left[\Sigma f_i \left(x_i^r - {}^rC_1 x_i^{r-1} \bar{x} + {}^rC_2 x_i^{r-2} (\bar{x})^2 - {}^rC_3 x_i^{r-3} (\bar{x})^3 + \ldots + \ldots + (-1)^r (\bar{x})^r\right)\right]$$

$$= \frac{1}{N}\left[\Sigma f_i x_i^r - {}^rC_1 \bar{x} \Sigma f_i x_i^{r-1} + {}^rC_2 (\bar{x})^2 \Sigma f_i x_i^{r-2} + \ldots + (-1)^r (\bar{x})^r \Sigma f_i\right]$$

$$= \mu_r' - {}^rC_1 \mu_{r-1}' \mu_1' + {}^rC_2 \mu_{r-2}' {\mu_1'}^2 + {}^rC_3 \mu_{r-3}' {\mu_1'}^3 + \ldots$$

$$+ (-1)^{r-1} {}^rC_{r-1} {\mu_1'}^r + (-1)^r {\mu_1'}^r$$

The above relations also hold true for individual observations. Proofs can be given on similar lines.

Note : In the above relations we observe the following facts :
(i) Sum of the coefficients on R.H.S. of each of the relations is zero.
(ii) The final expression of μ_r contains r terms.
(iii) First term in the expression of μ_r is positive and alternative terms are negative.
(iv) The last term in the expression of μ_r is $(\mu_1')^r$.

5.5 Moments About 'a'

Suppose 'a' is any arbitrary constant, then r^{th} moment about a is denoted by $\mu_r (a)$ and it is defined as follows :

$$\mu_r (a) = \Sigma(x_i - a)^r/n \text{ for individual observations}$$

$$= \Sigma f_i (x_i - a)^r/\Sigma f_i \text{ for frequency distributions}$$

Note : (i) If $a = 0$, then $\mu_r (a) = \mu_r'$

(ii) If $a = \bar{x}$, then $\mu_r (a) = \mu_r$

Relation between moments about 'a' and central moments are given below :

$$\mu_1 = 0$$

$$\mu_2 = \frac{\sum f_i (x_i - \bar{x})^2}{N} = \frac{\sum f_i \left[(x_i - a) - (\bar{x} - a)\right]^2}{N}$$

$$= \frac{\sum f_i (x_i - a)^2}{N} - 2(\bar{x} - a) \frac{\sum f_i (x_i - a)}{N} + \frac{\sum f_i (\bar{x} - a)^2}{N}$$

$$= \mu_2(a) - 2\mu_1^2(a) + \mu_1^2(a) = \mu_2(a) - \mu_1^2(a)$$

Similarly, $\mu_3 = \frac{\sum f_i (x_i - \bar{x})^3}{N} = \frac{\sum f_i [(x_i - a) - (\bar{x} - a)]^3}{N}$

$$= \frac{1}{N} \sum f_i (x_i - a)^3 - \frac{3(\bar{x} - a) \sum f_i (x_i - a)^2}{N}$$

$$+ \frac{3(\bar{x} - a)^2}{N} \sum f_i (x_i - a) - \frac{(\bar{x} - a)^3}{N} \sum f_i$$

$$= \mu_3(a) - 3\mu_2(a)\mu_1(a) + 3\mu_1^3(a) - \mu_1^3(a)$$

$$= \mu_3(a) - 3\mu_2(a)\mu_1(a) + 2\mu_1^3(a)$$

$$\mu_4 = \frac{1}{N} \sum f_i (x_i - \bar{x})^4 = \frac{1}{N} \sum f_i \left[(x_i - a) - (\bar{x} - a)\right]^4$$

$$= \frac{1}{N} \sum f_i (x_i - a)^4 - \frac{4(\bar{x} - a)}{N} \sum f_i (x_i - a)^3$$

$$+ \frac{6(\bar{x} - a)^2}{N} \sum f_i (x_i - a)^2$$

$$- \frac{4(\bar{x} - a)^3}{N} \sum f_i (x_i - a) + \frac{(\bar{x} - a)^4}{N} \sum f_i$$

$$= \mu_4(a) - 4\mu_3(a)\mu_1(a) + 6\mu_2(a)\mu_1^2(a) - 4\mu_1^4(a) + \mu_1^4(a)$$

$$= \mu_4(a) - 4\mu_3(a)\mu_1(a) + 6\mu_2(a)\mu_1^2(a) - 3\mu_1^4(a)$$

Properties of Central Moments :

1. Effect of change of origin :

The central moments are invariant to the change of origin. In other words, if $u = x - a$ then μ_r of $u = \mu_r$ of x.

Proof : Let $u = x - a$, hence $\bar{u} = \bar{x} - a$

By definition, μ_r of $u = \sum(u_i - \bar{u})^r/n$

$$= \sum[(x_i - a) - (\bar{x} - a)]^r/n = \sum(x_i - \bar{x})^r/n$$

$$= \mu_r \text{ of } x$$

2. **Effect of change of origin and scale :**

If $u = \dfrac{x-a}{h}$ then μ_r of $u = \dfrac{1}{h^r} \mu_r$ of x.

Proof : Since $u = \dfrac{x-a}{h}$, we get $\bar{u} = \dfrac{\bar{x}-a}{h}$

By definition, μ_r of $u = \dfrac{\sum(u_i - \bar{u})^r}{n}$

$$= \dfrac{1}{n} \sum \left[\dfrac{x_i - a}{h} - \dfrac{\bar{x} - a}{h} \right]^r$$

$$= \dfrac{1}{h^r} \dfrac{\sum (x_i - \bar{x})^r}{n} = \dfrac{1}{h^r} \mu_r \text{ of } x.$$

Note :

(i) If $a = 0$ then we get $u = x/h$, it is equivalent to only change of scale.

(ii) If $h = 1$ then we get $u = x - a$, it is equivalent to only change of origin.

(iii) Due to change of origin and scale actual computations of moments are simplified to a considerable extent.

Illustrative Examples

Example 5.1 : Compute the first four central moments for the following frequency distribution.

| No. of jobs completed | 0-10 | 10-20 | 20-30 | 30-40 | 40-50 |

| No. of workers | 6 | 26 | 47 | 15 | 6 |

Solution :

Class	Mid Pts. (x)	Freq. (f)	$u = \dfrac{x-25}{10}$	fu	fu²	fu³	fu⁴
0-10	5	6	– 2	– 12	24	– 48	96
10-20	15	26	– 1	– 26	26	– 26	26
20-30	25	47	0	0	0	0	0
30-40	35	15	1	15	15	15	15
40-50	45	6	2	12	24	48	96
Total	–	100	–	– 11	89	– 11	233

Raw Moments of u :

$$\mu'_1 = \Sigma f_i x_i / \Sigma f_i = \dfrac{-11}{100} = -0.11$$

$$\mu'_2 = \Sigma f_i x_i^2 / \Sigma f_i = \dfrac{89}{100} = 0.89$$

$$\mu'_3 = \Sigma f_i x_i^3 / \Sigma f_i = \dfrac{-11}{100} = -0.11$$

$$\mu'_4 = \Sigma f_i x_i^4 / \Sigma f_i = \dfrac{233}{100} = 2.33$$

Central Moments of u :

$\mu_1 = 0$

$\mu_2 = \mu'_2 - {\mu'_1}^2 = 0.89 - (-0.11)^2 = 0.8779$

$\mu_3 = \mu'_3 - 3\mu'_2 \mu'_1 + 2{\mu'_1}^3$

$= -0.11 - 3 \times 0.89 \times (-0.11) + 2 \times (-0.11)^3$

$= -0.11 + 0.2937 - 0.002662 = 0.181038$

$\mu_4 = \mu'_4 - 4\mu'_3 \mu'_1 + 6\mu'_2 {\mu'_1}^2 - 3{\mu'_1}^4$

$= 2.33 - 4 \times (-0.11) \times (-0.11)$

$\quad + 6 \times 0.89 \times (-0.11)^2 - 3 (0.11)^4$

$= 2.33 - 0.0484 + 0.064614 - 0.00043923 = 2.3457748$

Central Moments of x :

Since $u = \dfrac{x-25}{10}$, we get $x = 25 + 10u$, hence μ_r of $x = (10)^r \mu_r$ of u

∴ μ_1 of $x = 0$

μ_2 of $x = 10^2 \times 0.8779 = 87.79$

μ_3 of $x = 10^3 \times 0.181038 = 181.038$

μ_4 of $x = 10^4 \times 2.3457748 = 23457.748$

Example 5.2 : The first four moments of a distribution about the value '5' are 2, 20, 40 and 200 respectively.
(i) Find the first four central moments.
(ii) Find the arithmetic mean and S.D.

Solution : (i) Let $u = x - 5$.

Raw moments of u are $\mu_1' = 2$, $\mu_2' = 20$, $\mu_3' = 40$ and $\mu_4' = 50$. Let us compute central moments of u. Notice that the central moments are invariant to the change of origin, hence central moments of u and x are same.

Central Moments :

$\mu_1 = 0$

$\mu_2 = \mu_2' - \mu_1'^{2} = 20 - 2^2 = 16$

$\mu_3 = \mu_3' - 3\mu_2' \mu_1' + 2\mu_1'^{3}$

$\quad = 40 - 3 \times 20 \times 2 + 2 \times 2^3 = -64$

$\mu_4 = \mu_4' - 4\mu_3' \mu_1' + 6\mu_2' \mu_1'^{2} - 3\mu_1'^{4}$

$\quad = 200 - 4 \times 40 \times 2 + 6 \times 20 \times 2^2 - 3 \times 2^4 = 312$

(ii) Note that

$u = x - 5$

∴ $\bar{u} = \bar{x} - 5$

∴ $2 = \bar{x} - 5$ ∴ $\bar{x} = 7$ ($\because \mu_1'$ of $u = \bar{u}$)

∴   S.D. $= \sqrt{\mu_2} = \sqrt{16} = 4$.

5.6 Sheppard's Corrections for Central Moments

In order to compute arithmetic mean and S.D. of frequency distribution of a continuous variable, we assume that all the items in a class interval are concentrated at the mid-point of the class. The same assumption is made for calculating moments. This enables us to compute moments but it introduces some amount of error. Such error is known as error due to grouping.

If the classes are larger in width, then the error in computing higher order moments becomes considerable. Therefore, it needs to be corrected.

In calculating odd order central moments, the errors possessing negative signs and those possessing positive signs mostly tend to cancel each other. Hence, in case of odd order moments the sum of errors being small it is negligible. Therefore, odd order moments need not be corrected.

On the other hand, while computing even order central moments, errors are raised to even power, hence all errors are effectively positive. The accumulated errors will be considerably large. In this case W.F. Sheppard suggested the following corrections :

$$\mu_2^* = \mu_2 - h^2/12$$

$$\mu_3^* = \mu_3$$

$$\mu_4^* = \mu_4 - \frac{h^2}{2}\mu_2 + \frac{7h^4}{240}$$

where, μ_r^* is corrected r^{th} central moment and h is the class width.

The Sheppard's corrections are applied under the following conditions.

(i) The frequency distribution is related to continuous variable.

(ii) The total frequency is sufficiently large. Generally it should be larger than 1000.

(iii) The class-intervals are of uniform width say h and h is quite large.

Skewness & Kurtosis

5.7 Introduction

In the previous chapters we have studied two aspects in the study of frequency distribution viz. average and dispersion. However, in order to compare two frequency distributions, average and dispersion are not adequate. Sometimes two frequency distributions have same average and dispersion, however they differ in symmetry. Therefore, symmetry is the third aspect in the study of frequency distribution. The term skewness carries the meaning opposite to symmetry i.e. lack of symmetry. In this chapter we study various measures of skewness.

5.8 symmetry

A frequency distribution is symmetric about a value 'a', if the corresponding frequency curve is symmetric about 'a' (See Fig. 5.1). In other words, the ordinate at x = a divides frequency curve into two equal parts. For a symmetric frequency curve these two parts are mirror images of each other. The point 'a' turns out to be arithmetic mean, mode as well as median.

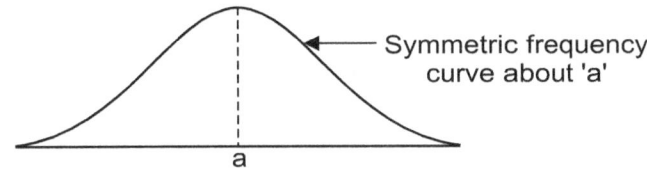

Symmetric frequency curve about 'a'

Fig. 5.1

In case of symmetric frequency distribution, frequencies of classes equidistant from central class on either side are same. For example :

Class	0-10	10-20	20-30	30-40	40-50
Frequency	5	12	20	12	5

Here, the frequency of first is the same as that of the last class. Similarly second and second last classes have equal frequencies and so on.

Properties of Symmetric Distribution

(i) In case of bell shaped unimodal symmetric frequency distributions, arithmetic mean, mode, median coincide.

(ii) The quartiles of symmetric distribution are equispaced. By that we mean $Q_3 - Q_2 = Q_2 - Q_1$.

(iii) The odd order central moments of symmetric distribution are zero. i.e. $\mu_1 = \mu_3 = \mu_5 = \ldots\ldots = 0$.

Proof : In case of symmetric frequency distribution, we know that the frequencies equidistant from the central class or from the point of symmetry ($\bar{x}$) are same. Moreover, the deviations ($x_i - \bar{x}$) are equal in magnitude and opposite in sign. Clearly odd powers of ($x_i - \bar{x}$) are negative if $x_i > \bar{x}$ and positive if $x_i < \bar{x}$. Therefore, $(x_i - \bar{x})^r f_i$ are equal in magnitude and opposite in sign for every odd power r. Therefore,

$$\therefore \sum_{x_i < \bar{x}} f_i (x_i - \bar{x})^r = \sum_{x_i > \bar{x}} f_i (x_i - \bar{x})^r$$

$$\therefore \sum_{x_i < \bar{x}} f_i (x_i - \bar{x})^r + \sum_{x_i > \bar{x}} f_i (x_i - \bar{x})^r = 0$$

$$\therefore \sum f_i (x_i - \bar{x})^r = 0$$

$$\therefore \mu_r = \frac{\sum f_i (x_i - \bar{x})^r}{\sum f_i} = 0$$

In day-to-day life we come across several distributions which are not symmetric. For example, distribution of income of individuals, distribution of agricultural land holdings, distribution of number of misprints per page. In these situations we require to measure the extent of departure from symmetry.

5.9 Skewness

Skewness is a lack of symmetry or departure from symmetry. If the distribution is skew, the corresponding frequency curve is elongated on either side. If the curve is elongated towards right side (Fig. 1.3), then the distribution is said to possess positive skewness. On the other hand, if it is elongated towards left side (Fig. 1.4), the distribution is said to possess negative skewness. In other words, in case of positive skewness, the frequency increases rapidly to reach the maximum and further decreases slowly. Exactly reverse process is observed in case of the distribution with negative skewness.

In case of positively skewed distribution we observe that,

Mode < Median < Arithmetic mean

Whereas, in case of negative skew distribution we observe that –

Arithmetic Mean < Median < Mode.

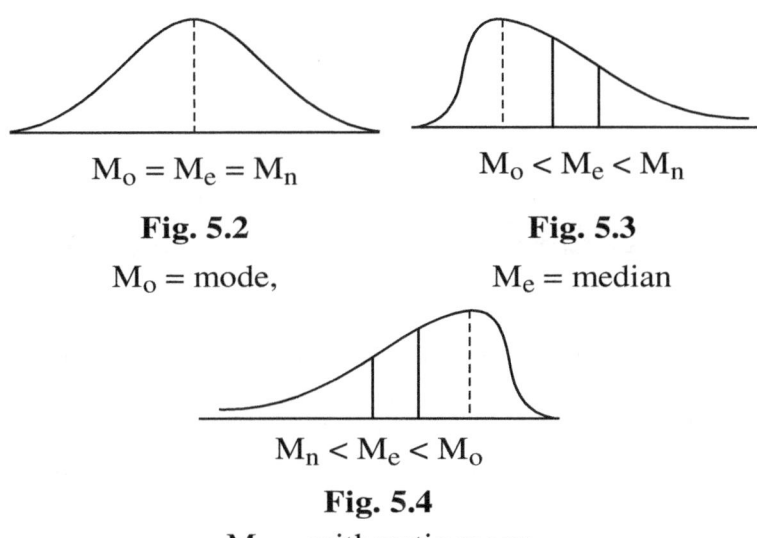

$M_o = M_e = M_n$ $M_o < M_e < M_n$

Fig. 5.2   **Fig. 5.3**

M_o = mode, M_e = median

$M_n < M_e < M_o$

Fig. 5.4

M_n = arithmetic mean

Examples :

(1) The frequency curve of annual income is positively skewed.

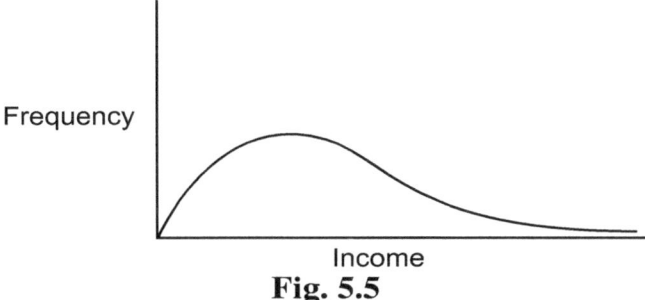

Fig. 5.5

(2) The frequency curve of deaths among adults is negatively skewed.

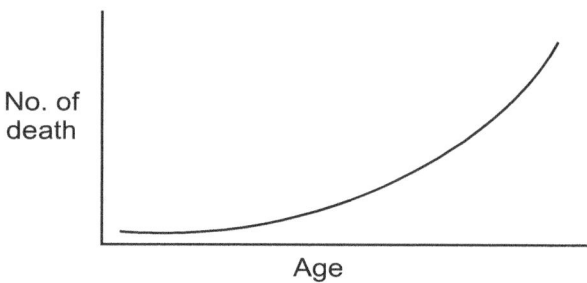

Fig. 5.6

(3) The frequency curve of intelligence quotient is symmetric.

5.10 Karl Aearson's Coefficient of Skewness

Mode is the most sensitive average to departure from symmetry. Larger the skewness, larger is the difference between arithmetic mean and mode. In case of positively skew data we observe, A.M. − mode > 0 and in case of negatively skew data A.M. − mode < 0. Therefore, the quantity (A.M. − mode) gives the extent of skewness as well as the type of skewness. Thus using the quantity (A.M. − mode), a relative measure of skewness is given below :

Karl Pearson's coefficient of skewness (S_k) : $\dfrac{\text{A.M.} - \text{mode}}{\sigma}$

If, $S_k < 0$, distribution is negatively skew

$S_k = 0$, distribution is symmetric

$S_k > 0$, distribution is positively skew

Remark :

(i) Karl Pearson's coefficient of skewness (S_k) is independent of change of origin and scale.

(ii) It cannot be computed for a distribution with open end classes as well as for qualitative data.

(iii) Theoretically, there is no limit on the value of S_k. However, in majority of the cases it lies between − 1 and 1. It rarely goes beyond − 3 and 3.

(iv) Sometimes, mode is ill-defined. It cannot be computed, hence there is difficulty in computing Karl Pearson's coefficient of skewness. In such a case, we use the following empirical relation $(\bar{x} - \text{mode}) \simeq 3\,(\bar{x} - \text{median})$ for moderately skew distribution. Hence,

$$S_k = \frac{3(\bar{x} - \text{median})}{\sigma}$$

(v) S_k is a unitless pure number.

In case of qualitative data and frequency distribution with open end classes we cannot compute arithmetic mean and S.D. In order to overcome this difficulty, we measure skewness using quartiles.

5.11 Bowley's Coefficient of Skewness

The first and third quartiles of symmetric distribution are equidistant from median. (Fig. 1.4). If the frequency curve is elongated towards right side then the third quartile goes away from the median as compared to the first quartile. Accordingly for positively skew distribution $Q_3 - Q_2 > Q_2 - Q_1$ (Fig. 1.6). In case of negatively skew distribution left side tail of frequency curve is elongated, which influences the first quartile to go away from the median. This results into $Q_3 - Q_2 < Q_2 - Q_1$ (Fig. 5.7).

The amount of skewness and the type of skewness is reflected by the quantity $(Q_3 - Q_2) - (Q_2 - Q_1)$. A relative measure based on this quantity is called as **Bowley's Coefficient of Skewness (S_B),** which is given by the following formula

$$S_B = \frac{(Q_3 - Q_2) - (Q_2 - Q_1)}{(Q_3 - Q_2) + (Q_2 - Q_1)} = \frac{Q_3 - 2Q_2 + Q_1}{Q_3 - Q_1}$$

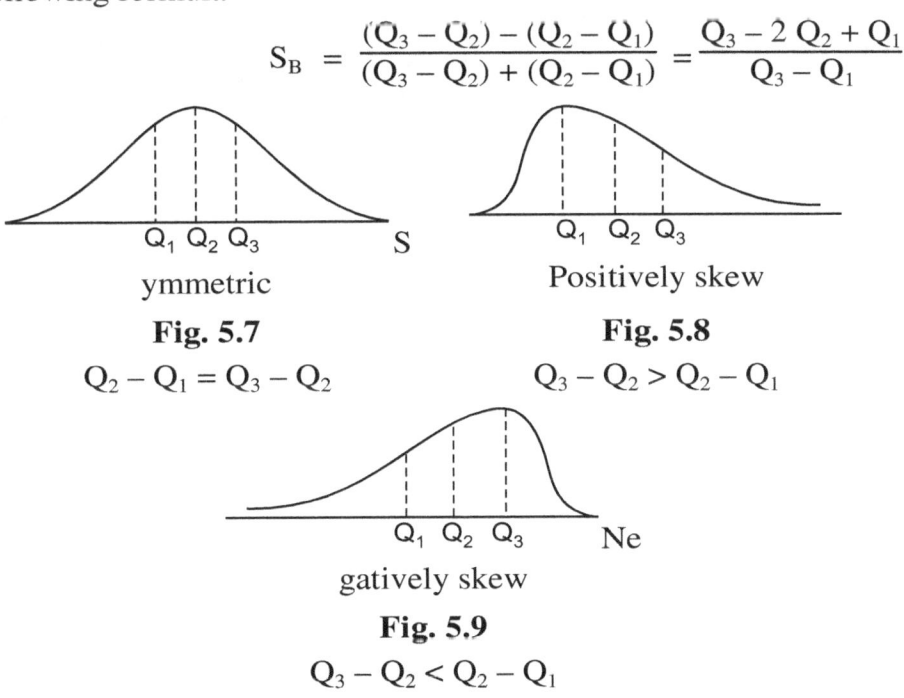

Symmetric

Fig. 5.7

$Q_2 - Q_1 = Q_3 - Q_2$

Positively skew

Fig. 5.8

$Q_3 - Q_2 > Q_2 - Q_1$

Negatively skew

Fig. 5.9

$Q_3 - Q_2 < Q_2 - Q_1$

The corresponding box plots will look like as follows :

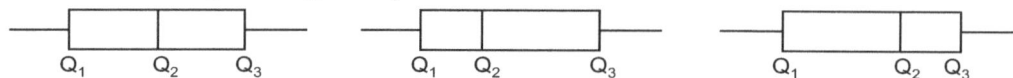

Result : The Bowley's coefficient of skewness S_B lies between -1 and 1.

Proof : For simplicity let $Q_3 - Q_2 = b$, $Q_2 - Q_1 = a$ then $S_B = \dfrac{b-a}{b+a}$.

Since, $a > 0$, $b > 0$ we can say

$$b - a \leq b + a$$

$$\therefore \quad \frac{b-a}{b+a} \leq 1 \quad \ldots (1)$$

Note that
$$-b \leq b \quad (\because b > 0)$$
$$\therefore \quad -b - a \leq b - a$$
$$\therefore \quad -(b+a) \leq b - a$$
$$\therefore \quad -1 \leq \frac{b-a}{b+a} \quad \ldots (2)$$

From (1) and (2) we get $-1 \leq S_B \leq 1$.

If, $S_B < 0$, the distribution is negatively skew

$S_B = 0$, the distribution is symmetric

$S_B > 0$, the distribution is positively skew.

5.12 Pearsonian Coefficient of Skewness (β_1) (Based on Moments)

In the earlier discussion we have studied that, the odd order central moments of a symmetric distribution are zero. Further, those are positive for positively skew distribution and negative for negatively skew distribution (except μ_1). Hence odd order moments can be used to define a measure of skewness.

The first odd order central moment $\mu_1 = 0$, therefore we use μ_3 for measuring the amount of skewness. The Pearsonian coefficient of skewness is denoted by γ_1. It is a relative measure of skewness given by the following formula :

$$\gamma_1 = \sqrt{\beta_1} \quad \text{where } \beta_1 = \mu_3^2 / \mu_2^3$$

Note that β_1 is always positive, so it fails to exhibit the type of skewness. Therefore γ_1, a measure which considers this fact is obtained by simply taking square root of β_1.

$$\therefore \quad \gamma_1 = \sqrt{\frac{\mu_3^2}{\mu_2^3}} = \frac{\mu_3}{\mu_2^{3/2}}$$

Since $\mu_2 > 0$, we take $\mu_2^{3/2} > 0$. Thus, γ_1 possesses the sign of μ_3.

If $\quad \gamma_1 < 0$, the distribution is negatively skew.

$\gamma_1 = 0$, the distribution is symmetric

$\gamma_1 > 0$, the distribution is positively skew.

Remark :
(i) It can be shown that, the various measures of skewness which we have discussed earlier are invariant to change of origin and scale. These measures are based on the differences of similar quantities. Note that S_k is based on $(\bar{x} - \text{mode})$, S_B is based on $(Q_3 - Q_2) - (Q_2 - Q_1)$, γ_1 is based on $(x_i - \bar{x})$. Hence, these measures are invariant to the changes of origin. Moreover these measures are expressed in terms of ratios of quantities possessing same unit. Therefore, measures of skewness are invariant to the change of scale also.

(ii) Skewness is a lack of symmetry. This lack may be either positive or negative. Hence, while comparing two frequency distributions one has to compare the magnitudes of skewness. For example, consider two frequency distributions with the coefficient of skewness as 0.5 and − 0.8. Then the latter has larger skewness, since |− 0.8| > |0.5|. The nature of skewness however is different, former is positively skew, while the later is negatively skew.

(iii) **Choice of measure of skewness :** The Pearsonian coefficient of skewness γ_1 is the best among all the measures. However, it is not simple to compute. Hence, Karl Pearson's coefficient of skewness S_k is preferred. If the frequency distribution has open end classes or qualitative data is under study then both of the above referred measures cannot be computed. Under these situations, Bowley's coefficient of skewness is the only measure which can be used.

Illustrative Examples

Example 5.3 : Compute (i) the Karl Pearson's coefficient of skewness (ii) Bowley's coefficient of skewness, (iii) Pearsonian coefficient of skewness for the following frequency distribution.

Marks	0-20	20-40	40-60	60-80	80-100
No. of students	5	12	32	40	11

(i) In this case we need to compute mean, mode and S.D.

Marks	Mid Pts. x_i	Freq. f_i	$u_i = \dfrac{x_i - 50}{20}$	$f_i u_i$	$f_i u_i^2$	$f_i u_i^3$	Cumulative freq. less than type
0-20	10	5	–2	–10	20	–40	5
20-40	30	12	–1	–12	12	–12	17
40-60	50	32	0	0	0	0	49
60-80	70	40	1	40	40	40	89
80-100	90	11	2	22	44	88	100
Total	–	100	–	40	116	76	–

Modal class : $(60 - 80)$, $f_m = 40$, $f_1 = 32$, $f_2 = 11$, $l = 60$, $h = 20$, hence

$$\text{Mode} = l + \frac{f_m - f_1}{2f_m - f_1 - f_2} \times h = 60 + \frac{40 - 32}{80 - 32 - 11} \times 20$$

$$= 64.3243$$

Note that $u = \dfrac{x - 50}{20}$, $\therefore$ $x = 20u + 50$

$\therefore$ $\bar{x} = 20\bar{u} + 50$ and $\sigma_x = 20\sigma_u$

$\therefore$ $\bar{u} = \dfrac{\sum f_i u_i}{\sum f_i} = \dfrac{40}{100} = 0.4$

$\therefore$ $\bar{x} = 50 + 20\bar{u} = 50 + 20 \times 0.4 = 58$

$$\sigma_u^2 = \frac{\sum f_i u_i^2}{\sum f_i} - (\bar{u})^2 = \frac{116}{100} - (0.4)^2 = 1$$

$\therefore$ $\sigma_u = 1$, $\sigma_x = 20\sigma_u = 20 \times 1 = 20$

$\therefore$ Karl Pearson's coefficient of skewness

$$S_k = \frac{\bar{x} - \text{mode}}{\sigma} = \frac{58 - 64.3243}{20} = -0.3162$$

Interpretation : The distribution is negatively skew.

(ii) For determining Bowley's coefficient of skewness we need to compute the quartiles.

Q_1 = The value of $\left(\dfrac{N}{4} = \dfrac{100}{4} = 25\right)^{th}$ item

Q_1 class : 40 – 60

∴ $Q_1 = l + \dfrac{N/4 - c.f.}{f} \times h = 40 + \dfrac{25 - 17}{32} \times 20 = 45$

Q_2 = The value of $(N/2 = 100/2 = 50)^{th}$ item

Q_2 class : 60 – 80

$Q_2 = l + \dfrac{N/2 - c.f.}{f} \times h = 60 + \dfrac{50 - 49}{40} \times 20 = 60.5$

Q_3 = The value of $\left(\dfrac{3N}{4} = \dfrac{300}{4} = 75\right)^{th}$ item

Q_3 class : 60 – 80

∴ $Q_3 = l + \dfrac{3N/4 - c.f.}{f} \times h = 60 + \dfrac{75 - 49}{40} \times 20 = 73$

Bowley's coefficient of skewness :

$$S_B = \dfrac{Q_3 - 2Q_2 + Q_1}{Q_3 - Q_1} = \dfrac{73 - 2 \times 60.5 + 45}{73 - 45}$$

$$= -\dfrac{3}{28} = -0.1071$$

∴ The distribution is negatively skew.

(iii) To find Pearsonian coefficient of skewness first we find the moments.

Note that u = (x – 50) / 20

Raw moments of u :

$\mu_1' = \Sigma f_i u_i / \Sigma f_i = 40/100 = 0.4$

$\mu_2' = \Sigma f_i u_i^2 / \Sigma f_i = 116/100 = 1.16$

$\mu_3' = \Sigma f_i u_i^3 / \Sigma f_i = 76/100 = 0.76$

Central moments of u :

$\mu_1 = 0$, $\mu_2 = \mu_2' - \mu_1'^2$ = variance = $1.16 - (0.4)^2 = 1$

$\mu_3 = \mu_3' - 3\mu_2' \mu_1' + 2\mu_1'^3 = 0.76 - 3 \times 1.16 \times 0.4 + 2(0.4)^3$

$= 0.76 - 1.392 + 0.128 = -0.504$

Since the coefficient of skewness is independent of both origin and scale we get β_1 of
x and β_1 of u same.

$$\beta_1 = \mu_3^2 / \mu_2^3 = (-0.504)^2/1^3 = 0.2540$$
$$\gamma_1 = \mu_3 / \mu_2^{3/2} = -0.504$$

Interpretation : The distribution is negatively skew.

Example 5.4 : From the information given below, compare the skewness of the two groups.

	Group I	Group II
Median	22	25
Arithmetic Mean	24	22
S.D.	10	12

Solution : Since mode is not given we use Karl Pearson's coefficient of skewness

$$S_k = (\bar{x} - \text{median})/\sigma$$

S_k for group I $= 3 (24 - 22) / 10 = 0.6$

S_k for group II $= 3 (22 - 25) / 12 = -0.75$

Interpretation : (i) Group I is positively skew whereas group II negatively skew (ii) since $|S_k| = 0.75$ for group II is larger than that of group I, group II possesses more skewness.

Example 5.5 : A distribution has mean 30, coefficient of variation 20% and coefficient of skewness 0.3. Find its mode.

Solution : $\text{C.V.} = \dfrac{\sigma}{(\bar{x})} \times 100 = \dfrac{\sigma}{30} \times 100 = 20 \quad \therefore \sigma = 6.$

Further, coefficient of skewness $= \dfrac{\bar{x} - \text{mode}}{\sigma} = 0.3$

$\therefore \quad \dfrac{30 - \text{mode}}{6} = 0.3$

$\therefore \quad 30 - \text{mode} = 1.8$

$\therefore \quad \text{mode} = 28.2$

Example 5.6 : In a certain frequency distribution the sum of supper and lower quartiles is 45 and the difference between them is 15. If the median is 20, find the coefficient of skewness.

Solution : Note that $Q_3 + Q_1 = 45$, $Q_3 - Q_1 = 15$, $Q_2 = 20$.

The Bowley's coefficient of skewness is

$$S_B = \frac{Q_3 - 2Q_2 + Q_1}{Q_3 - Q_1} = \frac{(Q_3 + Q_1) - 2Q_2}{Q_3 - Q_1} = \frac{45 - 40}{15} = 0.3333$$

Example 5.7 : In a certain frequency distribution upper quartile exceeds the median by 10 units, whereas the median exceeds the lower quartile by 7 units. Compute the coefficient of skewness.

Solution : $Q_3 - Q_2 = 10$, $Q_2 - Q_1 = 7$

∴ Bowley's coefficient of skewness

$$= \frac{(Q_3 - Q_2) - (Q_2 - Q_1)}{(Q_3 - Q_2) + (Q_2 - Q_1)} = \frac{10 - 7}{10 + 7} = \frac{3}{17}$$

Example 5.8 : Given the following summary, draw box plots and compare the data sets. State your interpretations.

	Min.	Q_1	Q_2	Q_3	Max.
Set A	12	15	20	25	28
Set B	0	8	10	14	20
Set C	3	9	17	27	32

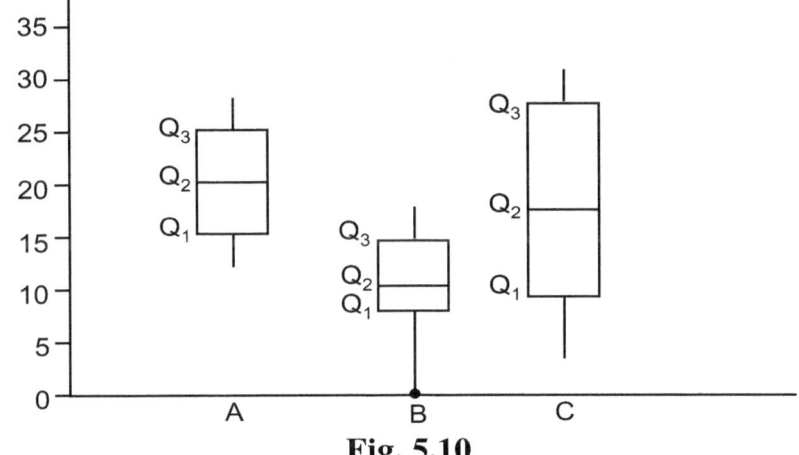

Fig. 5.10

Interpretations :

(1) Average of B < Average of C < Average of A.

(2) Spread of B < Spread of A < Spread of C.

(3) A is symmetric

B positively skew

C positively skew

5.13 Kurtosis

We have studied in preceding chapters the various three aspects of comparison of frequency distributions viz. average, dispersion and symmetry. However, the above three aspects are not enough for comparison. Two bell shaped, unimodal frequency distributions may have same average, dispersion and same amount of skewness still they may differ in the fourth aspect viz. the relative height of the curve. This is referred to as Kurtosis. Detailed discussion is given below.

Definition : Clark and Schkade defined **kurtosis** as the property of a distribution which expresses its relative peakedness.

Types of Kurtosis :

Thus, kurtosis is a height of unimodal, bell shaped curve or according to Karl Pearson, convexity of curve. The main reason of variation in height is variation in the concentration or proportion of observations around mode. If the proportion of observations around mode is more then the curve will exhibit sharper peak or higher peak. On the other hand, lower concentration around the mode will cause the curve to have blunt peak or peak with small height. The curves are classified in three groups according to the relative peakedness.

In this regard, normal distribution is considered to be a standard. The distributions having peakedness equal to that of normal distributions are called mesokurtic distributions. The distribution having more peak than that of normal distribution, is called as **leptokurtic** distribution, if it has less peak than that of normal distribution then the distribution is called as platykurtic (See Fig. 5.11).

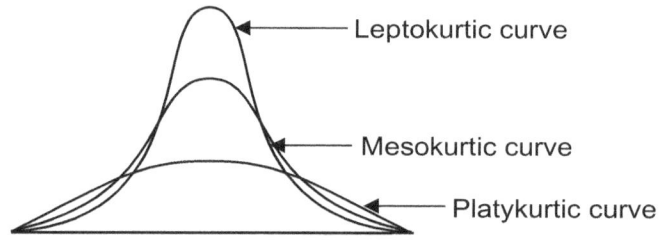

Fig. 5.11

5.14 Measures of Kurtosis

Measurement of kurtosis using figure poses several difficulties such as inaccuracy, subjectivity, lack of uniformity in scales.

Moreover, curves with larger variance tend to have small peak and vice-versa. By considering all these facts measures based on central moments called as Pearsonian coefficients β_2 and γ_2 are used to measure the kurtosis and are defined as follows :

$$\beta_2 = \frac{\mu_4}{\mu_2^2} \text{ and } \gamma_2 = \beta_2 - 3$$

Note :

1. γ_2 is called kurtosis or excess of kurtosis.
2. β_2 and γ_2 are invariant to change of origin and scale.
3. β_2 and γ_2 are both free from units.
4. β_2 and γ_2 cannot be used for qualitative data and frequency distribution having open end classes. A measure based on quartiles and percentiles is used in this situation. It is denoted by K_u and is given by

$$K_u = \frac{(Q_3 - Q_1)/2}{P_{90} - P_{10}}$$

For normal distribution $K_u = 0.263$.

The detailed discussion is out of scope of the book.

5. The moments used to find β_2, γ_2 are corrected ones.

Interpretation of β_2 and γ_2 :

If $\beta_2 < 3$ i.e. $\gamma_2 < 0$, the distribution is platykurtic.

If $\beta_2 = 3$ i.e. $\gamma_2 = 0$, the distribution is mesokurtic.

If $\beta_2 > 3$ i.e. $\gamma_2 > 0$, the distribution is leptokurtic.

Illustrative Examples

Example 5.9 : The first four raw moments of a frequency distribution are 2, 20, 40, 200 respectively. Comment on the nature of Kurtosis.

Solution : We are given that $\mu_1' = 2$, $\mu_2' = 20$, $\mu_3' = 40$, $\mu_4' = 200$. We need to find μ_2 and μ_4.

$$\mu_2 = \mu_2' - {\mu_1'}^2 = 20 - 4 = 16$$

$$\mu_4 = \mu_4' - 4\mu_3' \mu_1' + 6\mu_2' {\mu_1'}^2 - 3{\mu_1'}^4$$
$$= 200 - 4 \times 40 \times 2 + 6 \times 20 \times 4 - 3 \times 2^4 = 312$$

$$\therefore \quad \beta_2 = \frac{\mu_4}{\mu_2^2} = \frac{312}{16^2} = 1.2188 \text{ and } \gamma_2 = \beta_2 - 3 = -1.7812$$

Interpretation : Since $\beta_2 < 3$, the distribution is platykurtic.

Result 1 : The Pearsonian coefficient $\beta_2 \geq 1$.

Proof : Suppose, $x_1, x_2, \ldots, x_n$ are the observations, then,

$$\mu_4 = \frac{\sum (x_i - \bar{x})^4}{n} \text{ and } \mu_2 = \frac{\sum (x_i - \bar{x})^2}{n}$$

Let $(x_i - \bar{x})^2 = y_i$

Note that, $\quad \text{Var}(y) \geq 0$

$$\therefore \quad \frac{\sum y_i^2}{n} - (\bar{y})^2 \geq 0$$

$$\therefore \quad \frac{\sum (x_i - \bar{x})^4}{n} - \left[\frac{\sum (x_i - \bar{x})^2}{n} \right]^2 \geq 0$$

$$\mu_4 - \mu_2^2 \geq 0$$

$$\therefore \quad \mu_4 \geq \mu_2^2$$

$$\therefore \quad \mu_4 / \mu_2^2 \geq 1, \text{ hence } \beta_2 \geq 1.$$

Alternative method : Cauchy-Schwartz's inequality states that for real numbers $a_1, a_2, \ldots a_n$ and $b_1, b_2, \ldots b_n$

$$(\sum a_i b_i)^2 \leq \sum a_i^2 \times \sum b_i^2$$

Choosing $a_i = (x_i - \bar{x})^2$ and $b_i = \frac{1}{n}$, we get

$$\left(\sum (x_i - \bar{x})^2 \times \frac{1}{n} \right)^2 \leq \sum (x_i - \bar{x})^4 \times \sum \frac{1}{n^2}$$

$$\mu_2^2 \leq \sum (x_i - \bar{x})^4 \times \frac{1}{n} = \mu_4$$

$$\therefore \quad 1 \leq \frac{\mu_4}{\mu_2^2} = \beta_2$$

Note : The above result can be proved for frequency distribution also.

Result 2 : If β_1 and β_2 are the Pearsonian coefficients then $\beta_2 \geq \beta_1 + 1$.

Proof : Let $x_1, x_2 \ldots x_n$ be the observations, $y_i = x_i - \bar{x}$, hence

$$\mu_r = \frac{\sum y_i^r}{n}$$

Note that $\frac{1}{n} \sum (ay_i^2 + by_i + c)^2 \geq 0$

$\therefore \quad \frac{1}{n} \left[a^2 \sum y_i^4 + b^2 \sum y_i^2 + \sum c^2 + 2ab \sum y_i^3 + 2bc \sum y_i + 2ac \sum y_i^2 \right] \geq 0$

$\therefore \quad \mu_4 a^2 + \mu_2 b^2 + c^2 + 2ab\,\mu_3 + 2bc\,\mu_1 + 2ac\,\mu_2 \geq 0 \quad \ldots (1)$

We use the following result : The expression

$$Ax^2 + By^2 + Cz^2 + 2Hxy + 2Gxz + 2Fyz \geq 0 \quad \ldots (2)$$

if
$$\begin{vmatrix} A & H & G \\ H & B & F \\ G & F & C \end{vmatrix} \geq 0$$

Comparing (1) and (2) we get,
$A = \mu_4, B = \mu_2, C = 1, H = \mu_3, G = \mu_2, F = \mu_1 = 0$
Expression is always non-negative if

$$\begin{vmatrix} \mu_4 & \mu_3 & \mu_2 \\ \mu_3 & \mu_2 & 0 \\ \mu_2 & 0 & 1 \end{vmatrix} \geq 0$$

$\therefore \quad \mu_4 \mu_2 - \mu_3^2 + \mu_2(-\mu_2^2) \geq 0$

$\therefore \quad \mu_4 \mu_2 \geq \mu_3^2 + \mu_2^3 \quad \text{(dividing by } \mu_2^3\text{)}$

$\therefore \quad \frac{\mu_4}{\mu_2^2} \geq \frac{\mu_3^2}{\mu_2^3} + 1$

$\therefore \quad \beta_2 \geq \beta_1 + 1 \text{ or } \beta_2 - \beta_1 - 1 \geq 0$

Points to Remember

The relation between raw and central moments :

$$\mu_1 = 0$$
$$\mu_2 = \mu_2' - \mu_1'^2 = \text{variance}$$
$$\mu_3 = \mu_3' - 3\mu_2'\mu_1' + 2\mu_1'^3$$
$$\mu_4 = \mu_4' - 4\mu_3'\mu_1' + 6\mu_2'\mu_1'^2 - 3\mu_1'^4$$

EXERCISE 5 (A)

Moments :

1. Define raw and central moments of (i) frequency distribution (ii) series of individual observations.
2. Describe the utility of moments.
3. Express first four central moments in terms of raw moments.
4. Show that the central moments are invariant to the change of origin.
5. Write a note on 'Sheppard's correction'.
6. If $u = kx$, show that μ_r of $u = k^r \mu_r$ of x.

EXERCISE 5 (B)

1. Find the third central moment of the following observations : 1, 2, 3, ... , n.
2. Show that the third moment of the following series of observations is zero : $a, a+d, a+2d, \ldots, a+(n-1)d$.
3. Find the first four central moments of the following observations : 4, 0, 2, 6, 3, 1, – 7, – 5, 1, 5
4. Compute the first four central moments of the following frequency distribution :

x	1	2	3	4	5	6	7
f	2	9	25	35	20	8	1

5. Find the first four central moments of the frequency distribution given below :

Class	100-105	105-110	110-115	115-120	120-125
Frequency	7	13	25	25	30

6. Given that : $\sum f_i = 125$, $\sum f_i (x_i - 10) = -46$, $\sum f_i (x_i - 10)^2 = 306$, $\sum f_i (x_i - 10)^3 = -292$ $\sum f_i (x_i - 10)^4 = 1962$, find the first four central moments of x.

7. The first two moments of a distribution about the value 4 are 3 and 34. Find the mean and variance.
8. The first three moments of a distribution about 2 are 1, 22, 10. Find its mean, S.D. and the third central moment.
9. Given that $\bar{x} = 1$, $\mu_2 = 3$, $\mu_3 = 0$, $\mu_4 = 27$ find the first four raw moments.

EXERCISE 5 (C)

Skewness :
1. Explain the term 'skewness', using suitable diagrams. Explain the different types of skewness.
2. Explain the following measures of skewness (i) Karl Pearson's coefficient of skewness (ii) Bowley's coefficient of skewness (iii) Pearsonian coefficient of skewness based on moments.
3. If the mode is indeterminate, how Karl Pearson's coefficient of skewness is computed.
4. Show that Bowley's coefficient of skewness lies between −1 and 1.
5. Write a note on skewness.
6. Show that the measures of skewness are independent of both change of origin and scale.
7. Define skewness, state the types of skewness, state the various measures of skewness. Which of the measures are suitable for qualitative data ?
8. State the use of box plot in order to compare symmetry and skewness.

Kurtosis :
9. State what is 'Kurtosis'.
10. What are the types of kurtosis ?
11. Explain the use of moments in measuring kurtosis.
12. State the Pearsonian measure of kurtosis.
13. Show that $\beta_2 \geq 1$, $\beta_2 \geq \beta_1 + 1$. Notation have usual meanings.

EXERCISE 5 (D)

1. For a group of 10 items, $\sum x = 452$, $\sum x^2 = 24270$ and mode = 43.7. Find the coefficient of skewness by appropriate formula.

2. Given that, A.M. = 160, mode = 157, σ = 50, find (i) Karl Pearson's coefficient of skewness (ii) median (iii) coefficient of variation.

3. The arithmetic mean, standard deviation and Karl Pearson's coefficient of skewness of a frequency distribution are 29.5, 6.5 and 0.32 respectively. Find the mode and median.

4. The first three moments of a certain variable about the value of '1' are 2, 25 and 80. Find the coefficient of skewness γ_1 and interpret the result.

5. Show that the following series of observations is symmetric using Pearsonian coefficient of skewness γ_1.

    1, 2, 3, ..., n.

6. For a moderately symmetrical distribution the arithmetic mean, median and Karl Pearson's coefficient of skewness are 86, 80, 0.42 respectively. Find the mode and coefficient of variation.

7. The first three moments about the value 3 for a certain distribution are 1, 16, − 40 respectively. Find the mean, variance, third central moment. Also find γ_1 and comment on the nature of skewness.

8. For a symmetric distribution, with usual notation, prove that :
$$\frac{\mu_3'}{\mu_1'} = 3\mu_2' + {\mu_1'}^2$$

9. For a frequency distribution, Bowley's coefficient of skewness is 0.6. The sum of first and third quartiles is 100 and the median is 38. Find the two quartiles.

10. For the following frequency distribution of marks of candidates, find the Bowley's coefficient of skewness. Also draw box plot and interpret.

Marks	0-10	10-20	20-30	30-40	40-50	50-60	60-70	70-80
No. of candidates	5	25	40	70	90	40	20	10

11. Compute coefficient of skewness for the following frequency distribution using appropriate formula :

Age (Year)	No. of deaths

under 10	15
under 20	25
under 30	48
under 40	70
under 50	95
under 60	105
under 70	110
under 80	120

Also draw box plot and comment on the symmetry.

12. Obtain (i) Karl Pearson's coefficient of skewness (ii) Pearson's coefficients of skewness γ_1 based on moments for the following data :

Height (in inches)	59-61	61-63	63-65	65-67	67-69
No. of students	4	30	45	15	6

13. For two distributions A and B following summary statistics are available.

	A	B
Median	20	24
Q_1	13	14
Q_3	30	31

Compare the skewness of two distributions (i) using appropriate measure of skewness, (ii) using box plot.

14. The first four moments about '4' of a certain distribution are 1.5, 17, – 30 and 308. Find coefficient of skewness and coefficients of kurtosis and interpret.

15. Find the coefficient of skewness and kurtosis based on moments for the following frequency distribution.

Class :	0-10	10-20	20-30	30-40
Frequency :	1	3	4	2

16. Given that n = 100, $\sum x = -10$, $\sum x^2 = 140$, $\sum x^3 = -40$, $\sum x^4 = 560$. Find β_1, β_2 and comment upon the nature of skewness and kurtosis of the distribution.

17. If $\mu_1' = 1$, $\mu_2' = 4$, $\mu_3' = 10$, $\mu_4' = 46$, compute β_1, β_2, hence comment upon the nature of distribution regarding the skewness and kurtosis.

18. Is the following information consistent ?
    $\mu_1' = 2, \mu_2' = 20, \mu_3' = 40, \mu_4' = 50$
    Justify your answer.

19. Given that $\beta_2 = 2.6$, $\beta_1 = 0.19$, $\mu_2 = 1.2$. Find μ_3 and μ_4.

20. Variance of a mesokurtic distribution is 4. Find μ_4.

21. The first four moments about '5.2' are 0, 5.16, – 2.3 and 60; find β_1 and β_2 and interpret.

22. Given that $\Sigma f = 100$, $\Sigma fu = 100$, $\Sigma fu^2 = 4000$.
    $\Sigma fu^3 = 24,500$, $\Sigma fu^4 = 1386000$. Find β_1 and β_2.

23. Find $\beta_1, \beta_2, \gamma_1, \gamma_2$ for the following frequency distribution.

Daily wages :	70-90	90-110	110-130	130-150	150-170
No. of workers :	16	22	36	18	8

ANSWERS 5 (B)

1. 0
3. $\mu_2 = 10.6$, $\mu_3 = -35.4$, $\mu_4 = 607.2$
4. $\mu_2 = 1.39$, $\mu_3 = 0.018$, $\mu_4 = 5.5237$
5. $\mu_2 = 38.09$, $\mu_3 = -110.772$, $\mu_4 = 3229.7056$
6. $\mu_2 = 2.3122$, $\mu_3 = 0.2769$, $\mu_4 = 14.1915$
7. 7, 25
8. $\bar{x} = 3$, $\sigma = \sqrt{21}$, $\mu_3 = -54$
9. $\mu_1' = 1, \mu_2' = 4, \mu_3' = 10, \mu_4' = 46$.

ANSWERS 5 (C)

1. 0.08
2. (i) $S_k = 0.06$ (ii) Median = 159, (iii) C.V. = 31.25%
3. Mode = 27.52, median = 28.9
4. – 0.5619
5. 0

6. C.V. = 49.8339%, Mode = 68
7. Mean = 4, Variance = 15, $\mu_3 = -86$, $\gamma_1 = -1.4803$
9. $Q_1 = 30$, $Q_3 = 70$
10. -0.1101
11. -0.02846
12. (i) 0.1238 (ii) 0.4926
13. S_B for A = 0.1765, S_B for B = -0.1765.

ANSWERS 5 (D)

14. 1.5734, platykurtic. $\beta_1 = 0.7917$, negatively skew.
15. $\gamma_1 = -0.1975$, $\beta_2 = 2.258$, negatively skew and platykurtic.
16. $\beta_1 = 0.000121$, $\beta_2 = 2.8589$, moderate positively skew and platykurtic.
17. $\beta_1 = 0$, $\beta = 3$, symmetric and mesokurtic.
18. Inconsistent, $\mu_4 < \mu_2^2$.
19. 0.573, 3.744
20. 48
21. 0.0385, 2.2537, negatively skew and platykurtic.
22. 0.255, 8.6239.
23. $\beta_1 = 0.006261$, $\gamma_1 = 0.0791$, $\beta_2 = 2.3058$, $\gamma_2 = -0.6942$.

Objective Type Questions : Moments

I. Multiple Choice Questions

- **Choose the correct alternative out of four alternatives given below for each questions.**

1. Which one of the following is a raw moment ?
   (a) moment about a
   (b) moment about 4
   (c) moment about zero
   (d) moment about mean

2. The first order moment about origin is equal to
   (a) zero
   (b) one
   (c) three
   (d) mean

3. The first order moment about mean is equal to
   (a) zero   (b) one
   (c) three   (d) −1
4. In case of symmetric distribution the odd order central moments are :
   (a) zero   (b) one
   (c) positive   (d) negative
5. The central moments are invariant to the change of :
   (a) origin   (b) scale
   (c) origin and scale   (d) scale but not on origin
6. The raw moments are invariant to :
   (a) change of scale only
   (b) change of origin only
   (c) change of origin and scale
   (d) none of the above
7. The statement that 'the variance is equal to the second central moment'
   (a) always true   (b) some times true
   (c) never true   (d) ambiguous
8. If the mean and S.D. are 2 and 4 respectively then the second moment about origin is
   (a) 24   (2) 20
   (c) 22   (d) none of the above
9. If the first order moment about 5 is 2 then mena is
   (a) 5   (b) 2
   (c) 7   (d) none of the above
10. If μ_r is r^{th} central moment then μ_0, μ_1, μ_2 are .... respectively.
    (a) 0, 1, σ,   (b) 0, 1, σ^2
    (c) 1, 0, σ^2 (d) 1, 1, σ^2
11. If μ_r' is a rth moment about a then
    (a) $\mu_2 = \mu_2' + \mu_1'^2$ (b) $\mu_2' = \mu_2 + \mu_1'^2$
    (c) $\mu_2' = \mu_2 + \mu_1^2$ (d) $\mu_2 = \mu_2' - \mu_1'^2$
12. With usual notion which one of the following is correct :
    (a) $\mu_4 = \mu_4' - 4\mu_3' \mu_1' - 6\mu_2' (\mu_1')^2 + (\mu_1')^4$

(b) $\mu_4 = \mu_4' - 4\mu_3' \mu_1' + 6\mu_2' (\mu_1')^2 - 3(\mu_1')^4$

(c) $\mu_2' = \mu_2 - \mu_1'$

(d) $\mu_3' = \mu_3 - 3\mu_2 \mu_1 + \mu_1^3$

II. State whether the following statements are True or False :

1. The central moments are based on deviation from mean.
2. The deviations of the items in raw moments are always measured from zero.
3. Central moments of order r means arithmetic mean of rth power of deviation of the items taken from median.
4. The first order central moment is always zero.
5. For symmetric distribution all the even order central moments are zero.
6. The square of standard deviation is always equal to second order cental moment.
7. The central moments are independent of change of origin.
8. The central moments are affected by change of scale.
9. The raw moments depend on change of origin and also on change of scale.
10. Sheppard's corrections for central moments can be applied when frequency distribution is related to continuous variable.
11. When the calss intervals are of uniform width, total frequency generally larger than 1000 and frequency distribution is related to continuous variable then we can apply Sheppard's correction for central moments.
12. The Sheppard's correction formula
    $\mu_2^* = \mu_2 - h^2/21$, $\mu_3^* = \mu_3$ and
    $\mu_4^* = \mu_4 - h^2/12 \mu_2 + 7/240 h^4$, where h is class width.
13. While applying Sheppard's correction formula for central moments, in case of odd order moments the sum of errors being small it is negligible. Therefore, odd order moments need not be corrected.
14. The value of μ_2 always non-negative.
15. The even order central moments are always non-negative.
16. The third order central moment may be negative.
17. The formula for second order central moment in terms of moments about origin is $\mu_2 = \mu_2' - \mu_1'$

18. Mean is equal to first order moment about origin.
19. The first and second central moments of a variable are called mean and variance respectively.
20. When the origin of a moment is taken at the arithmetic mean of the variable, it is called a central moment.

Answers : Objective Type Questions

I. Multiple Choice Questions :

(1) d (2) d (3) a (4) a
(5) a (6) c (7) a (8) b
(9) c (10) c (11) d (12) b

II. True or False :

(1) True (2) True (3) False (4) True
(5) False (6) True (7) False (8) True
(9) True (10) True (11) True (12) False
(13) True (14) True (15) True (16) True
(17) False (18) True (19) False (20) True

Objective Type Questions : Skewness & Kurtosis

(A) Multiple Choice Questions

- **Choose the correct alternative out of four alternatives given below for each questions.**

1. If mean and S.D. are 2 and 4 respectively then second order moment about origin is :
   (a) 24
   (b) 20
   (c) 22
   (d) none of the above

2. If first order moment about 5 is 2 then mean is equal to :
   (a) 5
   (b) 2
   (c) 7
   (d) none of the above

3. Karl pearson's coefficient of skewness is :
   (a) $(\bar{x} - Me)/\sigma$
   (b) $(\bar{x} - Mo)/\sigma$
   (c) $3(\bar{x} - Mo)/\sigma$
   (d) $3(\bar{x} - Me)/\sigma^2$

4. The Bowley's coefficient of skewness of is :
   (a) $[Q_3 - Q_1 + 2Q_2]/[Q_3 + Q_1]$

(b) $[Q_3 - Q_2 + Q_1] / [Q_3 - Q_1]$
(c) $[Q_3 + Q_1 - 2Q_2] / [Q_3 - Q_1]$
(d) $[Q_3 - Q_1] / [Q_3 + Q_1 - 2Q_2]$

5. The coefficient of skewness determines departure from :
   (a) normal curve
   (b) average
   (c) standard deviation
   (d) symmetry

6. Bowley's coefficient of skewness can have :
   (a) values generally lying between +1 or −1 only
   (b) any value
   (c) no negative value
   (d) no fractional value

7. If the coefficient of skewness is negative, the distribution :
   (a) is of negative values of variate
   (b) has a negative mean
   (c) negative standard deviation
   (d) excess tail towards the negative side

8. A positive coefficient of skewness implies that :
   (a) Mean is greater than Mode
   (b) Mean is less than Median
   (c) Mean is equal to Median and Mode
   (d) Mean is related to Median or Mode only if standard deviation is negative

9. A positive coefficient of skewness imples that :
   (a) $Q_3 + Q_1 > 2Q_2$
   (b) $Q_3 + Q_2 > Q_1$
   (c) $Q_3 + Q_1 > 2Q_2$ if $Q_3 > Q_1$
   (d) $Q_3 > Q_1$

10. A negative coefficient of skewness imples that :
    (a) mode < median
    (b) mean < median
    (c) mean < mode
    (d) none of the above

11. If the extreme values lie to the right tail then the distribution is :
    (a) negatively skewed
    (b) positively skewed

(c) zero skewed (d) symmetric
12. The skewness is measured by :
    (a) fourth order moment about mean
    (b) fourth order moment about any point
    (c) cube root of thrid order moment about any point
    (d) square of third order central moment divided by cube of second order central moment
13. If the extreme values lie to the left tail then the distribution is :
    (a) negatively skewed (b) positively skewed
    (c) zero skewed (d) symmetric skewed
14. For a moderately skew distribution, the empirical relation between mean ($\bar{X}$), median (Me) and mode (Mo) is :
    (a) $3(Me - \bar{X}) = (Mo - \bar{X})$
    (b) $3(Me - \bar{X}) = (Mo - \bar{X})$
    (c) $2(Mo - \bar{X}) = 3(Me - \bar{X})$
    (d) $3(\bar{X} - Me) = (\bar{X} - Mo)$
15. If the mode of a frequency distribution Mo = 25 and its mean $\bar{X}$ = 25, the median of the distribution is :
    (a) 15 (b) zero
    (c) 25 (d) 32
16. If a moderately skewed distribution has mean 35 and median is equal to 27, the mode of the distribution is :
    (a) 11 (b) 15
    (c) 25 (d) 30
17. Given coefficient of skewness is 0.8, Q_3 = 85 and Q_1 = 40 of a frequency distribution. The median of the distribution is :
    (a) 44.5 (b) 22
    (c) 12.5 (d) 42.5
18. For a positively skewed distribution, the correct relation between mean, median and mode is :
    (a) mean > median > mode (b) median > mean > mode
    (c) mean = median = mode (d) none of the above
19. For negatively skewed distribution the correct relation between mean, median and mode is :

(a) mean < median < mode
(b) mode < mean < median
(c) median < mean < mode
(d) mean = median = mode

20. Given $\bar{X} = 50$, $\sigma = 35$ and coefficient of skewness of a frequency distribution is –0.8, the mode of the frequency distribution.
    (a) 72 (b) 76
    (c) 78 (d) 80

21. In case of negatively skewed frequency distribution curve, the algebraic sign of value of third central moment μ_3 :
    (a) is equal to zero (b) is positive
    (c) is negative (d) cannot be decided

22. The value of coefficient of skewness based on momnets γ_1 for symmetrical distribution is equal to :
    (a) –1 (b) 0
    (c) 1 (d) 3

23. The limits for coefficient of skewness based on quartiles are :
    (a) ± 3 (b) 0 and 3
    (c) ± 1 (d) $\pm \infty$

24. The Kurtosis is :
    (a) deviation from symmetry
    (b) departure from normality
    (c) peakedness as compared with a normal curve
    (d) dispersion as compared with a standard normal curve

25. For any discrete frequency distribution, the coefficient of Kurtosis is :
    (a) 3 (b) less than 3
    (c) more than 3 (d) can be any value

26. The measure of Kurtosis β_2 for a platykurtic curve is :
    (a) greater than 3 (b) less than 1
    (c) equal to 3 (d) less than 3

27. The measure of Kurtosis β_2 for a leptokurtic curve is :
    (a) greater than 3   (b) less than 1
    (c) equal to 3   (d) less than 3

28. The coefficient of skewness of a series A and B are 0.5 and –0.8 then series B has :
    (a) less skew than A   (b) more skew than A
    (c) same skewness as that of A
    (d) none of the above

29. The value of measure of Kurtosis β_2 can be :
    (a) less than 3   (b) equal to 3
    (c) greater than 3   (d) all the above

30. If coefficeint of Kurtosis based on moments γ_2 is negative, then frequency curve is :
    (a) mesokurtic   (b) playkurtic
    (c) leptokurtic   (d) any of the above

31. If coefficient of Kurtosis based on moments γ_2 is equal to zero the frequency curve is :
    (a) mesokurtic   (b) playkurtic
    (c) leptokurtic   (d) any of the above

32.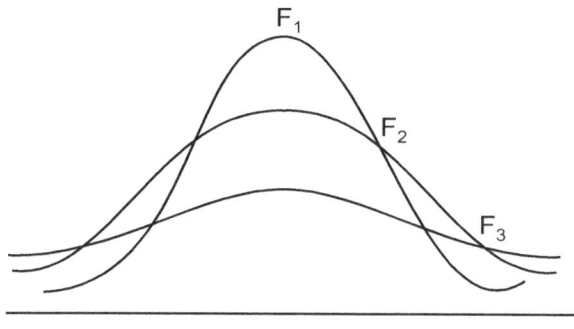

Fig. 5.12

The coefficient of Kurtosis (γ_2) for the curves F_2, F_3, F_1 are respectivley 5, 3 and 2. Which one of the following statement is time ?

(a) all the curves are platykurtic
(b) all the curves are leptokurtic
(c) F_2 is platykurtic and F_3 is leptokurtic
(d) F_1 is leptokurtic and F_3 is platykurtic

33. Which one of the following sketch indicates a positively skewed distribution ?

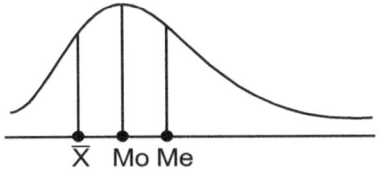
Fig. 5.13 (a)

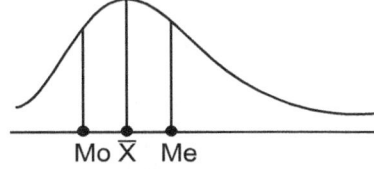
Fig. 5.13 (b)

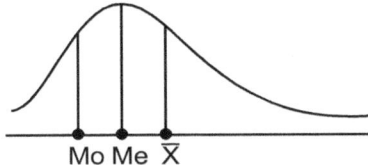
Fig. 5.13 (c)

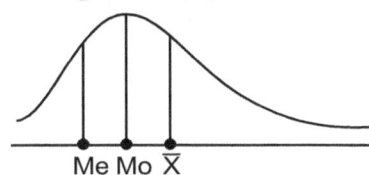
Fig. 5.13 (d)

34. Which one of the following sketches indicates a negatively skewed distribution ?

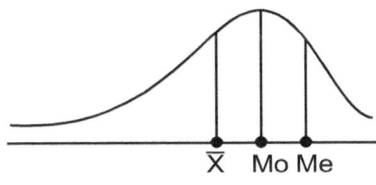
Fig. 5.14 (a)

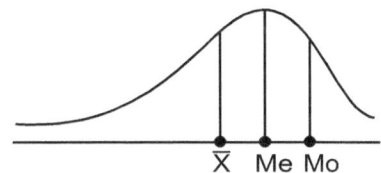
Fig. 5.14 (b)

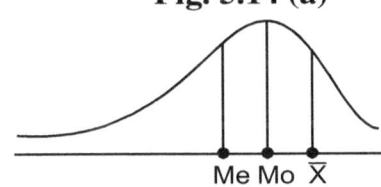
Fig. 5.14 (c)

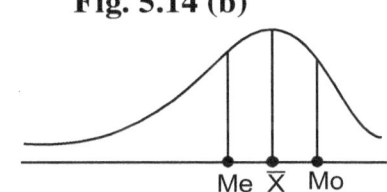
Fig. 5.14 (d)

35. For a distribution to be symmetrical, it should have same :
(a) median and mode and mean
(b) Q.D. and M.D.
(c) mean and mode and not necessarily the same median
(d) mean and median and not necessarily the same mode

36. When frequency curve is asymmetric which one of the following statement is false ?
    (a) quartiles are not equidistant from median
    (b) the frequency curve stretches on one side
    (c) mean, median and mode fall at different points
    (d) none of the above

37. For measuring skewness and Kurtosis, Karl Pearson defined :
    (a) two coefficients based on first two moments
    (b) two coefficients based on first four moments
    (c) four coefficients based on first three moments
    (d) four coefficients based on first four moments

38. When the coefficient of skewness is zero, then the nature of curve of distribution :
    (a) L shaped   (b) J shaped
    (c) U shaped   (d) none of the above

39. Let L : Leptokurtic, M : mesokurtic and P : platykurtic in the following diagram, sketches F_1, F_2 and F_3 are :

    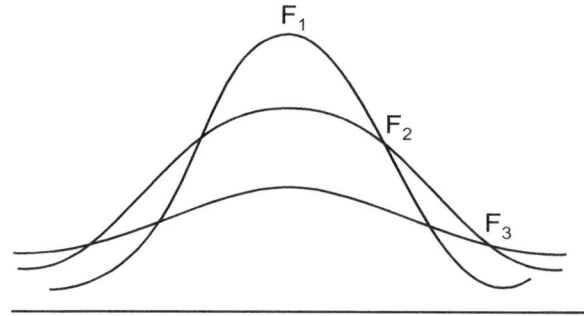

    Fig. 5.15

    (a) L, M and P respectively
    (b) M, P, and L respectively
    (c) P, M, and L respectively
    (d) P, L and M respectively

40. Which one of the following statement is true ?
    (a) third moment about origin is a measure skewness
    (b) second moment about origin is variance
    (c) first moment about origin is variance
    (d) all the above are false

41. Which one of the following distribution is positively skew, given the following box plot.

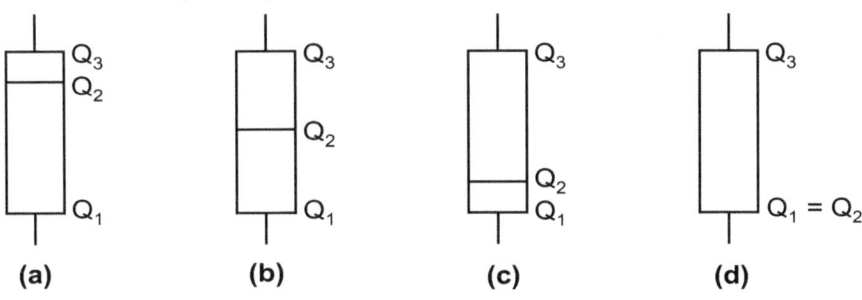

Fig. 1.16

42. The formula of coefficient of skewness γ_1 and coefficient of Kurtosis γ_2 involve β_1 and β_2 respectively, where
    (a) $\beta_1 = \mu_3^2 / (\mu_2)^3$ and $\beta_2 = (\mu_2)^2 / \mu_4$
    (b) $\beta_1 = \mu_3^2 / (\mu_2)^2$ and $\beta_2 = \mu_4 / (\mu_2)^2$
    (c) $\beta_1 = (\mu_2)^3 / (\mu_3)^2$ and $\beta_2 = (\mu_2)^2 / \mu_4$
    (d) $\beta_1 = (\mu_3)^2 / (\mu_2)^3$ and $\beta_2 = \mu_4 / (\mu_2)^2$

43. Let measures of skewness β_1 and measures of Kurtosis β_2 are pure number which are independent of the units of measurement then
    (a) $\beta_2 - \beta_1$ is greater than one
    (b) $\beta_2 - \beta_1$ is less than one
    (c) $\beta_2 - \beta_1$ is equal to one
    (d) $\beta_2 + \beta_1$ is equal to one

44. In practice β coefficients for a frequency distribution we find that coefficient of skeweness is less than unity and
    (a) Kurtosis is greater than unity
    (b) Kurtosis is less than unity
    (c) Kurtosis is less than three

(d) Kurtosis is greater than three

45. In a certain frequency distribution upper quartile exceeds the median by 10 units, where as the median exceeds the lower quartile by 7 units then coefficient of skewness is :
(a) 3/17 (b) 3/7
(c) 13/17 (d) 6/17

46. A distribution has mean 30, coefficient of variation 20% and coefficient of skewness 0.3 then value of mode is :
(a) 28.2 (b) 22.8
(c) 28.4 (d) 28.6

47. In a certain frequency distribution the sum of upper and lower quartiles is 45 and the difference between them is 15. If the median is 20 then coefficient of skewness is :
(a) 1/3 (b) 2/3
(c) 1/2 (d) 1/4

48. From the information given below :

	mean	median	S.D.
Group I	24	25	10
Group II	22	22	12

Which one of the following is true ?
(a) coefficient of skewness for group I = 0.6
(b) coefficient of skewness for group II = – 0.75
(c) group II possess more skewness
(d) all the above are true

49. The first four raw moments of a frequency distribution are 2, 20, 40 and 200 respectively then
(a) the distribution is positively skewed
(b) the distribution is negatively skewed
(c) the distribution is symmetricaly skewed
(d) inconclusive

50. Given that mean = 1, variance = 3, $\mu_3 = 0$ and $\mu_4 = 27$, then given distribution is :
(a) positively skewed (b) negatively skewed
(c) symmetric (d) none of the above

(B) State whether the following statements are True or False

1. Odd order third central moment is positive for a positively skewed distribution and negative for a negatively skewed distribution.

2. A measure of the peakedness of a distribution curve is its skewness.
3. If lower quartile is nearer to median than the upper quartile then the distribution is negatively skewed.
4. The first central moment is zero only if the distribution is symmetrical.
5. The Karl Pearsons coefficient for measuring skewness lies between -1 and $+1$.
6. For a negatively skew distribution, concentreation of frequencies on left.
7. For any distribution $\bar{x} - Mo = 3(\bar{x} - Me)$
8. Bowley's coefficient of Skewness can not be calculated for open end class intervals.
9. If skewness of frequency distribution A is -0.5 and B is -0.9, B is more skewed than A.
10. The frequency curve of I.Q. is symmetric.
11. The frequency curve of deaths among adults is negatively skewed.
12. For negativly skewed distribution $Q_3 - Q_2 < Q_2 - Q_1$
13. If coefficient of skewness γ_1 is positive the distribution is positively skewed.
14. In case of positively skew distribution mode < median < mean.
15. β_2 is an appropriate measure of Kurtosis for all distributions.
16. Kurtosis is the peakedness of the curve depicting the distribution.
17. The distribution having larger peak than that of normal distribution is called as leptokurtic distribution.
18. With usual notation $\beta_2 \geq \beta_1 + 1$ always holds.
19. With usual notation $\beta_2 \geq 1$ always holds.
20. The distribution having smaller peak than that of normal distribution is called as platykurtic distribution.
21. If the cofficient of Kurtosis γ_2 is positive then frequency distribution is Leptokurtic.
22. If $\gamma_1 = 0$ then distribution is symmetric.
23. β_2 and γ_2 are both are free from units.

24. β_2 and γ_2 are dependent on change of origin and scale.
25. β_2 and γ_2 can not be used for qualitative data and frequency distribution having open end classes.
26. For any distribution $\beta_2 \geq 3$.
27. Variance of a mesokurtic distribution is 4 then $\mu_4 = 38$

Answers : Objective Type Questions

(A) Multiple Choice Questions :

(1) b	(2) c	(3) b	(4) c	(5) d
(6) a	(7) d	(8) a	(9) c	(10) c
(11) b	(12) d	(13) a	(14) d	(15) c
(16) a	(17) a	(18) a	(19) a	(20) c
(21) c	(22) b	(23) c	(24) c	(25) d
(26) a	(27) a	(28) b	(29) d	(30) b
(31) a	(32) b	(33) c	(34) b	(35) a
(36) d	(37) d	(38) d	(39) a	(40) a
(41) c	(42) d	(43) a	(44) a	(45) a
(46) a	(47) a	(48) d	(49) b	(50) c

(B) True or False

(1) True	(2) False	(3) False	(4) False
(5) False	(6) False	(7) False	(8) False
(9) True	(10) True	(11) True	(12) True
(13) True	(14) True	(15) False	(16) True
(17) True	(18) True	(19) True	(20) True
(21) True	(22) True	(23) True	(24) False
(25) True	(26) False	(27) False	

SECTION - II

Chapter 6...
Sample Space and Events

John Venn (1834-1923), a British mathematician introduced the frequency interpretation of probability in his *'The Logic of Chance'* in 1866. Venn had other skills and interests too, including a rare skill in building machines. He used his skill to build a machine for bowling cricket balls which was so good that when the Australian Cricket team visited Cambridge in 1909, Venn's machine clean bowled one of its top stars four times.

John Venn

Contents ...

6.1 Introduction
6.2 Sample Space
6.3 Events
6.4 Types of Events

Key Words :

Random experiment, Uncertainty, Sample space, Discrete sample space, Continuous sample space, Events.

Objectives :

- To distinguish between deterministic and non-deterministic experiments.
- To write the sample space and related events.
- To express the events in set notations.

6.1 Introduction

You are familiar with the word 'experiment'. You perform experiments in Physics, Chemistry or Biology.

For example, in Chemistry, you estimate the exact amount of alkali required to neutralize acid using titration method. In Physics, velocity (v) of a particle at time (t) can be determined using v = u + at, where u is the initial velocity and a is the acceleration. In Biological experiments, a type of diet is fed to animals and increase in their weights are recorded.

However, in Statistics, the word 'experiment' is used in a wider sense. It is not necessarily restricted to laboratory experiments.

Experiment : An experiment is virtually any operation that results in one or more outcomes.

For instance,

(i) Appearing for F.Y. B.Sc. examination is an experiment with possible outcomes as PASS or FAIL.

(ii) Casting a vote in the election is an experiment with outcomes; the party you voted for wins or looses.

(iii) Releasing a stone from hand is an experiment with the outcome that 'it will fall on the ground'.

(iv) Tossing a coin is an experiment with two possible outcomes, 'Head up' or 'Tail up'.

Head   Tail

Fig. 6.1

(v) Rolling a six faced die; outcomes are 1, 2, 3, 4, 5, 6.

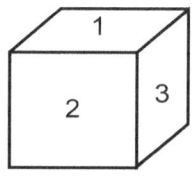

Fig. 6.2

Trial of an experiment : A trial of an experiment is nothing but performing the experiment once. So 'n' trials of an experiment means that the experiment is performed 'n' times either sequentially (or simultaneously). Experiments are classified into (i) Deterministic Experiments and (ii) Non-deterministic or Random Experiments.

(i) Deterministic Experiments : A deterministic experiment is an experiment for which the outcome is unique; hence certain. The outcome can therefore be predicted before performing the experiment. In other words, deterministic experiments are predictable phenomena. Following are some examples of deterministic experiments.

   (i)   Throwing a ball in the sky; Outcome : It falls down.

   (ii)   Cooling water below 0° centigrade; Outcome : It will freeze.

   (iii)   Determining the pressure of a gas using Boyle's law.

$$\text{Outcome : P} = \frac{\text{Constant}}{\text{Volume of the gas}}$$

Observe that, in all the above experiments, the outcome is certain, unique and predictable.

Such experiments are known as deterministic experiments. All the deterministic experiments can be described by mathematical formulae. These mathematical formulae are called as deterministic models. For example, $PV = \text{constant}$, $S = \frac{1}{2} gt^2$ are deterministic models used in Physics. Since, there is no uncertainty in the result of the experiment, probability theory does not play any role.

(ii) Non-deterministic (Random) Experiments : A non-deterministic experiment or a random experiment is an experiment, for which there are more than one possible outcomes and the result of the experiment cannot be predicted in advance.

For instance,

   (i)   Sex of a new born baby is recorded. Outcomes : Male or Female.

   (ii)   Rolling a die. Outcomes : 1, 2, 3, 4, 5, 6.

   (iii)   Tossing of a coin. Outcomes : Head or Tail.

   (iv)   Blood group of a person recorded in a blood donation camp. Outcomes : O, A, B, AB.

In random experiments, 'chance' element plays a vital role in determining the outcome. No mathematical formula can describe these experiments. These are the experiments we are interested in.

Though, we cannot predict the outcome of a single trial of the experiment, we can get some knowledge about the pattern among the outcomes, when the experiment is performed repeatedly for a large number of times. For example, we can't say whether 'head' or 'tail' will come up when a fair coin is tossed. However, if we toss the coin say 1000 times, what will we expect ? *About* 500 times 'head' will turn up and *about* 500 times 'tail' will turn up. If we further increase the number of tossings, we expect that the proportion of getting 'head' should approach the value $\frac{1}{2}$.

Thus, though the outcome of any particular experiment may be uncertain, there exists a long term regularity. This is the basis for the development of random models. These models help in predicting the outcome of the non-deterministic experiment in probabilistic terms. Therefore, these models are also known as probabilistic models. For example, using a non-deterministic i.e. random model, one can make the statement as 'Probability of death of an individual at the age of 80 years is 0.9.

These models are helpful in dealing with groups of cases. Random models are used in almost all branches of physical and social sciences. In fact, application of random models in different fields have given rise to several branches of Statistics such as Industrial Statistics, Econometrics, Statistical Ecology, Medical Statistics, Biometry, Acturial Science, Demography etc.

We cite here some situations where random models are applied.

(i) In industries, quality of the product manufactured is maintained.

(ii) Decision on whether to start an additional booking counter at railway station is taken by using random models in queueing theory.

(iii) A physicist studies the motion of particles emitted by a radioactive substance.

(iv) An economist, using random models can study the changes in price levels and construct index numbers.

(v) In a sociological survey, these models may be used to investigate the relationship between women literacy and success of family planning programmes.

(vi) In ecology, changes in the population of endangered species can be studied with a view to provide remedial measures.

Probability theory deals with non-deterministic or random models which describe and study the various phenomena happening in the world. We shall learn some of the simplest types of random models in this course in later chapters.

We are now in the position of learning some terminologies and concepts used in the theory of probability.

6.2 Sample Space

In the previous section, we talked about random experiments which have more than one possible outcome. In order to develop the probability theory, naturally, the first step is to *group* all possible outcomes of the experiment in a set. This set is called as 'Sample Space'.

Sample Space : The set of all possible distinct outcomes of an experiment is called a sample space.

Sample space is denoted by Ω or S. Thus, a sample space is nothing but the universal set concerned with the experiment. For example, consider the experiment of tossing a coin. The corresponding sample space will be;

$$\Omega = \{\text{Head, Tail}\} = \{H, T\}$$

The elements of sample space are different outcomes which are called as *sample points*. Thus, H and T are sample points of the above sample space Ω.

Depending upon the number of sample points, the sample spaces are categorized into two types (i) Discrete (ii) Continuous.

(i) Discrete Sample Space : A sample space containing a finite number of points or countably infinite points is called a discrete sample space. In other words a discrete sample space is either (a) a finite sample space or (b) a countably infinite sample space.

(a) Finite Sample Space : A sample space Ω is called a finite sample space if the number of elements contained in Ω is finite. Such a sample space can be denoted as

$$\Omega = \{\omega_1, \omega_2, \ldots \omega_n\}$$

where, n = number of elements i.e. number of possible outcomes of the experiment. $\omega_1, \omega_2, \ldots \omega_n$ are the outcomes.

For instance,

(i) Suppose two coins are tossed. Then,
$$\Omega = [HH, HT, TH, TT], \quad n = 4$$
where, H : Head,   T : Tail.

(ii) A die is rolled, then $\Omega = [1, 2, 3, 4, 5, 6], n = 6$

(iii) Suppose a pair of dice is rolled and the numbers on the uppermost faces are noted. Then,

$$\Omega = \begin{Bmatrix} (1,1) & (1,2) & \ldots & (1,6) \\ (2,1) & (2,2) & \ldots & (2,6) \\ (3,1) & (3,2) & \ldots & (3,6) \\ (4,1) & (4,2) & \ldots & (4,6) \\ (5,1) & (5,2) & \ldots & (5,6) \\ (6,1) & (6,2) & \ldots & (6,6) \end{Bmatrix} ; \quad n = 36$$

(iv) If a card is drawn from a well shuffled pack of playing cards and suit is recorded, then

$\Omega = \{Hearts, Spades, Diamonds, Clubs\}; n = 4$

(v) If a card is drawn from a pack of cards and denomination is noted, then

$\Omega = [ace, 2, 3, 4, 5, 6, 7, 8, 9, 10, jack, queen, king\}; n = 13$

(vi) Three coins are tossed,

$\Omega = \{HHH, HHT, HTH, THH, HTT, THT, TTH, TTT\}; n = 8$

(b) Countably Infinite Sample Space : A sample space Ω is called a countably infinite sample space if the number of elements in Ω are countably infinite. This means that there is a one-one correspondence between Ω and the set of natural numbers. It may be represented as

$$\Omega = \{\omega_1, \omega_2, \omega_3, \ldots, \omega_n, \ldots\}$$

For example,

(i) A student appears for an examination till he passes. Then
$$\Omega = \{P, FP, FFP, FFFP, \ldots\}$$
where F : Fail, P : Pass.

(ii) Number of accidents on the Nagpur-Pune Road in a month.

$$\Omega = \{0, 1, 2, 3, ...\}$$

(iii) Number of customers arriving at a telephone booth during a day.

$$\Omega = \{0, 1, 2, 3, ...\}$$

Note that, in all the above three examples, although possibility of infinite number of elements may not seem practicable, theoretically, we have to consider all possibilities in Ω.

(ii) Continuous Sample Space : A sample space Ω is called a continuous sample space, if the number of elements in Ω are uncountably infinite.

For example, consider the experiment of measuring height of a person. We may take $\Omega = (0, \infty)$. If we know that the lowest height is say 130 cm and highest is say 190 cm, we may as well consider $\Omega = (130, 190)$. Note that for both these sample spaces, the elements in the interval cannot be arranged in a sequence. Thus, there are uncountably infinite elements in Ω.

In other words, whenever, the observations on a characteristic can take any values in an interval, the concerned sample space is countably infinite.

The following diagram in Fig. 6.3 represents the different categories of sample spaces.

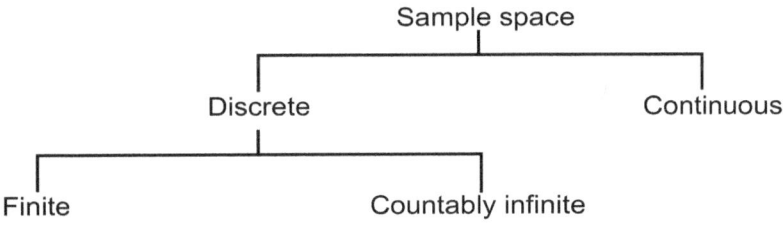

Fig. 6.3

In this book, we shall be concerned with only the discrete sample spaces and mostly with finite sample spaces.

6.3 Events

Consider the experiment of tossing two coins. Then the sample space is Ω = {HH, HT, TH, TT}. We might be interested in getting a single head. i.e. in the set {HT, TH}. Thus, we can associate the *event* of 'getting a single head' with the set {HH, TH} which is the subset of Ω.

Definition : Event : An event is a subset of the sample space. It consists of some or all points of the sample space.

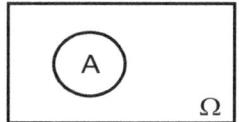

Fig. 6.4

Events are denoted by capital letters, A, B, C, ...

Remark : For a sample space containing n elements, there are 2^n events (including ϕ and Ω).

Occurrence of an event : We say that an event A has occurred, if after performing the experiment, the outcome belongs to the set A.

For example, suppose the experiment is of rolling a die. Then, $\Omega = \{1, 2, 3, 4, 5, 6\}$.

Let A be the event that even number appears on the upper face of the die.

$$\therefore \quad A = \{2, 4, 6\}.$$

Suppose, we roll the die, and 4 comes; then we shall say that 'event A has occurred'. If any of 1, 3, 5 appears, then we shall say that 'event A has not occurred' as 1, 3 or 5 are not the elements of A. On the other hand, if we only know that the event A has occurred, then all we know is that the outcome is one of the points of A.

We give below some examples to clarify the meaning of event.

Examples :

1. Experiment : Tossing two coins.

$$\Omega = \{HH, HT, TH, TT\}$$

event A = Occurrence of single head.

$$= \{HT, TH\}$$

2. Experiment : Rolling two dice.
   Ω contains 36 elements.
   Let the event A = Sum on the two uppermost faces is 10.
   Then, A = {(6, 4), (5, 5), (4, 6)}
   Let the event B = Getting sum of 13 of the numbers on uppermost faces.
   B = { } = ϕ.

6.4 Types of Events

According to the nature of the set, types of events are defined as follows.

1. Elementary event or simple event : An event containing only one element is called as *elementary event* or *simple event*. In other words, a singleton set is called as elementary event.

For example, A = Getting a multiple of 5 on a die. A = {5}.

2. Compound or contingent event : An event obtained through the combination of several simple events is called compound or contingent event.

For example : In an experiment of rolling a die, let A be the event of setting even number, B be the event of getting a number odd or multiple of 3. Thus, A = {2, 4, 6}, B = {1, 3, 5, 6}. Both A and B are not simple events, however they are compound events.

3. Impossible event : An event corresponding to empty set is called as an impossible event. In other words, an event which does not contain any sample point is called as an impossible event.

For example, if a single coin is tossed, then getting two heads is an impossible event.

3. Sure event or certain event : An event containing all the points of Ω is called a *sure event or certain event*. In other words, an event corresponding to the entire sample space is called a sure event. For example, getting a number either even or odd on a rolled die is a sure event.

We have seen in previous sections what is meant by sample space and events. As events are subsets of sample space, using set theory, we can generate new events from specified events. We shall use very often the following set of identities.

Set Identities :

(i) $(A')' = A$ where, A' denotes the complement of A.
    $\Omega' = \phi$. $\phi' = \Omega$

(ii) $A \cup B = B \cup A$, $A \cup \phi = A$, $A \cup \Omega = \Omega$, $A \cup A' = \Omega$, $A \cup A = A$.

(iii) $A \cap B = B \cap A$, $A \cap \phi = \phi$, $A \cap \Omega = A$
        $A \cap A' = \phi$, $A \cap A = A$
(iv) De Morgan's laws :
        $(A \cup B)' = A' \cap B'$ and $(A \cap B)' = A' \cup B'$
(v) If $A \subset B$, then
        $A \cup B = B$ and $A \cap B = A$
(vi) $A = (A \cap B) \cup (A \cap B')$
       $B = (A \cap B) \cup (A' \cap B)$

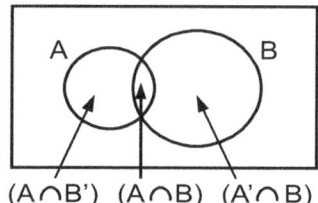

Fig. 6.5

(vii) $(A \cup B) = (A \cap B') \cup (A \cap B) \cup (A' \cap B)$

4. Mutually Exclusive Events : (Disjoint events) Events A and B are said to be mutually exclusive if there is no common element in A and B. That is,

$$A \cap B = \phi$$

For example : In an experiment of drawing a card from a well-shuffled pack of playing cards, if A = occurrence of red card and B = occurrence of a spade card, then

$$A \cap B = \phi.$$

Hence, A and B are mutually exclusive events. See figure 6.6

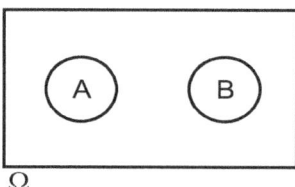

Fig. 6.6

5. Complement of an event : If A is an event on Ω then complement of A is the event corresponding to the set A'. In other words A' is the event containing all points in Ω which are not in A. (Fig. 6.7).

For example, if in the experiment of rolling a die, A = occurrence of an even number. Then complement of event A is A' = occurrence of an odd number.

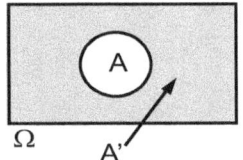

Fig. 6.7

Note that A and A' are mutually exclusive events.

6. Exhaustive events : Events A and B on Ω are said to be exhaustive events, if $A \cup B = \Omega$. In general, events $A_1, A_2, .., A_n$ are said to be exhaustive if $A_1 \cup A_2 ... \cup A_n = \Omega$.

For example, if $\Omega = \{1, 2, 3, 4, 5, 6\}$
$$A_1 = \{1, 3\} \quad A_2 = \{2, 3, 5\} \quad A_3 = \{4, 5, 6\}$$
Then, $A_1 \cup A_2 \cup A_3 = \Omega$ Therefore, A_1, A_2, A_3 are exhaustive events.

Remark : 1. A and A' are exhaustive.

2. By mutually exclusive and exhaustive events we mean a partition of Ω.

For example, with the above Ω, if
$$A_1 = \{1, 3\}, A_2 = \{2, 5\} \quad A_3 = \{4, 6\}$$
then, $A_1 \cap A_2 = \phi, A_1 \cap A_3 = \phi, A_2 \cap A_3 = \phi,$
$A_1 \cup A_2 \cup A_3 = \Omega$

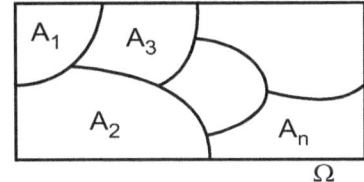

Fig. 6.8

If $A_1, A_2, ..., A_n$ are mutually exclusive and exhaustive events, then they can be represented as in the Venn diagram given in Fig. 6.8.

Union and intersection of two or more events give rise to the following different concepts.

1. Occurrence of at least one of the given events : If A and B are two events on Ω, then occurrence of at least one of the events A and B is defined as $A \cup B$. (Fig. 6.9)

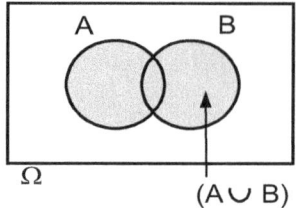

Fig. 6.9

For example, let $\Omega = \{1, 2, 3, 4, 5, 6, 7, 8\}$

A = Occurrence of an even number.
  = $\{2, 4, 6, 8\}$

B = Occurrence of a multiple of 3 = $\{3, 6\}$

Here occurrence of number either even or multiple of 3 is given by,

$$A \cup B = \{2, 3, 4, 6, 8\}$$

On similar lines, occurrence of *at least one* of the events of $A_1, A_2, \ldots A_n$ is given by

$$A_1 \cup A_2 \cup A_3 \ldots \cup A_n = \bigcup_{i=1}^{n} A_i$$

2. Occurrence of all of the given events or simultaneous occurrence of the events : If A and B are events on Ω, then $A \cap B$ is the occurrence of both the events A and B. It is also called as the simultaneous occurrence of events A and B (Fig. 6.10).

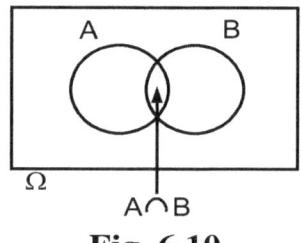

Fig. 6.10

For example, let $\Omega = \{1, 2, 3, 4, 5, 6\}$.

Event A : Occurrence of number of multiple of 3.
B : Occurrence of even number.

Then, $A = \{3, 6\}$ $B = \{2, 4, 6\}$

$A \cap B = \{6\}$.

We say that A and B occur simultaneously if '6' appears.

Similarly, occurrence of all the events $A_1, A_2, \ldots, A_n$ is given by,

$$A_1 \cap A_2, \ldots, \cap A_n = \bigcap_{i=1}^{n} A_i$$

3. Occurrence of none of the given events : Let A and B be two events on Ω. Occurrence of none of the events A and B is given by,

$$(A \cup B)' = A' \cap B' \text{ by De Morgan's law (Fig. 6.11)}.$$

Similarly, occurrence of none of the given events $A_1, A_2, \ldots A_n$ is given by,

$$\left(\bigcup_{i=1}^{n} A_i \right)' = \bigcap_{i=1}^{n} A_i'$$

For example,

Let, $\Omega = \{1, 2, 3, 4, 5, 6\}$

A = Even number appears.

B = Multiple of 3 appears.

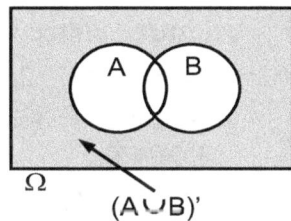

(A∪B)'

Fig. 6.11

Then none of the events A and B appear is

$$(A \cup B)' = \{1, 5\} = A' \cap B'$$

4. Relative complementation : Let A and B be two events on Ω. The relative complement of A with respect to B is given by $A' \cap B$. That is, it is the set of all points which are *not in* A but *in* B. Similarly, the relative complement of B with respect to A is given by $A \cap B'$. (Fig. 6.12).

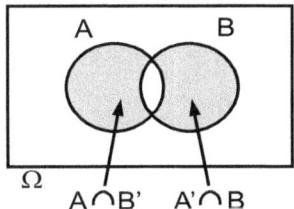

Fig. 6.12

Illustrative Examples

Example 6.1 : Write down the sample spaces for the following experiments. Also, state the type of the sample space.

(i) Examination results (P : Pass, F : Fail) are noted for three students.

(ii) Ten radio sets are checked and number of defective sets are noted.

(iii) Items coming-off a production line are marked defective (D) or non-defective (N). This is continued until two consecutive defectives are produced or four items have been checked, whichever occurs first.

(iv) A coin is tossed until 'head' appears for the first time.

(v) Life of an electric tube produced by a company is measured.

Solution : (i) Ω = {PPP, PPF, PFP, FPP, PFF, FPF, FFP FFF}

Sample space is finite, hence discrete.

(ii) Ω = {0, 1, 2, ..., 10}

Sample space is finite, hence discrete. NNNN, NNND, DNNN.

(iii) Ω = {DD, NDD, NNDD, DNDD, NDND, DNDN, NDNN, NNND, DNNN, NNDN, NNNN}

Sample space is finite, hence discrete. NNDN,

(iv) Ω = {H, TH, TTH, TTTH, ...}

Sample space is countably infinite, hence discrete.

(v) Ω = [0, ∞]

Sample space is continuous or uncountably infinite.

Example 6.2 : Let A, B, C be any three events on a sample space Ω. Write expressions for the events.

(a) At least one of the events A, B, C occurs.

(b) Only A occurs.

(c) A and B occur but not C.

(d) All three events occur.

(e) None of A, B, C occurs.

(f) Exactly one occurs.

(g) Exactly two occur.

Solution : (a) $A \cup B \cup C$

(b) $A \cap B' \cap C'$

(c) $A \cap B \cap C'$

(d) $A \cap B \cap C$

(e) $(A \cup B \cup C)' = A' \cap B' \cap C'$

(f) $(A \cap B' \cap C') \cup (A' \cap B \cap C') \cup (A' \cap B' \cap C)$

(g) $(A \cap B \cap C') \cup (A \cap B' \cap C) \cup (A' \cap B \cap C)$

Example 6.3 : A committee of 3 persons is to be formed from 5 persons A, B, C, D, E.

(a) Write down an appropriate sample space for this experiment.

(b) Write down the events corresponding to the following :

(i) E_1 = A is not selected in the committee.

(ii) E_2 = B and C are both selected in the committee.

(iii) E_3 = B and C but not D is selected in the committee.

(iv) E_4 = at least one of A and B is selected in the committee.

Solution : As 3 persons are to be selected from 5, the total number of ways in which this can be done is $\binom{5}{3}$ = 10.

The sample space is,

Ω = {ABC, ABD, ABE, ACD, ACE, ADE, BCD, BCE, BDE, CDE}

(i) Event E_1 = {BCD, BCE, BDE, CDE}

(ii) E_2 = {ABC, BCD, BCE}

(iii) E_3 = {ABC, BCE}

(iv) E_4 = {ABC, ABD, ABE, ACD, ACE, ADE, BCD, BCE, BDE}

Points to Remember

- Random experiments are ones which can result in more than one outcome.
- Sample space is the set of all possible outcomes of a random experiment.
- An event is a subset of sample space.

    $A \cup B$: Occurrence of at least one among A and B

$A \cap B$: Simultaneous occurrence of both A and B
$A' \cap B$: Occurrence of only B
$A \cap B'$: Occurrence of only A
$A' \cap B'$: Occurrence of neither A nor B
$(A \cap B)' = A' \cup B'$ De Morgan's law
$(A \cup B)' = A' \cap B'$ De Morgan's law

EXERCISE 6 (A)

Theory Questions :

1. Distinguish between deterministic and non-deterministic experiments. Give two illustrations of each.
2. Give an example of a random phenomenon that would be studied by (i) a physicist, (ii) an engineer, (iii) an economist, (iv) an environmentalist, (v) a sociologist.
3. Explain with suitable illustrations, the following (i) Sample space, (ii) Finite sample space, (iii) Discrete sample space, (iv) Countably infinite sample space, (v) Continuous sample space.
4. Explain with suitable illustrations, the following (i) Event (ii) Occurrence of an event.
5. Explain what is meant by (i) Simple event, (ii) Impossible event. (iii) Certain event.
6. Explain with one illustration each of the following :
   (i) Mutually exclusive events.
   (ii) Complement of an event.
   (iii) Exhaustive events.
   (iv) Mutually exclusive and exhaustive events.
7. Explain with illustrations and Venn diagrams how union and intersection of events give rise to the following :
   (i) At least one of the events A and B.
   (ii) Simultaneous occurrence of A and B.
   (iii) None of the events A and B.
   Also write the expressions for (i), (ii) and (iii) for n given events $A_1, A_2, ..., A_n$.
8. What is meant by relative complementation ? Explain with the help of an example.

EXERCISE 6 (B)

Numerical Problems :

9. Determine which of the following are (i) deterministic experiments and (ii) Non-deterministic experiments.
   - (i) The agriculturist uses different types of fertilizers to see which maximizes the yield of a crop.
   - (ii) Marketing manager conducts market survey to measure the effect on advertising on sales.
   - (iii) Water is heated upto 100°C.
   - (iv) A coin is tossed to decide the team which would bat first in a cricket match.
   - (v) An object is released from a fixed height and the time it takes to reach the ground is measured.

10. Write down the sample spaces for the following experiments. Also write the nature of the sample space.
    - (i) Answers to an objective question which has 4 multiple choices A, B, C, D. Student ticks a single answer.
    - (ii) Number of tossings of a die is recorded when it is tossed until '6' occurs.
    - (iii) Ten seeds are planted and total number of seeds germinated are recorded after a week.
    - (iv) T.V. viewers were asked to give ratings to 3 programmes.
    - (v) A two digit number is formed from the digits 4, 5, 6 using each digit only once.
    - (vi) A card is drawn from a pack of 52 playing cards and its suit as well as denomination is noted.
    - (vii) A student studying Mathematics, Statistics, Physics, Chemistry, Electronics offers only 3 subjects for the next year.
    - (viii) A point is randomly placed inside a circle with radius 10 cm. It's distance from the centre is measured.
    - (ix) Number of attempts required to kill a cockroach in the kitchen.

11. Let A, B, C be any three events on a sample space Ω. Write expressions for the following events.
    (i) A occurs but not B and C occur.
    (ii) B and C occur but not A.
    (iii) Only one of A and C occurs.
    (iv) At least one of A and C occur.
    (v) (A∪B) and (B∩C)' occur simultaneously.

12. Given three events A, B, C defined on Ω, find simpler expressions for
    (i) (A∪B) ∩ (A∪B') (ii) (A∪φ) ∩B (iii) (A∪B) ∩ (B∪C)
    (iv) (A∪B) ∩ (C∪C') (v) (A∩φ) ∩ (B∪C)

13. Three coins are tossed and whether each shows head or tail is recorded. Write the following events.
    (i) A : Exactly two coins show tails.
    (ii) B : At least two coins show tails.
    Write down also the sets corresponding to the complementary events. Determine whether the events A and B are mutually exclusive ? Are A and B exhaustive ?

14. Let,   Ω = {a, b, c, d, e, f, g, h, i}
           A = {a, c, e, f}, B = {b, d, e, g, h}, C = {e, h, i}
    List the elements of the following events.
    (i) A∩B'   (ii) (A∪B∪C)'
    (iii) (A∩B)∪C   (iv) [A∪ (B∪C)]'

15. A card is drawn from a pack of 52 playing cards. Consider the following events :
    A : An ace is drawn.   B : A face card is drawn.
    (i) List the elements of A and B.
    (ii) List the elements of A∩B'
    (iii) Are A and B mutually exclusive ? Justify.
        [A face card is a king, queen or a jack]

16. Consider the following sample space.
               Ω = {1, 2, 3, 4, 5, 6, 7, 8}
    Write down the following events : (list the elements)
    (i) A : An odd number appears.
    (ii) B : Number is greater than 4.

(iii) A∪B
(iv) Both A and B occur.
(v) None of A and B occurs.
(vi) Relative complement of A w.r.t. B occurs.
(vii) A occurs but not B.

17. Describe the event A' in each of the following cases.
    (i) a die is thrown; A = a number greater than 3 is obtained.
    (ii) Three shots are fired at the target.
        A = no shot hits the target.

18. If A = (0, 3) B = (1, 5) C = (0, 8)
    Describe the events.
    (i) A∪B   (ii) A ∪ (B∩C')
    (iii) (A∪B)' ∩ C (iv) (A∩B) ∪ C
    (v) A∩B∩C

EXERCISE 6 (C)

19. In a survey conducted by a Music club, it was observed that, 45% people out of 1000 liked Indian classical music, while 50% liked Western music and 15% liked neither Indian nor Western music. How many individuals liked both the types of music ?

20. A student appears for an examination. Consider the following events :
    A : He reaches late to the examination hall.
    B : He forgets his I - card.
    C : He completes the paper in the allotted time.
    Describe the following events in words :
    (i) A'∩B'∩ C (ii) B'∩C' (iii) A∩B∩C (iv) A∩B ∩C'

21. Write (A∪B∪C) as a union of mutually exclusive events. Draw Venn diagram.

22. A person will shoot at a target until he hits the target. Write the events corresponding to the following.
    (a) He needs 3 attempts to hit the target.
    (b) He needs less than 6 attempts to hit the target.
    (c) He hits the target.
    (d) He never hits the target.

23. A family consists of 3 children. Write the sample space and the following events.
    (i) Eldest is a boy.
    (ii) Youngest is a girl.
    (iii) There are at least two boys in the family.
    (iv) There are at the most two girls in the family.
    (v) Eldest is a boy and youngest is a girl.
24. For k = 1, 2, 3, 4, let A_k be the event A has at least k aces in a game of bridge. Let B_k, C_k, D_k be the analogous events for B, C and D respectively. How many aces has D in events
    (i) D_1' (ii) $B_2 \cap C_2$ (iii) $A_3 \cap D_1$ (iv) $A_1 \cap B_1 \cap D_1 \cap C_1$?

Objective Types Questions

I. Multiple Choice Questions (MCQ).

- **Choose the correct alternative :**

1. A sample space is ....
   (a) a set of data space in which a sample experiment can be performed to resolve a particular problem.
   (b) the set of all possible outcomes of a random experiment.
   (c) a space from which a sample for study may be drawn.
   (d) the set of all possible outcomes that belong to a particular sample.

2. A ball is drawn at random from a bag containing green, red and yellow balls in the ratio 2 : 3 : 1. Define the events A : Getting a green ball, B : Getting a red ball,
   C : Getting a yellow ball. Which of the following statements is false ?
   (a) A, B, C are exhaustive and equally likely events.
   (b) A, B, C are mutually exclusive and exhaustive events.
   (c) B and C are not exhaustive but mutually exclusive events.
   (d) A, B and C are mutually exclusive, exhaustive but not equally likely events.

3. Three coins are tossed and whether each shows head or tail is recorded. Let A be the event that exactly two coins show heads, and B be the event that exactly two coins show tails. Which of the following is true ?
   (a) A and B are sure events.
   (b) A and B are mutually exclusive events.
   (c) A and B are mutually exclusive as well as exhaustive events.
   (d) A and B are exhaustive events.

4. The sample space corresponding to the experiment "five seeds are planted and total number of seeds germinated are recorded after a week" is ....
   (a) (0, 5)
   (b) {0, 1, 2, 3, 4, 5}
   (c) {1, 2, 3, 4, 5}
   (d) [0, 5].

5. Relative complement of A w.r.t. B is given by ....
   (a) $A \cap B'$
   (b) $A' \cup B$
   (c) $A' \cap B$
   (d) $(A \cap B)'$.

6. A coin is tossed three times in succession and the outcomes are noted. The number of sample points in the sample space is ....
   (a) 6
   (b) 8
   (c) 3
   (d) 9.

7. Which of the following is a pair of mutually exclusive events in the drawing of a single card from a deek of 52 playing cards ?
   (a) A heart and a queen
   (b) An even number and a spade
   (c) A club and red card
   (d) An ace and an odd number.

8. Which of the following is not a random experiment ?
   (a) Number of runs scored by Sachin Tendulkar are noted in an over bowled by Shoeib Akhtar.
   (b) You watch T.V. for five hours on the day of the examination, and whether you pass or fail is noted.
   (c) You tie a friendship band to your friend who is your friend indeed !
   (d) You get up in the morning at 5.00 a.m.
   (e) When you walk on the ground, the earth pushes you.
9. Consider the experiment of rolling a die. Suppose A is the event that an odd number appears and B is the event that a prime number appears. Which of the following statements is true ?
   (a) $A \subset B$.
   (b) $B \subset A$.
   (c) A and B are mutually exclusive events.
   (d) A and B are not mutually exclusive events.
10. If a discrete sample space contains 5 elements that the total number of events on this sample space is ....
    (a) 10
    (b) 5
    (c) 32
    (d) 25

II. State whether the following statements are true or false.

11. An elementary event is an event containing only one element.
12. It is impossible to define an impossible event.
13. Occurrence of at least one of the two events is the event corresponding to the union of the two events.
14. The event Ω and ϕ are mutually exclusive.
15. A discrete sample space must contain a finite number of elements.

HINTS AND ANSWERS

9. (i) ND, (ii) ND, (iii) D, (iv) ND, (v) D.
10. (i) $\Omega = \{A, B, C, D\}$, finite, discrete.

(ii) $\Omega = \{1, 2, 3, 4, ...\}$, countably infinite, discrete.

(iii) $\Omega = \{0, 1, 2, ... 10\}$, finite.

(iv) $\Omega = \{$I II III, I III II, II I III, II III I, III I II, III II I$\}$, finite.

(v) $\Omega = \{45, 46, 54, 56, 64, 65\}$, finite.

(vi) $\Omega = \left\{\begin{array}{llllll} H1, & H2, & ... & H10, & HJ, & HQ, & HK \\ D1, & D2, & ... & D10, & DJ, & DQ, & DK \\ C1, & C2, & ... & C10, & CJ, & CQ, & CK \\ S1, & S2, & ... & S10, & SJ, & SQ, & SK \end{array}\right\}$,

Finite

where, H : Hearts, D : Diamonds, C : Club, S : Spade, J : Jack, Q : Queen, K : King.

(vii) $\Omega = \{$MSP, MSC, MSE, MPC, MPE, MCE, SPC, SPE, SCE, PCE$\}$, finite.

(viii) $\Omega = [0, 10]$ continuous, or uncountably infinite.

(ix) $\Omega = \{1, 2, 3, ... \}$

11. (i) $A \cap B' \cap C'$ (ii) $A' \cap B \cap C$ (iii) $(A \cap C') \cup (A' \cap C)$
    (iv) $A \cup C$ (v) $(A \cup B) \cap (B \cap C)'$

12. (i) A (ii) $A \cap B$ (iii) $B \cup (A \cap C)$ (iv) $A \cup B$ (v) ϕ

13. $\Omega = \{$HHH, HHT, HTH, THH, HTT, TTH, THT, TTT$\}$
    A = $\{$HTT, THT, TTH$\}$
    B = $\{$HTT, THT, TTH, TTT$\}$ No, No

14. (i) $\{a, c, f\}$ (ii) ϕ (iii) $\{e, h, i\}$, (iv) $\{b, d, g, i\}$

15. (i) A = $\{$S1, H1, C1, D1$\}$
    B = $\{$SJ, SQ, SK, HJ, HQ, HK, DJ, DQ, DK, CJ, CQ, CK$\}$
    (ii) $\{$S1, H1, C1, D1$\}$ (iii) yes.

16. (i) A = $\{1, 3, 5, 7\}$, (ii) B = $\{5, 6, 7, 8\}$, (iii) $\{1, 3, 5, 6, 7, 8\}$, (iv) $\{5\}$ (v) $\{2, 4\}$, (vi) $\{6, 8\}$ (vii) $\{1, 3\}$

17. A' = a number less than 4 is obtained.
    A' = at least one shot hits the target.

18. (i) (0, 5) (ii) (0, 3), (iii) (5, 8), (iv) (0, 8), (v) (1, 3).

19. 100.

20. (i) He reaches in time and has his I-card with him and also completes the paper in the allotted time.

    (ii) He takes his I-card but can't complete the paper in allotted time.

    (iii) Goes late, forgets I-card but completes the paper.

    (iv) Goes late, forgets I-Card and can't complete paper.

21.

I : A∩B'∩C'

II : A∩B∩C'

III : A∩B∩C

IV : A∩B'∩C

V : A'∩B∩C

VI : A'∩B∩C'

VII : A'∩B'∩C

Fig. 6.13

A∪B∪C = I ∪ II ∪ III ∪ IV ∪ V ∪ VI ∪ VII.

22 (a) {FFH}, (b) {H, FH, FFH, FFFH, FFFFH}

(c) Ω (d) φ (where F : Fails to hit; H : Hits)

23. Ω = {BBB, BBG, BGB, GBB, BGG, GBG, GGB, GGG}

    (i) {BBB, BBG, BGB, BGG}

    (ii) {BBG, BGG, GBG, GGG}

    (iii) {BBB, BBG, BGB, GBB}

    (iv) {BBB, BBG, BGB, GBB, BGG, GBG, GGB}

    (v) {BBG, BGG}

24. (i) zero, (ii) zero, (iii) one, (iv) one.

Answers of Objective Questions

I. (1) b, (2) a, (3) b, (4) b, (5) c, (6) b, (7) c, (8) e, (9) d, (10) c,

II. (11) T, (12) F, (13) T, (14) T, (15) F.

Chapter 7...
Probability

Abraham De Moivre (1667-1754) was a French mathematician famous for his work on probability theory and normal distribution. De Moivre first discovered the closed-form expression for Fibonacci numbers. As he grew older, he became increasingly lethargic and needed longer sleeping hours. He noted that he was sleeping an extra 15 minutes each night and correctly calculated the date of his death on the day when the additional sleep time accumulated to 24 hours, November 27, 1754.

Abraham De-Moivre

Contents ...
7.1 Introduction
7.2 Classical Definition of Probability
7.3 Limitations of Classical Definition of Probability
7.4 Probability Model : (Probability Assignment Approach)
7.5 Axiomatic Approach (Modern Approach) to Probability
7.6 Important Theorems on Probability

Key Words :
Equiprobable sample space, Classical definition of probability, Axioms, Probability model. Addition theorem of probability.

Objectives :
- Understand the basic concept of probability and different approaches.
- Learn theorems on probability, compute probabilities of different events.
- Solve elementary numerical problems on probability.

7.1 Introduction

The theory of probability has its origin in the seventeenth century. The king of France, who was fond of gambling, consulted the great mathematicians Pascal and Fermat for solving the gambling problems. These two scientists tried to solve the problems using probability concepts which laid the foundations of the probability theory.

Later on during eighteenth century, great mathematicians like Bernoulli, De-Moivre, Laplace and several others made valuable contributions to the theory. Prof. R. A. Fisher, who can be called as the father of Statistics, introduced the empirical approach to the theory of probability and expanded its use in biology, agriculture, genetics and medicine.

Now-a-days, there is hardly any discipline left, in which probability theory is not used. It is extensively applied in all fields such as business, life insurance agencies, Psychology, Ecology, Medicine, Physics, Astronomy and even in linguistics, nutrition and music etc.

In Chapter 1, we learned that a random experiment has a number of possible outcomes. Also, the outcome cannot be predicted before performing the experiment. However, we find ourselves making certain statements as :

(i) My chances of getting first class are good.

(ii) It may rain today.

(iii) Possibility of Indians entering the World Cup Cricket finals is high.

The probability theory tries to measure the *possibility* of an outcome in numeric terms. Thus probability of an outcome is a numeric measure of the possibility or chance of the occurrence of that outcome. Unless, we have numbers, measuring the chances of various outcomes, we cannot analyze them mathematically.

There are several definitions of 'probability'. We shall consider only (i) the classical definition and (ii) the axiomatic approach.

7.2 Classical Definition of Probability

Classical definition assumes that the sample space under consideration is equiprobable.

Equiprobable Sample Space : Consider a random experiment which has n mutually exclusive outcomes. The sample space Ω, is said to be an equiprobable sample space if all the outcomes are equally likely. Or there is no reason to say that, their chances of occurrence are different. In other words, probability of occurrence of every outcome is the same.

For example, when we toss a fair coin, probability of getting 'head' is the same as that of getting 'tail'. Therefore, if the total probability is assumed to be equal to 1,

$$P\{\text{Head}\} = P\{\text{Tail}\} = \frac{1}{2}.$$

Similarly, if $\Omega = \{\omega_1, \omega_2, ..., \omega_i, ..., \omega_n\}$ then Ω is 'equiprobable' would mean that probability of each ω_i is $\frac{1}{n}$ for $1 \leq i \leq n$.

If we denote probability of ω_i by $P\{\omega_i\}$, then we have

$$P\{\omega_1\} = P\{\omega_2\} ... = P\{\omega_i\} = ... = P\{\omega_n\} = \frac{1}{n}.$$

Probability of an event : If a random experiment results in n mutually exclusive and equally likely outcomes; out of which m are favourable to the event A, then the probability of occurrence of the event A is denoted by P(A) and is given by,

$$P(A) = \frac{m}{n} \; ; \; 0 \leq m \leq n$$

In other words,

$$P(A) = \frac{\text{Number of elements belonging to A}}{\text{Total number of elements in the sample space } \Omega}$$

Remark : 1. Note that for any event A,

$$0 \leq P(A) \leq 1 \quad \text{since} \quad 0 \leq m \leq n.$$

Thus, probability of any event always lies between 0 and 1.

2. The classical definition of probability does not require the performance of the experiment. Probability is obtained using logical reasoning without conducting the experiment.

3. n is total number of mutually exclusive, equally likely and exhaustive outcomes in Ω.

4. **Relative frequency :** Probability of an event A can be looked upon as relative frequency. Relative frequency gives proportion of the favourable cases to event A. The relative frequency tends to probability of the respective event when you perform the experiment infinitely many times (very large number of times).

Illustrative Examples

Example 7.1 : If a pair of unbiased coins is tossed, obtain probability of occurrence of (i) both heads (ii) single head (iii) at least one head.

Solution : Here, Ω = {HH, TH, HT, TT} $\therefore$ n = 4.

(i) Suppose : A = Occurrence of both heads = {HH}

$\therefore$ m = 1 and $P(A) = \dfrac{m}{n} = \dfrac{1}{4}$

(ii) B = Occurrence of single head = {HT, TH}

$\therefore$ m = 2 and $P(B) = \dfrac{m}{n} = \dfrac{2}{4} = \dfrac{1}{2}$

(iii) C = Occurrence of at least one head = {HT, TH, HH}

$\therefore$ m = 3 and $P(C) = \dfrac{m}{n} = \dfrac{3}{4}$

Example 7.2 : Four cards are drawn at random from a well shuffled pack of 52 cards. Find the probability that (i) two cards are red and two are black (ii) all cards are of different suits (iii) all are of same suit (iv) one is king.

Solution : The total number of ways in which 4 cards can be selected from 52 cards is given by $\binom{52}{4}$. Hence, Ω contains $n = \binom{52}{4}$ elements. [See Appendix for the formulas on combinations and permutations.]

(i) A = Occurrence of two red and two black cards.

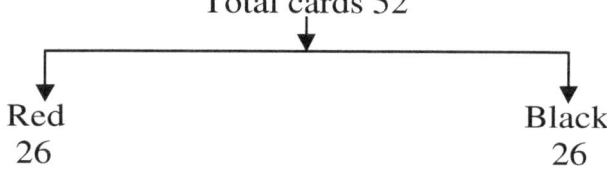

Two red cards can be drawn in $\binom{26}{2}$ ways. Two black cards can be drawn in $\binom{26}{2}$ ways. Since, both red and black cards are to be selected, the number of favourable cases to event A will be;

$$m = \binom{26}{2}\binom{26}{2}$$

$$\therefore \quad P(A) = \frac{m}{n} = \frac{\binom{26}{2}\binom{26}{2}}{\binom{52}{4}} = 0.3902$$

(ii) Let event B = All cards are of different suits

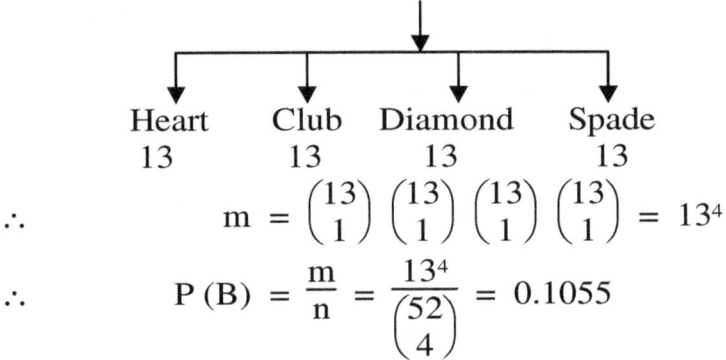

$$\therefore \quad m = \binom{13}{1}\binom{13}{1}\binom{13}{1}\binom{13}{1} = 13^4$$

$$\therefore \quad P(B) = \frac{m}{n} = \frac{13^4}{\binom{52}{4}} = 0.1055$$

(iii) Let event C = Occurrence of all cards of the same suit. That is, all cards are either hearts, spades, club or diamond. Using the addition principle of counting we get,

$$m = \binom{13}{4} + \binom{13}{4} + \binom{13}{4} + \binom{13}{4} = 4\binom{13}{4}$$

$$\therefore \quad P(C) = \frac{m}{n} = \frac{4\binom{13}{4}}{\binom{52}{4}} = 0.0106$$

(iv) Let event D = Occurrence of a king among selected cards.

Total cards 52
- King 4
- Others 48

$$\text{Favourable cases} = m = \begin{pmatrix} \text{Number of} \\ \text{ways of} \\ \text{occurrence of} \\ \text{a king} \end{pmatrix} \times \begin{pmatrix} \text{Number of} \\ \text{ways of} \\ \text{occurrence of} \\ \text{3 other cards} \end{pmatrix}$$

$$= \binom{4}{1}\binom{48}{3}$$

$$\therefore \quad P(D) = \frac{m}{n} = \frac{4\binom{48}{3}}{\binom{52}{4}} = 0.2556$$

Example 7.3 : A committee of four is to be formed from 3 engineers, 4 economists, 2 statisticians and 1 chartered accountant.
  (i) What is the probability that each of the four categories of profession is included in the committee ?
  (ii) What is the probability that the committee consists of the chartered accountant and at least one engineer ?

Solution : The sample space consists of all possible combinations of four persons from 10 persons. Hence, the total number of elements in the sample space = n = $\binom{10}{4}$ = 210.

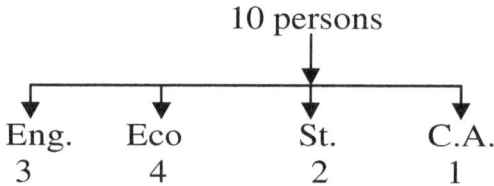

(i) Suppose A is the event that one engineer, one economist, one statistician and the chartered accountant forms the committee. Hence, the number of favourable cases for A is,

$$\binom{3}{1}\binom{4}{1}\binom{2}{1} \cdot 1 = 24$$

$\therefore$ Required probability = $\frac{24}{210} = \frac{4}{35}$

(ii) The committee should consist of the chartered accountant and at least one engineer. Therefore, this can be done in either of the following ways.

		No. of ways	
(a)	1 C. A. + 1 Engineer + 2 others	$1 \binom{3}{1}\binom{6}{2}$	= 45
(b)	1 C. A. + 2 Engineers + 1 others	$1 \binom{3}{2}\binom{6}{1}$	= 18
(c)	1 C.A + 3 Engineers + None other	$1 \binom{3}{3}\binom{6}{0}$	= 1

Using the addition principle of counting, we get,
$$m = 45 + 18 + 1 = 64$$
∴ Required probability $= \dfrac{64}{210} = 0.3048$

Example 7.4 : The letters of the word 'Seminar' are arranged at random. Find the probability that the vowels occupy the even places.

Solution : n = total number of permutations of the seven letters in the word 'seminar' = 7!.

Now, there are three vowels e, i and a in the word. These are to be placed in three even places, viz, 2nd, 4th and 6th. This can be done in 3! ways. The remaining 4 letters can be permuted in the odd places in 4! ways. Hence, m = total number of favourable cases for the event = 3! 4!.

Hence, required probability $= \dfrac{3!\,4!}{7!} = \dfrac{1}{35}$

Example 7.5 : If a three digit number is formed out of 4, 6, 7, 8, 5 without repeating any digit, find probability that it is divisible by 5.

Solution : Since, different order of selection produces different numbers, we need to use permutations. Hence, total numbers formed $= n = {}^5P_3 = 60$. If the last digit is 5, then only the number will be divisible by 5. Remaining two digits can be filled in using four digits out of 4, 6, 7, 8. This can be done in ${}^4P_2 = 12$ ways.

∴ $m = 1 \times {}^4P_2 = 12$

∴ Required probability $= \dfrac{12}{60} = \dfrac{1}{5}$

Example 7.6 : A committee consisting of 3 gents and 2 ladies wants to sit in a row for a photograph. What is the probability that the ladies will occupy extreme positions at two ends ?

Solution : n = Total number of arrangements.
$= {}^5P_5 = 5! = 120$

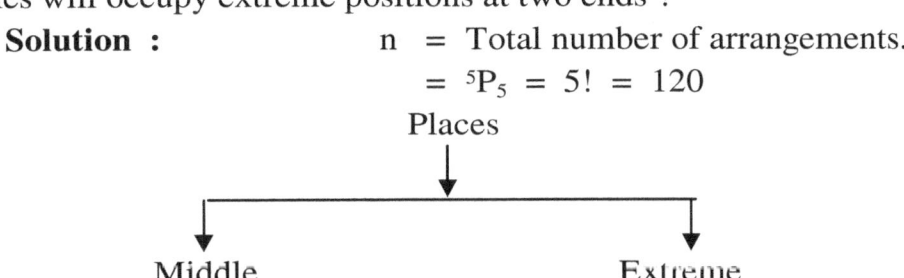

$$m = \begin{pmatrix} \text{Number of ways of} \\ \text{selecting extreme} \\ \text{positions for ladies} \end{pmatrix} \times \begin{pmatrix} \text{Number of ways of} \\ \text{selecting middle} \\ \text{positions for gents} \end{pmatrix}$$

$$= {}^2P_2 \times {}^3P_3 = 2! \times 3! = 12$$

∴ Required probability $= \dfrac{m}{n} = \dfrac{12}{120} = 0.1$

Odds Ratio and Probability : Sometimes, probability of an event is expressed in terms of odds ratios as follows.

(i) Odds *in favour* of an event A are a : b means

$$P(A) = \dfrac{a}{a+b}$$

(ii) Odds *against* an event A are a : b means

$$P(A') = \dfrac{a}{a+b}$$

or $\qquad P(A) = 1 - \dfrac{a}{a+b} = \dfrac{b}{a+b}$

Example 7.8 : Show that the odds are 6 : 4 against drawing 1 red and 1 white balls from a bag containing 2 red and 3 white balls.

Solution :

5 balls

2 R   3 W

$n = \binom{5}{2} = 10 \qquad m = \binom{2}{1}\binom{3}{1} = 6$

∴ If $\quad$ A = Getting 1 red and 1 white ball

then, $P(A) = \dfrac{6}{10} = \dfrac{6}{4+6} = \dfrac{b}{a+b}$

∴ Odds against A are 6 : 4.

7.3 Limitations of Classical Definition of Probability

(October 2012)

(i) In classical definition, it is assumed that all outcomes of the experiment under consideration are equally likely. This is not the case always. For instance, probability of passing the examination and failing in the examination are not same. In such cases, probabilities of events cannot be calculated using the classical definition. It violets the assumption that the outcomes are equiprobable.

(ii) Suppose a positive integer is drawn a random from a set of positive integers. To final probability that the number drawn is positive, we have to count number of favourable cases, it is ∞ and total number of cases is also ∞. Hence the P(Getting even integer) = $\frac{\infty}{\infty}$. The classical definition of probability does no work.

(iii) Sometimes, n, the total number of possible outcomes is infinite. For example, for the experiment of tossing coin until head appears, the sample space Ω = {H, TH, TTH, TTTH, ...}. Here also classical definition fails.

(iii) If the actual value of n is not known, then also probabilities cannot be computed using the classical definition.

For example, in the experiment of capturing fish from a pond, the total number of fish in the pond is not known. Hence, we cannot find probability of concerned events. Due to these drawbacks in the classical definition of probability, it is used only in limited situations.

A Russian mathematician, A. N. Kolmogorov in 1933 formulated the axiomatic approach to the modern probability theory. It overcomes the limitations of classical definition of probability. This approach begins with certain notions and axioms, based on which the further theory is developed using logical reasoning. For finite sample spaces, the axiomatic approach reduces to the probability assignment approach which we consider first.

7.4 Probability Model : (Probability Assignment Approach)

Let Ω be a finite sample space containing the points $\omega_1, \omega_2, ... \omega_n$. That is,

$$\Omega = \{\omega_1, \omega_2, ..., \omega_n\}$$

Assign a real number $P\{\omega_i\}$ to each $\omega_i \in \Omega$, such that

(i) $0 \leq P\{\omega_i\} \leq 1$, for i = 1, 2, ..., n and

(ii) $P\{\omega_1\} + P\{\omega_2\} + ... + P\{\omega_n\} = 1$

i.e. $\sum_{i=1}^{n} P\{\omega_i\} = 1$

$P\{\omega_i\}$ is called the probability of the elementary event $\{\omega_i\}$. In other words, $P\{\omega_i\}$ is the probability of occurrence of ω_i in anytrial of the experiment.

Note : The sample points $\omega_1, \omega_2, \ldots, \omega_n$ may not be equiprobable, hence $P\{\omega_i\}$ may differ from/point to sample point.

Probability Model : Suppose $\Omega = \{\omega_1, \omega_2, \omega_3, \ldots\}$ is a sample space then $(\omega_i, P\{\omega_i\}, i = 1, 2, 3, \ldots)$ is a probability model if $P\{\omega_i\} \geq 0 \ \forall i$ and $\sum P\{\omega_i\} = 1$.

Example 7.8 : Suppose $\Omega = \{\omega_1, \omega_2, \ldots, \omega_6\}$
Which of the following probability models are valid ?

Sample Points

Model	ω_1	ω_2	ω_3	ω_4	ω_5	ω_6
(i)	0	0	0	0	1/2	1/2
(ii)	1/4	1/4	1/4	1/4	1/4	1/4
(iii)	1	0	0	0	0	0
(iv)	$\frac{1}{8}$	$\frac{1}{8}$	$\frac{1}{2}$	$\frac{1}{8}$	0	$\frac{1}{8}$
(v)	$\frac{1}{6}$	$\frac{1}{6}$	$\frac{1}{6}$	$\frac{1}{6}$	0	$\frac{1}{6}$
(vi)	$\frac{-1}{3}$	$\frac{2}{3}$	0	$\frac{1}{3}$	0	0
(vii)	π	$1-\pi$	0	0	0	0
(viii)	$\frac{1}{20}$	$\frac{1}{20}$	$\frac{1}{20}$	$\frac{1}{20}$	$\frac{3}{4}$	$\frac{1}{20}$

Solution : Only (i), (iii) and (viii) are valid probability assignments.

(ii) is not valid as $\sum P(\omega_i) = \frac{3}{2} > 1$

(iv) is not valid as $\sum P(\omega_i) = \frac{3}{4} < 1$

(v) is not valid as $\sum P(\omega_i) = \frac{5}{6} < 1$

(vi) is not valid as $P(\omega_i) = \frac{-1}{3} < 0$

(vii) is not valid as $P(\omega_1) = \pi > 1$ and $P(\omega_2) = 1 - \pi < 0$

Probability of an event :

The probability P (A) of an event A is, the sum of the probabilities of the elements in A.

i.e. $$P(A) = \sum_{\omega_i \in A} P\{\omega_i\}$$

Example 7.9 : A loaded die has following probability assignment to the six faces.

$$\Omega = \{1, 2, 3, 4, 5, 6\}$$

with $P(1) = 0.1$; $P(2) = 0.2$, $P(3) = 0.3$, $P(4) = 0.25$, $P(5) = 0.1$, $P(6) = 0.05$

What is the probability of (i) an even number appears, (ii) a number less than 4 appears.

Solution : (i) Let event A = even number appears.

∴ $A = \{2, 4, 6\}$

∴ $P(A) = \sum_{\omega_i \in A} P(\omega_i) = P(2) + P(4) + P(6)$

$= 0.2 + 0.25 + 0.05$

$= 0.5$

(ii) Let, event B = a number less than 4 appears.

∴ $B = \{1, 2, 3\}$

∴ $P(B) = P(1) + P(2) + P(3) = 0.1 + 0.2 + 0.3$

$= 0.6$

Example 7.10 : Three girls and four boys take part in an antakshari competition. Those of same sex have equal probabilities of winning, but each girl is twice as likely to win as any boy. Find the probability that a boy wins in the competition.

Solution : Let B denote a boy and G a girl.

∴ $\Omega = \{G_1, G_2, G_3, B_1, B_2, B_3, B_4\}$

Let, $P(B_1) = P(B_2) = P(B_3) = P(B_4) = p$

∴ $P(G_1) = P(G_2) = P(G_3) = 2p$

Since, sum of probabilities of all points in Ω must be 1,

$4p + 6p = 1$

∴ $p = 0.1$

Now, let A be the event that a boy wins.

$$\therefore \quad A = \{B_1, B_2, B_3, B_4\}$$

$$\therefore \quad P(A) = \sum_{i=1}^{4} P(B_i) = 0.4$$

7.5 Axiomatic Approach (Modern Approach) to Probability

As stated earlier, we shall now introduce ourselves to the axiomatic approach given by A. N. Kolmogorov in 1933. An axiom is a statement which is accepted heuristically and not proved. Based on axioms further theory is developed.

Axioms of probability : Let Ω be a sample space concerning a random experiment. Let A be any event of Ω. Probability of A, denoted by $P(A)$, is defined as any real valued function on Ω, which satisfies the following axioms.

Axiom 1 : $\quad P(A) \geq 0$

Axiom 2 : $\quad P(\Omega) = 1$

Axiom 3 : If $A_1, A_2, ..., A_n$ are any mutually exclusive events of Ω, then,

$$P\left(\bigcup_{i=1}^{n} A_i\right) = \sum_{i=1}^{n} P(A_i)$$

In particular, if A and B are two mutually exclusive (disjoint) events, then

$$P(A \cup B) = P(A) + P(B)$$

Remark : The above definition applies to countably infinite as well as uncountably infinite sample spaces. These types of sample spaces are beyond the scope of this book. We shall always consider a finite sample space like

$$\Omega = \{\omega_1, \omega_2, ..., \omega_n\}$$

7.6 Important Theorems on Probability

We now learn some fundamental theorems on probability. Proofs of these theorems are based on the axioms given in 7.5. Application of these results makes the computation of probabilities of complex events very easy.

Theorem 1 : $P(A') = 1 - P(A)$ where A' is the complement of A.

Proof : Note that, for any event A, A and A' are mutually exclusive events.

∴ $\quad\quad\quad A \cap A' = \phi$

Also, $\quad\quad A \cup A' = \Omega$

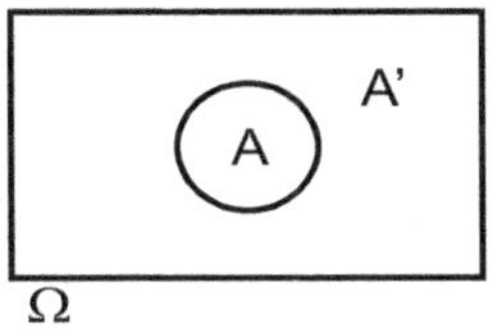

Fig. 7.1

Therefore, using Axiom 3,

$$P(A \cup A') = P(A) + P(A')$$
∴ $\quad\quad P(\Omega) = P(A) + P(A')$
∴ $\quad\quad 1 = P(A) + P(A')$

$\quad\quad\quad\quad\quad\quad\quad\quad\quad\quad \because P(\Omega) = 1$, by Axiom 2.

Hence, $\quad\quad P(A') = 1 - P(A)$

Theorem 2 : $P(\phi) = 0$, That is probability of an impossible event is zero.

Proof : We know that

$$\phi' = \Omega$$
∴ $\quad\quad P(\phi') = 1 - P(\Omega)$. $\quad\quad$ by theorem 1
$\quad\quad\quad\quad\quad = 1 - 1$ $\quad\quad\quad\quad\quad$ by Axiom 2
$\quad\quad\quad\quad\quad = 0$

Theorem 3 : For any event A of Ω,

$$0 \leq P(A) \leq 1$$

Proof : (i) $\quad\quad P(A) \geq 0$ $\quad\quad\quad\quad\quad\quad$ by Axiom 1

(ii) Also, if A' is the complement of A, then

$\quad\quad\quad\quad P(A') \geq 0$ $\quad\quad\quad\quad\quad\quad$ by Axiom 1
∴ $\quad\quad 1 - P(A) \geq 0$ $\quad\quad\quad\quad\quad$ by theorem 1
∴ $\quad\quad P(A) \leq 1$

Hence, $\quad\quad 0 \leq P(A) \leq 1$

Theorem 4 : If $A \subset B$, then $P(A) \leq P(B)$.

Proof : Observe Fig. 7.2. The event B is composed of two disjoint events A and $A' \cap B$.

i.e. $\quad B = A \cup (A' \cap B)$

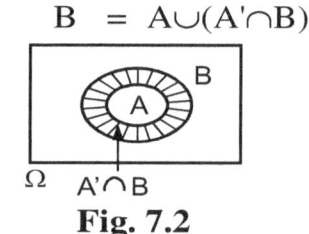

Fig. 7.2

∴ Using Axiom 3,

$$P(B) = P(A) + P(A' \cap B)$$

Now, $\quad P(A' \cap B) \geq 0$ by Axiom 1

∴ $\quad P(B) \geq P(A)$

Theorem 5 : Addition theorem of Probability (Theorem of total probability)

If A and B are any two events defined on Ω, then,

$$P(A \cup B) = P(A) + P(B) - P(A \cap B)$$

Proof : Since, A and B are any two events, we assume that they are not disjoint. For such general case the Venn diagram will be as follows.

Note that the event $A \cup B$ is composed of three mutually exclusive events $A \cap B'$, $A \cap B$ and $A' \cap B$.

Therefore, using Axiom 3, we write,

$$P(A \cup B) = P(A \cap B') + P(A \cap B) + P(A' \cap B) \quad \ldots (1)$$

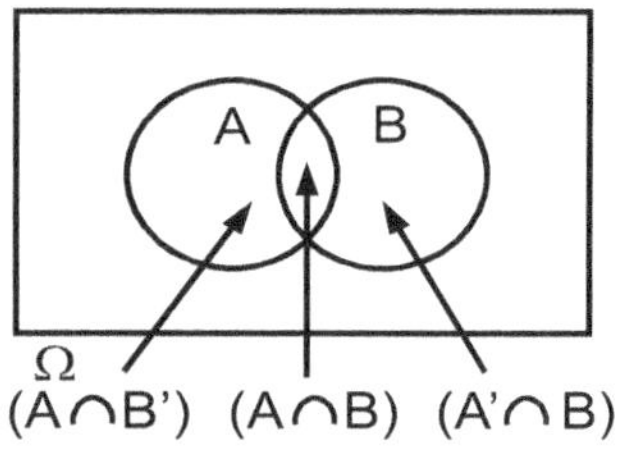

Fig. 7.3

Similarly, A is the union of the disjoint event $A \cap B'$ and $A \cap B$

∴ $\quad P(A) = P(A \cap B') + P(A \cap B) \quad \ldots (2)$

On similar lines, we see that

$$P(B) = P(A \cap B) + P(A' \cap B) \quad \ldots (3)$$

Adding (2) and (3), we get,

$$P(A) + P(B) = P(A \cap B') + P(A' \cap B) + 2P(A \cap B)$$
$$= P(A \cap B') + P(A \cap B) + P(A' \cap B) + P(A \cap B)$$
$$= P(A \cup B) + P(A \cap B) \quad \text{... from (1)}$$
$$\therefore \quad P(A \cup B) = P(A) + P(B) - P(A \cap B)$$

Hence the proof.

Remark : Note that $P(A \cup B)$ is the probability of occurrence of at least one of the events A and B.

Example 7.11 : Consider an experiment of rolling a fair die. Let A be the event that an even number appears. B = a number bigger than 3 occurs. Find the probability that the number appearing on the uppermost face is either even or bigger than 3.

Solution : Here, $\Omega = \{1, 2, 3, 4, 5, 6\}$

Since, the die is fair,

$$P(i) = \frac{1}{6} \text{ for } i = 1, 2, \ldots, 6.$$
$$A = \{2, 4, 6\}$$
$$B = \{4, 5, 6\}$$
$$A \cup B = \{2, 4, 5, 6\} \qquad A \cap B = \{4, 6\}$$
$$P(A) = \frac{3}{6} = \frac{1}{2} = P(B)$$
$$P(A \cup B) = \frac{4}{6} = \frac{2}{3} \qquad P(A \cap B) \frac{2}{6} = \frac{1}{3}$$

Also using theorem 5,

$$P(A \cup B) = P(A) + P(B) - P(A \cap B)$$
$$= \frac{1}{2} + \frac{1}{2} - \frac{1}{3} = \frac{2}{3}$$

Theorem 5 can be generalised to three events as follows.

Theorem 6 : If A, B, and C are any three events defined on Ω, then

$$P(A \cup B \cup C) = P(A) + P(B) + P(C) - P(A \cap B) - P(B \cap C) - P(A \cap C) + P(A \cap B \cap C)$$

Proof : Let, $B \cup C = D$, therefore,

$$P(A \cup B \cup C) = P(A \cup B)$$
$$= P(A) + P(D) - P(A \cap D)$$
$$= P(A) + P(B \cup C) - P[A \cap (B \cup C)]$$
$$= P(A) + P(B) + P(C) - P(B \cap C)$$
$$\quad - P[(A \cap B) \cup (A \cap C)]$$
$$= P(A) + P(B) + P(C) - P(B \cap C) - P(E \cup F)$$

where, $E = A \cap B$ and $F = A \cap C$

$$= P(A) + P(B) + P(C) - P(B \cap C)$$
$$\quad - P(E) - P(F) + P(E \cap F)$$
$$= P(A) + P(B) + P(C) - P(B \cap C) - P(A \cap B)$$
$$\quad - P(A \cap C) + P(A \cap B \cap C)$$

$[\because (A \cap B) \cap (A \cap C) = A \cap B \cap C]$

Note : The above result can also be proved by alternative method. In this method we express $(A \cup B \cup C)$ in 7 different mutually exclusive events viz. $A \cap B' \cap C'$, $A \cap B \cap C'$, $A' \cap B \cap C$, $A \cap B' \cap C$, $A \cap B \cap C$, $A' \cap B \cap C'$, $A' \cap B' \cap C$ and using axioms we can prove the result.

Extension of addition theorem for $n > 3$ events is also possible. Here we state only the statement of the possibel generalisation.

Generalisation : For any events, $A_1, A_2, \ldots, A_n$ on Ω, we have the following extension.

$$P\left(\bigcup_{i=1}^{n} A_i\right) = \sum_{i=1}^{n} P(A_i) - \sum_{i<j=1}^{n} P(A_i \cap A_j)$$
$$+ \sum_{i<j<k=1}^{n} P(A_i \cap A_j \cap A_k)$$
$$- \sum_{i<j<k<r=1}^{n} P(A_i \cap A_j \cap A_k \cap A_r)$$
$$+ \ldots + (-1)^{n-1} P(A_1 \cap A_2 \ldots \cap A_n)$$

Theorem 7 : Boole's inequality : If A and B are any two events defined on Ω, then
$$P(A \cup B) \leq P(A) + P(B)$$
Proof : $P(A \cup B) = P(A) + P(B) - P(A \cap B)$ and $P(A \cap B) \geq 0$
$\therefore \quad P(A \cup B) \leq P(A) + P(B)$

Extension of Boole's inequality is given in the following theorem.

Theorem 8 : If $A_1, A_2, \ldots, A_n$ are n events, then
$$P\left(\bigcup_{i=1}^{n} A_i\right) \leq \sum_{i=1}^{n} P(A_i)$$

Proof : We prove the theorem by the method of Induction.
(i) We note that the result is true for n = 2.
(ii) Let us assume that the result holds for n = m say.
$$\therefore \quad P\left(\bigcup_{i=1}^{m} A_i\right) = \sum_{i=1}^{m} P(A_i)$$
(iii) Now to prove that the result is true for n = m + 1, consider.
$$\bigcup_{i=1}^{m+1} A_i = \left[\bigcup_{i=1}^{m} A_i\right] \cup A_{m+1}$$

Let, $\quad B = \bigcup_{i=1}^{m} A_i$

$$\therefore \quad P\left[\bigcup_{i=1}^{m+1} A_i\right] = P[B \cup A_{m+1})]$$

$$\leq P(B) + P(A_{m+1}) \qquad \text{from Theorem 6.}$$

$$\leq \sum_{i=1}^{m} P(A_i) + P(A_{m+1}) \qquad \text{from (ii)}$$

$$= \sum_{i=1}^{m+1} P(A_i)$$

Hence, by induction,
$$P\left[\bigcup_{i=1}^{n} A_i\right] \leq \sum_{i=1}^{n} P(A_i) \qquad \text{for all } n \geq 2$$

Theorem 9 : If $A_1, A_2, \ldots, A_n$ are any n events defined on Ω, then
$$P\left(\bigcap_{i=1}^{n} A_i\right) \geq \sum_{i=1}^{n} P(A_i) - (n-1)$$

Proof : This result also we prove by induction.
Step (i) : Let n = 2.
We know that,

$$P(A_1 \cup A_2) \leq 1 \quad \text{by Theorem 3}$$

Using the addition theorem, we get,

$$P(A_1) + P(A_2) - P(A_1 \cap A_2) \leq 1$$
$$\Rightarrow P(A_1 \cap A_2) \geq P(A_1) + P(A_2) - 1$$

Thus the result holds for n = 2.

Step (ii) : Let us assume that the theorem holds for n = m.

Hence, $\quad P\left(\bigcap_{i=1}^{m} A_i\right) \geq \sum_{i=1}^{m} P(A_i) - (m-1)$

Step (iii) : Now to prove that the result is true for n = m + 1. Consider,

$$P\left(\bigcap_{i=1}^{m+1} A_i\right) = P\left(\bigcap_{i=1}^{m} A_i \cap A_{m+1}\right)$$

$$\geq P\left(\bigcap_{i=1}^{m} A_i\right) + P(A_{m+1}) - 1 \quad \ldots \text{ by (i)}$$

$$\geq \sum_{i=1}^{m} P(A_i) - (m-1) + P(A_{m+1}) - 1$$

$$\ldots \text{ by (ii)}$$

$$= \sum_{i=1}^{m+1} P(A_i) - m$$

$$= \sum_{i=1}^{m+1} P(A_i) - (m + 1 - 1)$$

Thus, the result holds for n = m + 1.

Hence, the theorem is true for all n ≥ 2.

Example 7.12 : If P(A) = 0.6, P(B) = 0.5, P(A∩B) = 0.3. Compute P(A'), P(A∪B), P(A'∩B), P(A'∩B') and P(A'∪B')

Solution : (i) P(A') = 1 − P(A) = 1 − 0.6 = 0.4

(ii) $\quad P(A \cup B) = P(A) + P(B) - P(A \cap B)$
$\quad\quad\quad\quad\quad = 0.6 + 0.5 - 0.3 = 0.8$

(iii) $\quad P(A' \cap B) = P(B) - P(A \cap B) = 0.5 - 0.3 = 0.2$

(iv) Since, $(A \cup B)' = A' \cap B'$, by De Morgan's law, we get,
$$P(A' \cap B') = P(A \cup B)'$$
$$= 1 - P(A \cup B)$$
$$= 1 - 0.8 = 0.2$$

(v) $\quad P(A' \cup B') = P(A \cap B)' \quad$ using De Morgan's law.
$$= 1 - P(A \cap B)$$
$$= 1 - 0.3$$
$$= 0.7$$

Example 7.13 : Arrange the following probabilities in ascending order.

$$P(A \cup B), \; P(A), \; P(A) + P(B), \; P(A \cap B)$$

Solution : $\quad\quad A \cap B \subset A$

$\therefore \quad\quad P(A \cap B) \leq P(A) \quad\quad$ by Theorem 4

Further, $\quad\quad A \subset A \cup B$

$\therefore \quad\quad P(A) \leq P(A \cup B)$

And $\quad\quad P(A \cup B) \leq P(A) + P(B)$ by Boole's inequality

$\therefore \quad\quad P(A \cap B) \leq P(A) \leq P(A \cup B) \leq P(A) + P(B)$

Example 7.14 : Let A and B be two events defined on a sample space Ω, such that

$$P(A) = \frac{3}{4} \quad \text{and} \quad P(B) = \frac{5}{8}$$

Show that $\quad \frac{3}{8} \leq P(A \cap B) \leq \frac{5}{8}$

Solution : Since, $(A \cap B) \subset B$, therefore,

$$P(A \cap B) \leq P(B) = \frac{5}{8}$$

Now $\quad\quad P(A \cap B) \geq P(A) + P(B) - 1 \quad$ from Theorem 9

$\therefore \quad\quad P(A \cap B) \geq \frac{3}{4} + \frac{5}{8} - 1$

$$\therefore \quad P(A \cap B) \geq \frac{3}{8}$$

$$\therefore \quad \frac{3}{8} \leq P(A \cap B) \leq \frac{5}{8}$$

Remark : $\text{Max}\{0, P(A) + P(B) - 1\} \leq P(A \cap B) \leq \min\{P(A), P(B)\}$

Example 7.15 : If A and B are any two events of Ω, show that,
$$\max\{P(A), P(B)\} \leq P(A \cup B) \leq \min\{P(A) + P(B), 1\}$$

Solution : Since both A and B are subsets of $A \cup B$,

$\therefore \quad P(A) \leq P(A \cup B)$

and $\quad P(B) \leq P(A \cup B)$ ... (1)

$\therefore \quad \max\{P(A), P(B)\} \leq P(A \cup B)$

Also $\quad P(A \cup B) \leq P(A) + P(B)$

by Boole's inequality

and $\quad P(A \cup B) \leq 1$ by Theorem 3

$\therefore \quad P(A \cup B) \leq \min\{P(A) + P(B), 1\}$ ... (2)

From (1) and (2) we get,
$$\max\{P(A), P(B)\} \leq P(A \cup B) \leq \min\{P(A) + P(B), 1\}$$

Example 7.16 : A and B are two events defined on a sample space Ω. Can the following statements be regarded as true ? Justify your answer.

(i) $P(A) = 0.8, P(B) = 0.7, P(A \cap B) = 0.8$

(ii) $P(A) = 0.8, P(B) = 0.7, P(A \cap B) = 0.3$

Solution : (i) is false as $P(A \cap B) > P(B)$ which is wrong as $(A \cap B) \subset B$

$\therefore \quad P(A \cap B) \leq P(B)$

(ii) is also false as

$P(A \cup B) = P(A) + P(B) - P(A \cap B)$
$= 0.8 + 0.7 - 0.3 = 1.2 > 1.$

Example 7.17 : If $P(A) = P(B) = 1$, show that
$$P(A \cup B) = P(A \cap B) = 1$$

Solution : We know that,

$P(A \cap B) \geq P(A) + P(B) - 1$
$= 1 + 1 - 1 = 1$

$\therefore \quad P(A \cap B) \geq 1$; but $P(A \cap B) \leq 1$

$\therefore \quad P(A \cap B) = 1$

$\therefore \quad P(A \cup B) = P(A) + P(B) - P(A \cap B)$
$= 1 + 1 - 1 = 1$

Example 7.18 : The probability that a contractor will get a plumbing contract is 0.4 and the probability that he will not get an electric contract is 0.7. If the probability of getting at least one contract is 0.6, what is the probability that he will get (i) both the contracts and (ii) exactly one contract ?

Solution : Let, A = Contractor gets plumbing contract.

B = Contractor gets electric contract.

∴ $P(A) = 0.4$, $P(B') = 0.7$ $P(B) = 0.3$

(i) $P(A \cup B) = P(A) + P(B) - P(A \cap B)$

$0.6 = 0.4 + 0.3 - P(A \cap B)$

∴ $P(A \cap B) = 0.1$

which is the probability that he gets both the contracts.

(ii) Exactly one contract means, if the contractor gets the plumbing contract, then he will not get the electric contract and vice versa.

∴ The required probability is $P[(A \cap B') \cup (A' \cap B)]$

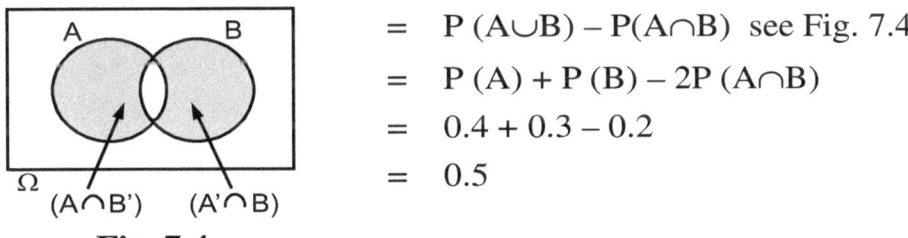

$= P(A \cup B) - P(A \cap B)$ see Fig. 7.4

$= P(A) + P(B) - 2P(A \cap B)$

$= 0.4 + 0.3 - 0.2$

$= 0.5$

Fig. 7.4

Example 7.19 : Suppose A, B, C are three events defined on Ω such that

$$P(A) = P(B) = P(C) = \frac{1}{4}, P(A \cap C) = \frac{1}{8}$$

$$P(A \cap B) = P(B \cap C) = 0$$

Calculate (i) $P(A \cup B \cup C)$ (ii) $P(A \cup C)$ (iii) $P(A' \cap B' \cap C')$ (iv) $P(A \cap C')$

Solution : (i) By the addition theorem,

$P(A \cup B \cup C) = P(A) + P(B) + P(C) - P(A \cap B) - P(B \cap C)$

$- P(A \cap C) + P(A \cap B \cap C)$

$$= \frac{1}{4} + \frac{1}{4} + \frac{1}{4} - 0 - 0 - \frac{1}{8} + 0$$

$$= \frac{5}{8}$$

Note that $(A \cap B \cap C) \subset (A \cap B)$

∴ $P(A \cap B \cap C) = 0$ since $P(A \cap B) = 0$

(ii) $P(A \cup C) = P(A) + P(C) - P(A \cap C)$

$$= \frac{1}{4} + \frac{1}{4} - \frac{1}{8} = \frac{3}{8}$$

(iii) $P(A' \cap B' \cap C') = P(A \cup B \cup C)'$

$$= 1 - P(A \cup B \cup C)$$

$$= 1 - \frac{5}{8} = \frac{3}{8}$$

(iv) $P(A \cap C') = P(A) - P(A \cap C) = \frac{1}{4} - \frac{1}{8} = \frac{1}{8}$

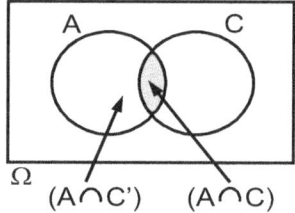

Fig. 7.5

Points to Remember

- In case of equiprobable sample space, probability of an event is the ratio of number of elements in the event to those of sample space.
- Axioms of probability are statements which are accepted heuristically and not proved. Theorems are based on these axioms.
- $P(A) = \dfrac{\text{Number of elements in A}}{\text{Number of elements in } \Omega}$ for equiprobable sample space.
- $P(A \cup B) = P(A) + P(B) - P(A \cap B)$
- If $A < B$ then $P(A) \leq P(B)$
- $P(\cap A_i) \geq \sum P(A_i) - (n - 1)$.

EXERCISE 7 (A)

Theory Questions :

1. What is meant by probability of an 'outcome' of an experiment ? Explain.
2. Give the classical definition of probability. What are its assumptions ?
3. Define Equiprobable Sample Space. If A is an event defined on an equiprobable sample space, how probability of A is calculated. Explain with an illustration.
4. What are the limitations of classical definition of probability ?
5. Specify the probability assignment approach (probability model). Describe with an example, how probability of an event is obtained in this case.
6. State the axioms of probability.
7. For an event A on a sample space Ω, prove the following theorems.
   (i) $P(A') = 1 - P(A)$ where, A' is the complement of A.
   (ii) $0 \leq P(A) \leq 1$
8. Prove that $P(\phi) = 0$, where ϕ is an impossible event.
9. Prove
   (i) If $A \subset B$ then $P(A) \leq P(B)$
   (ii) $P(A \cap B) \leq \min[P(A), P(B)]$
   (iii) $\max(0, P(A) + P(B) - 1) \leq P(A \cap B)$
10. State and prove the addition theorem of probability concerning two events A and B.
11. State and prove Boole's inequality for two events A and B.
12. If A, B and C are any three events defined on Ω, then prove that
    $P(A \cup B \cup C) = P(A) + P(B) + P(C) - P(A \cap B) - P(B \cap C)$
    $- P(A \cap C) + P(A \cap B \cap C)$
13. State the extention of the addition theorem for n events.
14. Prove the following Boole's inequality. If $A_1, A_2, ..., A_n$ are n exents, then,
    $$P\left(\bigcup_{i=1}^{n} A_i\right) \leq \sum_{i=1}^{n} P(A_i)$$

15. Prove that for any n events $A_1, A_2, \ldots, A_n$ on Ω,

$$P\left(\bigcap_{i=1}^{n} A_i\right) \geq \sum_{i=1}^{n} P(A_i) - (n-1)$$

16. Explain what is meant by saying
    (i) Odds in favour of an event are a : b
    (ii) Odds against an event are a : b.

EXERCISE 7 (B)

Numerical Problems :

17. Find the probability that three cards drawn at random, without replacement, from a well shuffled pack of 52 playing cards are all spades.

18. Two fair dice are rolled simultaneously. Find the probabilities of the following events.

    A : the sum of the two numbers is even.

    B : the sum of the two numbers is at least 8.

    C : the product of the two numbers is not greater than 9.

19. Three books are selected at random from a shelf containing 4 novels, 2 books of poems and a dictionary. What is the probability that : (i) 2 novels and 1 poem book is selected, (ii) dictionary is not selected.

20. In a group of 10 men, 6 are graduates. If 3 men are selected at random, what is the probability that they consist of (i) all graduates (ii) at least one graduate ? (iii) at most two graduates (iv) no graduate ?

21. A fair coin is tossed 4 times. Find the probability that we will get 2 heads and 2 tails.

22. There are 4 letters and 4 addressed envelopes. The letters are put into envelopes at random. Find the probability that all letters are despatched in the right envelopes.

23. A bag contains 4 white and 2 black balls. Another bag contains 3 white and 3 black balls. One ball is drawn from each bag at random. What is the probability that they are of different colours ?

24. There are 3 different pairs of socks in a box. If two socks are chosen at random, what is the probability that they form an exact pair?
25. Two cards are drawn from a pack of 52 well shuffled cards. Find the probability that both are king when (i) first card drawn is replaced, (ii) first card drawn is not replaced.
26. Three books of Accountancy and two books on Statistics are arranged on a shelf. Find the probability that (i) two statistics books are side by side (ii) two statistics books are not side by side.
27. An integer is chosen at random from 1 to 100. What is the probability that the number is not divisible by 7?
28. A die has two of its sides painted red, two green and two yellow. If the die is rolled twice, what is the probability that the same colour appears both the times?
29. Find the probability of the event A, if the odds in its favour are 3 : 2.
30. Find the probability of the event A, if the odds against it are 1 : 4.
31. Two cards are drawn from a well shuffled pack of playing cards. Determine the probability that (a) both are aces, (b) both are spades (c) both belong to the same suit.
32. Ten students are seated at random in a row. Find the probability that two particular students are not seated side by side.
33. In a random arrangement of the letters of the word 'BACKLOG', find the probability that all the two vowels come together.
34. The letters of the word ORANGE are arranged at random. Find the probability that the vowels may occupy the even places.
35. The first twelve letters of the English alphabet are written down at random. What is the probability that
    (a) there are 4 letters between A and B
    (b) A and B are written down side by side
36. Which of the following define a probability model on
$$\Omega = \{\omega_1, \omega_2, \omega_3\} ?$$

Sample Points

Model	ω_1	ω_2	ω_3
(i)	$\frac{1}{3}$	$\frac{1}{2}$	$\frac{1}{4}$
(ii)	$\frac{1}{3}$	$\frac{1}{6}$	$\frac{1}{2}$
(iii)	0	$\frac{1}{3}$	$\frac{2}{3}$
(iv)	$\frac{2}{3}$	$\frac{2}{3}$	$-\frac{1}{3}$

37. Let A, B, C be three mutually exclusive and exhaustive events defined on Ω. If $3P(A) = 2P(B) = P(C)$, find $P(A \cup B)$.

38. Let A and B be two events defined on Ω. Arrange the following probabilities in ascending order of magnitude ?

    $P(A), P(A \cup B), P(A) + P(B), P(A \cap B)$.

39. Suppose A and B are two events defined on Ω with $P(A) = \frac{2}{3}$ and $P(B) = \frac{3}{5}$. Show that

    (i) $\frac{4}{15} \leq P(A \cap B) \leq \frac{3}{5}$ (ii) $P(A \cup B) \geq \frac{2}{3}$

    (iii) $\frac{1}{15} \leq P(A \cap B') \leq \frac{2}{5}$

40. A die is loaded so that probability of an even number is twice the probability of an odd number. Even numbers are equally likely as well as odd numbers are equally likely. Find the probability that (i) an even number appears, (ii) a prime number appears uppermost (iii) an odd number appears uppermost, and (iv) a perfect square appears uppermost.

41. Let $P(A) = 0.38$, $P(A \cap B \cap C) = 0.10$, $P(A \cap B' \cap C') = 0.17$ and $P(A' \cap B \cap C) = 0.12$, find the probability of the occurrence of at least two of the three events A, B, and C on Ω.

42. An event A is such that it is five times as probable as the event A'. Determine P (A).

43. A certain company encourages its employees to participate in cricket and hockey. A survey indicates that 40% play cricket, 50% play hockey and 25% play cricket and hockey both. Find the probabilities of the following events.
    (i) An employee plays only hockey.
    (ii) An employee plays only cricket.
    (iii) An employee takes part in at least one of the games, cricket and hockey.
    (iv) An employee does not play either game.

44. An office has three xerox machines X_1, X_2, X_3. The probability that on a given day; X_1 works is 0.60; X_2 works is 0.75; X_3 works is 0.80; both X_1 and X_2 work is 0.50; both X_1 and X_3 work is 0.40; both X_2 and X_3 work is 0.70.

    The probability that all of them work is 0.25. Find the probability that on a given day at least one of the three machines works.

45. For any three events A, B, C on Ω, prove that
    (i) $1 - P(A) - P(B) - P(C) + P(A \cap B)$
    $$+ P(B \cap C) + P(A \cap C) \geq 0$$
    (ii) When $P(A \cap B \cap C) = P(A' \cap B' \cap C')$, Prove that
    $$2P(A \cap B \cap C) = 1 - P(A) - P(B) - P(C) + P(A \cap B)$$
    $$+ P(A \cap C) + P(B \cap C).$$

46. A factory employs both male and female workers. The probability that a worker chosen at random is male is 0.65, that the worker is married is 0.7 and that the worker is a married male is 0.47. Find the probability that a worker chosen at random is (i) a married female and (ii) a male or married or both.

47. A card is drawn at random from a well shuffled pack of playing cards. What is the probability that it is a heart or a queen ?

48. Let A, B, C be three events defined on Ω with the following probabilities P (A) = 0.3, P (B) = 0.2, P (C) = 0.5, P (A∩C) = 0.25, P (B∩C) = 0.15, P(A∩B) = 0.17, P (A∩B∩C) = 0.1. Compute (i) P (A∪B∪C), (ii) P (A∪B), (iii) P (A'∩B∩C), (iv) P (A'∩B'∩C), (v) P (A'∩B'∩C').

EXERCISE 7 (C)

49. An integer between 1 and 100 (both inclusive) is selected at random. Find the probability of selecting a perfect square if (a) all integers are equally likely (b) an integer between 1 and 50 is twice as likely to occur than an integer between 51 and 100.
50. Suppose a real number is to be selected at random from the interval (0, 100). Further let A_1 be the event that a real number is selected between (25, 65); let A_2 be the event that a real number is selected between (40, 90). Determine P ($A_1 \cup A_2$) assuming that all real numbers have equal chance of being selected.
51. A government prints 10 lakh lottery tickets of the value of ₹ 2 each. How many tickets must a person buy to have a chance of 0.5 or more to win the first prize of lakhs ?
52. What is the probability that a leap year selected at random will contain 53 Sundays ?
53. Which event has the greatest probability ? (i) Throwing 4 with one die, (ii) Getting a sum 8 on two dice, (iii) Getting a sum 12 on three dice ?

Objective Type Questions

I. Multiple Choice Questions (MCQ).

- **Choose the correct alternative.**

1. A number is selected at random from the set of numbers {11, 12, ..., 99}. What is the probability that selected number contains the digit 9 ?

    (a) $\dfrac{19}{89}$ (b) $\dfrac{18}{89}$

    (c) $\dfrac{1}{10}$ (d) $\dfrac{11}{100}$

2. For a sample space $\Omega = \{\omega_1, \omega_2, \omega_3, \omega_4\}$, $P\{\omega_1\} = \dfrac{1}{8} = P\{\omega_2\}$, $P\{\omega_3\} = k$, $P\{\omega_4\} = \dfrac{3}{8}$. For what value of 'k' will this be a probability model ?
   (a) 0
   (b) 1
   (c) – 1
   (d) $\dfrac{3}{8}$

3. If A and B are any two events defined as Ω, which of the following is a valid statement ?
   (a) $P(A \cup B) = P(A) + P(B) - P(A \cap B)$
   (b) $P(A \cup B) = P(A) + P(B)$
   (c) $P(A \cup B) = P(A) \cdot P(B)$
   (d) $P(A \cup B) = P(A) + P(B) - 2P(A \cap B)$.

4. Give that $P(A) = 0.8$, $P(B) = 0.7$, $P(A \cup B) = 0.9$, what is $P(A \cap B)$?
   (a) Can be any number between 0 and 0.7.
   (b) 0.56.
   (c) 0.06
   (d) 0.6

5. A card is drawn from a pack of 52 playing cards. What is the probability that it is a king, given that it is a face card ? [A face card is a jack, a queen or a king].
   (a) 1/3
   (b) 1/13
   (c) 1/52
   (d) 0

6. If A and B are two mutually exclusive event defined as Ω, then $P(A \cup B)$ is equal to ....
   (a) $P(A) + P(B) + P(A \cap B)$
   (b) $P(A) \cdot P(B)$
   (c) $P(A) + P(B)$
   (d) 0

7. In the simultaneous tossing of two fair coins, the probability of having at least one head is ....
   (a) 0.5
   (b) 0.25
   (c) 0.75
   (d) 1

8. The probability of drawing one white ball randomly from a bag containing 6 red, 8 black, 10 yellow and 1 green ball is ....
   (a) 1/25
   (b) 0
   (c) 1
   (d) 14/25

9. The classical approach to probability assumes that all possible outcomes of an experiment are ....
   (a) independent
   (b) dependent
   (c) mutually exclusive
   (d) equally likely.

10. Nine persons sit for a photograph in a row. Find the probability that a family of three always sits together ....
    (a) 1/12
    (b) 1/24
    (c) 1/48
    (d) 1/3.

11. The probability that a person shall not die is ....
    (a) 0
    (b) 1
    (c) 0.5
    (d) depends on the age of the person.

II. State whether the following statements are true or false.

12. We can not use the classical definition of probability in case the sample space is countably infinite.

13. $P(\phi) = 0$ is one of the axioms of probability theory.

14. $P(A \cup B \cup C) = P(A) + P(B) + P(C) - 2P(A \cap B) - 2P(B \cap C) - 2P(A \cap C) + P(A \cap B \cap C)$

15. If $P(A) = 0.4$, $P(B) = 0.3$ then $P(A \cap B)$ must be greater than or equal to 0.7.

HINTS AND ANSWERS

(17) $\frac{11}{850}$ (18) 0.5, $\frac{15}{36}$, $\frac{17}{36}$, (19) $\frac{12}{35}$, $\frac{4}{7}$ (20) $\frac{3}{18}$, $\frac{4}{5}$, $\frac{5}{6}$, $\frac{1}{30}$, (21) $\frac{3}{8}$, (22) $\frac{1}{24}$, (23) 0.5, (24) 0.5, (25) $\frac{1}{169}$, $\frac{1}{221}$, (26) $\frac{2}{5}$, $\frac{3}{5}$, (27) $\frac{43}{50}$, (28) $\frac{1}{3}$, (29) 0.6, (30) $\frac{4}{5}$, (31) $\frac{1}{221}$,

$\frac{1}{17}$, $\frac{4}{17}$, (32) $\frac{4}{5}$, (33) $\frac{2}{7}$, (34) $\frac{1}{20}$, (35) $\frac{7}{66}$, $\frac{1}{6}$, (36) (ii) and (iii) (37) P(A) + P(B) + P(C) = 1, P(A∪B) = $\frac{5}{11}$ (38) P(A∩B) ≤ P(A) ≤ P(A∪B) ≤ P(A) + P(B), (40) $\frac{2}{3}$, $\frac{4}{9}$, $\frac{2}{9}$, $\frac{1}{3}$, (41) 0.33, (42) $\frac{5}{6}$, (43) 0.25, 0.15, 0.65, 0.35, (44) 0.8, (45) 0.23, 0.88, (47) $\frac{4}{13}$, (48) 0.53, 0.33, 0.05, 0.2, 0.47, (49) (a) P(each int) = 0.01; There are 10 perfect squares between 1 to 100
∴ Prob = 10 × (0.01) = 0.1

(b) $\sum_{i=1}^{50} P(i) + \sum_{i=51}^{100} P(i) = 1$, and $\sum_{i=1}^{50} P(i) = 2 \sum_{i=51}^{100} P(i)$

∴ $P(i) = \frac{1}{75}$, $1 \leq i \leq 50$

$P(i) = \frac{1}{150}$, $51 \leq i \leq 100$.

7 integers whose squares ≤ 50 and 3 integers whose squares between 51 and 100.

∴ Required Prob. = $7\left(\frac{1}{75}\right) + 3\left(\frac{1}{150}\right) = \frac{17}{150}$.

(50) $P(A_1) = \frac{65-25}{100} = 0.4$

$(A_2) = \frac{90-40}{100} = 0.5$

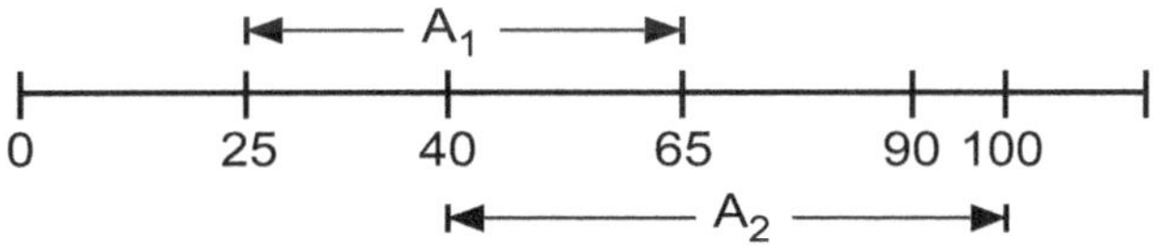

Fig. 7.6

$P(A_1 \cap A_2) = \frac{65-40}{100} = 0.25$

∴ $P(A_1 \cup A_2) = 0.65$

(51) x = no. of tickets. ∴ $\frac{x}{10^6} \geq \frac{1}{2} \Rightarrow \frac{10^6}{2} = 500{,}000$ tickets worth Rs. 10 lakhs.

(52) Leap year consists of 366 days. 52 weeks + 2 days. One of the two extra days must be sunday. Seven possibilities in all. (i) Mon. Tue., (ii) Tue. Wed., (iii) Wed Thu., (iv) Thu. Fri., (v) Fri. Sat., (vi) Sat. Sun., (viii) Sun. Mon. Only 2 satisfy ∴ ∴ Prob = $\frac{2}{7}$

(53) The first. $\frac{1}{6}, \frac{5}{36}, \frac{25}{216}$.

Answers of Objective Questions

I. (1) b   (2) d,   (3) a   (4) d
      (5) a   (6) c   (7) c   (8) b,
      (9) d   (10) a   (11) a.

II. (12) T   (13) F   (14) F   (15) F.

Chapter 8...
Conditional Probability and Independence of Events

Thomas Bayes (1701-1761) was an English mathematician known for having formulated the famous Bayes' theorem. Bayes worked on 'inverse probability' problems which further led to an important branch of probability known as Bayesian probability theory. His ideas have created much controversy and debate among statisticians over the years. His work has brought forth many new ideas that the world of Statistics continues to research and benefit from.

Thomas Bayes

Contents ...

8.1 Introduction
8.2 Independence of Two Events
8.3 Independence of Three Events
8.4 Conditional Probability
8.5 Comparison of Magnitudes of Conditional and Unconditional Probability
8.6 Multiplication Theorem (Theorem of Compound Probability)
8.7 Posterior Probabilities
8.8 Partition of a Sample Space
8.9 Bayes' Theorem

Key Words :

   Independent events, Conditional and unconditional probability, Theorem of compound probability, Prior and posterior probability, Bayes' theorem.

Objectives :

- Understand the concept of conditional probability of an event given the occurrence of other event.

(8.1)

- Understand when two events are called independent.
- Learn how Bayes' theorem can be used to update the probability of an event by utilizing prior probabilities.
- Solve numerical problems on conditional probability.

8.1 Introduction

In earlier chapter, we saw how to compute probability of events as well as their unions and intersections. Now, let us consider the following situation.

At the commencement of the academic year, suppose the probability that Raju will score distinction in Statistics at the annual examination is 0.5. At the end of the Ist term, Raju scores 80% marks in Statistics. The question is whether this information will change (increase or decrease) Raju's probability of scoring distinction at the annual examination ?

Such types of questions are answered with the help of conditional probability and independence. If the two events are independent, the probability 0.5 will remain as it is. On the other hand, if they are dependent, then conditional probability is to be calculated. Given the information that Raju has scored 80% marks at terminal examination, will affect his probability of scoring distinction at the annual examination.

We introduce first the concept of independence of events.

8.2 Independence of Two Events (Oct. 2012)

Two events are said to be independent if the occurrence or non-occurrence of one does not affect the occurrence of the other. This gives rise to the following definition of independent events.

Definition : Two events A and B defined on a sample space Ω are said to be *independent* if and only if

$$P(A \cap B) = P(A) \cdot P(B)$$

Illustration 1 : Consider the experiment of rolling a fair die

∴ $\Omega = \{1, 2, 3, 4, 5, 6\}$

Let, A = Occurrence of an even number.
   = $\{2, 4, 6\}$

   B = Occurrence of a number greater than 4.
   = $\{5, 6\}$

Note that $P(A) = \frac{3}{6} = \frac{1}{2}$, $P(B) = \frac{2}{6} = \frac{1}{3}$

and $P(A \cap B) = P\{6\} = \frac{1}{6} = P(A) \cdot P(B)$

∴ By definition, A and B are independent events.

Remark 1 : Note that here, $A \cap B \neq \phi$; therefore A and B are not mutually exclusive events, although A and B are independent.

Illustration 2 : Consider the experiment of tossing three fair coins simultaneously.

∴ Ω = {HHH, HHT, HTH, THH, HTT, THT, TTH, TTT}

Let A = Getting two heads
  = {HHT, HTH, THH}
 B = P (B) = Getting two tails.
  = {HTT, THT, TTH}

Observe that $P(A) = \frac{3}{8}$

and $A \cap B = \phi$ ∴ $P(A \cap B) = 0$
∴ $P(A \cap B) \neq P(A) \cdot P(B)$
∴ A and B are *not* independent.

Remark 2 : In the above example the events A and B are mutually exclusive (∵ $A \cap B = \phi$) but they are not independent.

Thus from the two illustrations it is clear that

(i) independence $\Rightarrow$ mutual exclusiveness and (ii) mutual exclusiveness $\Rightarrow$ independence. In fact what we have are the following results.

Result 1 : If A and B are independent events with P(A) and P(B) both non-zero, then A and B *cannot be* mutually exclusive.

Proof : Since A and B are independent,
 $P(A \cap B) = P(A) \cdot P(B)$
  $\neq 0$ ∵ $P(A) \neq 0, P(B) \neq 0$
∴ $A \cap B \neq \phi$ or A and B cannot be mutually exclusive.

Result 2 : If A and B are mutually exclusive with P(A) and P(B) both non-zero, then A and B *cannot* be independent; i.e. A and B are dependent.

Proof : Since A and B are mutually exclusive.

$$A \cap B = \phi$$
$$\therefore \quad P(A \cap B) = 0$$
However, $\quad P(A) \cdot P(B) \neq 0 \quad \because P(A) \neq 0, P(B) \neq 0$
$$\therefore \quad P(A \cap B) \neq P(A) \cdot P(B)$$

⇒ A and B are not independent. In other words A and B are dependent events.

The Fig. 8.1 depicts the relationship between independent events and mutually exclusive events.

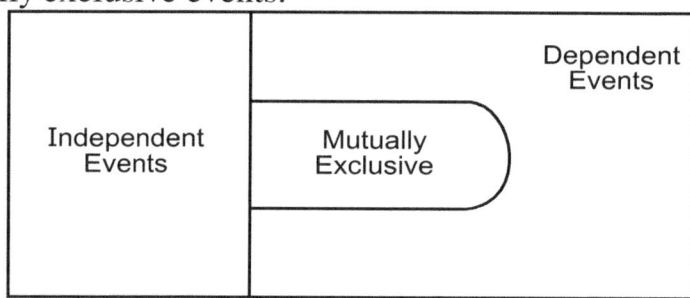

Fig. 8.1

Remark 3 : If one of the events of A and B is an impossible event (ϕ), then A and B are independent as well as mutually exclusive. For example, suppose $A = \phi$, then $A \cap B$ being a subset of A, $A \cap B = \phi$.

∴ A and B are mutually exclusive.

Also, $\quad P(A \cap B) = 0$
$$= P(A) \cdot P(B) \quad \because P(A) = 0$$

We shall now consider some of the important implications of independence of two events.

Theorem 1 : Suppose A and B are two events defined on a sample space Ω. If A and B are independent then,

(i) A and B' are independent.
(ii) A' and B are independent.
(iii) A' and B' are independent.

Proof : (i) Consider,
$$P(A \cap B') = P(A) - P(A \cap B)$$
$$= P(A) - P(A) \cdot P(B)$$
$$= P(A)[1 - P(B)] = P(A) P(B')$$

∴ A and B' are independent.

(ii) By changing the roles of A and B in (i), it can be proved that A' and B are independent.

(iii) Consider,

$$\begin{aligned} P(A' \cap B') &= P(A \cup B)' \quad \text{by De Morgan's Law} \\ &= 1 - P(A \cup B) \\ &= 1 - [P(A) + P(B) - P(A \cap B)] \\ &= 1 - P(A) - P(B) + P(A) \cdot P(B) \\ &= [1 - P(A)][1 - P(B)] \\ &= P(A') \cdot P(B') \end{aligned}$$

∴ A' and B' are independent.

Illustrative Examples

Example 8.1 : A and B are independent with $P(A) = 0.5$, $P(B) = 0.4$. Find : **(Oct. 2012)**

(i) $P(A \cap B)$
(ii) $P(A \cup B)$
(iii) $P(A \cap B')$
(iv) $P(A' \cap B)$
(v) $P(A' \cap B')$

Solution :

(i) $P(A \cap B) = P(A) \cdot P(B)$
$= 0.5 \times 0.4$
$= 0.2$

(ii) $P(A \cup B) = P(A) + P(B) - P(A \cap B)$
$= 0.5 + 0.4 - 0.2 = 0.7$

(iii) $P(A \cap B') = P(A) \cdot P(B')$

∵ A & B' are independent by Theorem 1.
$= 0.5 \times 0.6 = 0.3$

(iv) $P(A' \cap B) = P(A') P(B) = 0.5 \times 0.4 = 0.2$

(v) $P(A' \cap B') = P(A') P(B') = 0.5 \times 0.6 = 0.3$

Example 8.2 : Suppose a card is drawn at random from a well-shuffled pack of 52 playing cards. Let event A = getting a spade card; B = getting a king. Are A and B independent ?

Solution : $P(A) = \dfrac{13}{52} = \dfrac{1}{4}$; $P(B) = \dfrac{4}{52} = \dfrac{1}{13}$

$P(A \cap B) = \dfrac{1}{52}$ Also $P(A) \cdot P(B) = \dfrac{1}{4} \cdot \dfrac{1}{13} = \dfrac{1}{52}$

∴   A and B are independent.

Example 8.3 : Suppose A and B are two events defined on Ω. If $P(A) = 0.8$, $P(A \cup B) = 0.9$ and $P(B) = x$, find the value of x if A and B are (i) independent (ii) mutually exclusive.

Solution : (i) If A and B are independent, then

$$P(A \cup B) = P(A) + P(B) - P(A) \cdot P(B)$$
$$0.9 = 0.8 + x - 0.8x$$
∴ $0.2x = 0.1$
∴ $x = 0.5$

(ii) If A and B are mutually exclusive then,
$$P(A \cup B) = P(A) + P(B) = 0.8 + x = 0.9$$
∴ $x = 0.1$

Example 8.4 : A machine consists of two parts P_1 and P_2. Probability of defect in P_1 is 0.08 and that in P_2 is 0.05. What is the probability that the assembled machine will not have any defect ?

Solution : Let A be the event that P_1 does not have any defect

∴ $P(A) = 1 - 0.08 = 0.92$

Let B be the event that P_2 does not have any defect.

∴ $P(B) = 1 - 0.05 = 0.95$

The assembled product will not have any defect if both the parts are free from defect.

∴   Required probability $= P(A \cap B)$
$= P(A) \cdot P(B)$
$= 0.92 \times 0.95 = 0.8740$

Notice that here we assumed that the event 'P_1 being defective or not' has nothing to do with 'P_2 being defective.

Example 8.5 : The odds that A speaks the truth are 5 : 3 and the odds that B speaks the truth are 8 : 3. In what percentage of cases are A and B likely to contradict each other on an identical point ?

Solution : Let,   event C = A speaks the truth.
event D = B speaks the truth.

∴ $P(C) = \frac{5}{8}$ and $P(D) = \frac{8}{11}$

⇒ $P(C') = P(A \text{ telling a lie}) = \frac{3}{8}$

and $P(D') = P(B \text{ telling a lie}) = \frac{3}{11}$

They will contradict in following two mutually exclusive cases.
(i) A tells truth, but B tells a lie.   i.e. $C \cap D'$
(ii) A tells a lie, but B tells truth   i.e. $C' \cap D$

∴ Required probability $= P(C \cap D') + P(C' \cap D)$
$= P(C) \cdot P(D') + P(C') \cdot P(D)$

∵ independence

$= \frac{5}{8} \times \frac{3}{11} + \frac{3}{8} \times \frac{8}{11} = \frac{39}{88} = 0.4472$

∴ In 44.72% of cases A and B will contradict each other.

8.3 Independence of Three Events   (Oct. 2012)

Extension of the definition of independence of two events to the case of three events is not straight forward.

Definition 1 : Mutual independence of three events A, B, C, (Complete independence of A, B, C).   **(Oct. 2012)**

Let A, B, C be three events defined on Ω. The three events A, B, C are said to be mutually independent or completely independent if and only if the following conditions are satisfied.

(i) $P(A \cap B) = P(A) \cdot P(B)$
(ii) $P(B \cap C) = P(B) \cdot P(C)$
(iii) $P(A \cap C) = P(A) \cdot P(C)$
(iv) $P(A \cap B \cap C) = P(A) \cdot P(B) \cdot P(C)$

Definition 2 : *Pairwise independence of three events.* The three events A, B, C defined on Ω are said to be *pairwise independent* if and only if the following conditions are satisfied.

(i) $P(A \cap B) = P(A) \cdot P(B)$
(ii) $P(B \cap C) = P(B) \cdot P(C)$
(iii) $P(A \cap C) = P(A) \cdot P(C)$

Remark : Note that the definition of mutual independence needs the condition $P(A \cap B \cap C) = P(A) \cdot P(B) \cdot P(C)$, in addition to the pairwise independence of A, B and C. Therefore,

A, B, C are mutually independent.

$\Rightarrow$ A, B, C are pairwise independent.

The other way implication is not true; can be seen from the following example.

Example 8.6 : Consider the experiment of rolling two fair dice. Let A = odd number on the first die, B = odd number on the second die and C = sum of two points is odd. Show that A, B, C are pairwise independent but not mutually independent.

Solution : Recall that Ω contains 36 points.

$$\Omega = \begin{Bmatrix} (1,1) & (1,2) & \ldots & (1,6) \\ (2,1) & (2,2) & \ldots & (2,6) \\ \vdots & \vdots & \vdots & \vdots \\ (6,1) & (6,2) & \ldots & (6,6) \end{Bmatrix}$$

Observe that A will contain 18 points, B will contain 18 points.

For the sum to be an odd only one of the two scores should be odd for example, (1, 2), (1, 4), (2, 1) etc. which are also 18 in number.

$\therefore \qquad P(A) = P(B) = P(C) = \dfrac{18}{36} = \dfrac{1}{2}$

Now, $\quad A \cap B = \{(1, 1)\ (1, 3)\ (1, 5)\ (3, 1)\ (3, 3)\ (3, 5)$
$\qquad\qquad\qquad (5, 1)\ (5, 3)\ (5, 5)\}$

$\qquad\quad A \cap C = \{(1, 2)\ (1, 4)\ (1, 6)\ (2, 1)\ (2, 3)\ (2, 5)$
$\qquad\qquad\qquad (3, 2)\ (3, 4)\ (3, 6)\}$

$\qquad\quad B \cap C = \{(2, 1)\ (2, 3)\ (2, 5)\ (4, 1)\ (4, 3)\ (4, 5)$
$\qquad\qquad\qquad (6, 1)\ (6, 3)\ (6, 5)\}$

Thus, $\quad P(A \cap B) = P(A \cap C) = P(B \cap C) = \dfrac{9}{36} = \dfrac{1}{4}$

$\therefore \qquad P(A \cap B) = P(A) \cdot P(B)$

$\qquad\quad P(A \cap C) = P(A) \cdot P(C)$

$\qquad\quad P(B \cap C) = P(B) \cdot P(C)$ are satisfied.

Hence, A, B, C are pairwise independent.

However, A∩B∩C = φ since if both the dice show odd number, their sum cannot be odd.

∴ $P(A \cap B \cap C) = 0 \neq P(A) \cdot P(B) \cdot P(C)$

∴ A, B, C are not mutually independent.

Example 8.7 : Consider the experiment of tossing an unbiased coin three times. Let A_i denote the event that a head turns up on i^{th} toss, i = 1, 2, 3. Are events A_1, A_2, A_3 mutually independent ?

Solution :
Ω = {HHH, HHT, HTH, THH, HTT, THT, TTH, TTT}
A_1 = {HHH, HHT, HTH, HTT)
A_2 = {HHH, HHT, THH, THT}
A_3 = {HHH, HTH, THH, TTH}

Further
$A_1 \cap A_2$ = {HHH, HHT};
$A_2 \cap A_3$ = {HHH, THH};
$A_1 \cap A_3$ = {HHH, HTH};
$A_1 \cap A_2 \cap A_3$ = {HHH};

∴
$$P(A_1) = \frac{4}{8} = \frac{1}{2}$$
$$P(A_2) = \frac{1}{2}$$
$$P(A_3) = \frac{1}{2}$$
$$P(A_1 \cap A_2) = \frac{2}{8} = \frac{1}{4}$$
$$P(A_2 \cap A_3) = \frac{1}{4}$$
$$P(A_1 \cap A_3) = \frac{1}{4}$$
$$P(A_1 \cap A_2 \cap A_3) = \frac{1}{8}$$

Thus, (i) $P(A_1 \cap A_2) = P(A_1) \cdot P(A_2)$
(ii) $P(A_2 \cap A_3) = P(A_2) \cdot P(A_3)$
(iii) $P(A_1 \cap A_3) = P(A_1) \cdot P(A_3)$
(iv) $P(A_1 \cap A_2 \cap A_3) = P(A_1) \cdot P(A_2) \cdot P(A_3)$

are all satisfied.

∴ A_1, A_2, A_3 are mutually independent.

Remark : Note that the condition
P (A∩B∩C) = P (A) · P (B) · P (C) does not imply that the conditions required for pairwise independence are true.

For example, consider an event A defined on Ω with P (A) ≠ 0 and P (A) ≠ 1. Let B = A and C = ϕ.

Then,   P (A∩B∩C) = P (ϕ) = 0
                  = P (A) · P (B) · P (C)
since,   P (C) = 0
However, P (A∩B) = P (A) ≠ P (A) · P (B).

Example 8.8 : Show that if A, B and C are pairwise independent events and A is independent of (B∩C), then A, B and C are completely independent.

Solution : A, B, C are pairwise independent implies.

(i)   P (A∩B) = P (A) · P (B)
(ii)   P (B∩C) = P (B) · P (C)
(iii)   P (A∩C) = P (A) · P (C)

Further, A and (B∩C) are independent.

∴   P [A∩(B∩C)] = P (A) · P (B∩C)
∴   P (A∩B∩C) = P (A) · P (B) · P (C)   from (ii)

Thus all conditions of mutual independence are satisfied. Hence A, B, C are mutually independent.

Example 8.9 : A problem in Statistics is given to three students A, B, C whose chances of solving the same are $\frac{1}{2}, \frac{1}{3}, \frac{1}{4}$ respectively. If all the three students solve the problem independently, what is the probability that the problem will be solved ?

Solution : The problem will be solved if *at least* one of the three students solves the problem. Hence, if A, B, C denote the events that the respective student solves the problem, then $P(A) = \frac{1}{2}$; $P(B) = \frac{1}{3}$; $P(C) = \frac{1}{4}$ and we are interested in finding P (A∪B∪C).

Assuming mutual independence, we have $P(A \cap B) = P(A) \cdot P(B) = \frac{1}{6}$, $P(A \cap C) = \frac{1}{8}$, $P(B \cap C) = \frac{1}{12}$ and $P(A \cap B \cap C) = \frac{1}{24}$.

By the addition theorem,
$$P(A \cup B \cup C) = P(A) + P(B) + P(C) - P(A \cap B)$$
$$- P(A \cap C) - P(B \cap C) + P(A \cap B \cap C)$$
$$= \frac{3}{4}$$

8.4 Conditional Probability

Consider a family having two children. Suppose, we wish to find the probability of the event A; that both the children are males.

∴ Ω = {MM, MF, FM, FF} and A = {MM}

Assuming the sample space to be equiprobable; $P(A) = \frac{1}{4}$. Now suppose it is already known that at least one of the children is a boy. Then the sample space will not contain FF and reduce to a new sample space say, B = {MM, MF, FM}.

As there are only 3 elements in the sample space, probability of A with respect to the reduced sample space B will be $\frac{1}{3}$. Thus, the knowledge about the occurrence of some other event has altered the probability of the event under consideration. The above probability is called as conditional probability of A given B and is denoted by P(A|B).

Observe that, initially.
$$P(A) = \frac{\text{Number of elements in A}}{\text{Number of element in } \Omega} = \frac{n(A)}{n(\Omega)} \text{ say}$$

then, $$P(A|B) = \frac{\text{Number of elements in } A \cap B}{\text{Number of elements in B}} = \frac{n(A \cap B)}{n(B)}$$
$$= \frac{n(A \cap B)/n(\Omega)}{n(B)/n(\Omega)}$$

$$P(A|B) = \frac{P(A \cap B)}{P(B)} \qquad P(B) \neq 0$$

Remark 1 : This expression, though derived for events on an equiprobable finite sample space, remains valid for not equiprobable sample spaces such as countably infinite and continuous sample spaces.

Remark 2 : The probability P(A) is called unconditional probability of A.

Conditional probability of A given B : Suppose A and B are two events defined on a sample space Ω, then the conditional probability of A *given* B, denoted by P (A|B) is defined as,

$$P(A|B) = \frac{P(A \cap B)}{P(B)}, \quad P(B) > 0$$

Similarly, conditional probability of B *given* A is,

$$P(B|A) = \frac{P(A \cap B)}{P(A)}, \quad P(A) > 0$$

Illustrative Examples

Example 8.10 : A pair of fair dice is rolled. If the sum of 8 has appeared, find the probability that one of the dice shows 3.

Solution : The sample space contains 36 elements. Suppose B is the event that sum of 8 appears. Then,

$$B = \{(2,6), (3,5), (4,4), (5,3), (6,2)\}$$

Now, A = One of the dice shows 3.

$$\therefore \quad A \cap B = \{(3,5), (5,3)\}$$

By definition, the conditional probability of A given B will be

$$P(A|B) = \frac{P(A \cap B)}{P(B)} = \frac{2/36}{5/36} = \frac{2}{5}$$

Remark : In the above example, if we calculate P(B|A), i.e. conditional probability of B given the event A, it will be

$$P(B|A) = \frac{P(A \cap B)}{P(A)} = \frac{2/36}{2/36}$$

$$= 1$$

Thus, $P(A|B) \neq P(B|A)$

Theorem 2 : Conditional probability satisfies all the axioms of unconditional probability, viz, for event B defined on Ω, with $P(B) > 0$.

A·1 $0 \leq P(A|B) \leq 1$ for any $A \subset \Omega$

A·2 $P(\Omega|B) = 1$

A·3 If A and C are mutually exclusive events defined on Ω, then

$$P(A \cup C|B) = P(A|B) + P(C|B)$$

Proof : A·1 $P(A|B) = \dfrac{P(A \cap B)}{P(B)} \geq 0$

$\because$ ratio of non-negative numbers

and $P(A|B) = \dfrac{P(A \cap B)}{P(B)} \leq \dfrac{P(B)}{P(B)}$ $\quad \because A \cap B \subset B$

$\Rightarrow P(A \cap B) \leq P(B) = 1$

A·2 $\quad P(\Omega|B) = \dfrac{P(B \cap \Omega)}{P(B)} = \dfrac{P(B)}{P(B)} = 1 \;\; \because B \cap \Omega = B$

A·3 A and C are mutually exclusive events.

$\therefore \quad A \cap C = \phi$

$P(A \cup C|B) = \dfrac{P[(A \cup C) \cap B]}{P(B)}$

$= \dfrac{P(A \cap B) \cup (B \cap C)}{P(B)}$ $\;\; \because A \cap B$ and $B \cap C$ are disjoint (see Fig. 3.2)

$= \dfrac{P(A \cap B)}{P(B)} + \dfrac{P(B \cap C)}{P(B)} = P(A|B) + P(C|B)$

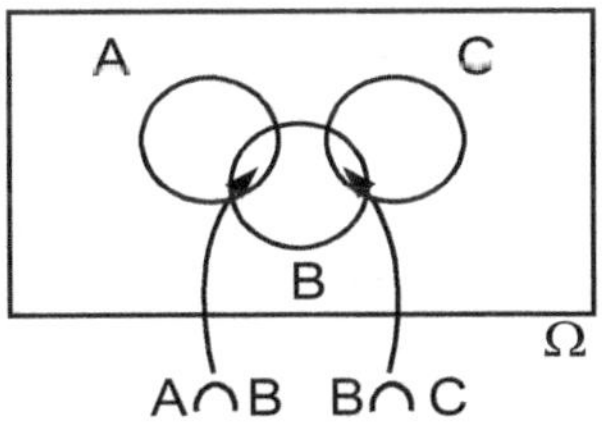

Fig. 8.2

In what follows the following properties of conditional probability.

Theorem 3 : If A, B, C are any three events defined on Ω, with $P(B) > 0$, then

$P(A \cup C|B) = P(A|B) + P(C|B) - P(A \cap C|B)$

Proof : Recall

$(A \cup C) \cap B = (A \cap B) \cup (B \cap C)$

$\therefore \quad P(A \cup C/B) = \dfrac{P[(A \cup C) \cap B]}{P(B)}$

$= \dfrac{P[(A \cap B) \cup (B \cap C)]}{P(B)}$

$$= \frac{P(A \cap B) + P(B \cap C) - P[(A \cap B) \cap (B \cap C)]}{P(B)}$$

by addition theorem

$$= P(A|B) + P(C|B) - \frac{P(A \cap B \cap C)}{P(B)}$$

$$= P(A|B) + P(C|B) - P(A \cap C|B)$$

Theorem 4 : If A and B are events defined on Ω then,

$$P(A'|B) = 1 - P(A|B); \quad P(B) > 0$$

Proof : Consider,

$$P(A'|B) = \frac{P(A' \cap B)}{P(B)} = \frac{P(B) - P(A \cap B)}{P(B)}$$

$$= 1 - \frac{P(A \cap B)}{P(B)}$$

$$= 1 - P(A|B)$$

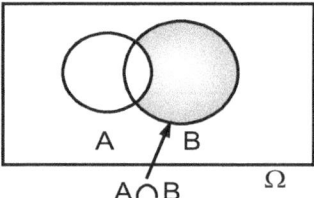

Fig. 8.3

Example 8.10 : Let A and B be two events defined on Ω; P(A), P(B) > 0; Prove the following :

(i) $P(A|A') = 0$

(ii) If A and B are mutually exclusive, then $P(A|B) = 0$.

(iii) If $B \subset A$, then $P(A|B) = 1$.

(iv) If $A \subset B$, then $P(A|B) = \dfrac{P(A)}{P(B)}$

Solution : (i) $\quad P(A|A') = \dfrac{P(A \cap A')}{P(A')} = 0 \quad \therefore A \cap A' = \phi$

(ii) $\quad P(A|B) = \dfrac{P(A \cap B)}{P(B)} = \dfrac{P(\phi)}{P(B)} = 0$

(iii) $\quad P(A|B) = \dfrac{P(A \cap B)}{P(B)} = \dfrac{P(B)}{P(B)} = 1$

(iv) $\quad P(A|B) = \dfrac{P(A \cap B)}{P(B)} = \dfrac{P(A)}{P(B)}$

8.5 Comparison of Magnitudes of Conditional and Unconditional Probability

Let A and B be two events defined on Ω. We wish to consider the magnitudes of $P(A|B)$ and $P(A)$ in each of the following different cases.

(i) A and B are mutually exclusive (Fig. 8.4).

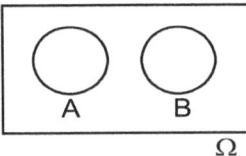

Fig. 8.4

$P(A) > 0$

$P(A|B) = \dfrac{P(A \cap B)}{P(B)} = \dfrac{P(\phi)}{P(B)} = 0$

$\therefore P(A|B) \leq P(A)$

(ii) $A \subset B$

$P(A|B) = \dfrac{P(A \cap B)}{P(B)} = \dfrac{P(A)}{P(B)}$

$\therefore P(A|B) \geq P(A)$

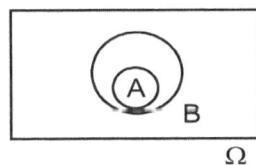

Fig. 8.5

(iii) $A \supset B$ (Fig. 8.6)

$P(A|B) = \dfrac{P(A \cap B)}{P(B)} = \dfrac{P(B)}{P(B)} = 1$

$\therefore P(A|B) \geq P(A)$

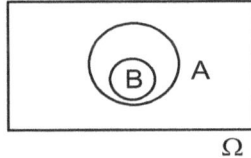

Fig. 8.6

(iv) $A \cap B \neq \phi$ (Fig. 8.7)

$P(A|B) = \dfrac{P(A \cap B)}{P(B)}$ may or may not be bigger than $P(A)$

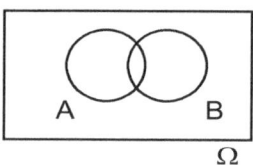

Fig. 8.7

(v) A and B are independent.

$$P(A|B) = \frac{P(A \cap B)}{P(B)} = \frac{P(A) \cdot P(B)}{P(B)} \quad \because \text{ independence}$$
$$= P(A)$$

∴ $P(A|B) = P(A)$ when A and B are independent.

Remark : The above relation is also stated as the definition of independent events.

Definition : Events A and B defined on a sample space Ω are called independent iff,

$$P(A|B) = P(A);$$
or $$P(B|A) = P(B).$$

The statement $P(A|B) = P(A)$ means that the information that 'event B has occurred' does not have any effect on the probability of A. In other words, whenever occurrence or non-occurrence of one event does not have any impact on the occurrence of other event, the two events are said to be independent. Therefore in practice, when we *feel* that the two events are not related in the above sense, we assume independence and calculate probability of their joint occurrence by taking the product of the individual probabilities. i.e. we use $P(A \cap B) = P(A) \cdot P(B)$. Whenever the two events are not independent, they are said to be *dependent*. In that case, we can't use $P(A \cap B) = P(A) \cdot P(B)$ but have to use the theorem of compound probability which we shall study in Section 8.6.

Example 8.12 : A random experiment results in an integer outcome between 1 and 10 (both inclusive). All numbers are equally likely. Let A be the event that an odd number occurs and B be the event that a number divisible by 3 occurs. Obtain (i) P(A|B) (ii) P(B|A) (iii) P(A'|B) (iv) P(A|B') (v) P(A'|B').

Solution : The sample space will be

$$\Omega = \{1, 2, 3, 4, 5, 6, 7, 8, 9, 10\}$$

and A = {1, 3, 5, 7, 9}   B = {3, 6, 9}
A∩B = {3, 9}   A' = {2, 4, 6, 8, 10}
B' = {1, 2, 4, 5, 7, 8, 10}
A'∩B = {6}, A∩B' = {1, 5, 7}, A'∩B' = {2, 4, 8, 10}

Therefore,

(i) $P(A|B) = \dfrac{P(A \cap B)}{P(B)} = \dfrac{0.2}{0.3} = \dfrac{2}{3}$

(ii) $P(B|A) = \dfrac{P(A \cap B)}{P(A)} = \dfrac{0.2}{0.5} = \dfrac{2}{5}$

(iii) $P(A'|B) = \dfrac{P(A' \cap B)}{P(B)} = \dfrac{0.1}{0.3} = \dfrac{1}{3}$

(iv) $P(A|B') = \dfrac{P(A \cap B')}{P(B')} = \dfrac{0.3}{0.7} = \dfrac{3}{7}$

(v) $P(A'|B') = \dfrac{P(A' \cap B')}{P(B')} = \dfrac{0.4}{0.7} = \dfrac{4}{7}$

Example 8.13 : A card is drawn from an ordinary pack of 52 playing cards. What is the probability that it is a king; given that it is a face card ? [A face card is either a jack, a queen or a king].

Solution : Let event, A = The card drawn is a king.
B = The card drawn is a face card.

∴ $P(A|B) = \dfrac{P(A \cap B)}{P(B)}$

$= \dfrac{4/52}{12/52}$ ∵ A∩B = A

$= \dfrac{4}{12} = \dfrac{1}{3}$ ∵ there are in all 12 face cards.

Example 8.14 : The personnel department of a company has 100 engineers whose distribution is as given below.

Age (year)	B.E.	M.E.	Total
20 – 30	20	5	25
30 – 40	25	10	35
≥ 40	10	30	40
Total	55	45	100

If one engineer is selected at random, find :
(i) The probability that he is only B.E.
(ii) The probability that he has master's degree given that his age is beyond 40.
(iii) The probability that he is under 30, given that he has M.E. degree.

Solution : Let us define the events A, B, C as follows :
A : An engineer is only a B.E.
B : An engineer has master's degree.
C : An engineer's age is beyond 40.
D : An engineer's age is below 30.
Therefore,

(i) $P(A) = \dfrac{55}{100} = 0.55$

(ii) $P(B|C) = \dfrac{P(B \cap C)}{P(C)} = \dfrac{30/100}{40/100} = \dfrac{3}{4}$

(iii) $P(D|B) = \dfrac{P(B \cap D)}{P(B)} = \dfrac{5/100}{45/100} = \dfrac{5}{45} = \dfrac{1}{9}$

Example 8.15 : Computers PC-386 and PC-486 are to be sold. A salesman has 50% and 40% chances of finding customers for the above two types of computers respectively. The computers can be sold independently. Given that he was able to sell at least one of the above two computers, what is the probability that computer PC-386 has been sold ?

Solution : Let A = selling PC – 386; B = selling PC – 486
∴ $P(A) = 0.5 \qquad P(B) = 0.4$

Required probability = $P(A | A \cup B)$

$= \dfrac{P[A \cap (A \cup B)]}{P(A \cup B)}$

$= \dfrac{P(A)}{P(A) + P(B) - P(A \cap B)}$

$= \dfrac{P(A)}{P(A) + P(B) - P(A) \cdot P(B)}$

$= \dfrac{0.5}{0.5 + 0.4 - 0.5 \times 0.4}$

$= \dfrac{0.5}{0.7} = \dfrac{5}{7}$

8.6 Multiplication Theorem (Theorem of Compound Probability)

Theorem 4 : Let A and B be any two events defined on a sample space Ω.

Then,
$$P(A \cap B) = P(A|B) \cdot P(B)$$
$$= P(B|A) \cdot P(A)$$

Proof : From the definition of conditional probability,

$$P(A|B) = \frac{P(A \cap B)}{P(B)}$$

$\therefore \quad P(A \cap B) = P(A|B) \cdot P(B)$

Similarly, $\quad P(A \cap B) = P(B|A) \cdot P(A)$

Remark 1 : The theorem holds even if $P(B) = 0$, provided we interpret $P(A|B) = 0$ if $P(B) = 0$. This is so because $A \cap B \subset B \Rightarrow P(A \cap B) = 0$.

Remark 2 : The multiplication theorem is used for obtaining probability of simultaneous occurrence of two events, whenever conditional probability is given. This will be clear from the examples we discuss in this section.

Example 8.16 : A lot contains 12 items of which 4 are defective. Two items are drawn at random from the lot one after other (without replacement). Find the probability that both items are non-defective.

Solution : Let,

A : Event that the item drawn first is non-defective (ND).

B : Event that the item drawn at the second draw is non-defective.

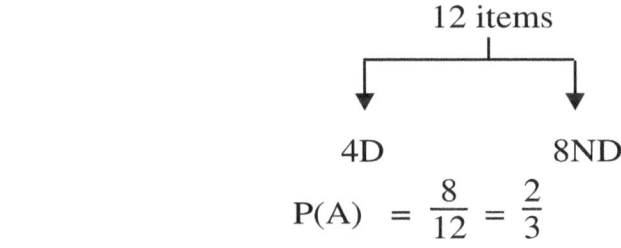

$\therefore \quad P(A) = \frac{8}{12} = \frac{2}{3}$

Now probability that second item is ND given that first item is ND is

$$P(B|A) = \frac{7}{11}$$

Since, the item drawn at first draw is kept aside,

∴ P (both items non-defective) = $P(A \cap B)$
= $P(B|A) \cdot P(A)$

... by theorem 4

$= \frac{7}{11} \times \frac{2}{3} = \frac{14}{33}$

The multiplication theorem can be extended to more than two events. Here we give the theorem for three events A, B, C.

Theorem 5 : If A, B, C are any three events defined on a sample space Ω, then

$P(A \cap B \cap C) = P(A) \cdot P(B|A) \cdot P(C|A \cap B)$

Proof : Let us call the events $A \cap B$ as D

∴ $P(A \cap B \cap C) = P(D \cap C)$
= $P(D) P(C|D)$
= $P(A \cap B) \cdot P(C|A \cap B)$
= $P(A) \cdot P(B|A) \cdot P(C|A \cap B)$

Example 8.17 : Find the probability of drawing an ace, a king and a queen in this order from a pack of 52 playing cards. The cards are not replaced back to the pack.

Solution : Define the events A : the first card is an ace,
B : the second card is a king, C : the third card is a queen.

∴ $P(A) = \frac{4}{52}$, $P(B|A) = \frac{4}{51}$, $P(C|A \cap B) = \frac{4}{50}$

∴ $P(A \cap B \cap C) = P(A) \cdot P(B/A) \cdot P(C|A \cap B)$

$= \frac{4}{52} \times \frac{4}{51} \times \frac{4}{50}$

$= \frac{8}{16075} = 0.0005$

8.7 Posterior Probabilities

One of the important applications of conditional probability and multiplication theorem is computation of posterior probabilities on the basis of the information supplied by the experiment. For example, consider the following situation.

A certain factory has three machines M_1, M_2 and M_3. From past experience it is observed that the probabilities of producing defective articles by M_1, M_2, M_3 are 0.01, 0.03 and 0.05 respectively. These probabilities are called as prior probabilities. Now, suppose an item is drawn at random at the end of the day's production. This item is found to be *defective*. Then, naturally, the quality control engineer will be interested in knowing the probabilities that the defective item is produced by M_1, M_2 or M_3. This enables him to maintain the quality of the product. These probabilities, which are computed after performance of the experiment using the information on the outcome, are called as posterior probabilities.

These calculations are facilitated by the famous Bayes' theorem. Bayes', a British mathematician postulated this theorem in 1763. Bayes' theorem is of extreme help to business and management executives in arriving at valid decisions.

Let us first introduce ourselves to the concept of partition of sample space as a prerequisite to the Bayes' theorem.

8.8 Partition of a Sample Space

A collection of mutually exclusive and exhaustive events is called a partition of sample space. More specifically, the events $A_1, A_2 \ldots, A_n$ defined on a sample space Ω are said to form a partition of Ω if and only if and only if.

(i) $\quad A_i \cap A_j = \phi$ for all i and j; $i \neq j$

(ii) $\quad \bigcup_{i=1}^{n} A_i = \Omega$

Illustration : Let $\Omega = \{1, 2, 3, 4, 5, 6\}$
Let, $\quad A = \{2, 4, 6\}$ and $B = \{1, 3, 5\}$
Then, $\quad A \cap B = \phi$ and $A \cup B = \Omega$
Thus A and B form a partition of Ω.
Here note that $\quad B = A'$

8.9 Bayes' Theorem

Suppose events $A_1, A_2, \ldots, A_n$ form a partition of a sample space Ω of a random experiment. Suppose B is any other event with $P(B) > 0$, defined on Ω. Then,

$$P(A_i|B) = \frac{P(A_i) \cdot P(B|A_i)}{\sum_{j=1}^{n} P(A_j) \cdot P(B|A_j)} \quad \text{for all } i = 1, 2, \ldots, n$$

Proof : Events $A_1, A_2, \ldots, A_n$ from a partition of Ω

$$\therefore \quad \bigcup_{j=1}^{n} A_j = A_1 \cup A_2 \ldots \cup A_n = \Omega.$$

Consider, $\quad B = \Omega \cap B$

$$= \left[\bigcup_{j=1}^{n} A_j \right] \cap B$$

$$= \bigcup_{j=1}^{n} (A_j \cap B) \quad \text{by distributive property}$$

Now $(A_j \cap B)$, $j = 1, 2, \ldots, n$ are mutually exclusive events. (See Fig. 8.8).

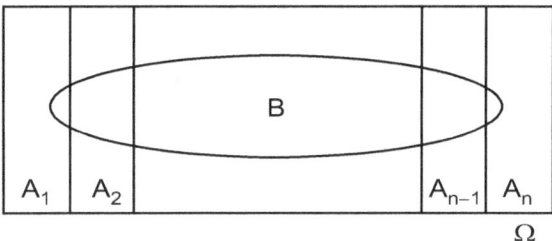

Fig. 8.8

$$\therefore \quad P(B) = \sum_{j=1}^{n} P(A_j \cap B) \quad \text{by Axiom 3.}$$

$$= \sum_{j=1}^{n} P(B|A_j) \, P(A_j)$$

by multiplication theorem... (1)

We write, for any A_i,

$$P(A_i|B) = \frac{P(A_i \cap B)}{P(B)}$$

$$= \frac{P(A_i) \, P(B|A_i)}{\sum_{j=1}^{n} P(A_j) \, P(B|A_j)} \quad i = 1, 2, \ldots, n$$

Illustrative Example

Example 8.18 : Bag I contains 6 blue and 4 red balls. Bag II contains 2 blue and 6 red balls. Bag III contains 1 blue and 8 red balls.

(i) A bag is chosen at random; a ball is drawn randomly from this bag. It turns out to be blue. Find the probability that bag I was chosen.

(ii) A bag is chosen at random; two balls are drawn without replacement from this bag. Both the balls were blue. Find the probability that bag II was chosen.

Solution : (i) Let A_1 : Event that bag I is chosen.

A_2 : Event that bag II is chosen.

A_3 : Event that bag III is chosen.

$$\therefore \quad P(A_1) = P(A_2) = P(A_3) = \frac{1}{3} \text{ ; prior probabilities.}$$

Let event B = The ball drawn is blue. Using Bayes' theorem,

Required probability = $P(A_1|B)$

$$= \frac{P(A_1) \cdot P(B|A_1)}{\sum_{j=1}^{3} P(A_j) P(B|A_j)} \quad \ldots (1)$$

Now, $P(B|A_1)$ = Probability that the ball is blue given that bag I was selected.

$= \frac{6}{10}$; as there are 6 blue balls among 10 balls.

Similarly, $P(B|A_2) = \frac{2}{8}$; and $P(B|A_3) = \frac{1}{9}$

$\therefore$ Substituting these values in (1), we get,

$$\text{Required probability} = \frac{\frac{1}{3} \cdot \frac{6}{10}}{\frac{1}{3} \cdot \frac{6}{10} + \frac{1}{3} \cdot \frac{2}{8} + \frac{1}{3} \cdot \frac{1}{9}}$$

$$= \frac{108}{173} = 0.6243$$

(ii) Define   C = Event that both balls are blue.

∴ As before, $P(A_1) = P(A_2) = P(A_3) = \frac{1}{3}$

$$P(B|A_1) = \frac{\binom{6}{2}}{\binom{10}{2}}, \quad P(B|A_2) = \frac{\binom{2}{2}}{\binom{8}{2}} = \frac{1}{\binom{8}{2}}$$

$P(B|A_3) = 0$

∴ there is only one blue ball in bag III.

Using Bayes' theorem,

$$\text{Required probability} = \frac{P(A_2) \cdot P(B|A_2)}{\sum_{j=1}^{3} P(A_j) \cdot P(B|A_j)}$$

$$= \frac{\frac{1}{3} \cdot \frac{1}{\binom{8}{2}}}{\frac{1}{3}\left[\left(\binom{6}{2} + \binom{10}{2}\right) + \left(1 + \binom{8}{2}\right)\right]} = \frac{3}{31}$$

Example 8.19 : An explosion in a factory manufacturing explosives can occur due to (i) short circuit (ii) defects in machinery (iii) negligence of workers and (iv) sabotage. The probabilities of these four causes are known to be 0.3, 0,2, 0.4 and 0.1 respectively. The engineers feel that an explosion can occur with probability (i) 0.3 if there is a short circuit, (ii) 0.2 if there are defects in machinery, (iii) 0.25 if the workers are negligent and (iv) 0.8 if there is a sabotage. Given that an explosion has occurred, determine the most likely cause of it.

Solution : Define the events

A_1 : Short circuit,

A_2 : Defects in machinery,

A_3 : Negligence of workers;

A_4 : Sabotage.

Hence, the prior probabilities are

$P(A_1) = 0.3$, $P(A_2) = 0.2$, $P(A_3) = 0.4$, $P(A_4) = 0.1$. Let B be the event that there is explosion in the factory.

∴ $P(B|A_1) = 0.3$, $P(B|A_2) = 0.2$, $P(B|A_3) = 0.25$, $P(B|A_4) = 0.8$

To determine the most likely cause of explosion we have to compute $P(A_1|B)$, $P(A_2|B)$, $P(A_3|B)$ and $P(A_4|B)$ and identify the largest among these.

From Bayes' theorem,

$$P(A_i|B) = \frac{P(A_i) \cdot P(B|A_i)}{\sum_{j=1}^{n} P(A_j) P(B|A_j)} \quad ; \quad i = 1, 2, 3, 4.$$

$P(A_1) \cdot P(B|A_1) = 0.3 \times 0.3 = 0.09$

$P(A_2) \cdot P(B|A_2) = 0.2 \times 0.2 = 0.04$

$P(A_3) \cdot P(B|A_3) = 0.4 \times 0.25 = 0.1$

$P(A_4) \cdot P(B|A_4) = 0.1 \times 0.8 = 0.08$

$\therefore \sum_{j=1}^{4} P(A_j) \cdot P(B|A_j) = 0.09 + 0.04 + 0.1 + 0.08 = 0.31$

$$P(A_1|B) = \frac{0.09}{0.31} = 0.2903$$

$$P(A_2|B) = \frac{0.04}{0.31} = 0.1290$$

$$P(A_3|B) = \frac{0.1}{0.31} = 0.3226$$

$$P(A_4|B) = \frac{0.08}{0.31} = 0.2581$$

Comparing the above probabilities, it is clear that $P(A_3|B) = 0.3704$. This means that negligence of workers is the most likely cause of explosion in the factory.

Example 8.20 : Two urns identical in appearance, contain respectively 3 white and 2 black balls; and 2 white and 5 black balls. One urn is selected at random, and a ball is drawn from it. What is the probability that it is black ?

Solution : Let event A_1 : urn I is selected; A_2 : urn II is selected, B = ball drawn is black. We want to find P (B).

Now, $P(B) = \sum_{j=1}^{2} P(A_j) P(B|A_j)$

(See the proof of Bayes' theorem)

$= P(A_1) P(B|A_1) + P(A_2) \cdot P(B|A_2)$

$= \frac{1}{2} \cdot \frac{2}{5} + \frac{1}{2} \cdot \frac{5}{7}$

$= \frac{1}{2} \left(\frac{2}{5} + \frac{5}{7}\right) =$ **0.5571**

8.10 Sensitivity and Specificity of a Procedure (as an Application of Bayes' Theorem)

The terms sensitivity and specificity are the terms used relating to outcome of a test which predicts that the disease is present or not i.e. It is positive or negative. The results of the test of each individual are as follows :

(i) The person actually have the disease and hence correctly diagnosed as suffering from it. It may be called as 'true positive'.

(ii) The individual actually may not have the disease and wrongly diagnosed as sick. It is called as 'false positive'.

(iii) The person has not the disease and correctly diagnosed as healthy. In short this result can be described as 'true negative'.

(iv) The remaining possibility is that the person may be sick and wrongly identified as healthy.

Thus we have 4 types of identification in clinical tests.

True positive ≡ 'Correctly' classified as 'possessing' the disease.

False positive ≡ 'Wrongly' classified as 'possessing' the disease.

True negative ≡ 'Correctly' classified as not possessing the 'disease'.

False negative ≡ 'Wrongly' classified as not possessing the 'disease'.

Based on these results we shall define sensitivity and specificity of a procedure.

Sensitivity : It is defined as the proportion of ill persons who are identified to have the disease.

i.e. Sensitivity of a procedure = $\dfrac{\text{Number of true positive cases}}{\begin{pmatrix}\text{Number of true positive cases}\\+\text{ Number of false positive cases}\end{pmatrix}}$

Thus sensitivity gives the probability that a test is positive given that the person is sick. It can be expressed in percentage form by multiplying it by 100 e.g. sensitivity of a test is 100% means that all ill persons are correctly identified.

It is 90% for a test indicates that 90% of patients are correctly identified as having +ve test but 10% wrongly show that test is –ve.

In this way sensitivity of a test measures its ability to correctly identify the patients with a certain disease.

Specificity : It measures the ability of the test to identify the patients who do not have the disease.

∴ Specificity of a procedure = $\dfrac{\text{Number of true negative cases}}{\begin{pmatrix}\text{Number of true negative cases}\\+\text{ Number of false negative cases}\end{pmatrix}}$

For example, a test has 95% specificity means that 95% of patients are correctly identified as not suffering from the disease but 5% patients not having the disease are wrongly identified as possessing the disease. Ideally if a test has 100% specificity then 100% patients (all patients) are correctly identified as not possessing the disease.

Illustrative Examples

Example 8.22 : The outcome clinical trail (test) and actual status of the patients are given in the following table. Obtain the values of sensitivity and specificity of the test.

Outcome of test	Actual status (condition)	
	Positive	**Negative**
Positive	40	360
Negative	10	1640

Solution : Positive Positive = True Positive (T.P.) = 40
Negative Positive = False Negative (F.N.) = 10
Positive Negative = False Positive (F.P.) = 360
Negative Negative = True Negative = 1640

∴ Sensitivity of the test = $\dfrac{TP}{TP+FN} = \dfrac{40}{40+10} = 0.8$

⇒ Sensitivity of tthe test = 80%

Similarly specificity the test = $\dfrac{TN}{TN + FP} = \dfrac{1640}{1640 + 360} = \dfrac{1640}{2000} = 0.82$

∴ Specificity of test = 82%.

Points to Remember

1. Two events are said to be independent if the occurrence or non-occurrence of one does not affect the occurrence of the other. Two events A and B defined on a sample space Ω are said to be independent if and only if $P(A \cap B) = P(A) \cdot P(B)$.
2. If two events are independent they cannot be mutually exclusive.
3. If two events are mutually exclusive, they cannot be independent.
4. If one of the events A and B is impossible event (φ) then A and B are mutually exclusive as well as independent.
5. Suppose A and B are two events defined on a sample space Ω. If A and B are independent then
   (i) A and B' are independent.
   (ii) A' and B are independent.
   (iii) A' and B' are independent.
6. Conditional probability satisfies all axioms of probability.
7. For independent events, conditional probability is the same as unconditional probability.
8. $P(A|B) = \dfrac{P(A \cap B)}{P(B)}$.
9. $P(A \cap B) = P(A) \cdot P(B|A) = P(B) \cdot P(A|B)$.
10. Bayes' theorem : $P(A_i|B) = \dfrac{P(A_i) \cdot P(B|A_i)}{\sum\limits_{j=1}^{n} P(A_j) \cdot P(B|A_j)}$.
11. If A and B are independent then $P(A \cap B) = P(A) \cdot P(B)$.

EXERCISE 8 (A)

1. Explain the concept of independence of two events.
2. Define independence of two events A and B on Ω. Give an illustration.
3. Does independence of two events imply that the events are mutually exclusive ? Justify your answer.

4. Does mutually exclusiveness of two events imply independence ? Justify.
5. When are two events independent as well as mutually exclusive ?
6. Given A and B two independent events defined on Ω, prove that (i) A and B' are independent (ii) A' and B are independent, (iii) A' and B' are independent.
7. Given three events A, B, C defined on a sample space Ω, define (i) Pairwise independence, (ii) mutual or complete independence of A, B, C.
8. Show that if A, B, C are mutually independent, then $A \cup B$ and C are independent.
9. Prove or disprove the following :
   (i) Mutual independence of 3 events $\Rightarrow$ Pairwise independence
   (ii) Pairwise independence $\Rightarrow$ mutual independence.
10. Explain the concept of conditional probability.
11. For two events defined on a sample space Ω, define conditional probabilities $P(A|B)$ and $P(B|A)$.
12. Prove or disprove : $P(A|B) = P(B|A)$; where A and B are any two events defined on Ω.
13. Show that conditional probability satisfies all the axioms of probability.
14. If A, B, C are any three events defined on Ω, with $P(B) > 0$ then prove that
    $$P(A \cup C|B) = P(A|B) + P(C|B) - P(A \cap C|B)$$
15. For A and B events defined on Ω, prove the following results.
    (i) $\quad P(A'|B) = 1 - P(A|B)$
    (ii) $\quad P(A|A') = 0$
    (iii) If $A \cap B = \phi$, $P(A|B) = 0$
    (iv) If $B \subset A$, then $P(A|B) = 1$
    (v) If $A \subset B$, then $P(A|B) = \dfrac{P(A)}{P(B)}$
16. Compare the magnitude of $P(A|B)$ and $P(A)$ in each of the following cases.
    (i) $A \cap B = \phi$, (ii) $A \subset B$, (iii) $B \subset A$, (iv) $A \cap B \neq \phi$.

17. State and prove the multiplication theorem for two events A and B defined on a sample space Ω.
18. State the extension of the theorem of compound probability for three events.
19. What are 'posterior' and 'prior' probabilities ? Explain.
20. Define partition of a sample space.
21. State and prove Bayes' theorem.
22. If $A_1, A_2, \ldots, A_n$ is a partition of a sample space Ω and if B is any event defined on Ω, prove that
$$P(B) = \sum_{j=1}^{n} P(A_j) \cdot P(B|A_j)$$
23. Explain with an illustration, how the Bayes' theorem is applied in practical situations.

EXERCISE 8 (B)

24. If A is an event on a sample space Ω, show that (i) A and Ω are independent (ii) A and ϕ are independent.
25. Of the three events A, B, C; A and B are mutually exclusive; A and C are independent; B and C are independent. If $P(A) = \frac{1}{4}, P(B) = \frac{1}{3}, P(C) = \frac{1}{6}$, find (i) $P(A\cup B)$ (ii) $P(A\cap C)$ (iii) $P(A\cup B\cup C)$.
26. In a certain school, examination results showed that 20% students failed in Mathematics, 5% failed in English while 10% failed in both Mathematics and English. Are the two events 'failing in Mathematics' and 'failing in English' independent ?
27. An article manufactured by a company consists of two parts A and B. In the manufacturing process of part A, 9 out of 100 are likely to be defective, similarly 5 out of 100 are likely to be defective in the process of part B. Calculate the probability that the assembled parts will not be defective.
28. A husband and wife appear for two vacancies in the same post. The probability of husband's selection is 1/7 and that of wife's selection is 1/5. What is the probability that
    (a) both of them will be selected ?
    (b) only one of them will be selected ?
    (c) none of them will be selected ?

29. Let A and B be two independent events defined on a sample space Ω. The probability that at least one event out of A and B occurs is 0.7, while the probability that A occurs is 0.5, determine the probability that B occurs.
30. The probability of an accident in a factory in year is 0.2 in Delhi, 0.3 in Pune and 0.1 in Mumbai. Find the probability that an accident may happen in (i) at least one of the three cities (ii) all the three cities.
31. Probability that a man will be alive 20 years hence is 0.3 and probability that his wife will be alive 20 years hence is 0.4. Find the probability that after 20 years (i) both will be alive (ii) only the man will be alive (iii) only the wife will be alive (iv) at least one of them will be alive.
32. Let $\Omega = \{\omega_1, \omega_2, \omega_3\}$ be a sample space associated with a certain experiment. If $P(\omega_1) = k$, $P(\omega_2) = 2k^2$, $P(\omega_3) = k^2 + k$, find k. Also examine whether $A = \{\omega_1, \omega_2\}$ and $B = \{\omega_2, \omega_3\}$ are independent events.
33. Prove that if $P(A) = 0$, then A and B are independent for any event B.
34. A bag contains 4 tickets numbered 445, 454, 544 and 555. One ticket is drawn randomly. Let A_i (i = 1, 2, 3) be the event that the ith digit of the number of the ticket is 4. Are A_1, A_2, A_3 (i) Pairwise independent ? (ii) mutually independent ?
35. A town has 3 doctors A, B and C operating independently. The probability that doctor A is available is 0.9 and that for B is 0.6, for C 0.7; what is the probability that at least one doctor is available when needed ?
36. There are two Sections I and II Statistics paper. The probability that a candidate passes in Section I is 0.6 and that he passes in Section II is 0.7. What is the probability that a particular candidate passes only in any one of the two sections ?
37. A man wants to marry a girl having qualities : white complexion – the probability of getting such a girl is 0.1; convent educated-probability of which is one if fifty; handsome dowry the probability of getting this is one is hundred. Find the probability that the man gets married to a girl who possesses all the above three independent qualities.

38. If A and B are mutually exclusive non-empty events of Ω, show that
$$P(A|A\cup B) = \frac{P(A)}{P(A)+P(B)}$$

39. Let A and B be two events defined on a sample space Ω such that $P(A) = \frac{1}{4}$, $P(B|A) = \frac{1}{2}$ and $P(A|B) = \frac{1}{4}$. Prove that
   (i) A and B are independent (ii) $P(A'|B') = \frac{3}{4}$.

40. Let Ω {a, b, c, d, e, f, g, h}. A function P on Ω defines a probability model by assigning probabilities in the following manner.

Element	a	b	c	d	e	f	g	h
Probability	0.1	0.2	0.15	0.05	0.25	0.1	0.1	0.05

Determine the conditional probability of
   (i) {a, b, c} given {b, c, e, f}
   (ii) {c, d, g, h} given {b, c, h}
   (iii) {a, f, g, h} given {g}

41. The probability that a construction job will be finished on time is 0.7, the probability that there will be no strikes is 0.6 and the probability that the job will be finished on time given that there are no strikes is 0.8.
   (i) What is the probability that the job will be finished on time and there will be no strikes ?
   (ii) What is the probability that there will have been no strikes given that the job is finished on time ?

42. In a group of equal number of men and women, 10% men and 45% women are unemployed. What is the probability that a person selected at random is employed ?

43. A coin is tossed until a head appears, or until it has been tossed three times. Given that the head does not appear on the first toss, find the probability that the coin is tossed three times.

44. A pair of fair dice is thrown. If the two numbers appearing on the top faces are different, find the probability that the sum of numbers on the top faces is (i) 4, (ii) at most 4.

45. Given that $P(A_1) = P(A_2) = P(A_3) = \frac{1}{3}$ and $P(B|A_1) = \frac{2}{7}$, $P(B|A_2) = \frac{4}{9}$, $P(B|A_3) = \frac{1}{5}$, find $P(A_1|B)$

46. A and B are two events on a sample space Ω. Prove with usual notation,
$$P(A) = P(A|B) \cdot P(B) + P(A|B') \cdot P(B')$$

47. A and B are two events defined on a sample space Ω. State the nature of relationship between A and B in each of the following :

    (a) $P(A|B) = 0$, (b) $P(A|B) = P(A)$.

48. A, B, C form a partition of Ω. If $3P(A) = 2P(B) = P(C)$ find $P(A \cup B)$.

49. A certain item is manufactured by three factories F_1, F_2, F_3. It is known that F_1 turns out twice as many items as F_2 and that F_2 and F_3 turn out the same number of items during a specified period. It is also known that 2% of the items produced by F_1 and by F_2 are defective, while 4% of those manufactured by F_3 are defective. One item is chosen at random from the lot of items produced by those factories together, and found defective. Find the probability that it is produced by F_1.

50. The probabilities of A, B and C becoming managers are $\frac{4}{9}$, $\frac{2}{9}$ and $\frac{1}{3}$ respectively. The probabilities that the employment insurance scheme will be introduced if A, B, C become managers are $\frac{3}{10}$, $\frac{1}{2}$ and $\frac{4}{5}$ respectively. (i) What is the probability that the employment insurance scheme will be introduced and (ii) If the employment insurance scheme has been introduced, what is the probability that the manager appointed was not A.

51. There are 4 boys and 2 girls in Room No. 1 and 5 boys and 3 girls in Room No. 2. A girl from one of the two rooms laughed loudly. What is the probability that the girl who laughed loudly was from Room No. 2.

52. In a community 5 percent of people suffer from cancer. The probability that a doctor is able to correctly diagnose a person with cancer with suffering from cancer is 0.9. The doctor wrongly diagnoses a person without cancer as having cancer with probability 0.1. What is the probability that a randomly selected person diagnosed as having cancer is really suffering from cancer ?

EXERCISE 8 (C)

53. The occurrence of two independent events is known to be each greater than $\frac{1}{2}$. It is given that the probability that the first event will happen simultaneously with the second not occurring is $\frac{3}{25}$. Also, the probability of the second occurring simultaneously with the first not occurring is $\frac{8}{25}$. Find the probabilities of the respective events.

54. Let A_1, A_2, A_3 be 3 completely independent events defined on Ω.

    If $P(A_i') = \left(\frac{1}{2}\right)^i$, $i = 1, 2, 3$ find $P\left(\bigcup_{i=1}^{3} A_i\right)$.

55. Let A, B and C be three events on Ω such that

    $P(A \cap B \cap C') = P(A \cap B' \cap C) = P(A' \cap B \cap C') = P(A' \cap B' \cap C)$
    $= \frac{1}{4}$. Are A, B, C (i) mutually independent, (ii) pairwise independent ?

Objective Type Questions

I. Multiple Choice Questions (MCQ).

Choose the correct alternative.

1. A number is selected at random from 1, 2, 3. Define A = {1, 2}, B = {2, 3}, C = {1, 3}. Then ....
   (a) A, B, C are mutually independent events.
   (b) A, B, C are pairwise but not mutually independent events.
   (c) A, B, C are mutually independent but not pairwise independent events.
   (d) None of the above.

2. Urns I and II respectively contain 5 white, 5 black and 2 white, 8 black balls. An urn is selected at random and a ball is drawn at random from the selected urn. If the ball drawn is white, then the probability that the selected urn was II is given by ....
   (a) 0.5 (b) 0
   (c) 1/7 (d) 2/7

3. If $A_1, A_2, \ldots, A_n$ form a partition of Ω, then
   (a) $\bigcap_{i=1}^{n} A_i = \Omega, \quad A_i \cap A_j = \phi \quad i = j$
   (b) $\bigcap_{i=1}^{n} A_i = \Omega, \quad A_i \cap A_j = \phi \quad i \neq j$
   (c) $\bigcap_{i=1}^{n} A_i = \Omega, \quad A_i \cup A_j = \phi \quad i \neq j$
   (d) $\bigcap_{i=1}^{n} A_i = \Omega, \quad A_i \cap A_j = \phi \quad i \neq j$

4. Which of the following statement is true ?
   (a) A and A' form partition of Ω.
   (b) A and Ω form partition of Ω.
   (c) A and A' do not form partition of Ω.
   (d) Only two events can not form a partition of Ω.

5. For two events A and B, if P (A) = P (A|B) = 0.25 and P (B|A) = 0.5, then ....
    (a) A and B are mutually exclusive events.
    (b) A and B are independent.
    (c) A is subset of B.
    (d) P (A'|B) ≠ 0.75.

6. If A and B are independent events with P (A) = 0.4 and P (B) = 0.25, then P (A ∪ B) is ....
    (a) 0.65
    (b) 0.55
    (c) 0.1
    (d) not enough information is given to answer this question.

7. If A and B are independent events with P(A) = 0.4, P(B) = 0.5, then P(A' ∩ B) is ....
    (a) 0.03
    (b) 0.9
    (c) 0.1
    (d) 0.3.

8. Suppose you pass a certain examination with probability 0.6 and your friend passes the examination with probability 0.7. Both of you share the same bench and get the same education, hence the events are not independent. What is the probability that both of you pass the examination ?
    (a) 0.42
    (b) can't determine, but must be ≤ 0.6.
    (c) can't determine but must be ≤ 0.7.
    (d) 1 as you both guarantee to study hard.

9. Which of the following statement is true ?
    (a) P (A|B) ≥ P (A)
    (b) P (A|B) ≤ P (A)
    (c) P (A|B) = P (A)
    (d) Nothing can be said about the magnitudes of P (A) and P (A|B).

10. Given that a student has scored distinction in Xth standard, probability that he will score distinction in XIIth is 0.8. Suppose probability that he scores distinction in Xth is 0.4, what is the probability that he will score distinction in both Xth and XIIth standard ?

   (a) 0.12   (b) 0.32
   (c) 0.032   (d) 0.4

II. State whether the following statement are true or false.

11. Independence implies mutual exclusiveness.

12. If A' and B' are independent, then A and B are independent.

13. Bayes' theorem is used to calculate posterior probabilities of events.

14. If $B \subset A$, then $P(A|B) = 1$.

15. If $A_1, A_2, \ldots, A_n$ form a partition of Ω, then $A_1 \cap B, A_2 \cap B, \ldots, A_n \cap B$ form a partition of B.

HINTS AND ANSWERS

(25) $\frac{7}{12}, \frac{1}{24}, \frac{7}{12}$. 26) No. (27) 0.8645; (28) $\frac{1}{35}, \frac{2}{7}, \frac{24}{35}$. (29) 0.4. (30) 0.696, 0.006. (31) 0.12, 0.18, 0.28, 0.58. (32) k = 1/3, No. (34) yes, no. (35) 0.494. (36) 0.46. (37) 0.00002. (40) 0.5, 0.5, 1. (41) 0.48, 0.6857. (42) 0.725. (43) 1/2. (44) $\frac{1}{15}, \frac{2}{15}$. (45) 0.3072. (47) (a) mutually exclusive, (b) independent; (48) $\frac{5}{11}$. (49) $\frac{1}{7}$. (50) $\frac{23}{45}$, $\frac{17}{23}$. (51) $\frac{9}{17}$. (52) 0.3214. (53) **Hint :** $P(A) \cdot P(B') = \frac{3}{25} \Rightarrow P(A) = \frac{3}{25(1-B)}$ ∴ $P(A' \cap B) = \frac{8}{25}$ = quadratic equation in P (B) ∵ $P(B) > \frac{1}{2}$, $P(A) = \frac{3}{5}$, $P(B) = \frac{4}{5}$. (54) $\frac{63}{64}$. (55) The four events form partition.

∴ $P(A'\cap B\cap C) = P(A\cap B'\cap C) = P(A\cap B\cap C') = 0$

not mutually independent, but pairwise independent.

Answers of Objective Questions

I. (1) d, (2) d, (3) b, (4) a, (5) b, (6) b, (7) d, (8) b, (9) d, (10) b.

II. (11) F, (12) T, (13) T, (14) T, (15) T.

Chapter 9...
Univariate Probability Distribution

Andrey Kolmogorov (1903-1987) was a Russian mathematician who advanced various scientific fields, among them probability theory, topology, intuitionistic logic etc. In 1933, Kolmogorov published his book, *Foundations of the Theory of Probability*, laying the modern axiomatic foundations of probability theory and establishing his reputation as the world's leading expert in this field. A quotation attributed to Kolmogorov is "Every mathematician believes that he is ahead over all others. The reason why they don't say this in public, is because they are intelligent people."

Andrey Kolmogorov

Contents ...
9.1 Introduction
9.2 Definition : Discrete Random Variable
9.3 Probability Distribution
9.4 Cumulative Distribution Function (c.d.f.) or Distribution Function (d.f.)
9.5 Properties of Distribution Function F (·)
9.6 Median of a Discrete Probability Distribution
9.7 Mode of a Discrete Probability Distribution
9.8 Probability Distribution of a Function of a Discrete R.V.

Key Words :
Random variable, Discrete random variable, Probability mass function, Cumulative distribution function, Discrete probability distribution.

Objectives :
- Understand the concept of random variables as a function from sample space to real line.
- Understand the concept of probability distribution of a discrete random variable.
- Calculation of probabilities for a discrete random variable.
- Understand the concept of cumulative distribution function.

9.1 Introduction

We are introduced to the concept of random experiments, sample space and probability in previous chapters. Many a times, sample space S or Ω contains non-numeric elements. For example, in an experiment of tossing a coin, $\Omega = \{H, T\}$. However, in practice it is easier to deal with numerical outcomes. In turn, we associate real number with each outcome. For instance, we may call H as 1 and T as 0. Whenever we do this, we are dealing with a *function* whose *domain* is the sample space Ω and whose range is the set of real numbers. Such a function is called a *random variable (r.v.)*.

Random Variable : Let Ω be a discrete sample space corresponding to a random experiment. A function $X : \Omega \to R$ (where R is a real line) is called as a random variable.

Remark 1 : If $\Omega = \{-4, 0, 4\}$ and $X(\omega) = \sqrt{\omega}$, then $X(-4) = \sqrt{-4}$ is an imaginary number.

$\therefore \quad X(-4) \notin R$. Hence, X is not a real valued mapping. Hence, X is not a random variable.

Remark 2 : If $\Omega = \{a, b, c\}$ and X is a mapping between Ω to A as follows :

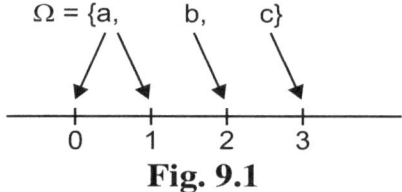

Fig. 9.1

Then $X(a) = 0$ also $X(a) = 1$.

i.e. X is a one-many correspondence.

$\therefore$ X is *not* a function. Recall that a function can either be one-one correspondence or a many-one correspondence. Hence, X is not a random variable.

9.2 Discrete Random Variable

A random variable X is said to be discrete if it takes finite or countably infinite number of values. Thus discrete random variable takes only isolated values.

Remark : In this course, we shall deal with only discrete sample spaces containing finite number of elements. For example, $\Omega = \{\omega_1, \omega_2, \ldots, \omega_n\}$.

Therefore, in this setup, a discrete random variable is a function X which assigns a real number = X (ω_i) to every sample point $\omega_i \in \Omega$.

Remark : X : $\{\omega_1, \omega_2, \omega_3, \ldots, \omega_n\} \to$ A, where A is a finite set of real numbers.

Illustration 1 : Suppose two coins are tossed simultaneously.
$$\Omega = \{HH, TH, HT, TT\}$$
Let X be number of heads obtained tossing two coins. Then we have,
$$X : \Omega \to R \text{ in the following manner.}$$
$$X(HH) = 2, \quad X(TH) = 1, \quad X(HT) = 1, X(TT) = 0.$$
Here random variable X takes three distinct values 0, 1, 2.

Following diagram will help in understanding the concept of random variable.

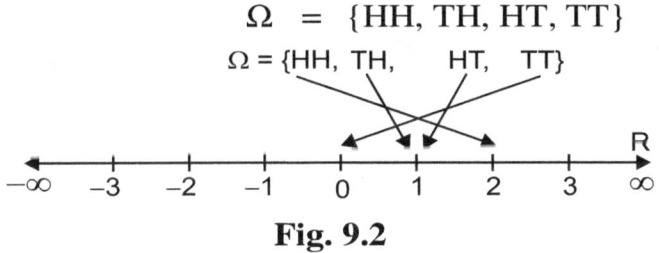

Fig. 9.2

Note : Random variables are denoted by capital letters X, Y, Z etc. whereas the values taken by them are denoted by corresponding small letter x, y, z etc.

Remark : Several random variables can be defined on the same sample space Ω. For example in the Illustration 1, one can define Y = number of tails or Z = difference between number of heads and number of tails. Following are some of the examples of discrete variable.

(i) Number of students present in the class.
(ii) Number of accidents on a highway.
(iii) Number of days of rainfalls in Pune city.
(iv) Number of patients cured by using a certain drug.
(v) Number of attempts required to pass the examination.

Range set of a discrete random variable : Let X be a discrete random variable defined on a sample space Ω. Since Ω contains either finite or countably infinite elements, and X is a function on Ω, therefore, X can take either finite or countably infinite values. Suppose X takes values $x_1, x_2,\ldots$, then the set $\{x_1, x_2, \ldots\}$ is called the range set of X.

For the illustrative example 1, observe that the range set of X = number of heads is $\{0, 1, 2\}$.

9.3 Probability Distribution

Consider again the experiment of tossing two unbiased coins. X = number of heads observed in each tossing. Then range set of X = $\{0, 1, 2\}$. Although, we cannot in advance predict what value X will take, we can certainly state the probabilities with which X will take the three values 0, 1, 2. The following table helps to determine such probabilities.

Outcome	Probability of outcome	Value of X
HH	$\frac{1}{4}$	2
TH	$\frac{1}{4}$	1
HT	$\frac{1}{4}$	1
TT	$\frac{1}{4}$	0

Observe that the following events are associated with the distinct values of X.

$$(X = 0) \Rightarrow \{TT\}$$
$$(X = 1) \Rightarrow \{TH, HT\}$$
$$(X = 2) \Rightarrow \{HH\}$$

Therefore, probabilities of various values of X are nothing but the probabilities of the events with which the respective values are associated.

∴ $P(X = 0) = P\{TT\} = \frac{1}{4}$

$P(X = 1) = P\{TH, HT\} = \frac{1}{4} + \frac{1}{4} = \frac{1}{2}$

$P(X = 2) = P\{HH\} = \frac{1}{4}$

Note that these probabilities add upto 1 (why ?).

Probability Mass Function : Let X be a discrete random variable defined on a sample space Ω. Suppose $\{x_1, x_2, ..., x_n\}$ is the range set of X. With each of x_i, we assign a number $p_i = P(X = x_i)$, called the probability of x_i such that

(i) $\quad p_i \geq 0 \; ; \; i = 1, 2, ..., n$

and (ii) $\quad \sum_{i=1}^{n} p_i = 1$

Then the function P defined above is called the *probability mass function* (p.m.f.) of X.

The table containing the values of X along with their probabilities given by probability mass function is called as *probability distribution* of the random variable X. For example,

X	x_1	x_2	...	x_i	...	x_n	Total
$P(X = x_i)$	p_1	p_2	...	p_i	...	p_n	1

Remark 1 : Properties of a random variable can be studied only in terms of its p.m.f. We need not refer to the underlying sample space Ω, once we have the probability distribution of the random variable.

Remark 2 : If A is any subset of the range set of X, then $P(X \in A) = \sum_{x_j \in A} p(x_j)$; where the sum is taken over all points in A.

For example, if the range set of X is $\{1, 2, 3, 4, 5, 6\}$ and we want to find $P(X \leq 3)$. Then,

$P(X \leq 3) = P(X = 1) + P(X = 2) + P(X = 3)$
$= p_1 + p_2 + p_3$

Illustration 2 : A symmetric die is rolled and number on uppermost face is noted. Find its probability distribution.

Solution : X = number on uppermost face.

∴ Range set of X = {1, 2, 3, 4, 5, 6}

Probability of each of the elements = $\frac{1}{6}$.

∴ The probability distribution of X is

X	1	2	3	4	5	6	Total
P (X = x)	$\frac{1}{6}$	$\frac{1}{6}$	$\frac{1}{6}$	$\frac{1}{6}$	$\frac{1}{6}$	$\frac{1}{6}$	1

Illustration 3 : A pair of fair dice is thrown. Let X = sum of numbers on the uppermost faces.

Range set of X = {2, 3, ..., 12}

Since, X (1, 1) = 2 and X (6, 6) = 12.

We know that Ω contains 36 elements (ordered pairs).

The following table displays the subsets corresponding to the events (X = j) j = 2,..., 12 as well as the corresponding probabilities p_j.

Value of X	Subsets of Ω	$p_j = P(X = j)$
2	{(1, 1)}	1/36
3	{(1, 2), (2, 1)}	2/36
4	{(1, 3), (2, 2), (3, 1)}	3/36
5	{(1, 4) (2, 3), (3, 2), (4, 1)}	4/36
6	{(1, 5), (2, 4), (3, 3), (4, 2), (5, 1)}	5/36
7	{(1, 6) (2, 5), (3, 4), (4, 3), (5, 2), (6, 1)}	6/36
8	{(2, 6), (3, 5), (4, 4), (5, 3), (6, 2)}	5/36
9	{(3, 6), (4, 5), (5, 4), (6, 3)}	4/36
10	{(4, 6) (5, 5), (6, 4)}	3/36
11	{(5, 6) (6, 5)}	2/36
12	{(6, 6)}	1/36

Note that (i) $p_j \geq 0$, $\forall_j = 2, 3, ..., 12$ and (ii) $\sum_{j=2}^{12} p_j = 1$.

Illustrative Examples

Example 9.1 : For the following probability distribution of X.

X	0	1	2	3	4
P (X = x)	k	3k	5k	2k	k

(i) Find the value of k.

(ii) Find $P(X \geq 2)$, $P(X < 3)$, $P(X \leq 1)$.

Solution : (i) In order that the function P (·) should be p.m.f. it should satisfy the properties.

(i) $p_i \geq 0$ $\forall i$ and (b) $\sum p_i = 1$

$\therefore k > 0$ and $12k = 1 \Rightarrow k = \frac{1}{12}$

(ii) $P(X \geq 2) = P(X = 2) + P(X = 3) + P(X = 4)$

$= 8k = \frac{8}{12} = \frac{2}{3}$

$P(X < 3) = P(X = 0) + P(X = 1) + P(X = 2)$

$= 9k = \frac{9}{12} = \frac{3}{4}$

$P(X \leq 1) = P(X = 0) + P(X = 1)$

$= 4k = \frac{4}{12} = \frac{1}{3}$

Example 9.2 : Verify whether the following functions can be regarded as the p.m.f. for the given values of X.

(i)

X	1	2	3	4
P(x)	0.2	0.4	0.3	0.5

(ii)

X	−1	2	3	4
P(x)	0.5	−0.3	0.3	0.5

(iii) $P(x) = \frac{x^2}{14}$; if $x = 1, 2, 3$

$= 0$; otherwise

(iv) $P(x) = \frac{x-1}{2}$; if $x = 0, 1, 2,$

$= 0$; otherwise

Solution : (i) $\sum P(x) = 0.2 + 0.4 + 0.3 + 0.5$

$= 1.4 \neq 1$

$\therefore$ P (x) is not a p.m.f.

(ii) $P(X = 1) \leq 0$ $\therefore$ P (x) is not a p.m.f.

(iii) $P(x) \geq 0$ $\forall x$ and $\sum P(x) = \frac{1}{4} + \frac{4}{14} + \frac{9}{14} = 1.$

$\therefore$ P (x) is a p.m.f.

(iv) $P(0) = -\frac{1}{2} < 0$ $\therefore$ P (x) is not a p.m.f.

Example 9.3 : Determine c such that the following function is a p.m.f.

$$P(x) = c\binom{5}{x}; \quad x = 0, 1, 2, 3, 4, 5.$$

Solution : (i) $c > 0$, (ii) $\sum P(x) = 1$.

$$\Rightarrow \quad c\left[\binom{5}{0} + \binom{5}{1} + \binom{5}{2} + \binom{5}{3} + \binom{5}{4} + \binom{5}{5}\right] = 1$$

$$\therefore \quad c \cdot 2^5 = 1 \quad \text{using the result}$$

$$\binom{n}{0} + \binom{n}{1} + \ldots + \binom{n}{n} = 2^n$$

$$\therefore \quad c = \frac{1}{2^5} = \frac{1}{32} \quad \text{(See Appendix)}$$

9.4 Cumulative Distribution Function (c.d.f.) or Distribution Function (d.f.)

Definition 5 : Let X be a discrete random variable taking values $x_1, x_2, \ldots, x_i, \ldots, x_n$ with probabilities $p_1, p_2, \ldots, p_i, \ldots, p_n$ respectively. Then *cumulative distribution function* (c.d.f.) which is also called as *distribution function* (d.f.) is denoted by F(x) and is defined as follows.

$$F(x) = P[X \leq x] \; ; \; -\infty < x < \infty$$

In particular, $\quad F(x_i) = P[X \leq x_i]$

$$= \sum_{j=1}^{i} p_j \; ; \; i = 1, 2, \ldots, n.$$

Remark : (1) The c.d.f. is defined for all values of $x \in R$. However, since the random variable takes only isolated values, the function is constant in between two successive values of X and have jumps at the points x_i, $i = 1, 2, \ldots, n$. Hence, the distribution function for a discrete random variable is a **step function** as shown in Fig. 9.3.

(2) Since F(x) is a step function we write it as follows :

$$\begin{aligned}
f(x) &= 0 & &\text{if } -\infty < x < x_1 \\
&= p_1 & &\text{if } x_1 < x < x_2 \\
&= p_1 + p_2 & &\text{if } x_2 \leq x \leq x_3 \\
&= p_1 + p_2 + \ldots + p_i & &\text{if } x_i \leq x \leq x_{i+1} \\
&\quad \ldots \\
&= 1 & &\text{if } x \geq x_n
\end{aligned}$$

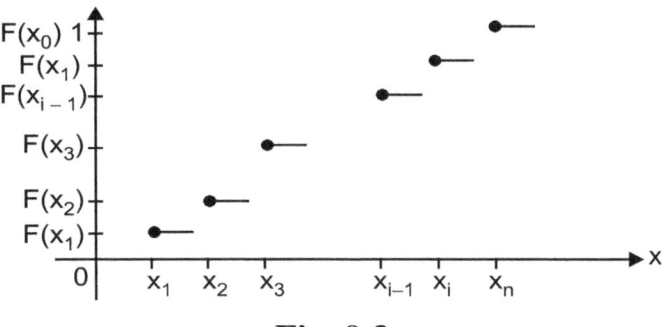

Fig. 9.3

Example 9.4 : Consider the following probability distribution of a discrete random variable X. (i) Obtain the c.d.f. of X. (ii) Draw a graph of the c.d.f. and p.m.f.

x_i	1	2	3	4	5
p_i	0.1	0.2	0.3	0.2	0.2

Solution : Since $F(x_i) = \sum_{j=1}^{i} p_j$, we obtain $F(x_i)$ by taking cumulative sum of probabilities p_i as follows :

x_i	1	2	3	4	5
$F(x_i)$	0.1	0.1 + 0.2 = 0.3	0.3 + 0.3 = 0.6	0.6 + 0.2 = 0.8	0.8 + 0.2 = 1

Note that $F(x_n) = F(5) = 1$ since there is no value of X beyond 5 with positive probability.

While describing the function $F(x)$; we write

$$F(x) = \begin{cases} 0 & x < 1 \\ 0.1 & 1 \leq x < 2 \\ 0.3 & 2 \leq x < 3 \\ 0.6 & 3 \leq x < 4 \\ 0.8 & 4 \leq x < 5 \\ 1 & x \geq 5 \end{cases}$$

The graph of F (X) would be as shown in Fig. 9.4.

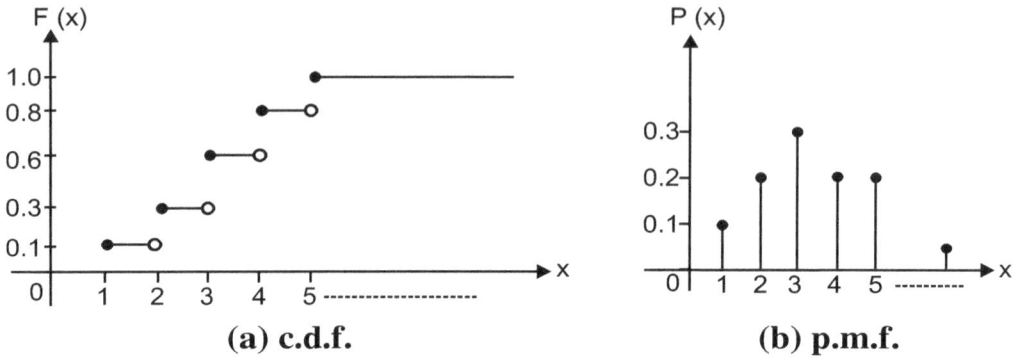

(a) c.d.f. (b) p.m.f.

Fig. 9.4

● : the point is included; ○ : the point is excluded.

9.5 Properties of Distribution Function F (.)

The distribution function is a very important entity in Statistics. It is used extensively in Statistical Inference, the main branch of Statistics; in which inferences are drawn regarding population on the basis of information collected in a sample. Now, we shall study some of the important properties of c.d.f. F (x) of a discrete random variable.

(i) F (x) is defined for all $x \in R$, real line.

(ii) $0 \leq F(x) \leq 1$; obvious, as it is *probability* of the event $(X \leq x)$.

(iii) F (x) is a non-decreasing function of x.
   i.e. if a < b, then F (a) ≤ F (b).
   This is clear from the graph.

(iv) It has jumps at $x_1, x_2, \ldots, x_n$, the values taken by the random variable X and is constant between two successive values of X. Moreover size of jump at x_i is $P(X = x_i)$.

(v) $F(-\infty) = 0$ and $F(\infty) = 1$.
   where $F(-\infty) = \lim_{x \to -\infty} F(x)$, $F(\infty) = \lim_{x \to \infty} F(x)$.

(vi) Let a and b be two real numbers where a < b; then using distribution function, we can compute probabilities of different events as follows.

1. $P(a < X \leq b) = P[X \leq b] - P[X \leq a]$
   $= F(b) - F(a)$

   ○————————●
   a   b

2. $P(a \leq X \leq b) = P[X \leq b] - P(X \leq a) + P(X = a)$
    $= F(b) - F(a) + P(a)$

    •────────•
    a   b

3. $P(a \leq X < b) = P[X \leq b] - P[X \leq a] - P[X = b] + P[X = a]$
    $= F(b) - F(a) - P(b) + P(a)$

    •────────◦
    a   b

4. $P(a < X < b) = P[X \leq b] - P[X \leq a] - P(X = b)$
    $= F(b) - F(a) - P(b)$

    ◦────────◦
    a   b

5. $P(X > a) = 1 - P(X \leq a) = 1 - F(a)$

    ◦────────→
    a   ∞

6. $P(X \geq a) = 1 - P[X \leq a] + P[X = a]$
    $= 1 - F(a) + P(a)$

    •────────→
    a   ∞

Example 9.5 : The following is the cumulative distribution function of a discrete random variable.

X	−3	−1	0	1	2	3	5	8
F(x)	0.1	0.3	0.45	0.65	0.75	0.90	0.95	1.00

(i)   Find the p.m.f. of X.   (ii) $P(0 < X < 2)$
(iii) $P(1 \leq X \leq 3)$ (iv) $P(-3 < X \leq 2)$
(v) $P(-1 \leq X < 1)$ (vi) $P(X = \text{even})$
(vii) $P(X > 2)$ (viii) $P(X \geq 3)$
(ix) $P(X = -3 | X < 0)$ (x) $P(X \leq 3 | X > 0)$

Solution : (i) Since,

$$F(x_i) = \sum_{j=1}^{i} p_j,$$

$$F(x_{i-1}) = \sum_{j=1}^{i-1} p_j$$

$\therefore \quad p_i = \sum_{j=1}^{i} p_j - \sum_{j=1}^{i-1} p_j = F(x_i) - F(x_{i-1})$

∴ The p.m.f. of X is given by –

X	− 3	− 1	0	1	2	3	5	8
P (x)	0.3	0.2	0.15	0.2	0.1	0.15	0.05	0.05

(ii) $P(0 < X < 2) = F(2) - F(0) - P(2)$
    from property (vi), (4)
    $= 0.75 - 0.45 - 0.1 = 0.2$

(iii) $P(1 \leq X \leq 3) = F(3) - F(1) + P(1)$
    $= 0.9 - 0.65 + 0.2$ from (vi), (2)
    $= 0.45$

(iv) $P(-3 < X \leq 2) = F(2) - F(-3)$ from (vi), (1)
    $= 0.75 - 0.1$
    $= 0.65$

(v) $P(-1 \leq X < 1) = F(1) - F(-1) - P(1) + P(-1)$
    from (vi) (3)
    $= 0.65 - 0.3 - 0.2 + 0.2$
    $= 0.35$

(vi) $P(X = \text{even}) = P(x = 0) + P(x = 2) + P(x = 8)$
    $= 0.15 + 0.1 + 0.05$
    $= 0.3$

(vii) $P(X > 2) = 1 - F(2)$ from (vi) (5)
    $= 1 - 0.75 = 0.25$

(viii) $P(X \geq 3) = 1 - F(3) + P(3)$ from (vi) (6)
    $= 1 - 0.9 + 0.15 = 0.25$

(ix) To compute $P(X = -3 | X < 0)$, let us define A : event $(X = -3)$ and B : event $(X < 0)$.

∴ We have to determine P (A|B)

Now, $P(A|B) = \dfrac{P(A \cap B)}{P(B)}$

and $A \cap B = (X = -3) \cap (X < 0)$
    $= (X = -3)$

∴ $P(X = -3 | X < 0) = \dfrac{P(X = -3)}{P(X < 0)} = \dfrac{0.3}{P(-3) + P(-1)}$
    $= \dfrac{0.3}{0.3 + 0.2} = 0.6$

(x) $P(X \leq 3 | X > 0) = \dfrac{P(X \leq 3, X > 0)}{P(X > 0)} = \dfrac{P(0 < X \leq 3)}{P(X > 0)}$

$= \dfrac{0.45}{1 - 0.45}$

$= 0.8182$

9.6 Median of a Discrete Probability Distribution

Let X be a discrete random variable with c.d.f. F(x). The median, M of the probability distribution of X is defined as that value of X, such that

$$P(X \leq M) \geq \dfrac{1}{2} \text{ and } P(X \geq M) \geq \dfrac{1}{2}$$

In other words,

$F(M) \geq \dfrac{1}{2}$ and $1 - F(M) + P(M) \geq \dfrac{1}{2}$. For calculation purposes, median is the first value of X for which $F(X) \geq 0.5$.

Illustration 1 : Consider the following probability distribution.

X	1	2	3	4	5
P (x)	0.1	0.2	0.3	0.25	0.15

The c.d.f. F (x) is given as follows :

X	1	2	3	4	5
F (x)	0.1	0.3	0.6	0.85	1

Hence, X = 3 is the median;

since $F(3) = 0.6 \geq 0.5$

and $1 - F(3) + P(3) = 1 - 0.6 + 0.3 = 0.7 \geq 0.5$

∴ $\quad M = 3$

Illustration 2 : Consider the following probability distribution.

X	1	2	3	4
P (x)	$\dfrac{1}{4}$	$\dfrac{1}{4}$	$\dfrac{1}{4}$	$\dfrac{1}{4}$

Observe that, $P(X \leq 2) = \frac{1}{2} \geq \frac{1}{2}$ and $P(X \geq 2) = \frac{3}{4} \geq \frac{1}{2}$

Median = 2

Also, $P(X \leq 3) = \frac{3}{4} \geq \frac{1}{2}$ and $P(X \geq 3) = \frac{1}{2} \geq \frac{1}{2}$

Hence, Median = 3.

Thus median may not be unique.

9.7 Mode of a Discrete Probability Distribution

Let X be a discrete random variable with c.d.f. F(x). The mode, M_o of the probability distribution of X is defined as the value of X for which the p.m.f. is *maximum*.

Illustration 1 : Determine mode for the following probability distribution.

X	5	10	15	20	25
P(x)	0.13	0.15	0.24	0.37	0.11

Observe that the maximum p.m.f. is 0.37 = P(20). Hence, Mode = 20.

Remark : The mode may not be *unique*. If there are more than one value of X, for which the p.m.f. is maximum, then all these values of X are modes. If there are two modes, the distribution is called *bimodal*. If there are more than two modes, say 3, 4, …, then the distribution is called multimodal.

9.8 Probability Distribution of a Function of a Discrete R.V.

Let X be a discrete r.v. with the following probability distribution.

X	x_1	x_2	…	x_i	…	x_n
P(X = x)	p_1	p_2	…	p_i	…	p_n

Suppose, Y = g(x) is a real valued function of X. Then Y takes values

$y_1 = g(x_1), y_2 = g(x_2), \ldots y_i = g(x_i), \ldots, y_n = g(x_n)$.

Hence, the probability distribution of Y will be as follows :

Y	$y_1 = g(x_1)$	…	$y_i = g(x_i)$	…	$y_n = g(x_n)$
P(Y = y)	p_1	…	p_i	…	p_n

Illustration : Consider the following probability distribution of X.

X	0	1	2	3
P(x)	0.2	0.5	0.2	0.1

Let Y = 5X − 2 then possible values of Y are − 2, 3, 8, 12 with probabilities as of corresponding values of X.

Y	− 2	3	8	12
P(y)	0.2	0.5	0.2	0.1

9.9 Symmetry of Random Variable

A discrete random variable X is said to be symmetric if the graph of probability mass function P(x) against x is symmetric. In other words the height of bars of P(x) equidistant from certain value are of equal height. Or the bars equidistant from two extreme values of random variables X are of equal heights. If $P(a - x) = P(a + x) \forall x$ the random variable X is symmetric around X = a.

Illustrative Examples

Example 9.5 : Suppose X is a random variable with probability mass function as follows :

X	1	2	3	4	5
P(x)	0.05	0.25	0.40	0.25	0.05

Solution : The random variable X has symmetric distribution around X = 3. Since the graph is symmetric.

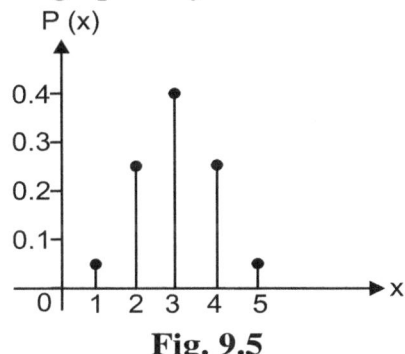

Fig. 9.5

We also observe that :

$$P(3 - x) = P(3 + x) \quad \text{for } x = 1, 2$$

For x = 1 $P(3 - 1) = P(3 + 1) \Rightarrow P(2) = P(4) = 0.25$
For X = 2 $P(3 - 2) = P(3 + 2) \Rightarrow P(1) = P(5) = 0.05$

Note :

(1) If X is symmetric around a, then mean of X is a.

(2) If median and mode are unique then, for symmetric distribution mean = mode = median.

In the above example we can verify that median = 3, mode = 3.

Example 9.6 : Verify whether the following probability distribution symmetric.

X	1	2	3	4
P(x)	0.2	0.3	0.3	0.2

Solution : The graph of P(x) is symmetric around 2.5.

Also $P(2.5 - x) = P(2.5 + x)$ for $x = 0.5, 1.5$

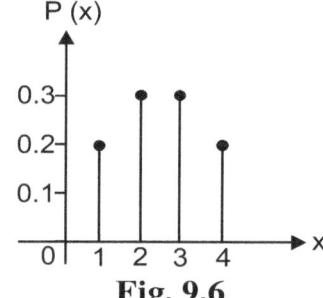

Fig. 9.6

The random variable X is symmetric about 2.5.

Note : Median and mode are not unique, hence

$$\text{mean} \neq \text{mode} \neq \text{median}.$$

Points to Remember

- A discrete random variable is a function, which assigns a real number to every sample point.
- Properties of a random variable are studied using its p.m.f.
- Cumulative distribution function has jumps at the values of the discrete random variable and the size of the jump is equal to the probability of that specific value.
- $P(x_i)$ is p.m.f. if (i) $p(x_i) \geq 0 \ \forall \ x_i$ and (ii) $\sum_i p(x_i) = 1$.
- M is median. $P(X \leq m) \geq \frac{1}{2}$ and $P(X \geq m) \geq \frac{1}{2}$.
- Mode is that value of r.v. at which probability is maximum.
- Median and mode may not be unique.

EXERCISE 9 (A)

Theory Questions :

1. Explain the following terms :

   (a) random variable, (b) discrete random variable, (c) range set of a discrete random variable, (d) probability mass function (p.m.f.), (e) probability distribution of a discrete r.v.

2. Explain with illustration, how to determine probability of an event A, whenever the p.m.f. is available.

3. Give three examples of a discrete random variable.

4. Define cumulative distribution function (c.d.f.) of a discrete r.v. and state its important properties.

5. Define median of a discrete probability distribution.

6. Define mode of a discrete probability distribution.

7. Is the mode always unique ? It not, give an example of a bimodal probability distribution.

EXERCISE 9 (B)

Numerical Problems :

8. Suppose three balanced coins are tossed simultaneously. If X denotes the number of heads, find the probability distribution of X.

9. Obtain the probability distribution of the number of sixes in two tosses of a die.

10. If the variable X denotes the maximum of the two numbers, when a pair of unbiased die is rolled, find the probability distribution of X.

11. A box of 20 mangoes contain 4 bad mangoes. Two mangoes are drawn at random without replacement from this box. Obtain the probability distribution of the number of bad mangoes in the sample.

12. Three cards are drawn at random successively, with replacement, from a well shuffled pack of 52 playing cards. Getting 'a card of diamonds' is termed as a success. Obtain the probability distribution of the number of successes.

13. A person has 4 keys out of which only one key can open a lock. He tries keys one by one, discarding the keys already used. Obtain the probability distribution of the number of attempts to open the lock.

14. Determine k such that the following functions are p.m.f.s
    (i) $f(x) = kx$, $x = 1, 2, 3, \ldots 10$.
    (ii) $f(x) = k\dfrac{2^x}{x!}$, $x = 0, 1, 2, 3$
    (iii) $f(x) = k(2x^2 + 3x + 1)$, $x = 0, 1, 2, 3$

15. Verify whether the following can be looked upon as p.m.f. for the given values of X.
    (i) $P(x) = \dfrac{1}{4}$;   for $x = 0, 1, 2, 3, 4$
    (ii) $P(x) = \dfrac{x+1}{10}$; $x = 0, 1, 2, 3$
    (iii) $P(x) = \dfrac{x^2}{30}$; $x = 0, 1, 2, 3, 4$
    (iv) $P(x) = \dfrac{x-2}{5}$; $x = 1, 2, 3, 4, 5$

16. A random variable X has the following probability distribution.

X	0	1	2	3	4	5	6
P(x)	k	3k	5k	7k	9k	11k	13k

(i) Find k, (ii) Find $P(X \geq 2)$, (iii) $P(0 < X < 5)$, (iv) What is the minimum value of C for which $P(X \leq C) > 0.5$, (v) What is the distribution function of X ?

17. A random variable X takes values 0, 1, 2, 3, 4 such that $P(1 < X \leq 4) = 0.55$, $P(X \leq 1) = 0.25$, $P(X = 2) = 2 P(X = 1)$, $P(X > 3) = 0.2$ and $P(0 < X \leq 2) = 0.45$. Find the probability distribution of X.

18. A random variable X assumes the values 1, 2, 3, 4, 5 such that
    $P(X = 1) = P(X = 2)$; $P(X = 4) = P(X = 5)$
    $P(X < 3) = P(X = 3) = P(X > 3)$.

    Write down the p.m.f. of X and evaluate $P(X \leq 3)$.

19. Let P (x) be the p.m.f. of a discrete random variable X which assumes the values x_1, x_2, x_3, x_4 such that
    $$2P(x_1) = 3P(x_2) = P(x_3) = 5P(x_4)$$
    Find the p.m.f. of X.
20. The. p.m.f. of a random variable X is as follows :
    P (0) $=3k^3$, P (1) = 4k – $10k^2$, P (2) = 5k – 1
    P (x)   =0 elsewhere.
    Find (i) k, (ii) P(X < 1), (iii) P(1 < X ≤ 2), (iv) P(0 < X < 3), (v) Obtain the c.d.f.
    F (x). Describe it and sketch its graph.
21. A discrete random variable X has the p.m.f. given by

X	2	4	6	8	10
P (x)	$\frac{1}{12}$	$\frac{1}{6}$	$\frac{1}{4}$	$\frac{1}{3}$	$\frac{1}{6}$

    Find (i) mode, (ii) median, (iii) P (4 ≤ X < 8).
22. A scooter coming-off the production line can have 0, 1, 2, 3 or 4 defects according to the following p.m.f. P (0) = 0.4, P (1) = 0.25, P (2) = 0.15, P (3) = 0.1, P (4) = 0.1. Find the probability that (i) a scooter has two or more defects (ii) less than 3 defects (iii) not more than 1 defect (iv) at most one defect (v) no defect given that the scooter has not more than 1 defect.
23. Given the following distribution function of a random variable X.

X	– 3	– 2	– 1	0	1	2	3
F (x)	0.05	0.15	0.38	0.57	0.72	0.88	1

    Obtain :

    (i)   P (– 2 ≤ X ≤ 1)

    (ii)   P (X > 0)

    (iii)   P (– 1 < X < 2)

    (iv)   P (– 3 ≤ X < – 1)

    (v)   P (– 2 < X ≤ 0)

    (vi)   P.m.f. of X

    (vii)   Median of X

    (viii) Mode of X

(ix) $P(|X| < 2)$.

(x) $P(|X| \geq 1)$.

24. Given the following c.d.f. $F(x)$ of a discrete random variable X, obtain the p.m.f. of X.

    Also obtain the median of X.

    $$\begin{aligned} F(x) &= 0 & ; & \quad x < 0 \\ &= 0.2 & ; & \quad 0 \leq x < 2 \\ &= 0.5 & ; & \quad 2 \leq x < 4 \\ &= 0.7 & ; & \quad 4 \leq x < 6 \\ &= 0.8 & ; & \quad 6 \leq x < 8 \\ &= 1 & ; & \quad x \geq 8 \end{aligned}$$

25. A discrete random variable X assumes values $-2.5, -1.5, 0.5, 1.5$ and 2.5. If

    $P(X = -2.5) = P(X = -1.5)$
    $P(X = 1.5) = P(X = 2.5)$
    $P(X < 0.5) = P(X > 0.5) = P(X = 0.5)$

    Obtain the (i) p.m.f. of X (ii) the distribution function of X.

26. The distribution function $F(x)$ is

    $$\begin{aligned} F(x) &= 0 & ; & \quad x < \frac{1}{4} \\ &= \frac{1}{8} & ; & \quad \frac{1}{4} \leq x < \frac{1}{2} \\ &= \frac{1}{4} & ; & \quad \frac{1}{2} \leq x < \frac{3}{4} \\ &= \frac{1}{2} & ; & \quad \frac{3}{4} \leq x < 1 \\ &= \frac{3}{4} & ; & \quad 1 \leq x < \frac{5}{4} \\ &= 1 & ; & \quad \frac{5}{4} \leq x < \frac{3}{2} \end{aligned}$$

    Find mode of the distribution.

27. Following is the distribution function $F(\bullet)$ of a discrete random variable X.

X	1	2	3	4	5	6	7	8
F (x)	0.08	0.12	0.23	0.37	0.48	0.62	0.85	1

    (i)   Find the probability distribution of X.
    (ii)   Find $P(X \leq 4)$ and $P(2 \leq X \leq 6)$
    (iii) Find $P(X = 5 | X \geq 3)$
    (iv) Find $P(X \geq 6 | X \geq 4)$
    (v)   Find the values of median and mode of the distribution.

28. A random variable X has the following probability distribution.

X	0	1	2	3
P (x)	$\frac{1}{5}$	$\frac{2}{5}$	$\frac{1}{5}$	$\frac{1}{5}$

Find probability distribution of
    (i) $W = X - 1$, (ii) $Y = \frac{3X + 2}{2}$, (iii) $Z = X^2 + 2$.

29. Let a discrete random variable X assume values 5, 10, 15, 20 with equal probability. Obtain the probability distribution of $Y = \frac{X - 5}{5}$. Also determine the median of Y. Can you determine the mode of Y ? Explain.

30. State, giving reasons, whether the following statements are true or false.
    (i)   A discrete random variable assumes only finite number of values.
    (ii)   A discrete random variable is defined on a discrete sample space.
    (iii) A discrete random variable takes only positive integral values.
    (iv) Sum of probabilities of all values of a discrete random variable is less than one.
    (v)   The p.m.f. of a discrete random variable is a non-decreasing function.
    (vi) We cannot find the probability of an interval for a discrete variable.
    (vii) A distribution function is an increasing function.

(viii) The graph of a distribution function of a discrete random variable contains of number of steps.

(ix) Median M of a discrete r.v. is that value of the random variable for which

$$F(M) = \frac{1}{2}$$

31. State the random variable and its range set in each of the following cases.
    (i) A pair of fair dice is rolled and difference between the two numbers in noted.
    (ii) Four unbiased coins are tossed simultaneously and number of runs observed.
    (A run is an unbroken chain of same symbol for example, HHTT has two runs).
    (iii) A bag contains 3 red and 4 black balls. Three balls are drawn at random without replacement and number of red balls recorded.
    (iv) A random sample of 5 mangoes is taken from a dozen mangoes which contains 3 bad mangoes. Number of good mangoes in the sample is noted.

EXERCISE 9 (C)

32. A weighted coin $\left[P(H) = \frac{2}{3}, P(T) = \frac{1}{3}\right]$ is tossed three times. If the variate X denotes the number of heads produced in three tosses, find
    (i) the p.m.f. of X
    (ii) the c.d.f. of X
    (iii) $P[X = 2]$.

33. Suppose a function F is defined by

$$F(x) = \begin{cases} 0 \ ; & x \leq 2 \\ \frac{1}{3} \ ; & 2 < x < 3 \\ 1 \ ; & x \geq 3 \end{cases}$$

Show why F does not represent a d.f.

34. An organism of n cells contains variable number of live cells. Suppose X denotes this number of live cells out of n cells, then its p.m.f. is given by;

$$P(x) = \theta^x(1-\theta), \quad x = 0, 1, 2, \ldots, n-1$$
$$= \theta^n \qquad x = n$$

where $0 < \theta < 1$. On this basis, find the probability that an organism contains both dead and live cells.

Objective Types Questions

I. Multiple Choice Questions (MCQ).

- **Choose the correct alternative.**

1. Which of the following can be regarded as p.m.f. for given values of X ?

    (a)

X	1	2	3	4
P (x)	0.2	0.4	0.3	0.5

    (b)

X	−1	0	1
P (x)	1/2	0	1/2

    (c)

X	0	1	2	3
P (x)	0.3	− 0.1	0.6	0.2

    (d) $\quad P(x) = \dfrac{(x-1)}{2} \; ; \quad x = 0, 1, 2$
    $\qquad\qquad\quad = 0 \qquad ; \quad$ elsewhere.

2. The p.m.f. of a discrete random variable X is given by,

X	1	2	3	4	5
P (x)	0.1	0.25	0.25	0.2	0.2

    What is P (2 < X < 5) ?

    (a) 0.9 (b) 0.5
    (c) 0.45 (d) 0.3

3. If X and Y denote the points obtained when two six face unbiased dice are thrown, then $P(X = Y)$ is
   (a) 1/2 (b) 1/6
   (c) 1/24 (d) 1/36

4. Let X take values –1, 0, 1 and 2 with probabilities 0.2, 0.4, 0.1 and 0.3 respectively. Then X^2 takes values 0, 1 and 4 with respective probabilities.
   (a) 0.4, 0.3, 0.3 (b) 0.4, 0.2, 0.5
   (c) 0.16, 0.02, 0.82 (d) 0.2, 0.4, 0.1, 0.3

5. Suppose we toss a biased coin twice. Probability of getting 'head' is twice that of getting 'tail' for this coin. What will be the probability of getting no head?
   (a) 0 (b) 1/3
   (c) 1/9 (d) 4/9

6. Suppose the values of distribution function $F(x)$ at $X = x_i$ are as a given below :

X	0	1	2	3	4	5	6
$F(x_i)$	0.2	0.3	0.5	0.65	0.75	0.9	1

   What is $P(X = 2)$?
   (a) 0.5 (b) 0.2
   (c) 0 (d) can not determine.

7. Give the following probability distribution of a discrete random variable X,

x_i	– 3	– 2	– 1	0	1
$P(x_i)$	0.1	0.2	0.25	0.3	0.15

   What is the median of X ?
   (a) Median does not exist (b) 0
   (c) – 1 (d) 0.25

8. Given the following values of $F(x_i)$; what is the mode of X ?

x_i	0	1	2	3
$F(x_i)$	0.1	0.5	0.7	1

   (a) 2 (b) 1
   (c) 3 (d) 2

9. Which of the following is not a discrete random variable ?
   (a) Number of students present in the class.
   (b) Number of persons possessing 'O –ve' blood group in a blood donation camp.
   (c) Number of daughters born to a couple until they get son.
   (d) Weight of a new born baby.

10. For the following p.m.f. P (x), what is the value of median of X ?
    p (x) = kx; x = 1, 2, 3, 4, 5.
    (a) 3   (b) 4
    (c) 5   (d) 1

II. State whether the following statements are true or false.

11. A discrete random variable cannot take negative values.
12. A distribution function F (x) is defined only at the values, the variable takes.
13. The median M of a discrete random variable is defined as that value of X such that
    $P(X \leq M) \geq \frac{1}{2}$ and $P(X \geq M) \geq \frac{1}{2}$.
14. Mode of a random variable X is the maximum value that X takes.
15. A function $X : \Omega \to R$ is called as a random variable.

HINTS AND ANSWERS

8.

X	0	1	2	3
P (x)	1/8	3/8	3/8	1/8

9.

X	0	1	2
P (x)	25/36	10/36	1/36

10.

X	1	2	3	4	5	6
P (x)	1/36	3/36	5/36	4/36	9/36	11/36

11.

X	0	1	2
P (x)	95/138	40/138	3/138

12.

X	0	1	2	3
P (x)	27/64	27/64	9/64	1/64

13.

X	1	2	3	4
P (x)	1/4	1/4	1/4	1/4

14. (i) $\frac{1}{55}$, (ii) $\frac{3}{19}$, (iii) $\frac{1}{40}$

15. (i) No, (ii) Yes, (iii) Yes, (iv) No.

16. (i) $\frac{1}{49}$, (ii) $\frac{45}{49}$, (iii) $\frac{24}{49}$, (iv) 4.

(v)

X	0	1	2	3	4	5	6
P (x)	1/49	4/49	9/49	16/49	25/49	36/49	1

17.

X	0	1	2	3	4
P (x)	0.1	0.15	0.3	0.25	0.2

18. (i)

x	1	2	3	4	5
P (x)	1/6	1/6	2/6	1/6	1/6

(ii) 2/3

19.

X_i	x_1	x_2	x_3	x_4
P (x_i)	15/61	10/61	30/61	6/61

20. (i) $k = \frac{1}{3}$, (ii) $\frac{1}{9}$, (iii) $\frac{2}{3}$, (iv) $\frac{8}{9}$.

(v)

X	0	1	2
P (x)	1/9	3/9	1

21. (i) mode = 8, (ii) median = 6, (iii) $\frac{5}{12}$.

22. (i) 0.35; (ii) 0.8; (iii) 0.65; (iv) 0.65; (v) 0.6154

B.Sc. Part-I : Statistics : P-I   9.27   **Univariate Probability Distributions**

23. (i) 0.67, (ii) 0.43, (iii) 0.34, (iv) 0.15, (v) 0.42.
    (vi)

x	− 3	− 2	− 1	0	1	2	3
P (x)	0.05	0.1	0.23	0.19	0.15	0.16	0.12

(vii) median = 0, (viii) mode = − 1, (ix) 0.57, (x) 0.81.

24.

X	0	2	4	6	8
P (x)	0.2	0.3	0.2	0.1	0.2

median = 2.

25.

X	− 2.5	− 1.5	0.5	1.5	2.5
P (x)	1/6	1/6	2/6	1/6	1/6
F (x)	1/6	2/6	4/6	5/6	1

26. Mode does not exist.

27. (i)

X	1	2	3	4	5	6	7	8
P (x)	0.08	0.04	0.11	0.08	0.17	0.14	0.23	0.15

(ii) 0.31, 0.54; (iii) 0.1932; (iv) 0.6753, (v) mode = 7, median = 6.

28. (i)

W	− 1	0	1	2
P (w)	1/5	2/5	1/5	1/5

(ii)

Y	1	5/2	4	11/2
P (y)	1/5	2/5	1/5	1/5

(iii)

Z	2	3	6	11
P (z)	1/5	2/5	1/5	1/5

29.

Y	0	1	2	3
P (y)	1/4	1/4	1/4	1/4

30. (i) No, (ii) Yes, (iii) No, (iv) No, (v) No, (vi) No, (vii) No, (viii) Yes, (ix) No.

31. (i)   X = Difference between the two numbers.
R_X = {0, 1, 2, 3, 4, 5}

(ii)   X = Number of runs
R_X = {1, 2, 3, 4}

(iii)   X = Number of red balls
R_X = {0, 1, 2, 3}

(iv)   X = Number of good mangoes
R_X = {2, 3, 4, 5}

32. (i) and (ii)

X	0	1	2	3
P (x)	1/27	6/27	12/27	8/27
F (x)	1/27	7/27	19/27	1

(iii) 12/27

34. $\theta (1 - \theta^{n-1})$

Answers to Objective Questions

I. (1) b, (2) c, (3) b, (4) a, (5) c, (6) b, (7) – 1, (8) b, (9) d, (10) b.

II. (11) F, (12) F, (13) T, (14) F, (15) T.

Chapter 10...
Mathematical Expectation (Univariate)

Pierre-Simon Laplace (1749-1827) was a French mathematician and astronomer whose work on analytic theory of probability helped in creating foundation for mathematical statistics. In two important papers in 1810 and 1811, Laplace first developed the characteristic function as a tool for large-sample theory and proved the first general central limit theorem.

Pierre-Simon Laplace

We use moment generating function as a type of Laplace transform.

Contents ...

10.1 Introduction
10.2 Mathematical Expectation
10.3 Expectation of a Function of a Random Variable
10.4 Theorems on Expectation
10.5 Variance of a Random Variable
10.6 Effect of Change of Origin and Scale on Variance
10.7 Moments of Random Variable
10.8 Relations between Raw Moments and Moments about 'a'
10.9 Relations between Raw Moments and Central Moments
10.10 Relations between Central Moments and Moments about 'a'
10.11 Effect of Change of Origin and Scale on Central Moments
10.12 Measures of Skewness and Kurtosis Based on Moments
10.13 Factorial Moments
10.14 Moment Generating Function (M.G.F.)
10.15 Properties of Moment Generating Function
10.16 Cumulant Generating Function (C.G.F.)

Key Words :

Mean, Variance of a random variable, Moment generating function, Cumulant generating function, raw moments, Central moments, Factorial moments.

Objectives :

- Understand the concept of expectation of a random variable and its function.
- Learn the m.g.f. and c.g.f. and their properties.
- Compute raw and central moments of a random variable.
- Solve numerical problems on moments and compute coefficient of skewness and kurtosis.

10.1 Introduction

The probability distribution of a random variable (r.v.) specifies the chances (probabilities) of a r.v. taking different values. However, we might be interested in various characteristics of a probability distribution such as average, spread, symmetry, shape etc. In order to study these characteristics, statistical measures are developed. The development of measures such as mean, variance, moments, coefficients of skewness and kurtosis is on similar lines as that for a frequency distribution. The basis for all this is mathematical expectation. Mathematical expectation of a r.v. or its function provides a representative figure for the probability distribution. It takes into account probabilities of all possible values that the r.v. can take and summerizes them into a single average.

10.2 Mathematical Expectation

Definition : Let X be a discrete r.v. taking values $x_1, x_2, \ldots, x_i, \ldots, x_n$ with probabilities $p_1, p_2, \ldots, p_i, \ldots, p_n$ respectively. The mathematical expectation of X; denoted by E (X) is defined as,

$$E(X) = x_1 p_1 + x_2 p_2 + \ldots + x_n p_n$$

$$= \sum_{i=1}^{n} x_i p_i$$

E(X) is also called as the expected value of X.

Remark 1 : E (X) is the arithmetic mean (A.M.) of X. To see this, let us consider the following frequency distribution of X.

X	x_1	x_2	...	x_i	...	x_n
f	f_1	f_2	...	f_i	...	f_n

We know that the A.M. is given by

$$\bar{X} = \frac{\sum_{i=1}^{n} f_i x_i}{N} \quad \text{where,} \quad N = \sum_{i=1}^{n} f_i$$

$$= \frac{f_1 x_1 + f_2 x_2 \ldots + f_i x_i + \ldots + f_n x_n}{N}$$

$$= \left(\frac{f_1}{N}\right) x_1 + \left(\frac{f_2}{N}\right) x_2 + \ldots + \left(\frac{f_i}{N}\right) x_i + \ldots + \left(\frac{f_n}{N}\right) x_n$$

$$= \sum_{i=1}^{n} p_i x_i = E(X)$$

where, $p_i = \frac{f_i}{N}$; $i = 1, 2, \ldots, n$ are the relative frequencies of $x_1, x_2, \ldots, x_n$ respectively. Thus in $E(X)$, the relative frequencies are replaced by the probabilities of respective values of X.

Remark 2 : If the p.m.f. is in functional form $P(x)$, then $E(X) = \sum x\, P(x)$.

Remark 3 : If a random variable takes countably infinite values then $E(X) = \sum_{i=1}^{\infty} x_i\, p_i$. The expectation is well defined if the series $\sum |x_i|\, p_i < \infty$ (i.e. absolutely convergent). Otherwise we say $E(X)$ does not exist.

Remark 4 : The value of $E(X)$ may not be a possible value of the r.v. X. For example, when we toss a fair die, $P(x_i) = \frac{1}{6}$ for $i = 1, 2, \ldots, 6$, where X = number observed on the face of the die.

Hence, $E(X) = \sum_{i=1}^{6} x_i\, P(x_i) = \frac{1}{6}(1 + 2 + 3 + 4 + 5 + 6) = 3.5$

which is not a possible value of X.

Remark 5 : Arithmetic mean of X, i.e. $E(X)$ is considered to be the centre of gravity of the probability distribution of X. It is the average of values of X, if we perform the experiment several times and observe a large number of values of X.

Illustrative Examples

Example 10.1 : Obtain expectation of a r.v. X with the following probability distribution.

x_i	1	3	5	6
$P(x_i)$	0.1	0.2	0.4	0.3

Solution :

x_i	$P(x_i)$	$x_i P(x_i)$
1	0.1	0.1
3	0.2	0.6
5	0.4	2.0
6	0.3	1.8
Total	1.0	4.5

$\therefore \quad E(X) = \sum x_i P(x_i) = 4.5$

Example 10.2 : Obtain the expected value of number of heads when three fair coins are tossed simultaneously.

Solution : We know that in this case

$\Omega = \{HHH, HHT, HTH, THH, HTT, THT, TTH, TTT\}$

and hence if X denotes number of heads, the probability distribution of X is,

x	0	1	2	3
P(x)	$\frac{1}{8}$	$\frac{3}{8}$	$\frac{3}{8}$	$\frac{1}{8}$

Accordingly, $E(X) = \sum x P(x) = 0 + \frac{3}{8} + \frac{6}{8} + \frac{3}{8} = \frac{12}{8} = \frac{3}{2}$

Example 10.3 : A box contains 5 tickets. Two of the tickets carry a prize of ₹ 10 each, the other three carry prizes of ₹ 2 each. (i) If one ticket is drawn at random, what is the expected value of the prize ? (ii) If two tickets are drawn, without replacement, what is the expected value of the prize ?

Solution : (i) Let the tickets be numbered as 1, 2, 3, 4, 5.

$\therefore \quad \Omega = \{1, 2, 3, 4, 5\}$. Without loss of generality, let tickets numbered 1 and 2 carry prizes of ₹ 10/- and others carry prizes of ₹ 2/- each. Suppose X denotes the prize amount, then following is the probability distribution of X.

Mathematical Expectation (Univariate)

w	1	2	3	4	5
x	10	10	2	2	2
P(x)	1/5	1/5	1/5	1/5	1/5

$\therefore \quad P(X = 2) = \dfrac{3}{5}; \qquad P(X = 10) = \dfrac{2}{5}$

$\therefore \quad E(X) = \sum x P(x) = 2 \cdot \dfrac{3}{5} + 10 \cdot \dfrac{2}{5} = \dfrac{26}{5} = 5.2$

$\therefore$ The expected amount of prize is ₹ 5.20.

(ii) When we draw two tickets without replacement, the equiprobable sample space contains $^5C_2 = 10$ points. Now, let X denote the amount of prize when the experiment is performed. There are three possibilities.

(a) Both tickets drawn are of ₹ 10/-. This can happen in $\binom{2}{2} = 1$ ways i.e. when tickets numbered 1 and 2 are drawn.

$\therefore \quad P(X = 20) = \dfrac{1}{10}$

(b) One ticket is of ₹ 10 and the other is ₹ 2. This corresponds to $\binom{2}{1}\binom{3}{1} = 6$ sample points in Ω.

$\therefore \quad P(X = 12) = \dfrac{6}{10}$

(c) Both tickets are of ₹ 2. There are $\binom{3}{2} = 3$ ways in which this can happen.

$\therefore \quad P(X = 4) = \dfrac{3}{10}$

Hence, the probability distribution of X is

x	4	12	20
P(x)	$\dfrac{3}{10}$	$\dfrac{6}{10}$	$\dfrac{1}{10}$

and $\quad E(X) = \sum x P(x) = 10.40$

$\therefore$ Expected prize would be of ₹ 10.40.

Example 10.4 : There are three proposals before a manager to start a new project.

Proposal A : Profit of ₹ 50,000 with probability 0.6 or loss of ₹ 8,000 with probability 0.4.

Proposal B : Profit of ₹ 1,00,000 with probability 0.4 or otherwise a loss of ₹ 20,000.

Proposal C : Profit of ₹ 45,000 with probability 0.8 otherwise loss of ₹ 5,000.

Which proposal should the manager choose ? Justify ?

Solution : Let X = Profit in ₹ We assign positive sign to profit and negative sign to loss. We obtain the expected profit due to each proposal.

Proposal A			Proposal B			Proposal C		
x_i	p_i	$x_i\,p_i$	x_i	p_i	$x_i\,p_i$	x_i	p_i	$x_i\,p_i$
50000	0.6	30000	100000	0.4	40000	45000	0.8	36000
− 8000	0.4	− 3200	− 20000	0.6	− 12000	− 5000	0.2	− 1000
E (X)		26800			28000			35000

Expected profits from proposals A, B, C are 26,800; 28,000 and 35,000 respectively. Since proposal C is expected to give maximum profit, the manager should choose proposal C.

Example 10.5 : A r.v. X takes values 0, 1, 2, ..., n with probabilities proportional to the binomial coefficients $\binom{n}{0}, \binom{n}{1}, \ldots, \binom{n}{n}$ respectively. Find E (X).

Solution : Let, $p_i = P(X = i)$ where $i = 0, 1, \ldots, n$

$$= k \binom{n}{i}$$

$$\therefore \quad \sum_{i=0}^{n} p_i = 1 \Rightarrow k \sum_{i=0}^{n} \binom{n}{i} = 1$$

$$\Rightarrow k = 2^{-n} \qquad \because \sum_{i=0}^{n} \binom{n}{i} = 2^n$$

$$\therefore \quad E(X) = \sum x P(x)$$

$$= \frac{1}{2^n} \sum_{i=0}^{n} i \binom{n}{i}$$

$$= \frac{n}{2^n} \sum_{i=1}^{n} \binom{n-1}{i-1} \quad \because i\binom{n}{i} = n\binom{n-1}{i-1}$$

$$= \frac{n 2^{n-1}}{2^n} = \frac{n}{2}$$

Example 10.6 : Let the p.m.f. of a r.v. X be

$$P(x) = \frac{3-x}{10}, \quad x = -1, 0, 1, 2$$

Calculate E (X).

Solution : The probability distribution of X is

x	−1	0	1	2
P (x)	0.4	0.3	0.2	0.1

Hence, $E(X) = \sum x P(x) = -0.4 + 0 + 0.2 + 0.2 = 0$.

10.3 Expectation of a Function of a Random Variable

In earlier chapter we have seen that if Y = g (x) is a function of a r.v. X, then Y is also a r.v. with the same probability distribution of X viz. P(x). Using this property we can define the expectation of Y as follows :

$$E(Y) = E[g(x)] = \sum g(x) P(x)$$

For example, suppose X has the following probability distribution.

x	0	1	2
P (x)	0.3	0.3	0.4

Let, Y = 2X + 3. Hence values of Y are 3, 5, 7.

and $E(Y) = \sum y P(x) = 0.9 + 1.5 + 2.8 = 5.2$

The above concept is useful in deriving some important results.

10.4 Theorems on Expectation

Theorem 1 : Expected value of a constant is the constant itself. That is,
$$E(C) = C$$

Proof : Let $\{x_i, p_i\}$, $i = 1, 2, \ldots, n$ denote the probability distribution of a discrete r.v. X. Let $g(x) = C$, a constant.

$\therefore \quad E(C) = E[g(x)] = \sum g(x_i) p_i = c \sum p_i = c$

$$\because \sum p_i = 1$$

Theorem 2 : Effect of change of origin and scale on $E(X)$.

(i) $E(X + b) = E(X) + b$

(ii) $E(aX) = a E(X)$

(iii) $E(aX + b) = aE(X) + b$

Proof : (i) $g(X) = X + b$

$\therefore \quad E[g(X)] = \sum g(x_i) p_i = \sum (x_i + b) p_i$

$\qquad = \sum x_i p_i + b \sum p_i$

$\qquad = \sum x_i p_i + b \qquad \because \sum p_i = 1$

$\qquad = E(X) + b$

(ii) $E(aX) = \sum a x_i p_i = a \sum x_i p_i = a E(X)$

(iii) $E(aX + b) = \sum (a x_i + b) p_i$

$\qquad = a \sum x_i p_i + b \sum p_i$

$\qquad = a E(X) + b$

Remark : 1. In particular $E(-X) = -E(X)$ and $E(3X - 6) = 3E(X) - 6$ etc.

Remark : 2. If we define $Y = \dfrac{X-a}{h}$, then $E(Y) = \dfrac{E(X)-a}{h}$

or $E(X) = a + hE(Y)$ which is a property of a.m. You have studied it in paper I.

10.5 Variance of a Random Variable

The expected value of X, viz. $E(X)$ provides a measure of central tendency of the probability distribution. However, it does not provide any idea regarding the spread of the distribution. For this purpose, variance of a random variable is defined as follows.

Definition : Let X be a discrete r.v. with probability distribution $\{x_i, p_i\}$, $i = 1, \ldots, n$. Variance of X, denoted by σ^2 is defined as,

$$\sigma^2 = \text{Var}(X) = E[X - E(X)]^2$$

Note : (i) Var (X) is expected value of the function $g(X) = [X - E(X)]^2$. The mean of X, viz. E (X) is generally denoted by 'μ'. Using this notation, we can write

$$\sigma^2 = E(X - \mu)^2$$

(ii) The above formula for σ^2 is difficult to compute. For computational convenience, the following simplification is used.

$$\sigma^2 = E(x - \mu)^2$$

$$= \sum_{i=1}^{n} (x_i - \mu)^2 p_i$$

$$= \sum_{i=1}^{n} x_i^2 p_i - 2\mu \sum_{i=1}^{n} x_i p_i + \mu^2 \sum_{i=1}^{n} p_i$$

$$= E(X^2) - 2\mu^2 + \mu^2$$

$$= E(X^2) - \mu^2$$

Thus, $\quad \text{Var}(X) = E(X^2) - [E(X)]^2$

Remark 1 : Var (X) $\geq$ 0. This is because variance is expected value of the square, $[X - E(X)]^2$, which cannot be negative. Therefore, we get

$$E(X^2) \geq [E(X)]^2$$

Remark 2 : Variance of X is zero if and only if X is a degenerate r.v. That is, X takes only one value with probability 1. For example, if $P[X = C] = 1$, then E (X) = C.

and $\qquad \sigma^2 = E(X - C)^2 = (C - C)^2 \cdot 1 = 0$

Remark 3 : The positive square root of variance is called the standard deviation of X. It is denoted by σ.

$$\therefore \qquad \sigma = \sqrt{\text{Var}(X)} = \sqrt{E(X - \mu)^2}$$

Standard deviation is used to compare variability between two distributions.

Illustrative Examples

Example 10.7 : Calculate the variance of X, if X denotes the number obtained on the face of a fair die.

Solution : We know that,

$$P(x) = \frac{1}{6}, \qquad x = 1, 2, ..., 6$$

and $E(X) = 3.5$ (Ref. Remark 3 to 5.2)

Now, $\sigma^2 = E(X^2) - [E(X)]^2$

Consider, $E(X^2) = \sum x^2 P(x)$

$$= \frac{1}{6}(1^2 + 2^2 + 3^2 + 4^2 + 5^2 + 6^2)$$

$$= \frac{91}{6}$$

$$\therefore \quad \sigma^2 = \text{Var}(X) = \frac{91}{6} - (3.5)^2 = 2.9167$$

Example 10.8 : Obtain variance of r.v. X having following p.m.f.

x	0	1	2	3	4	5
P(x)	0.05	0.15	0.2	0.5	0.09	0.01

Solution :

x_i	p_i	$x_i p_i$	$x_i^2 p_i$
0	0.05	0	0
1	0.15	0.15	0.15
2	0.20	0.40	0.80
3	0.50	1.50	4.50
4	0.09	0.36	1.44
5	0.01	0.05	0.25
Total	1	2.46	7.14

$$E(X) = \sum x_i p_i = 2.46$$

$$\text{Var}(X) = \sum x_i^2 p_i - [E(X)]^2$$

$$= 7.14 - (2.46)^2 = 1.0884$$

Example 10.9 : Compute variance of X for the following probability distribution.

$$P(x) = \frac{x^2}{30}, \qquad x = 0, 1, 2, 3, 4$$

Solution : $E(X) = \sum x P(x)$

$$= \frac{1}{30} \sum_{x=0}^{4} x^3$$

$$= \frac{1}{30} (0 + 1 + 8 + 27 + 64)$$

$$= \frac{100}{30} = \frac{10}{3}$$

$$E(X^2) = \frac{1}{30} \sum x^4$$

$$= \frac{1}{30} (1 + 16 + 81 + 256) = \frac{354}{30} = 11.8$$

$$Var(X) = E(X^2) - [E(X)]^2$$

$$= 11.8 - \left(\frac{10}{3}\right)^2$$

$$= 0.6889$$

Example 10.10 : Consider the following probability distribution.

X	0	1	2
P(X)	p	1−2p	p

$0 \leq p \leq \frac{1}{2}$

For what value of p, is the Var (X) maximum ?

Solution : $E(X) = 1 - 2p + 2p = 1$

$E(X^2) = 1(1 - 2p) + 4p$

$= 1 + 2p$

∴ $Var(X) = E(X^2) - [E(X)]^2 = 1 + 2p - 1 = 2p$.

Since, $0 \leq p \leq \frac{1}{2}$, Var (X) will be maximum when $p = \frac{1}{2}$.

For $p = \frac{1}{2}$, Var (X) = 1.

10.6 Effect of Change of Origin and Scale on Variance

Theorem 3 : Let X be a discrete r.v. with mean μ and variance σ^2. Then,

(i) $\text{Var}(X + b) = \text{Var}(X) = \sigma^2$

(ii) $\text{Var}(aX) = a^2 \text{Var}(X) = a^2 \sigma^2$

(iii) $\text{Var}(aX + b) = a^2 \sigma^2$

Solution : By definition,

$$\begin{aligned}\text{Var}(X + b) &= E[(X + b) - E(X + b)]^2 \\ &= E[X + b - E(X) - b]^2 \\ &= E[X - \mu]^2 = \sigma^2\end{aligned}$$

Thus variance is invariant to the change of origin.

(ii) $\text{Var}(aX) = E[aX - E(aX)]^2$ by definition of variance of a r.v.

$$\begin{aligned} &= E[aX - aE(X)]^2 \\ &= E[a(X - E(X))]^2 \\ &= a^2 E(X - E(X))^2 \\ &= a^2 \sigma^2\end{aligned}$$

(iii) On similar lines,

$$\begin{aligned}\text{Var}(aX + b) &= E[aX + b - E(aX + b)]^2 \\ &= E[aX + b - aE(X) - b]^2 \\ &= E[a(X - E(X))]^2 \\ &= a^2 E[X - E(X)]^2 \\ &= a^2 \sigma^2\end{aligned}$$

Thus variance is *not* invariant to the change of scale.

Remark 1 : If we define $Y = \dfrac{X - a}{h}$, then

$$\sigma_y^2 = \frac{1}{h^2} \sigma_x^2$$

where σ_x^2 and σ_y^2 are Var (X) and Var (Y) respectively.

Remark 2 : Let X be a r.v. with mean μ and s.d. σ. Define $Y = \dfrac{X - \mu}{\sigma}$.

Then, $\quad E(Y) = E\left(\dfrac{X-\mu}{\sigma}\right) = \dfrac{1}{\sigma}[E(X) - \mu] = 0$

and $\quad Var(Y) = \dfrac{1}{\sigma^2}, \quad Var(X) = \dfrac{\sigma^2}{\sigma^2} = 1.$

$\therefore$ Y has mean 0 and variance 1. Therefore, $Y = \dfrac{X-\mu}{\sigma}$ is called a standardised r.v.

Remark 3 : If $Y = aX$, 'a' constant, then standard deviation of Y, is given by

$$\sigma_y = |a|\,\sigma_x$$

We know that $\sigma_y^2 = a^2\,\sigma_x^2$ and s.d. is defined to be the positive square root of variance.

$\therefore \quad \sigma_y = |a|\,\sigma_x$

Thus, $\quad Var(-3X + 5) = 9\,Var(X)$

and $\quad s.d.(-3X + 5) = 3\,s.d.(X).$

Theorem 4 : Variance of constant is zero.

Proof : $\quad Var(c) = E(c^2) = -[E(c)]^2 = c^2 - c^2 = 0$

Illustrative Examples

Example 10.11 : The mean and variance of marks in Statistics (X) are 60 and 25 respectively. Find the mean and variance of

(i) $Y = \dfrac{X-60}{5}$, (ii) $Z = \dfrac{X-50}{10}$.

Solution : (i) We know that, if $Y = \dfrac{X-a}{h}$ then,

$$E(Y) = \dfrac{E(X) - a}{h}$$

and $\quad V(Y) = \dfrac{V(X)}{h^2}$; V denotes variance

$\therefore$ Here, $\quad E(Y) = \dfrac{60 - 60}{5} = 0$

and $\quad Var(Y) = \dfrac{25}{25} = 1$

Thus Y is a standardised variable of X.

(ii) $\quad E(Z) = \dfrac{E(X) - 50}{10} = \dfrac{60 - 50}{10} = 1$

$\quad Var(Z) = \dfrac{V(x)}{100} = \dfrac{25}{100} = 0.25$

Example 10.12 : A r.v. X assumes n values 1, 2, ... , n with equal probability. If the ratio of Var (X) to E (X) is equal to 4, find the value of n. What will be the value of n if Var (X) = E (X) ?

Solution : The probability distribution of X is as follows :

X	1	2	...	n
P (x)	$\dfrac{1}{n}$	$\dfrac{1}{n}$	...	$\dfrac{1}{n}$

Hence, $\quad E(X) = \dfrac{1}{n} \sum_{i=1}^{n} i = \dfrac{n(n+1)}{n \cdot 2} = \dfrac{n+1}{2}$

$\quad E(X) = \dfrac{1}{n} \sum_{i=1}^{n} i^2$

$\quad\quad\quad = \dfrac{1}{n} \cdot \dfrac{n(n+1)(2n+1)}{6}$

$\quad\quad\quad = \dfrac{(n+1)(2n+1)}{6}$

$\therefore \quad Var(X) = E(X^2) - [E(X)]^2$

$\quad\quad\quad = \dfrac{(n+1)(2n+1)}{6} - \dfrac{(n+1)^2}{4}$

$\quad\quad\quad = \dfrac{(n+1)(n-1)}{12} = \dfrac{n^2-1}{12}$

Given : $\dfrac{Var(X)}{E(X)} = 4 \Rightarrow \dfrac{n^2-1}{12} \times \dfrac{2}{n+1} = \dfrac{n-1}{6} = 4$

$\therefore \quad n = 25$

To answer the second part of the problem, let

$\quad\quad Var(X) = E(X)$

$\Rightarrow \quad \dfrac{n^2-1}{12} = \dfrac{n+1}{2}$

$\Rightarrow \quad \dfrac{n-1}{6} = 1$

$\Rightarrow \quad n = 7$

Example 10.13 : Let X be a discrete r.v. with mean 5 and s.d. 3. Compute mean and s.d. of (i) $2X - 5$, (ii) $3 - 7X$, (iii) $\frac{X+1}{2}$.

Solution : Let $Y = 2X - 5$,

∴ $E(Y) = 2E(X) - 5$
$= 10 - 5 = 5$
$\sigma_y = |2|, \sigma_x = 6$

(ii) Let, $Y = 3 - 7X$
∴ $E(Y) = 3 - 7E(X) = 3 - 35 = -32$
s.d. $(Y) = \sigma_y = |7| \sigma_x = 21$

(iii) $Y = \frac{X+1}{2}$

∴ $E(Y) = \frac{1}{2} E(X) + \frac{1}{2} = \frac{5}{2} + \frac{1}{2} = 3$

s.d. of $Y = \sigma_y = \left|\frac{1}{2}\right| \sigma_x = \frac{1}{2} \cdot 3 = \frac{3}{2}$

Example 10.14 : Prove that $E(X-k)^2 = Var(X) + [E(X) - k]^2$, where k is any constant.

Proof : $Var(X) = Var(X-k)$ ... (From Theorem 3)
$= E(X-k)^2 - [E(X-k)]^2$
$= E(X-k)^2 - [E(X) - k]^2$

∴ $E(X-k)^2 = Var(X) + [E(X) - k]^2$

10.7 Moments of a Random Variable

So far we studied mean and variance of a random variable. The mean measures central tendency while the variance measures spread. In order to get the complete information on the probability distribution, we also have to study the shape of the probability distribution. For example, we need measures of Skewness (lack of symmetry) and Kurtosis (peakedness) of a probability distribution. Moments of a random variable (or probability distribution) serve this purpose.

We shall study four types of moments of a r.v. in this chapter. Let $\{x_i, p_i\}$, $i = 1, 2, \ldots, n$ represent a probability distribution of a discrete r.v. X.

1. Moments about any arbitrary point 'a' : The rth moment of X about 'a' is denoted by $\mu'_r(a)$ and is defined as,

$$\mu'_r(a) = E(X-a)^r = \sum_{i=1}^{n}(x_i - a)^r p_i$$

$$r = 1, 2, 3, \ldots$$

In particular, $\mu'_1(a) = E(X-a) = E(X) - a$

$\mu'_2(a) = E(X-a)^2$

2. Raw moments (Moments about the origin i.e. zero) : The rth raw moment of X is defined as the rth moment about 0. It is denoted by μ'_r.

Hence, $\mu'_r = \mu_r(0) = E(X)^r = \sum_{i=1}^{n} x_i^r p_i,\ r = 1, 2, 3, \ldots$

In particular, $\mu'_1 = E(X) = $ mean

$$\mu'_2 = E(x^2) = \sum_{i=1}^{n} x_i^2 p_i$$

$$\mu'_3 = E(X^3) = \sum_{i=1}^{n} x_i^3 p_i$$

$$\mu'_4 = E(X^4) = \sum_{i=1}^{n} x_i^4 p_i \quad \text{and so on.}$$

3. Central moments (Moments about the arithmetic mean) : The rth central moment of X is defined as the rth moment of X about E(X). It is denoted by μ_r. Hence,

$$\mu_r = \mu'_{r\ (E(x))} = E[X - E(X)]^r$$

$$= \sum_{i=1}^{n}[x_i - E(X)]^r p_i$$

$$r = 1, 2, 3, \ldots$$

In particular, $\mu_1 = E[X - E(X)] = E(X) - E(X) = 0$

Thus, the first central moment is always zero.

$$\mu_2 = E[X - E(X)]^2 = Var(X)$$
$$\mu_3 = E[X - E(X)]^3 \text{ and so on.}$$

10.8 Relations between Raw Moments and Central Moments

$$\mu_1 = 0$$
$$\mu_2 = E[X - E(X)]^2$$
$$\mu_2 = \sum (x_i - \mu_1')^2 p_i$$

It can be proved that

$$\mu_2 = \mu_2' - \mu_1'^2$$
$$\mu_3 = E[X - E(X)]^3$$
$$= E(X_i - \mu_1')^3 = \sum (x_i - \mu_1')^3 p_i$$

It can be shown that:

$$\mu_3 = \mu_3' - 3\mu_2' \mu_1' + 2\mu_1'^3$$
$$\mu_4 = E[X - E(X)]^4$$
$$= E(X - \mu_1')^4$$

It can be show that:

$$\mu_4 = \mu_4' - 4\mu_3' \mu_1' + 6\mu_2' \mu_1'^2 - 3\mu_1'^4$$

and so on.

10.9 Relations between Central Moments and Moments About 'a'

$$\mu_1 = 0$$

Consider, $\mu_2 = E(x - \mu_1')^2$

$$= \mu_{2(a)}' - [\mu_{1(a)}']^2$$

Similarly, $\mu_3 = E(x - \mu_1')^3$

$$= \mu_{3(a)}' - 3\mu_{2(a)}' \mu_{1(a)}' + 2\mu_{1(a)}'^3$$

Also, $\mu_4 = \mu_{4(a)}' - 4\mu_{3(a)}' \mu_{2(a)}' + 6\mu_{2(a)}' \mu_{1(a)}'^2 - 3\mu_{1(a)}'^4$.

10.10 Effect of Change of Origin and Scale on Central Moments

Let X be a discrete r.v. with r^{th} central moment $\mu_r(x)$. Define $Y = \dfrac{X-a}{h}$. Then r^{th} central moment of Y, denoted by $\mu_r(y)$ say, is given by,

$$\mu_r(y) = \frac{1}{h^r}\mu_r(x)$$

or $\quad \mu_r(x) = h^r \mu_r(y)$

Proof : $Y = \dfrac{X-a}{h} \quad \therefore X = a + hY \therefore E(X) = a + h\,E(Y)$

Now, $\mu_r(x) = E[X - E(X)]^r$
$= E[a + hY - a - h\,E(Y)]^r$
$= E[h(Y - E(Y))]^r$
$= h^r E[Y - E(Y)]^r$
$= h^r \mu_r(y).$

Thus central moments are invariant to the change of origin but not to the change of scale.

10.11 Measures of Skewness and Kurtosis Based on Moments

The concepts of skewness and kurtosis of a probability distribution are similar to those of a frequency distribution which you study in Statistics – Paper I.

Skewness means the *lack of symmetry* of the probability distribution while kurtosis means peakdedness of the distribution. Following are the measures based on moments.

1. Coefficient of skewness (γ_1) : The coefficient of skewness is defined as,

$$\gamma_1 = \sqrt{\beta_1} = \sqrt{\frac{\mu_3^2}{\mu_2^3}} = \frac{\mu_3}{\sigma^3} \quad \text{where } \mu_2 = \sigma^2, \text{ the variance.}$$

The sign of γ_1 is that of μ_3.

If, $\quad \gamma_1 = 0$, the distribution is symmetric.
$\quad \gamma_1 > 0$, the distribution is positively skew.
$\quad \gamma_1 < 0$, the distribution is negatively skew.

2. The coefficient of kurtosis (γ_2) : The coefficient of kurtosis is defined as

$$\gamma_2 = \beta_2 - 3 = \frac{\mu_4}{\mu_2^2} - 3$$

γ_2 is also called the 'excess of kurtosis'.

If, $\gamma_2 = 0$, the distribution is mesokurtic i.e. moderately peaked

$\gamma_2 > 0$, the distribution is leptokurtic i.e. more peaked

$\gamma_2 < 0$, the distribution is platykurtic i.e. is less peaked

Points to Remember

- The concept of expectation of random variable is same as that of arithmetic mean for a frequency distribution.
- M.g.f. and c.g.f. can be used to compute moments of the probability distribution.
- Coefficients of skewness and kurtosis based on moments give us the idea about the symmetry, spread, shape of the probability distribution.
- $E(X) = \sum xP(x)$
- $Var(X) = E(X^2) - [E(X)]^2$
- Variance is invariant to change of origin

EXERCISE 10 (A)

Theory Questions :

1. Define mathematical expectation of a discrete r.v. X.
2. Explain how $E(X)$ is the arithmetic mean of X. Can $E(X)$ always be one of the possible values of X ? Explain.
3. What is the physical interpretation of $E(X)$?
4. Define expectation of a function of random variable.
5. Define variance of a discrete r.v.
6. Let X be a discrete random variable. Define $E(X)$ and $E(X^2)$. Hence give formula for variance of X.
7. With usual notations prove that
   $E(X-k)^2 = var(X) + [E(X) - k]^2$, where k is a constant.

8. Define standard deviation of a r.v. X. What is its use?
9. If $Y = \dfrac{X-a}{h}$, prove that (i) $E(Y) = \dfrac{E(X)-a}{h}$,
   (ii) $V(Y) = V(X)/h^2$.
10. Show that variance is invariant to the change of origin but not of scale.
11. What is meant by standardised r.v.? Explain with the help of an illustration.
12. Prove that (i) Variance of a constant zero,
    (ii) $E(X^2) \geq [E(X)]^2$.
13. A discrete r.v. X assumes values 1, 2,…, n, with $P(x) \propto i$, $i = 1, 2, …, n$. Find $E(X)$.
14. Let X be a r.v. with following as the p.m.f.

x	0	1	2	3
P (x)	0.1	0.3	0.4	0.2

Find $E(X)$ and Var (X).

15. Let X be a discrete r.v. with p.m.f.

$$P(X = x) = \dfrac{x}{15} \quad ; \text{ for } x = 1, 2, 3, 4, 5$$
$$= 0 \quad ; \text{ otherwise.}$$

Find $E(X)$ and Var $(2X - 3)$.

16. The p.m.f. of a r.v. X is given by

$$P(X = x) = \dfrac{1}{10} \quad ; \text{ for } x = 11, 12, …, 20$$
$$= 0 \quad ; \text{ otherwise.}$$

Find $E(2X)$, $E(3X - 4)$.

17. If X is a r.v. with p.m.f.

$$P(x) = kX \quad ; \text{ for } x = 1, 2, 3$$
$$= 0 \quad ; \text{ otherwise.}$$

find k and $E(X)$.

18. The p.m.f. of a r.v. X is

$$P(x) = \dfrac{2x}{n(n+1)} \quad ; \text{ for } x = 1, 2, …, n$$
$$= 0 \quad ; \text{ otherwise.}$$

Find $E(X)$ and $E(X^2)$.

19. The p.m.f. of a r.v. X is,

    $P(x) = \frac{1}{15}$, ; for x = 1, 2, ..., 15

    $ = 0$; otherwise.

    Find E (X) and Var (X). Using these results find the values of (i) E (2X – 3),
    (ii) Var (3X + 5), (iii) E (5 – 4X), (iv) Var (– 3X + 2), (v) s.d. $\left(\frac{10-X}{2}\right)$.

20. A fair coin is tossed 3 times. A person receives ₹ X², if he gets X number of heads in all. Find his expected gain.

21. The probabilities that a man fishing at a particular place will catch 1, 2, 3, 4 fish are 0.4, 0.3, 0.15, 0.15 respectively. What is the expected number of fish caught ?

22. A bag contains 20 currency notes, 10 of ₹ 5, 5 of ₹ 10, 3 of ₹ 20 and 2 of ₹ 50. If the probability that any note is taken out is the same, find the expected value of the note drawn at random.

23. An urn contains 6 blue and 4 red balls. Three balls are drawn at random without replacement. What is the expected number of red balls that will be obtained ?

24. Calculate the expected value of the sum of the two numbers obtained when two fair dice are rolled.

25. Two cards are drawn at random from a box which contains five cards numbered 1, 1, 2, 2, and 3. Let X denote the sum of the numbers. Find the expected value of the sum.

26. A man wishes to open the door of his house in dark. He has a bunch of n keys out of which only one key works. He tries keys one by one, removing the unsuccessful keys. Find the expected number of keys he tries before the door is opened.

27. A bakerman sells 5 types of cakes. Profit due to sale of each type of cake is respectively ₹ 1, 1.5, 0.5, 0.75 and 0.25. The demands for these cakes are 10%, 5%, 20%, 50% and 15% respectively. What is the expected profit per cake ?

28. A player tosses two fair coins. He wins ₹ 5 if 2 heads appear, ₹ 2 if 1 head appears and Re. 1 if no head appears. Find his expected amount of winning and variance of winning.

29. For a discrete r.v. X, E (X) = 10 and Var (X) = 25. Find the positive values of a and b such that Y = aX − b has mean 0 and variance 1.

30. A r.v. X has the following probability mass function.

X	− 2	− 1	0	1	2	3
P (x)	0.1	k	0.2	2k	0.3	k

Find the value of k, and calculate mean and variance.

31. The probability distribution of weekly sales of TV sets in a shop is given below.

Demand (units)	10	11	12	13	14	15
Probability	0.05	0.10	0.25	0.40	0.15	0.05

The shop earns a profit of ₹ 700 per set. It is not sold, the loss is ₹ 300 per set. How many sets should be stocked ?

32. Find E (X) and V (X) for the following p.m.f.s.

(i) $P(x) = \dfrac{\binom{5}{x}\binom{4}{3-x}}{\binom{9}{3}}$; x = 0, 1, 2, 3

(ii) $P(x) = \binom{3}{x}\left(\dfrac{5}{9}\right)^x \left(\dfrac{4}{9}\right)^{3-x}$; x = 0, 1, 2, 3

33. The first three moments about the value 3 for a certain probability distribution are 1, 16 and − 40 respectively (i) Find the mean, variance and third central moment of the distribution. (ii) Compute γ_1 and comment on the nature of the skewness of the distribution.

34. The probability distribution of a r.v. X is given by,

X	0	1	2	3
P (x)	$\dfrac{1}{6}$	$\dfrac{1}{3}$	$\dfrac{1}{3}$	$\dfrac{1}{6}$

Calculate γ_1 and γ_2. Comment on the nature of the distribution.

35. The p.m.f. of a discrete r.v. X is

P (x) = $\dfrac{1}{n}$; for x = 1, 2, ..., n

= 0 ; otherwise.

Show that, $\mu'_{(r)} = \dfrac{(n+1)^{(r+1)}}{n(r+1)}$

36. For a certain distribution, $\mu_1' = 5$, $\mu_2 = 2$, $\gamma_1 = 1$, and $\beta_2 = 4$. Find the first four raw moments.

37. The first three central moments of a distribution are 0, 50 and 90. Calculate the coefficient of skewness and interpret the value.

38. Following is the probability distribution of number of children in a family in a certain city.

X	0	1	2	3	4	5
P (x)	0.10	0.15	0.40	0.30	0.03	0.02

Obtain the mean, first three central moments and γ_1 of X. Interpret the values of μ_1, μ_2 and γ_1.

39. A coin is tossed until a head or 5 tails occur. Find the expected value and variance of number of tosses of the coin.

40. A die is tossed twice. Getting a number > 4 is considered as a 'success'. Find the mean and variance of the number of successes.

41. A special die has (n + 1) faces marked with numbers $0, \frac{1}{n}, \frac{2}{n}, \ldots, \frac{n-1}{n}, 1$. The die is unbiased. Let X denote the number on the uppermost face. Find E (X) and Var (X).

42. If X is a discrete r.v. taking non-negative values $x_1, x_2, \ldots, x_n$ with probabilities $p_1, p_2, \ldots, p_n$ respectively. Show that
$$E\left(\frac{1}{X}\right) \geq \frac{1}{E(X)}$$

43. With usual notations, prove that
$$\mu_2 = \mu_2' - \mu_1'^2$$

44. Let the p.m.f. of X be
$$P(x) = \binom{3}{x} \left(\frac{1}{4}\right)^x \left(\frac{3}{4}\right)^{3-x} \quad ; \quad x = 0, 1, 2, 3.$$
$$= 0 \quad ; \quad \text{otherwise}$$
Obtain the first 3 factorial moments of X. Hence, compute mean and variance of X.

45. Let X be a r.v. with the following p.m.f.
$$P(x) = \frac{1}{n} \; ; \; x = 1, 2, \ldots, n \text{ where n is odd.}$$
$$= 0 \; ; \text{ otherwise}$$
If $g(x) = X - E(X)$, prove that
$$E[|g(x)|] = \frac{n^2 - 1}{4n}$$

Objective Type Questions

I. Multiple Choice Questions (MCQ).
- **Choose the correct alternative.**

1. If $E(X) = 5$ and $Var(X) = 5$, then $E(X + 6)$ and $Var(X)$ are equal to ....
   (a) 5, 4
   (b) 6, 6
   (c) 11, 4
   (d) 11, 10

2. If X is a discrete random variable, then ....
   (a) $E(X^2) = [E(X)]^2$
   (b) $E(X^2) \geq [E(X)]^2$
   (c) $E(X^2) \leq [E(X)]^2$
   (d) $E(X^2) \geq [E(X)]^2$

3. X takes values 1, 2, 3 with $P(X = 1) = 0.2$ and $E(X) = 2.2$. Then $P(X = 2)$ is ....
   (a) 0.5
   (b) 0.1
   (c) 0.3
   (d) 0.4

4. Suppose X is a discrete random variable with following p.m.f.
$$p(x) = kx^2 \; ; \; x = 1, 2, 3$$
$$= 0 \; ; \text{ elsewhere}$$
   What is the expected value of X ?
   (a) can't determine, since k is unknown.
   (b) 2 k
   (c) 18/7
   (d) 2

5. For the following probability distribution, calculate $E(3X + 2)$.

X	-2	-1	0	1
P(x)	0.3	0.2	0.4	0.1

   (a) 0.1
   (b) -0.1
   (c) -0.7
   (d) -1

Mathematical Expectation (Univariate)

6. If $E(Y) = 3$ where $Y = \dfrac{X-2}{5}$, what is $E(X)$?
   (a) 1/5 (b) 17/5
   (c) 5/17 (d) 17.

7. For the following probability distribution of a random variable X, obtain Var (X).

X	5000	5002	5004	5006
P(x)	0.3	0.1	0.3	0.3

   (a) 5.76 (b) 16
   (c) 10.24 (d) 5003

8. Let X be a random variable with mean 5 and variance 16. What are the values of mean and standard deviation of $(X-5)/16$?
   (a) 0, 1 (b) 0, 0.25
   (c) 5, 1 (d) 5, 0.25

9. If $\mu_1' = 3$, $\mu_2' = 11$, $\mu_3' = 25$, then the value of γ_1 is ....
   (a) 16.25 (b) 21.43
   (c) 4.63 (d) 14

10. The third factorial moment can be expressed as ....
    (a) $\mu_{(3)}' = \mu_3' - 3\mu_2' + 2\mu_1'$
    (b) $\mu_{(3)}' = \mu_3' - 3\mu_2'\mu_1' + 2\mu_1'^2$
    (c) $\mu_{(3)}' = \mu_3' - 3\mu_2'\mu_1' + 3\mu_2'\mu_1'^2 - 2\mu_1'^3$
    (d) $\mu_{(3)}' = \mu_3' + 3\mu_2' - 2\mu_1'$.

II. State whether the following statements are true or false.

11. Expected value of a constant is zero.
12. Variance of a random variable is never negative.
13. The first row moment of a variable is always zero.
14. If $\gamma_1 > \gamma_2$, then the distribution is positively skew.
15. If $\gamma_2 < 0$, the distribution is mesokurtic.

Hints and Answers

(13) $\dfrac{2n+1}{3}$ (14) 1.7, 0.81

(15) $\dfrac{11}{3}, \dfrac{56}{9}$ (16) $\dfrac{31}{2}, \dfrac{85}{2}$

(17) $\frac{1}{6}, \frac{7}{3}$ (18) $\frac{2n+1}{3}, \frac{n(n+1)}{2}$

(19) $8, \frac{56}{3}, 13, 168, -27, 168, 2.16,$

(20) ₹ 3   (21) 2.05

(22) ₹ 13   (23) $\frac{6}{5}$

(24) 7   (25) 3.6

(26) $\frac{n+1}{2}$ (27) ₹ 0.69

(28) 2.5, 2.25   (29) $a = \frac{1}{5}, b = 2$

(30) 0.1, 0.8, 2.16   (31) 13

(32) (i) $\frac{5}{3}, \frac{5}{9}$; (ii) $\frac{5}{3}, \frac{20}{27}$

(33) $1, 15, -86, -1.48, -$ vely skew

(34) $\gamma_1 = 0, \gamma_2 = -0.9424$, symmetric, platykurtic.

(35) $\frac{(x+1)^{(r+1)} - x^{(r+1)}}{r+1} = x^{(r)}$

(36) $\mu_1' = 5, \mu_2' = 27, \mu_3' = 157.83, \mu_4' = 985.6.$

(37) 0.036, positively skew

(38) $2.07, 1.1451, -0.1108, \gamma_1 = -0.069$

(39) 1.94, 5.09; (40) 2/3, 4/9 (42) $\frac{1}{2}, \frac{n+2}{12n}$

(44) 3/4, 3/8, 3/32, 3/14, 9/16

Answers of Objective Questions

I.   (1) c   (2) b   (3) d   (4) c
     (5) b   (6) d   (7) a   (8) b
     (9) c   (10) a

II. (11) F   (12) T   (13) F   (14) F
     (15) F

www.ingramcontent.com/pod-product-compliance
Lightning Source LLC
Chambersburg PA
CBHW080540230426

43663CB00015B/2656